A Clinician's Guide to Worki with Problem Gamblers

Problem gambling is a recognised mental disorder and a significant public health issue internationally. *A Clinician's Guide to Working with Problem Gamblers* introduces the reader to the concept of problem gambling as an illness, it describes the current gambling habits and explores the way problem gambling may present in an individual. This guide is the product of a collaboration between two of the country's most eminent experts on problem gambling as a psychiatric disorder.

Bowden-Jones and George bring together contributions from leading clinicians working in the field to provide an outline of the epidemiology, aetiology, research, assessment procedures and treatment practices, which are discussed and presented in an accessible and engaging manner. The inclusion of questionnaires and screening tools adds to the 'hands on' feel of the book. The book covers a range of topics that clinicians and trainees need in order to review and understand the disorder, including, amongst others:

* Cognitive behavioural models of problem gambling
* Psychiatric co-morbidity
* Family interventions
* Gambling and women
* Remote gambling.

A Clinician's Guide to Working with Problem Gamblers will be essential reading for mental health professionals working with problem gamblers, as well as those in training. It is a comprehensive reference point on all aspects of this psychiatric condition. It is also aimed at various other groups of people who have an interest in the field of problem gambling, including academics, researchers, policy makers, NHS commissioners, probation officers, other health care professionals, the lay reader and family members of those affected by gambling.

Henrietta Bowden-Jones is a doctor trained in psychiatry and neuroscience. She is Founder and Director of the National Problem Gambling Clinic CNWL NHS Trust and Honorary Senior Lecturer, Brain Science Division, Imperial College, UK.

Sanju George is a consultant in addiction psychiatry, Birmingham and Solihull Mental Health NHS Foundation Trust, and is an opinion leader in the field of gambling addiction.

A Clinician's Guide to Working with Problem Gamblers

Edited by Henrietta Bowden-Jones
and Sanju George

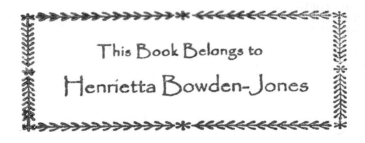

This Book Belongs to
Henrietta Bowden-Jones

Routledge
Taylor & Francis Group

LONDON AND NEW YORK

First published 2015
by Routledge
27 Church Road, Hove, East Sussex, BN3 2FA

and by Routledge
711 Third Avenue, New York, NY 10017

Routledge is an imprint of the Taylor & Francis Group, an informa business

British Library Cataloguing in Publication Data
A catalogue record for this book is available from the British Library

Library of Congress Cataloging in Publication Data
A clinician's guide to working with problem gamblers / edited by Henrietta
Bowden-Jones and Sanju George.
pages cm
1. Compulsive gambling. 2. Compulsive gambling--Treatment. 3. Compulsive
gambling--Psychological aspects. I. Bowden-Jones, Henrietta. II. George, Sanju.
RC569.5.G35C55 2015
616.85'841--dc23
2014027675

ISBN: 978-0-415-73283-3 (hbk)
ISBN: 978-0-415-73285-7 (pbk)
ISBN: 978-1-315-73427-9 (ebk)

Typeset in Times
by Saxon Graphics Ltd, Derby

Printed and bound in Great Britain by
TJ International Ltd, Padstow, Cornwall

To Marc Potenza and Nancy Petry for all their inspirational advice and support in the early years of the National Problem Gambling Clinic.

Contents

List of figures and tables   ix

List of contributors   xi

1   Introduction   1
    HENRIETTA BOWDEN-JONES AND SANJU GEORGE

2   Gambling behaviour in Britain: evidence from the British
    Gambling Prevalence Survey series   2
    HEATHER WARDLE

3   Gambling and public health   15
    ELEANOR ROAF

4   Aetiology of problem gambling   28
    ANDRE GEEL AND REBECCA FISHER

5   Cognitive-behavioural models of problem gambling   39
    NEIL SMITH AND SNEHAL SHAH

6   Neurobiology of pathological gambling   53
    LUKE CLARK

7   Psychiatric co-morbidity in gambling   75
    ROMINA LOPEZ GASTON

8   Effects of gambling on the family   90
    RICHARD VELLEMAN, JENNIFER COUSINS AND JIM ORFORD

9   Pathological gambling: screening, diagnosis and assessment   104
    PHOEBE KASPAR

10 Psychosocial treatments for problem and pathological
gambling 123
NANCY M. PETRY

11 Pharmacological treatments 134
SCOTT BULLOCK AND MARC N. POTENZA

12 Family interventions in gambling 163
SANJU GEORGE AND HENRIETTA BOWDEN-JONES

13 Women and gambling 172
JASBIR DHILLON

14 Young people and problem gambling 182
XENIA ANASTASSIOU-HADJICHARALAMBOUS AND CECILIA A. ESSAU

15 Remote gambling: an overview of Internet gambling,
mobile phone gambling and interactive television gambling 195
MARK GRIFFITHS

Appendix 1 219
National Problem Gambling Clinic CBT group programme

Appendix 2 221
Assessment form for problem gambling

Appendix 3 226
Client-administered questionnaire

Index 232

Figures and tables

List of figures

2.1   Profile of regular gambler sub-groups by number and type of
      activities engaged in.   7
2.2   Problem gambling prevalence rates by regular gambling sub-
      group.   10
5.1   A bio-psycho-social model of pathological gambling (Sharpe
      2002).   43
5.2   A cognitive-conceptualisation diagram of gambling loss-chasing
      behaviour.   48
5.3   Schema-drive theory of gambling loss-chasing behaviour.   49
7.1   Structured interviews that can be used as guidance to apply the
      ICD-10/DSM-IV criteria.   83
12.1 Risk factors for problematic gambling.   168
12.2 Types of support and their key features.   170
13.1 The woman gambler: summary of gender-specific issues.   175

List of tables

4.1   A Pathway model of problem gambling.   32
5.1   List of schema domains and Early Maladaptive Schemas (EMS).   47

Contributors

Xenia Anastassiou-Hadjicharalambous, CPsychol, is an Associate Professor of Developmental Psychopathology at the University of Nicosia, Cyprus. She is a Chartered Psychologist of the British Psychological Association and a member of the Society of Pediatric Psychology of the American Psychological Association. Dr Anastassiou-Hadjicharalambous is an editorial board member of the *Encyclopaedia of Child Behavior and Development*, and an editorial/advisory board member and ad hoc reviewer of several well-established psychology journals. She is the author of over 50 scholarly publications in the area of Development and Psychopathology.

Scott Bullock is a research associate and clinic coordinator working with Dr Marc Potenza in the Center of Excellence in Gambling Research at Yale University. He received his BA in Psychology with a research emphasis from the University of Connecticut in 2008, graduating summa cum laude. Over the past six years, he has taken on increasing responsibilities including data management and analysis of gambling-related data. He has co-authored two journal articles on the neuropsychopharmacology of pathological gambling/gambling disorder and contributed to additional articles related to gambling and gambling disorders.

Luke Clark is the Director of the Centre for Gambling Research at UBC, in Vancouver, Canada. Prior to moving to the University of British Columbia, he trained at the University of Oxford and was appointed to faculty at the University of Cambridge. His work on gambling behaviour has been funded by the Economic and Social Research Council and the Medical Research Council.

Jennifer Cousins has worked at the National Problem Gambling Clinic since it opened in 2008. In her role as Family Psychotherapist she has taken the lead in developing the family service at the clinic; she has created a family support group, been a part of developing the 'Gambling, Family and You' workbook for relatives affected by gambling, and provided both couples and family therapy for those who attend the service. Jenny has an Advanced Diploma in Humanistic Counselling, and has completed two years of Systemic Therapy training.

Jasbir Dhillon is a second-year Trainee Clinical Psychologist training with the University of Hertfordshire. Jasbir worked at the National Problem Gambling Clinic as an Assistant Psychologist in 2012, working with problem gamblers in individual and group formats, as well as supporting and contributing to the development of a new treatment pathway for female gamblers. Alongside this, Jasbir has also previously worked within health psychology services, as well as contributed to research on conflict and containment within inpatient mental health services at the Institute of Psychiatry.

Cecilia A. Essau is a Professor of Developmental Psychopathology and the Director of the Centre for Applied Research and Assessment in Child and Adolescent Wellbeing (CARACAW) at the University of Roehampton, UK.

Professor Essau was born and raised in the tropical jungle of Borneo Island. She obtained her Bachelor of Arts Degree, her Honours Bachelor of Arts Degree and her Master of Arts degree from Lakehead University (Canada), her PhD from the University of Konstanz (Germany), and her 'Habilitation' in Psychology (qualification for tenure-track professorships in Germany) from the University of Bremen (Germany).

She has held a number of academic positions in Canadian (Lakehead University), Austrian (Karl-Franzens University, Graz) and German (Max-Planck Institute of Psychiatry, University of Konstanz, University of Bremen, Technical University Braunschweig, University of Muenster) universities before joining the University of Roehampton in 2004 as a Professor of Developmental Psychopathology. With research grants from numerous national and international institutions, her research has focused on understanding the interacting factors that can lead children and adolescents to have serious emotional and behavioural problems, and she has used this research to (a) enhance the assessment of childhood and adolescent psychopathology and (b) design more effective interventions to prevent and treat such problems. She is author of 180 articles, and is author/editor of 17 books in the area of youth mental health.

Rebecca Fisher is a University of East London trainee clinical psychologist who worked at the National Problem Gambling Clinic from October 2011 to March 2012. Her work involved administering a manualised CBT treatment programme on both an individual and group level to those with a gambling addiction. Additional individualised psychological therapy was provided for clients with further complex mental health needs. Her research and clinical interests lie in complex mental health needs particularly with respect to attachment, emotion regulation and mentalization.

Romina Lopez Gaston works as a consultant psychiatrist in the NHS. She has specialised in addiction and worked in a dual diagnosis service for almost four years. She has developed a special interest in co-morbid conditions that affect those suffering from addictive behavior, as well as services aiming to address this cohort of patients. Her work around integrated dual diagnosis services and young persons services based on local experience has been welcomed in international forums. She has been involved in a variety of research projects to gain a better understanding of addiction careers. She has also been involved in harm-reduction initiatives such as the prevention of drug-related deaths through the distribution of naloxone. Her areas of interest are reflected in myriad publications.

Andre Geel is a Chartered and Consultant Clinical Psychologist in Substance Misuse with Central and North West London NHS Foundation Trust in London. He has worked in the National Problem Gambling Clinic as a Consultant as part of his role as Sector Lead Psychologist for the Trust, also being responsible for supervising and overseeing psychologists in the Addictions Directorate in seven Central London boroughs and working clinically in a number of Community Drug and Alcohol Services.

He was previously Chair of the British Psychological Society Faculty of Addictions and is currently their Project Lead for Addictions. He was a contributor to the National Institute for Clinical Excellence (NICE) 2012 Guidelines on Drug and Alcohol Services. He is a supervisor and lectures on the North Thames Clinical Psychology Doctoral Courses for University College London, the University of East London and Royal Holloway University, and is also a supervisor for City and University's Counselling Psychology Doctorate Course.

He has previously been Head of Adult Clinical Psychology services and has worked in community, rehabilitation, primary care and military psychology. He has presented numerous national and international conferences on psychological therapies, addictions and carer issues.

Mark Griffiths is a Chartered Psychologist and Professor of Gambling Studies at the Nottingham Trent University, and Director of the International Gaming Research Unit. He has spent almost 30 years in the field, and is internationally known for his work into gaming and gambling. He has published over 450 refereed research papers, three books, 120+ book chapters and over 1000 other articles. He has served on numerous national and international committees and gambling charities (e.g. National Chair of GamCare, Society for the Study of Gambling, Gamblers Anonymous General Services Board, National Council on Gambling, etc.). He has won 14 national and international awards for his work, including the John Rosecrance Prize (1994), CELEJ Prize (1998), Joseph Lister Prize (2004) and the US National Council on Problem Gambling Lifetime Research Award (2013). He also does a lot of freelance journalism and has appeared on over 2500 radio and television programmes.

Phoebe Kaspar graduated with a degree in Psychology from the University of Birmingham in 2011. After working as an Assistant Psychologist in the National Problem Gambling Clinic for two years, she began her training to be a Clinical Psychologist at the University of Birmingham. She will qualify in 2016 and hopes to continue working in the field of problem gambling in the future.

Jim Orford trained in clinical psychology and obtained his PhD at the Institute of Psychiatry in London. He has researched and written extensively about alcohol, drug and especially gambling problems. He was an academic advisor to the 1999, 2007 and 2010 British Gambling Prevalence Surveys. In 2011 his book, *An Unsafe Bet? The Dangerous Rise of Gambling and the Debate We Should Be Having* was published by Wiley-Blackwell, and in 2012 he set up the Gambling Watch UK website to campaign for a public-health approach to gambling. A special area of interest has always been research on the impact of gambling and other addiction problems on the family, and the development of methods, such as the 5-Step Method, for helping and supporting affected family members. In 2010 he received the International Jellinek Award for contributions to addiction studies. His latest books are *Addiction Dilemmas: Family Experiences in Literature and Research and their Lessons for Practice* (Wiley-Blackwell, 2012), and *Power, Powerlessness and Addiction* (Cambridge University Press, 2013). He is now Emeritus Professor of Clinical and Community Psychology at the University of Birmingham, England.

Nancy M. Petry earned a PhD in Psychology from Harvard University in 1994. In 1996, she joined the faculty of the University of Connecticut Health Center, where she is Professor of Medicine. Dr Petry conducts research on treatment of addictive disorders, ranging from substance use to gambling disorders, and she uses behavioral interventions to improve health behaviours. She has published over 250 articles in peer-reviewed journals, and her work is funded by the National Institute on Drug Abuse, the National Institute of Mental Health, the National Institute on Alcohol Abuse and Alcoholism, the Eunice Kennedy Shriver National Institute of Child Health and Human Development, and the National Institute of Diabetes and Digestive and Kidney Diseases. Dr Petry is a consultant and advisor for the National Institutes of Health and the Veterans Administration, she served on the DSM-5 committee for the American Psychiatric Association, and she is the Editor of *Psychology of Addictive Behaviors*. Her book, *Pathological Gambling: Etiology, Comorbidity, and Treatment*, received the *Choice* magazine award for Top Academic Title in 2005.

Marc N. Potenza is a board-certified psychiatrist with sub-specialty training and certification in addiction psychiatry. He has trained at Yale University receiving a combined BS/MS with Honors in Molecular Biochemistry and Biophysics and a PhD in Cell Biology, the latter concurrent with the MD through the Medical Scientist Training Program. He completed internship, psychiatric residency and addiction psychiatry fellowship training at Yale. Currently, he is a Professor of Psychiatry, Child Study and Neurobiology at the Yale University School of Medicine where he is Director of the Problem Gambling Clinic, the Center of Excellence in Gambling Research, and the Women and Addictive Disorders Core of Women's Health Research at Yale. He is on the editorial boards of ten journals and editor-in-chief of the *Current Addiction Reports* journal and has received multiple national and international awards for excellence in research and clinical care. He has consulted to the Substance Abuse and Mental Health Services Administration, National Institutes of Health, American Psychiatric Association and World Health Organization and has participated in two DSM-5 research work groups.

Dr Potenza's research has focused on the neurobiology and treatment of substance and non-substance addictions and other disorders characterised by impaired impulse control. This research has a developmental focus, with implications for adolescents, young adults and older adults considered in studies. Dr Potenza's interdisciplinary research has applied brain imaging, genetic, epidemiological and clinical trials methodologies to gain knowledge and improve prevention and treatment strategies. This work has also involved identifying potential intermediary phenotypes, like facets of impulsivity, that may in part explain the high rates of co-occurrence between addictions and other mental health conditions, and might represent novel targets for prevention and treatment strategies.

Eleanor Roaf is a Fellow of the Faculty of Public Health. She worked in the NHS for 24 years, and was in the first cohort of people from a non-medical background to undertake Public Health training in the North West. She has worked as both a Consultant and a Director of Public Health, spending much of her career in Manchester. She was a member of the Responsible Gambling Strategy Board from 2009–13, providing Public Health and safeguarding expertise to the Board. She has published a number of articles in peer-reviewed journals, including on mainstreaming gambling as a public-health issue. She is currently working as a freelance Consultant in Public Health.

Snehal Shah is a chartered clinical psychologist registered with the Health Professions Council and British Psychological Society. After qualifying as a clinical psychologist, she worked at the National Problem Gambling Clinic using a variety of individual- and group-based psychological interventions including cognitive behaviour therapy and acceptance and commitment therapy. She now works with children and young people in Hertfordshire.

Neil Smith is a chartered consultant clinical psychologist registered with the Health Professions Council and British Psychological Society. Since qualifying as a clinical psychologist he has worked with a variety of addictions populations. He joined the National Problem Gambling Clinic in 2008, where he is currently the lead psychologist and service manager.

Richard Velleman is a leading authority on substance misuse, and especially the impact of this misuse on other family members, including children. Richard is both a clinical and an academic psychologist, has always held simultaneous posts in Universities and in the NHS, and has worked in the addictions and mental health fields for over 35 years. He is a co-founder of the International Network, AFINet, concerned with Addiction and the Family (http://www.

afinetwork.info/) and of the UK component: AFINet UK (formerly the UK Alcohol Drugs and the Family research network); a Senior Research Consultant in India with the Sangath Community Health NGO, Goa, India (http://www.sangath.com/), where he is developing and researching the use of community lay health workers to deliver psychological interventions to people with severe depression or serious alcohol problems. He is also the Vice-President of ENCARE (http://www.encare.info/) – an EU-wide network which he co-founded, concerned with developing resources to assist professionals across the EU to improve the help they offer to children in families affected by substance misuse. He was for six years (2008–13) a member of the 15-person Scientific Committee of the EMCDDA (European Monitoring Centre on Drugs and Drug Addiction). He is now Emeritus Professor of Mental Health Research at the University of Bath, England.

Heather Wardle was Project Director of the British Gambling Prevalence Survey 2010 and is currently a Research Director at NatCen Social Research. As well as leading NatCen's gambling research programme, she is a public-health specialist and has a keen interest in research methodology. She has just submitted her PhD in Sociology at the University of Glasgow focusing on female gambling behaviour and tracing how it has changed during and since the early twentieth century.

Chapter 1

Introduction

Henrietta Bowden-Jones and Sanju George

The first time the idea of editing a UK-based textbook on problem gambling came to us was the day we reached 1000 patients at the National Problem Gambling Clinic. We wanted to celebrate with something tangible that would reflect our dedication to gathering knowledge about this group of patients.

Having founded the clinic in 2008 and set up its first treatment protocols by basing much of our work on the textbooks and research by American colleagues Nancy Petry and Marc Potenza, we felt that five years later, the knowledge base we had acquired at the clinic had become substantial and we wanted to share it.

Our work as members of the Government's Responsible Gambling Strategy Board further added to the realisation that a significant body of expertise and knowledge now existed in the UK and that it should be these sources the textbook needed to refer to.

The chapter topics will allow any colleague with a wish to learn about this subject to feel comfortable in assessing and treating problem gamblers. Please note that we use the terminology problem gambling wherever possible in this book except when referring to primary research where the term pathological gambling was used.

Nothing teaches you more about a specific psychiatric condition than listening to hundreds of personal accounts of how the illness developed, its impact on the individual, his/her friends and family and his/her career. The people who have contributed to the chapters have become experts by dedicating their careers to this field.

We hope this book will be a companion to many of our colleagues not just in the UK, but all over the world. Although specific references are made to the UK in parts of this book, many of the theories and principles discussed are equally applicable across the world. We are grateful to the problem gambling treatment community for having been, from the beginning, a sharing and nurturing one, and we feel privileged to have worked with such an eminent group of professionals in bringing this book together.

Chapter 2

Gambling behaviour in Britain

Evidence from the British Gambling Prevalence Survey series

Heather Wardle

Aims

1 To describe the historical development of gambling opportunities in Britain, with a particular focus on the impact of the introduction of the National Lottery in 1994 and the Gambling Act in 2005.

2 To describe the purpose and methods of the three British Gambling Prevalence Surveys (1999, 2007 and 2010).

3 To present key findings from the 2010 survey and offer interpretations.

4 To discuss changes in gambling behaviours and prevalence of problem gambling across the three surveys (1999 to 2010).

Introduction

The gambling landscape: pre- and post-introduction of the National Lottery (1994)

Great Britain arguably has one of the most diverse and accessible commercial gambling markets in the world. In every high street, in every community, opportunities to gamble exist. These provisions range from the purchase of lottery tickets and scratch cards, sold in over 28,800 retailers nationwide, to venues where the only or main product on offer is gambling – amusement arcades, betting shops, casinos, bingo halls – to free and open access to Internet gambling, which is heavily advertised. Development of mobile gambling and related applications, which streamline the gambling process, mean that for those who wish to engage with gambling, the opportunities to do so can be omnipresent.

However, it has not always been this way. Prior to the introduction of the National Lottery in 1994, gambling provisions were limited to certain venues, such as bookmakers, bingo halls, casinos, amusement arcades, racecourses, pubs and clubs or other venues where slot machines were allowed. Whilst for some, gambling was part of the nation's pastimes, it was arguably not as visible prior to the introduction of the National Lottery and was confined to certain spaces and locations within communities. That is not to say that gambling was not popular. Estimates produced from national surveys in 1951 and 1977 show that the vast majority of adults, both men and women, gambled (Hoinville et al., 1977; Kemsley & Ginsburg, 1951). In fact when the findings of the 1951 study were published, the national and international press reported that gambling was 'almost universal'. Therefore, the popularity of gambling and betting has clear historical antecedents. In particular, the late nineteenth and early twentieth centuries were boom times for gambling and betting. As Reith (1999) describes, technological advances in the nineteenth century, particularly the development of the telegraph system improving communication systems and the opening of the rail networks, served to democratise horse racing and betting. It was no longer the preserve of the elite and became embedded as a form of popular entertainment and recreation among the working classes (Clapson, 1992; Reith, 1999). The popularity of horse racing betting among the working classes is still evident today, with regular betting on horse races being most prevalent among those in routine and manual occupations. Similar patterns can be traced for other gambling activities, specifically the development and growth of commercial bingo and the football pools.

The introduction of the National Lottery in 1994 can be seen as a step change in the way gambling was provided, regulated and promoted, for two main reasons. The first is that it broadened access to gambling opportunities in a way that had not been seen before. Lottery tickets and subsequently scratch cards were made available in many different venues, ranging from corner shops and petrol stations to major high street chains. Secondly, the introduction of the National Lottery represented widespread government endorsement of gambling. This endorsement was actively promoted through advertising, as, at that point, the National Lottery and its related products were the only forms of gambling allowed to promote their services via television and radio campaigns. The net effect, according to one commentator, was to turn Britain into a 'Nation of Gamblers' overnight (Atherton, 2006), though, as can be seen from the 1951 and 1977 studies, arguably we already were.

However, Britain was somewhat behind the curve when it came to the implementation of a nationwide lottery. The majority of US states had established lotteries in the 1970s and 1980s, Canadian state lotteries were established within a similar timeframe, as too were those in Australia, France, Ireland and Germany. Therefore, the implementation of the National Lottery could be viewed as Britain simply catching up with other nations. However, combining this provision with a number of other land-based gambling opportunities served to create one of the most accessible gambling markets in the world.

The Gambling Act (2005)

A second step change in how gambling was provided, regulated and controlled was the implementation of the Gambling Act 2005. Depending on your viewpoint, this legislation was either a wholescale liberalisation of the gambling market or a badly needed update to allow government to meet the increasing challenges of modern gambling practice, or, indeed, was both (Light, 2007). The Act included the creation of a new regulator, the Gambling Commission, charged with the objectives to keep gambling crime free, to ensure gambling is conducted fairly and openly and to protect children and vulnerable people from harm. To meet these objectives, a whole new regulatory and licensing regime was implemented based on dual principles of compliance and enforcement. However, much commentary about the Act has focused on its more visible clauses. For example, a key aspect, which has received increasing attention, was the removal of the demand criterion in the licensing process. Previously, operators had to demonstrate that there was substantial unmet demand for their products before being granted a licence to operate in a local area. However, under the Gambling Act 2005 these restrictions were removed, with the explicit instruction that when considering applications for premises licences, Local Authorities should not have 'regard for the expected demand for facilities' (DCMS, 2005). Since the implementation of the Act, debate has raged about the consequences of this, with many high-profile politicians and other stakeholders arguing that this has led to clustering of gambling establishments on some local high streets (Harman, 2011; Orford, 2010). Another visible aspect was permission for all gambling operators from all sectors to advertise their products on television and radio, albeit with certain restrictions. The Act also included provisions for a so-called 'super casino', which dominated debate although never came to fruition. The Act itself was fully implemented on 1 September 2007 and arguably heralded a key shift by which commercial gambling was mandated to become an increasingly visible commodity.

It is against this backdrop that the British Gambling Prevalence Survey series was developed and conducted. This aimed to understand and measure gambling behaviour in Great Britain and, crucially, to measure prevalence rates of problem gambling. It is this series of research to which the rest of the chapter now turns.

Measuring gambling behaviour and problem gambling among adults: the British Gambling Prevalence Survey series (BGPS)

The British Gambling Prevalence Survey series (BGPS) was a nationally representative survey of gambling behaviour among adults aged 16 and over living in private households in Great Britain. It was the only national study that focused solely on this topic. The first study was conducted in 1999, commissioned by GamCare, a then newly created treatment service for problem gamblers. Up until that point, it was widely acknowledged that there was a distinct lack of reliable information about gambling behaviour in Britain and that this represented a major gap in the evidence base. Specifically, there was no information about the magnitude or otherwise of problem gambling in Britain, which represented a challenge when estimating resource need for treatment services. The 1999 study was designed to fill this gap. Further studies were conducted in 2007 and 2010, funded by the Gambling Commission.

The purpose of each study was to monitor participation rates in all forms of gambling, to estimate the extent of gambling problems, explore attitudes to gambling and investigate the socio-demographic and economic characteristics of both gamblers and problem gamblers. In 2010, a further remit was added, which was, where possible, to provide comparisons pre and post implementation of the Gambling Act 2005.

Methodology

All three surveys were conducted by NatCen Social Research. To ensure maximum comparability across survey years, the study design broadly followed that used for the first study in 1999. First, a random sample of private households was drawn from the Small Users Postcode Address File. Advance letters were sent to these addresses to inform residents that they had been selected. Trained NatCen interviewers visited each address and attempted to interview the primary householder to obtain broad demographic information about the household. All adults aged 16 and over within co-operating households were eligible to participate and were asked to complete an individual questionnaire using either a paper self-completion booklet (as used in 1999 and 2007) or using computer-assisted self-interviewing methods whereby the respondent reads and types responses directly into a laptop computer (as used in 2010).

In each study respondents were asked to consider a list of gambling activities and to indicate whether they had participated in them in the past 12 months or not. The activities included were intended to cover *all* types of gambling available in Britain and were updated to reflect changes in gambling activities and provisions in each study year. Types of commercial gambling included were the National Lottery, other lotteries, scratch cards, bingo, betting on any event or sports, casino table games, poker, machine gambling, football pools, spread betting, etc. Private betting or gambling was also included, as were questions about online gambling.

Response rates varied from 65% in 1999 to 47% in 2010 and in each year the survey data were weighted to match the age, sex and regional distribution of the British population. Responses were obtained from 7680 participants in 1999, 9003 participants in 2007 and 7756 participants in 2010. Fuller technical details can be found in the main report of survey findings (see Sproston et al., 2000; Wardle et al., 2007; Wardle et al. 2011a).

Limitations

As with any social survey, there are important measurement issues to bear in mind when reviewing results from this study series. The first relates to the sample frame used. The BGPS is a study of people living in private households. This means those living in institutions are excluded from the study. The most pertinent population groups for this study are the prison population and young people living in student halls of residence. Both of these groups are likely to experience higher rates of problem gambling, meaning that the estimates provided by the BGPS across all three studies are likely to be a marginal underestimate of the true population value. Secondly, the methods used to measure problem gambling prevalence rely on respondents answering a set of questions based on specific criteria (typically, in this case, based on the ten DSM-IV criteria for pathological gambling). Once data are summed and scored, a threshold is set above which a person is deemed to be a problem gambler or not. As with any screening instrument, the possibility of including either false positives (i.e. identification of people as problem gamblers who are not) or false negatives (people who are problem gamblers being identified as non-problem gamblers) exists. Finally, any survey estimate may be subject to sampling error; that is, the possibility that differences between survey years are observed by chance simply because a different sample of the population has been drawn.

The BGPS survey was designed to minimise the potential impact of these measurement issues. For example, self-completion methodologies were used to elicit more honest responses, a standard threshold for the identification of problem gamblers was used in every survey year, detailed analysis comparing the profile of the BGPS responding sample to the population of profile of Great Britain was conducted to provide information about how and in what ways the sampled respondents may vary year on year. Nevertheless, no social survey is without its limitations and it is important that these be recognised.

Given below are some of the key findings from these surveys.

Who gambles and what on?

Data from the BGPS series show that the majority of adults in Britain take part in some form of gambling. In 2010, 73% of adults gambled at least once in the past year. This ranged from buying a single lottery ticket to regularly betting with bookmakers or playing table games in a casino. In population terms, this equates to around 35.5 million adults, making gambling an activity that the majority engage in.

Across all survey years, the most popular form of gambling activity was, and remains, purchase of National Lottery tickets. In 2010, 59% of adults bought a lottery ticket at least once in the past year and 60% of this group bought tickets at least once a week or more often. The next most popular activity was other lotteries (25%) and then the purchase of scratch cards (24%), followed by betting on horse races (16%) and playing slot machines (13%). Aside from private betting, all other forms of gambling activity were undertaken by less than 10% of adults.

Whilst these figures are of interest in describing basic patterns of behaviour, it treats participation in gambling activities in an isolated way. The BGPS series shows that if people have gambled in the past year, they tend to take part in more than one activity. In 2010, nearly two thirds (65%) of past-year gamblers took part in more than one form of gambling, with nearly one in ten (9%) past-year gamblers taking part in at least six or more different types of gambling.

Focus on regular gamblers, those who gamble once a month or more often, provides further insight into how gambling activities cluster together. In 2010, over 50% of adults had gambled regularly. Of course, purchase of National Lottery tickets accounts for a large part of this. Indeed, over half of regular gamblers were those who only bought tickets for the National Lottery or other lotteries on a regular basis. However, around one in four (23.9%) regularly took part in two or more activities, and around one in five (18.5%) regularly took part in three or more activities, of whom some displayed clear game-types preferences. This is shown in Figure 2.1 and highlights, for example, the small proportion of regular gamblers whose activities focused mainly on betting, be it horse races, dog races, other sports or other events, or the proportion of regular gamblers (2.2%) who were multi-interest gamblers regularly taking part in seven or more activities.

Individual gambling behaviour, particularly among those most engaged in gambling, is complex. Gamblers are not a homogenous group, but rather take part in a different range of activities, have different levels of engagement with gambling and different ways of accessing gambling products (Wardle et al., 2011c). A key question therefore is how does the profile of these differing types of gambler vary? Understanding this may help to further understand some of the heterogeneity between gambler sub-groups.

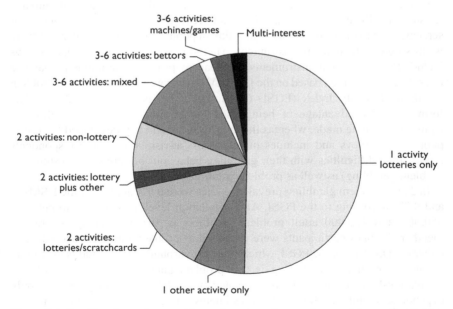

Figure 2.1 Profile of regular gambler sub-groups by number and type of activities engaged in.

To set the scene, evidence from the BGPS shows that the typical regular gambler is more likely to be male; to be older; to be from White/White-British ethnic groups; to be a cigarette smoker; to have lower levels of educational attainment; to be in a routine or manual occupation and to have parents who gambled. However, the profile of some of the regular gambling sub-groups significantly varies from this. Those who only regularly gambled on lotteries were more likely to be women, to have higher (not lower) levels of educational attainment and were less likely to have parents who gambled and less likely to smoke cigarettes. In this respect, their typical profile is generally opposite of all regular gamblers, although they were also more likely to come from lower-income households and to be older. By contrast, those who were multiple-interest regular gamblers were predominately male (87%), younger (58% were aged 16–35) adults, lived in lower-income households (45%) and were cigarette smokers (61%). They were also more likely to have parents who gambled.

As this brief analysis shows, gamblers are not a homogenous group; the demographic and socio-economic profile of gambler sub-groups varies, as do rates of gambling problems. It is to this which this chapter now turns.

Problem gambling prevalence rates

In the BGPS series, problem gambling was defined as gambling to a degree that compromises, disrupts or damages family, personal or recreational pursuits (Lesieur & Rosenthal, 1991). Many different questionnaire instruments, or screens, exist to measure problem gambling in population surveys, but as yet there is no single gold-standard instrument. Therefore, the BGPS series has always included two different instruments to measure problem gambling prevalence rates. In 2010, a screen based on the DSM-IV criteria was used, as was the Problem Gambling Severity Index (PGSI) (APA, 2000; Ferris & Wynne, 2001). The former has the advantage of being used in all three survey years, allowing comparisons to be made, whereas the latter was specifically developed for use in population surveys and includes measures of 'at-risk' (i.e. where respondents report some difficulties with their gambling behaviour but are sub-threshold for problem gambling) as well as problem gambling.

In 2010, problem gambling prevalence rates were 0.9% according the DSM-IV and 0.7% according to the PGSI. At a population level, this equates to between 360,000 and 450,000 adult problem gamblers in Britain. Taking the results together, 1.2% of participants were classified as problem gamblers according to either the DSM-IV or the PGSI, which equates to around 586,000 adults in Britain. What is particularly interesting is that problem gambling rates are similar to population-based estimates for drug dependence (0.9%) (excluding cannabis-only dependency) and are higher than estimates of moderate or severe alcohol dependence (0.4% and 0.1% respectively) (McManus et al., 2009).

In addition to those defined as problem gamblers, a further 7.3% of participants were classified as 'at-risk' gamblers (i.e. they had a PGSI score of 1 or more), meaning that these people had experienced some type of difficulty with their gambling behaviour in the past year. This equates to a further 3.5 million adults.

Of the different types of problems people experienced, chasing losses, being preoccupied with gambling, betting more than they can afford to lose and feeling guilty about gambling were the most common. Committing a crime to finance gambling, lying about gambling and risking a relationship, job or educational opportunity because of gambling were the least commonly reported problems. Whilst these problems were the least common, they were not unreported: in 2010, 0.2% of respondents had committed a crime to finance gambling in the past year and 0.4% respectively lied about the extent of their gambling or risked a relationship, job or educational opportunity because of their gambling.

Profile of problem gamblers

The profile of who experiences gambling problems has been fairly consistent across all three survey years. In 2010, problem gamblers were more likely to be male, to be younger adults, to be cigarette smokers, to be unemployed, to be in poorer health, to be from Asian or Asian-British ethnic groups and to have parents who had, themselves, experienced gambling problems. It is notable that this profile is similar to that of our multi-interest regular gamblers.

Of course, this is not to say that people with other demographic profiles do not also experience problems. For example, 1.5% of men and 0.3% of women were problem gamblers. Whilst there a strong correlation with age, with 2.1% of those aged 16–24 being categorised as problem gamblers, 0.3% of those aged 65 and over were also problem gamblers. Likewise, 3.3% of those who were unemployed were problem gamblers, but so too were 0.9% of those in paid employment. The pattern by ethnicity is of particular interest. Overall, those from Asian/Asian-British groups were less likely to gamble than their White/White-British counterparts and, correspondingly, had the most negative attitudes towards gambling. Yet problem gambling prevalence rates were significantly higher among this group (2.8%) than White/White-British (0.8%), indicating that those from Asian/Asian-British groups who do gamble were more likely to experience problems (Forrest & Wardle, 2011).

Finally, problem gambling rates varied significantly among the regular gambler sub-groups (select estimates are shown in Figure 2.2). Problem gambling rates ranged from 0.2% for those who only took part in the National Lottery on a regular basis, to 24.1% for multi-interest gamblers. Only 28.7% of multi-interest gamblers were not categorised as being, at least, an at-risk gambler. Equivalent estimates among those who were mainly bettors were 63.7%, and among those who only participated regularly in the National Lottery were 96.4%.

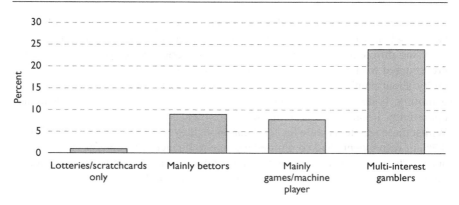

Figure 2.2 Problem gambling prevalence rates by regular gambling sub-group.

How has gambling behaviour changed from 1999 to 2010?

Evidence from the BGPS series shows that gambling behaviour in Britain has changed since 1999 (Wardle et al., 2011b). Among certain groups, such as women and older adults, the popularity of gambling is growing. More women than ever before participate in some form of gambling activity, and interestingly, in 2010 over 50% of women had gambled on some activity other than the National Lottery in the past year. The prevalence of past-year gambling participation also significantly increased among those aged 55 and over, rising from 65% in 1999 to 72% in 2010.

Excluding National Lottery-only gambling helps to identify broader patterns and trends in behaviour that are not obscured by the varying popularity of the National Lottery. This shows a clear upward trend in participation in other forms of gambling. In 1999 and 2007, around 52% of men gambled on activities other than the National Lottery. In 2010, this increased to 59%. The increase was even more marked among women, rising from 41% in 1999 to 53% in 2010. This means that for the first time in the survey's history, the majority of the British population either gambled on activities other than the National Lottery or bought tickets for the National Lottery and took part in some other form of gambling. The marked increase among women is of particular note. The latest survey shows that although gambling remains more popular among men than women, more women than previously now buy scratch cards (25%), take part in other lotteries (25%), play slot machines (10%) and gamble online on bingo, casino or slot-machine-style games (4%).

Furthermore, the proportion of people who gamble on a regular, at least monthly, basis significantly increased between 2007 and 2010, rising from 48% in 2007 to 54% in 2010. This increase in regular gambling activity was observed equally for both men and women. There were significant increases in regular gambling activity for the National Lottery Draw, scratch cards, other lotteries, football pools, betting on Fixed Odd Betting Terminals (FOBTs), betting on horse races, betting on other events, online gambling, spread betting and private gambling. For five activities, rates of regular participation were at least two times higher in 2010 than in 2007. These were: other lotteries, FOBTs, betting on other events or sports, online gambling and spread betting.

The changing distribution of what people gamble on and how often is evident among our regular-gambling sub-groups. Among both men and women, the proportion of regular gamblers who took part in more than one activity on a monthly basis rose from 45% in 2007 to 53% in 2010. The proportion of regular gamblers categorised as multi-interest significantly increased from 1.0% in 2007 to 2.2% in 2010. This pattern was evident for both men and women.

In short, in 2010 more people were gambling more regularly and they were gambling on a wider range of activities than previously. This highlights a shift among the British population, showing that they are increasingly more engaged with gambling and that this shift is particularly notable among some population groups, like women and older people, who had previously been less involved with gambling than their male or younger counterparts. Whilst men and younger people are still the groups most likely to gamble, the gap between men and women or older and younger people shows signs of narrowing.

Changes in the prevalence of problem gambling

Detecting changes in problem gambling prevalence rates as measured in surveys is difficult. The absolute number of problem gamblers identified in each BGPS survey year ranges from around 42–63, depending on the prevalence rate and sample size. This makes detecting statistically significant differences in problem gambling prevalence rates particularly sensitive to other changes between survey years, such as response biases or the changing profile of the population at large. The DSM-IV problem gambling estimate observed in 2010 (0.9%) was significantly higher than 2007 and 1999 (both 0.6%), though marginally so; the p-value was $p = 0.049$. (See Wardle et al., 2011a for further discussion of this data). However, by examining the overall patterns of gambling-related harm at a population level, corroborating evidence is provided by changes in average DSM-IV scores. The DSM-IV gives a score ranging from 0 to 10, a score of zero meaning that no problems were reported and a score of 10 meaning that all 10 items were endorsed. Mean DSM-IV scores among the total population significantly increased from 0.06 in 1999 to 0.08 in 2007 to 0.09 in 2010 ($p = 0.001$). The mean is skewed towards zero because of the large proportion of the population who do not gamble or who report no problems. However, these data show that distribution of DSM-IV scores within the population has shifted towards experiencing slightly greater levels of gambling-related harm than previously. Viewing these changes in context of the other changes in gambling behaviour described above, where people are gambling more often and on more activities, perhaps makes them less surprising and adds further contextual insight about how gambling behaviour has changed since the late 1990s.

Debate has raged about why these changes have occurred. Some have argued that this is a predictable result of the Gambling Act of 2005, whereas others have argued that they reflect broader shifts in attitudes, values and leisure preferences (see evidence presented to the 2011 Select Committee Inquiry into the Gambling Act for the range of opinion). The BGPS series is not able to untangle why these changes have happened. However, it is clear that we are living in an ever more complex world where physical and digital environments increasingly overlap and where gambling is increasingly visible and available for those who want it. It is important to continue to monitor gambling behaviour and to assess patterns, trends and direction of travel with these key metrics so that need for treatment services can be estimated and effective education and prevention strategies can be developed to reflect the current behavioural landscape.

Whilst this monitoring is clearly important, funding for the BGPS is no longer available, meaning there are currently no plans for BGPS trend series data to be extended beyond 2010. Some questions about gambling behaviour have since been included in the Health Survey for England (HSE) 2012 and the Scottish Health Survey 2012, to provide some information for these jurisdictions. These studies only collect past-year gambling rates and problem gambling prevalence, so analysis looking at frequent play is not possible. These studies have reported past-year rates of gambling for men of 65% and 70% respectively, and problem gambling rates of 0.5% and 0.7% (according to the DSM-IV criteria).

Conclusion

Stepping back from the debate about why behaviour has changed, the crucial message is that the BGPS series conservatively estimates that there are around 4–500,000 problem gamblers in Britain today and that 3.5 million adults are at risk of experiencing some kind of problem with their gambling behaviour. More recent data from the English and Scottish health surveys show more conservative figures but still estimates that somewhere in the region of 250,000 Scottish and English adults are likely to be problem gamblers. These are not insignificant numbers, nor are they shrinking numbers (notably, problem gambling rates from HSE 2012 are similar to rates from the BGPS 1999 and 2007). Problem gambling therefore should be acknowledged as an important public-health issue and deserves increasing recognition among healthcare professionals as an issue of equal prevalence to other substance abuse and misuse disorders.

Key points

---

1. Great Britain has one of the most diverse and accessible commercial gambling markets in the world, and opportunities for remote (TV, phone and Internet) gambling are on the increase.

2. Introduction of the National Lottery in 1994 and the Gambling Act in 2005 considerably deregulated and liberalised gambling opportunities in Great Britain.

3. The British Gambling Prevalence Survey series (1997, 2007 and 2010) was developed and conducted to understand and measure gambling behaviour in Great Britain and to measure the prevalence of problem gambling.

4. Some key findings of the 2010 survey were: 73% of adults gambled at least once in the past year; the most popular betting activities were the National Lottery, other lotteries, scratch cards and betting on horses, in that order; the typical regular gambler is more likely to be male, to be older, to be from White/White-British ethnic groups, to be a cigarette smoker, to have lower levels of educational attainment, to be in a routine or manual occupation and to have parents who gambled; problem gambling prevalence rates were between 0.7% and 0.9%.

5. In addition to the 0.7% to 0.9% problem gamblers, there are also another 6.5% of people who are 'at risk' of developing the problem.

6. The BGPS series clearly shows that more people were gambling more regularly, and they were gambling on a wider range of activities than previously; and that the popularity of gambling among women and older adults has grown.

7. Given these numbers of problem gamblers and 'at risk' gamblers, gambling needs to be acknowledged as an important public-health issue, and healthcare professionals need greater awareness of this potentially addictive behaviour.

References

Atherton, M. (2006). *Gambling: A Story of Triumph and Disaster.* London: Hodder.

American Psychiatric Association (APA) (2000). *Diagnostic and Statistical Manual of Mental Disorders, 4th edition, text revised.* Washington, DC: American Psychiatric Association.

Clapson, M. (1992). *A Bit of a Flutter: Popular Gambling and English Society c.1823–1961.* Manchester: Manchester University Press.

Department for Culture, Media and Sport (DCMS) (2005). *Gambling Act 2005.* London: DCMS.

Ferris, J. & Wynne, H. (2001). *The Canadian Problem Gambling Index: Final Report.* Canada: The Canadian Centre on Substance Abuse.

Forrest, D. & Wardle, H. (2011). Gambling in Asian communities in Great Britain. *Asian Journal of Gambling Studies*, 2(1): 2–16.

Harman, H. (2011). The problem of betting shops blighting our high street. Available at: http://www.harrietharman.org/uploads/d2535bc1-c54e-6114-a910-cce7a3eff966.pdf. Accessed 25 January 2012.

Hoinville, G., Collins M. & Smith, D. (1977). *National Lottery Survey*. London: Social and Community Planning Research.

Kemsley, W. & Ginsburg, D. (1951). *Betting in Britain*. London: Central Statistical Office.

Lesieur, H. R. & Rosenthal, M. D. (1991). Pathological gambling: a review of the literature (prepared for the American Psychiatric Association Task Force on DSM-IV Committee on disorders of impulse control not elsewhere classified). *Journal of Gambling Studies*, 7(1): 5–40.

Light, R. (2007). The Gambling Act 2005: regulatory containment and market control: the Gambling Act 2005. *Modern Law Review*, 70(4): 626–3.

McManus, S., Meltzer, H., Brugha, T., Bebbington, P. & Jenkins, R. (eds) (2009). *Adult Psychiatric Morbidity in England. Results of a Household Survey*. Leeds: NHS Information Centre for Health and Social Care.

Orford, J. (2010). *An Unsafe Bet: The Dangerous Rise of Gambling and the Debate We Should Be Having*. Oxford: Wiley.

Reith, G. (1999). *The Age of Chance: Gambling in Western Culture*. London: Routledge.

Sproston, K., Erens, B. & Orford, J. (2000). *Gambling in Britain: Evidence from the British Gambling Prevalence Survey 1999*. London: GamCare.

Wardle, H., Sproston, K., Orford, J., Erens, B., Griffiths, M., Constantine, R. & Piggot, S. (2007). *British Gambling Prevalence Survey 2007*. London: NatCen.

Wardle, H., Moody, A., Spence, S., Orford, J., Volberg, R., Griffiths, M., Jotangia, D., Hussey, D. & Dobbie, F. (2011a). *British Gambling Prevalence Survey 2010*. Birmingham: Gambling Commission.

Wardle, H., Griffiths, M.D., Orford, J., Moody, A. & Volberg, R. (2011b). Gambling in Britain: a time of change? *International Journal of Mental Health and Addiction*. doi: 10.1007/s11469-011-9319-4.

Wardle, H., Moody, A., Griffiths, M., Orford, J. & Volberg, R. (2011c). Defining the online gambler and patterns of behaviour integration: evidence from the British Gambling Prevalence Survey. *International Gambling Studies*, 11: 336–59.

Chapter 3

Gambling and public health

Eleanor Roaf

Aims

1 To explore whether problem gambling is an important public-health issue.
2 To describe why taking a public-health approach to tackling gambling-related harm is important.

Introduction

Gambling, while specifically banned in a number of religions, is commonly practised across the world. It enjoys a very mixed press, often attracting overt disapproval, but notwithstanding this, almost three quarters of British adults gamble on occasion, and many gamble regularly.

Few people experience any difficulty in controlling their spending (of either time or money) on gambling, and the prevalence of gambling-related harm in Britain is less than 1% (Wardle et al., 2010). Therefore, for most people, gambling is a pleasurable and harmless activity. It is a source of revenue to government, through taxes, and provides employment for many, at all skill levels. It is used as a fundraising tool for charities, leading to investment in the arts, local development and regeneration. Gambling in the UK has recently been liberalised through the Gambling Act (2005), but the Act continues to require that children and other vulnerable people be protected from being harmed or exploited by gambling.

Although only a small proportion of people who gamble suffer adverse consequences, the sheer number of people who gamble in the UK means that this small proportion creates, in numerical terms, a significant number of people where gambling is causing harm either directly to them or indirectly to their family or community. It comes as a surprise to many to discover that the number of individuals experiencing gambling-related harm is greater than the estimated number who misuse Class A drugs (Hay et al., 2010).

Terminology

The term 'gambling-related harm' is in general to be preferred to 'problem gambling' as the former phrase reflects that the person engaging in problematic gambling may be causing harm to their families and wider society, as well as to themselves. There is a danger that the phrase 'problem gambling', with its emphasis on the individual gambler and their needs, can lead to a focus on treatment services at the expense of addressing the wider impact of gambling.

'Responsible gambling' has been defined by the Responsible Gambling Strategy Board (2009) as being when 'operators provide socially responsible gambling products and players are able to control their play'.

Defining gambling-related harm

Gambling-related harm can be defined as gambling that disrupts or damages personal, family or recreational pursuits (Lesieur and Rosenthal, 1991). It is associated with a range of health and social problems, which include:

- mental ill-health, e.g. anxiety, depression, compulsive behaviour patterns;
- impact on family cohesion, including domestic violence;
- employment instability;
- debt problems;
- homelessness;
- criminality (e.g. theft or fraud to fund gambling activity).

In the main, gambling-related harm does not manifest itself in physical symptoms, which means that, unlike other dependent behaviours such as smoking or alcohol misuse, people with gambling-related problems rarely present to medical practitioners – or if they do, it may be because of symptoms caused by other behaviours. Because of this, gambling-related harm can remain invisible within the medical world, leading to an under-identification of it, and a lack of prioritisation of the problem. Consequently, within the UK health system, few resources are allocated to identifying or treating gambling-related harm, and within public health, it is usually ignored in favour of issues such as drugs, alcohol, smoking, obesity and risky sexual behaviour.

Is gambling a public-health issue?

For gambling to be of interest to public health, there needs to be clear evidence that **harm** is being caused, and that this **harm is significant** either across the whole population, or within identifiable sub-groups. Where the harm is limited to sub-groups within the population, public health will have a particular interest if this adds to other known **vulnerabilities** for that population. There is an interest in knowing where the **benefits** from the activity accrue, and if these benefits are spread equally across society (or equally across the groups that participate in the activity), or if one group is benefitting at the expense of others. Finally, there is interest in identifying the relative role of government, of society and culture, and of the individual, in mitigating these harms.

Having identified an issue, public health typically then considers two further elements. One is whether treatment of affected individuals (if relevant) is effective and whether it reaches people in need in an equitable manner. The second, and more overarching, element is to consider whether there are regulatory or organisational changes that could be made that would reduce the overall risks from the activity. To give an example of the two facets: in road safety, public-health advice would be that cyclists should wear helmets to reduce the risk of head injury in case of accidents. This provides some protection of compliant individuals. But reducing speed limits and promoting bicycle awareness among drivers will reduce the number of cycling accidents and thereby more effectively protect all cyclists. Most public-health practitioners would argue that the focus of their work must be on the latter, 'upstream', activities. Often, as in the example above, the issues tackled will be outside any medical sphere, with classic examples of public-health interventions including the provision of clean water and sewage, or immunisation programmes. More recently, public health in the industrialised world has focused on lifestyle factors, because of the contribution these make to morbidity and premature mortality. The ban on smoking in public places is a recent example of public-health-led legislation.

In this chapter, I will argue both that the data on the number of people affected by gambling demonstrates that reducing gambling-related harm is an important area for public health, and that taking a public-health approach to tackling gambling-related harm is the one that will have the greatest impact.

What is the public-health approach, and can it be justified?

Public health uses statistical and epidemiological evidence to identify risk factors within particular sub-groups of the population, and provides actions, advice and guidance on how these risks can be reduced, including examination of the types of harm prevention available and their impact and effectiveness. In addition, it interests itself with the evidence for the effectiveness of treatment, and on the access, availability and appropriateness of treatment offered. It will often focus as much on how to get equitable use of treatment as on the quality of treatment provided. This is where health economics becomes an important part of the public-health approach – and where public-health practitioners often come into disagreement with clinicians, who (understandably) tend to have more interest in their actual than their potential patients.

Because public health includes consideration of the impact of legislation and regulation on health, it is often accused of being an advocate of the 'nanny state', and of restricting the right of individuals or groups to exercise their freewill. Such restrictions can often incur direct economic costs on sections of society (although the restrictions may produce savings in other sectors). An example of this is the UK ban on smoking in public enclosed spaces: this has a negative effect on business profits and on the liberty of some individuals, but the NHS is seeing savings caused by a reduction in illnesses caused by smoking (Sims et al., 2010). Gostin (2007) described three general justifications for public-health regulation: firstly, to reduce risk to others; secondly, to protect 'incompetent' people, and thirdly, to reduce the risks to oneself. This third justification is the most hotly challenged area. While many would agree that the state interfering to curtail an individual's freewill is not to be taken lightly, there are instances where this right is routinely withheld (for example, compulsory seatbelts). In addition, many would argue that the ability to exercise one's freewill is very much affected by the beliefs and mores of the society that one inhabits. This is particularly true of behaviours such as smoking or drinking, where the behaviours of others in the area or the social group have an enormous influence, with, for example, the more people around you that smoke, the more likely you are to smoke, and the harder it is for you to stop. As Gostin says: 'state paternalism has the potential to alter culture in a positive direction, making it easier for individuals to make healthier or safer choices.'

Formulating the public-health response in order to reduce gambling-related harm – a 7-step approach

Having established that gambling is an issue that should be addressed by public health, the remainder of this chapter will focus on what steps should be taken to undertake this effectively.

I Understand the prevalence data and identify risk factors for harm

The link between the proportion of the population that gambles, and the proportion that has problems arising from its gambling, is not straightforward. It might be expected that the higher the proportion of people who gamble, the higher the absolute numbers of people who experience gambling-related harm will be (because 1% of 100 people is a smaller number than 1% of 1000 people). From this, it is argued that limiting the acceptability of or the opportunity for gambling are important prevention measures, as these will keep the absolute numbers of individuals affected low. However, not all groups in the population have the same prevalence of gambling-related harm. For example, Forrest and Wardle (2011) have shown that while participation in gambling is lower among people of Indian, Pakistani and Bangladeshi heritage living in Britain than among the white British population, the rates of gambling-related harm are significantly higher for these groups. Data from the British Gambling Prevalence Survey (BGPS) (Wardle et al., 2010) give pointers to the lifestyle, socio-economic and demographic features that correlate with problem gambling in the adult population. Using the criteria for problem gambling applied by the DSM-IV (American Psychiatric Association, 1994), the following points emerge regarding the current scale and distribution of problem gambling in the British population. These measures look at individual behaviours, rather than at the wider impact on family, friends or society.

- 0.9% of the British over-16 population can be classified as problem gamblers, which extrapolates to a figure of 451,000 adults across the population.
- The highest rates of problem gambling in Britain are among those aged 16–24 (2.1%) and 25–35 (1.5%). Whether this reduction in rates as people get older shows a 'natural recovery' needs to be explored.
- Problem gambling rates were significantly higher among those who were single (1.8%) or who were separated or divorced (1.1%), compared to those who were married or living with a partner (0.7%).
- In England only, problem gambling was lowest among least deprived individuals and highest among those who were close to the most deprived end of the social spectrum (1.8% for individuals in the Index of Multiple Deprivation (IMD) quintile 4).
- The prevalence of problem gambling was 3.3% among unemployed respondents compared to 0.9% among those who were in paid work.
- The prevalence was 6.1% among those who reported *'very severe money problems'*, compared to 0.5% among those who reported no money problems. Whether there is a causal link between the gambling and money problems is not known – nor, if there is a link, whether the gambling caused the money problems or vice versa.

It is clear from the variation in prevalence rates among different subpopulations that the risk of experiencing gambling-related harm, while remaining low in all groups, is far from evenly distributed. The data above also show a particular risk of the numbers experiencing gambling-related harm increasing during the current recession, given the association between low income, unemployment and gambling-related harm. Additionally, any increase in the prison population may increase the numbers experiencing gambling-related harm, as the recent study by May-Chahal et al. (2011) shows that prisoners are a very high-risk category.

Forrest and McHale (2012) identified that of those young people who gambled, 9% experienced problems, and many adult pathological gamblers report that they started gambling in childhood or adolescence. Correlation does not prove causation, and many of those who had problems as young gamblers, seem to have recovered by the time they are adults. But whatever the implications for later life, it appears that young people who gamble are more likely to experience immediate difficulties.

From Forrest and McHale's work, and from the Avon Longitudinal Study of Parents and Children (ALSPAC) report on gambling among 17-year-olds (Emond et al., 2012) a number of risk factors for children and young people are emerging. Deprivation (as measured by free school meals) does not increase the proportion of young people who gamble, but it does increase the risk of gambling-related harm. While gambling is strongly related to drinking alcohol, it is gambling associated with drugs or cigarettes that appears to lead to increased risk of harm. Boys are more likely to have problems with gambling than girls, and young people of 'Asian' ethnicity, while they are no more likely to gamble than the White population, are, if they gamble, three times as likely to have problems. Young people in the care of a guardian are at increased risk, as are those with no other siblings living in the household. Parental behaviour has been shown to be significant, and parental betting/lottery participation increases the chance that the child will gamble, as does living in a coastal area, where there are higher gambling rates but, interestingly, no increase in the proportion experiencing harm. The amount of pocket money given also strongly influences whether a child will gamble, with those given more money gambling more.

Many of these variables are hard (or even undesirable) to address: some children will always live in coastal areas; and most families, even where there is more than one child in the family, will have a time when there is only one child living at home. However, given the increased risk to children and adolescents, more attention should be given to young people's gambling, most of which takes place among friends, outside any regulated setting. In particular, it is important that parents understand the possible impact of their own behaviour, given the correlation between parental gambling and the increased likelihood of their children gambling, and the significance of the amount of pocket money they give. Despite this, parents do not often consider gambling to be a major concern, and evidence from the BGPS (Wardle et al., 2010) suggests that only 5% consider giving advice to their children regarding gambling.

2 Design interventions that increase resilience amongst high-risk groups

When addressing the needs of children and young people, **schools-based work and work with parents** seem obvious starting points. However, engaging with schools and parents is not simple, and often the parents with children at highest risk are the least likely to engage with any intervention. In addition, finding time within the school curriculum can be difficult. The evidence from substance misuse is that general programmes (e.g. via parents' evenings) are not very effective.

In terms of working with young people, while general advice could be given in schools, more specific work might focus on looked-after children, young people accessing drug or alcohol services, or young people in Young Offenders Institutions or known to youth offending services.

Measuring the outcomes of these interventions is always difficult. Experience in the drug and alcohol field suggests that information on its own has only a limited role, and that a focus on developing resilience, self-efficacy, and communication skills is more preventative than knowledge transmission.

There is evidence (Friend & Ladd, 2009) that **advertising bans** and counter-advertising increase anti-tobacco attitudes and reduce smoking prevalence in teenagers. **Social marketing campaigns** aimed at preventing youth gambling problems have been suggested as a method of reducing the incidence of gambling among young people. Messerlin and Derenevsky (2007) discuss the evidence for social marketing in relation to alcohol and drug prevention campaigns, and consider what lessons there may be for preventing gambling-related harm. Young focus-group participants in the study recommended that social marketing aimed at gambling prevention should demonstrate the harmful effects on the individual, the family, and on finances, with the largest impact expected from showing the personal consequences. They disliked campaigns that were seen as biased or authoritarian. Demonstrating how the government gets revenue from the gambling industry was also thought to be likely to have a deterrent effect (although one reason given for continuing to smoke is that without the revenue from tobacco products, the government would have to increase other taxes, which rather undermines this view). The authors do not recommend the use of social marketing as a standalone strategy, but felt it could form a part of a strategy that included school-based programmes and a public policy approach. Friend and Ladd (2009) summarise Cummings and Clarke's 1998 review of counter-advertising and contend that the most important elements were sufficient long-term funding, no political or tobacco company interference, and an approach that addressed the general population rather than focusing on children, teenagers or other specific vulnerable groups, as this increases the applicability of the message, reduces the risk of stigmatisation and reduces the risk that the behaviour becomes seen as a desirable, adult-only behaviour.

3 Promote early identification of those suffering gambling-related harm

Identifying gambling problems early, by means of simple screening questions, might help GPs to provide more appropriate interventions (George & Gerada, 2011). This follows the model used for other 'social' issues, such as domestic abuse or debt, where the GP is provided with a basic understanding, such that they can recognise the problem, provide information, and/or refer on for specialist help. This allows for a more holistic treatment of co-morbidities, and may reduce the level of need for 'medical' interventions. As with domestic abuse, the individual presenting to the GP may be suffering gambling-related harm as a consequence of actions of a family member rather than because of their own behaviour.

However, many individuals affected by gambling-related harm will not present to their GP, but instead may attend other services such as those offering financial advice or debt management. It is important that these services can identify gambling issues, and that they can also offer brief evidence-based advice, and refer or signpost on to appropriate treatment and support.

4 Provide adequate access to effective treatment services

As with other addictions such as smoking and alcohol use, there is a need to provide a range of treatments for gambling-related harm. Not all individuals will require the same input to address their problems, and a 'tiered' approach to service delivery should be explored, with, in general, the entry point for treatment being at the lowest tier. 'Brief interventions' have been shown to be effective in the treatment of both smoking and hazardous/harmful alcohol use, and the development of screening questions and follow-up brief interventions should be considered for addressing gambling-related harm.

Providing effective routes into services for all individuals affected is key to ensuring equitable access to treatment. Because most people presenting with gambling problems are male, many of the current services are heavily geared towards men. It is important the treatment providers consider not only the people whom they are successful in treating, but also the populations who are known to be affected but do not present for treatment, and those who present for treatment but drop out before completion. This can be achieved through treatment providers undertaking regular health-equity audits, comparing the characteristics (e.g. age, sex, ethnicity, deprivation, geographical location) of those likely to be suffering gambling-related harm with those who are presenting to their services. Commissioners of treatment services should be looking at this data, and at outcomes data, to see if particular services are especially good (or bad) at treating specific population groups, and should work with service providers to ensure that potential service users are able to access appropriate services in a timely manner.

5 Reduce the risks associated with the gambling environment

Gambling is not a uniform activity. It takes place in many different settings, such as casinos, betting shops, bingo halls and the Internet, and has many different forms such as sports betting, casino games, raffles and lotteries, and electronic gaming machines (EGMs). These different forms of gambling have different potential for causing gambling-related harm. EGMs are often regarded as the most harmful, because they are based on an 'intermittent reinforcement' model, which is dependency inducing. Evidence from Australia (Livingstone & Adams, 2010) shows that the machines are often calibrated so that they suit the characteristics of individuals in specific venues. Furthermore, the machines are more often located in areas of socio-economic disadvantage, which adds to the inherent risk. The Australian Productivity Commission (2010) reported that 41% of the EGMs revenue comes from severe problem gamblers (those with a Canadian Problem

Gambling Index (CPGI) score of 8+), with a further 20% coming from moderate risk gamblers (CPGI 3–7).

As part of most, if not all, treatment programmes, individuals are expected to refrain from gambling. This is often referred to as 'self-exclusion' and considerable attention has been given to how venues can support individuals to exclude themselves. One difficulty is that while a casino might require some personal identification, most other betting venues such as betting shops or bingo halls require no personal identification, and the data protection laws make data sharing across businesses problematic. In addition, the sheer number of betting shops in some areas has led to considerable concern that in such areas the temptation to bet may become overwhelming for vulnerable individuals.

There are a number of steps that venues can take to reduce the risk of gambling-related harm. These include reducing the size of the pay-out or the speed of play, changing the size of the stake or using less addictive reinforcement models. Training staff in casinos and other venues to recognise when someone has a problem and to signpost to services can be beneficial. Introducing breaks in play can also help reduce the likelihood of gambling beyond a player's means, as can restricting access to cash within the venue. While in the UK all machines must carry warning signs and also signpost to the helpline service, there is limited evidence of the impact of these warnings (Monaghan & Blaszczynski, 2010). In addition, gambling venues should be aware that their staff may be at risk from gambling-related harm themselves.

Betting operators therefore have a number of tools at their disposal, if they wish to reduce the risks from gambling. However, it is difficult for any individual operator to take the steps required to make a significant reduction in risk while still maintaining market share and making a profit for their shareholders.

6 Consider the role of regulation and legislation in reducing risk

Because it is against the interest of individual operators to act alone to reduce the risks from gambling, regulation of the industry is necessary. This regulation is generally welcomed by the industry, as it keeps a 'level playing field' between the various operators, and because it assists the industry to defend its practices by demonstrating its compliance with the regulations. However, as with the tobacco and alcohol industry, it is noticeable that the industry will fight fiercely to defend its profits.

This includes, for example, the resistance of the industry to proposed bans on advertising. Evidence from the USA (Friend & Ladd, 2009) shows that 'young people are disproportionately exposed to the marketing of products that present serious health risks, including smoking', and that this exposure increases the perceived attractiveness of smoking to young people, and reduces their perception of the risk. Given this, it is certainly a concern that much advertising of gambling, while not overtly targeting young people, is carried on websites and in events that predominantly attract a younger audience.

However, while there are many similarities between the tobacco and the gambling industries, there are also a number of significant differences, not the least of which is that while smoking is always harmful, many people gamble with no ill effect. Any advertising ban would come under considerable challenge from the fact that there are state lotteries that tend to be well promoted, including live draws on national TV, and therefore any ban would cause a conflict of interest within government.

A notable finding in relation to gambling is the interdependency between the gambling industry and the 'good causes' it supports. For example, the Australian gambling regulatory system means that companies can reduce their tax liability by demonstrating how they are putting money back into the local community. This has led to a dependency by local community organisations, such as sporting clubs, charities and schools, on the proceeds of gambling. However, as the people most likely to be harmed by gambling are those in the lowest socio-economic groups, this method of raising revenue or supporting good causes is highly regressive.

7 Ensure that the independent voice of public health is heard

The inter-dependence of the gambling industry and government adds a layer of complexity to any discussion about reducing gambling-related harm. Adams et al. (2009) investigated the implications of different methods of engagement between health, government agencies and what they describe as 'addictive consumption industries' such as tobacco, alcohol and gambling. In many jurisdictions, joint work between these three groups is promoted on the grounds that shared development of harm-reduction initiatives will be the most sustainable and efficient way of providing effective harm reduction. However, such joint work, while generally well intentioned, often has the unintended consequence of the harm-reduction message becoming compromised. There are a number of reasons for this. Firstly, there can be a conflict of interest. Where a health or research organisation is directly funded by the industry that it is meant to be evaluating, the independence of the voice becomes lost. Secondly, there is a power imbalance in terms of resources or influence, with health organisations being significantly weaker than either government or industry. This can lead to health organisations being pressured into endorsement of policies that they may only partially support. Thirdly, while some government departments want to reduce harm from gambling and other addictions, other departments may be more interested in the revenue gains from the activity. Thus harm-reduction methods that lead to a significant fall in consumption give a problem for government (unless there is a matching rise in taxation): on the one hand, there is a need to protect the vulnerable; on the other, the need to protect income streams. With the tobacco and alcohol industries, significant progress has been made in gaining tighter controls through campaigners demonstrating the hidden costs of the activity (for example, the cost to the NHS, the police, and social services of alcohol use). Arguably, within the anti-gambling campaigns, there has been little emphasis on the economic or health impact of gambling-related harm, which may weaken the case for tighter controls to government decision makers.

Adams et al. (2010) argue that government and the industry both share a dilemma – they wish to be seen to be acting responsibly without taking actions that would lead to a significant drop in income. This means that government and industry are both drawn to measures that appear to address harm without in fact reducing levels of revenue. This leads to the development of less effective methods such as school education programmes or public awareness campaigns, rather than arguably more effective measures such as regulating price or controlling advertising (or in the case of gambling, addressing the intermittent reinforcement techniques).

Sometimes, health organisations respond to the inherent difficulties of joint working by taking a stance of 'non-association', with a strict separation between health organisations and government/industry groups. This allows for discussion of the most effective harm-reduction techniques, rather than those that are most politically expedient. However, it also carries the significant danger that the health voice is ignored.

Conclusion

Because the harm done by gambling does not 'advertise' itself by visible signs, gambling does not yet have the prominence of other forms of damaging behaviour. This needs to change and gambling needs to be seen in context: that is, as an interaction between psychological, social, economic, business and government variables. Managing these effectively requires a more co-ordinated approach to recognising and treating gambling-related harm.

At the local level, to open the debate about how to recognise the impact of gambling-related harm, how best to prevent it, and to improve access to treatment services, gambling-related harm should fall under the remit of public health and be overseen by the new Health and Well-Being Boards. This would raise the profile of the issue within the NHS and the local authority, both of which have frameworks and structures which could be used to address gambling-related harm.

Nationally, there are a number of initiatives that could be taken to reduce gambling-related harm. For example, it would be possible to introduce 'smart' pre-commitment systems that would allow players to control their spending in terms of both time and money; to ban advertising; or to redesign EGMs to offer entertainment at a lower risk of inducing harmful gambling. There is also a need for a better understanding of the implications of new technologies and of the role of regulation in preventing harm. The Department of Health needs to work closely with the Department of Culture, Media and Sport, in order to reduce the harms caused by gambling in this country, while recognising that for the vast majority, gambling is a harmless and enjoyable pastime.

Key Points

1   Gambling is an important issue that should be addressed by public health.
2   In the UK public-health system, gambling-related harm is usually ignored in favour of issues such as drugs, alcohol, smoking, obesity and risky sexual behaviour, because the latter conditions cause more 'visible' harm.
3   A 7-step public-health response is proposed to reduce gambling-related harm.

Acknowledgements

Many thanks to Katrina Stephens, Specialty Registrar in Public Health, NHS Manchester, for carrying out the initial literature search; and to Sarah Doran, Richard Ives, Janet Mantle and David Regan for their comments on the draft of this chapter.

References

Adams, P. J., Raeburn, J. & de Silva, K. (2009). A question of balance: prioritizing public health responses to harm from gambling. *Addiction*, 104:688–91.
Adams, P. J., Buetow, S. & Rossen, F. (2010). Poisonous partnerships: health sector buy-in to arrangements with government and addictive consumption industries. *Addiction*, 105:585–90.
American Psychiatric Association (APA) (1994). *Diagnostic and Statistical Manual of Mental Disorders, 4th edition.* Washington, DC: American Psychiatric Association.
Australian Government Productivity Commission (2010). Gambling Inquiry, Report 50. Canberra.
Emond. A., Doerner, R. & Griffiths, M. D. (2012). Avon longitudinal study of parents and children (ALSPAC): gambling behaviour in adolescents aged 17 years. Bristol: Responsible Gambling Fund.
Forrest, D. & McHale, G. (2012). Gambling and problem gambling among young adolescents in Great Britain. *J Gambling Studies*, 28(4):607–22.
Forrest, D. & Wardle, H. (2011). Gambling in Asian communities in Great Britain. *Asian Journal of Gambling Issues and Public Health*, 2:13–16.
Friend, K. B. & Ladd, G. T. (2009). Youth gambling advertising: a review of the lessons learned from tobacco control. *Drugs: education, prevention and policy*, 16(4):283–97.
George, S. & Gerada, C. (2011). Problem gamblers in primary care: can GPs do more? *Brit J Gen Pract*, 61:248–9.
Gostin, L. O. (2007). General justifications for public health regulation. *Public Health*, 121:829–34.
Hay, G., Gannon, M., Casey, J. & Millar, T. (2010). National and regional estimates of the prevalence of opiate and/or crack cocaine use 2008/9: a summary of the key findings. National Treatment Agency, www.nta.nhs/uk/facts-prevalence.aspx.

Lesieur, H. R. & Rosenthal, M. D. (1991). Pathological gambling: a review of the literature (prepared for the American Psychiatric Association Task Force on DSM-IV Committee on disorders of impulse control not elsewhere classified). *J Gambl Stud*, 7(1):7–39.

Livingstone, C. & Adams, P. J. (2010). Harm promotion: observations on the symbiosis between government and private industries in Australasia for the development of highly accessible gambling markets. *Addiction*, 106:3–8.

May-Chahal, C., Reith, G. & Wilson, A. (2011). Offgam – an evidenced informed approach to addressing problem gambling in prison populations. www.rgfund.org.uk. Article of same name published in *Howard Journal of Criminal Justice* (2012), 51(4):372–86.

Messerlin, C. & Derenevsky, J. (2007). Evaluating the role of social marketing campaigns to prevent youth gambling problems. *Canadian Journal of Public Health*, 98(2):101–4.

Monaghan, S. & Blaszczynski, A. (2010). Electronic gambling machine warning messages: information versus self-evaluation. *Journal of Psychology*, 144(1):83–96.

Sims, M., Maxwell, R., Bauld, L. & Gilmore, A. (2010). Short term impact of smoke-free legislation in England: retrospective analysis of hospital admissions for myocardial infarction. *BMJ*, 340:c2161.

Wardle, H., Moody, A., Spence, S., Orford, J., Volberg, R., Jotangia, D. et al. (2010). *British Gambling Prevalence Survey National Centre for Social Research*. London: The Stationery Office.

Chapter 4

Aetiology of problem gambling

Andre Geel and Rebecca Fisher

Aims

1   To explore risk factors associated with gambling.
2   To describe a pathways model of problem gambling.

Introduction

The literature is both extensive and diverse when concerning the aetiology of problem gambling (PG) with numerous meta analyses finding multiple correlates to PG (see Goudriaan et al., 2004; Johansson et al., 2009; Raylu & Oei, 2002; Shafer & Hall, 1996; Welte et al., 2004). However, few of these factors have been found to be well established and causality has yet to be determined. The aim of this chapter, therefore, is to conceptualise and provide a general overview of this area. We shall investigate prevalence, demographics and other risk factors.

Demographics risk factors

Whilst the amount of gambling literature is ever increasing, there is no comparable increase in the amount of causal factors predicting the development of PG. The multiple risk factors and co-morbidity associated with problem gambling suggest it is not a homogenous illness nor is it found in a homogenous population, a conclusion made by numerous authors who advocate an alternative model proposing PG as a heterogeneous disorder with subtypes that share characteristics (Moreyra et al., 2000; Kalyoncu et al., 2003). The inclusive conceptualisation of problem gambling developed by Blaszczynski and Nower (2002) in their 'Pathways Model' provides one such useful framework in which to explore the risk factors for developing PG.

Age

Research has consistently demonstrated that a younger age is a risk factor for developing problem gambling (Johansson et al., 2009), specifically for those under 30 (Bondolfi et al., 2000; Clarke et al., 2006; Volberg et al., 2001), with higher incidence rates in those aged 16 to 24 years old (British Gambling Prevalence Survey (BPGS), 2010). This is an important factor for government health policy and psychological intervention, considering adult problem gamblers report gambling at a significantly younger age than those without problems (Abbott et al., 2000; Australian Productivity Commission, 1999). Moreover, Burge et al. (2006) found that those who started gambling in pre- or early adolescence (mean age 10.5 years) reported increased family, social, substance abuse and psychiatric problems as assessed by the Addiction Severity Index (ASI) (McLellan et al., 1980), in comparison with those starting gambling later in life (mean age 23 years), yet few adolescents, in this key developmental stage, seek help for gambling difficulties (Wilber & Potenza, 2006).

Countering this evidence, however, is research by Winters et al. (2002), who found that as age increased through adolescent years, so did at-risk gambling, but that the rate of problem gambling remained stable over time and across age ranges. In fact, the older adult population (65 years and above) has been found to be the group demonstrating the highest growth rate in participation of gambling (Desai et al., 2004; Morgan Research, 2000).

Gender

A strong gender bias is found within the PG literature, with males more likely to be problem gamblers than females (BGPS, 2010; Bondolfi et al., 2000; Chalmers & Willoughby, 2006; Clarke et al., 2006; Govoni et al., 1996; Johansson et al., 2009; Shead et al., 2010; Volberg et al., 2001; Winters et al., 1998, 2002), with comparative rates demonstrating significant differences between the two sexes across the literature, albeit inconsistent in size, e.g. 1.5% of men versus 0.3% of women (BGPS, 2010) and 11.8% of male versus 4.8% female PG (Govoni et al., 1996).

This appears to be borne out by some of the treatment services in the UK, who report that referrals are predominantly men. These anecdotal accounts also suggest that it might be due to women being less willing to admit to such a problem, and also possibly gambling online or privately compared to men. If problem gambling is more related to impulse control disorders, as both ICD-10 and DSM-IV suggest, then the gender bias might partially be explained, as men tend to present with a higher incidence of such. Another hypothesis is that there are gender differences in risk assessment and that women tend to take fewer risks than men, and as gambling is perceived as risky behaviour with an uncertain outcome, women tend to avoid it as such (Harris et al., 2006).

Socio-economic status and occupation

People from a disadvantaged neighbourhood are more likely to gamble. Welte et al. (2006) and the British Gambling Prevalence Survey (2010) found that those with no money or who had severe financial difficulties were significantly more at risk of developing PG. Perhaps going some way to explain this is the correlation that an excess of provision of gambling 'opportunity' (e.g. non-casino gaming machines) has been found in areas classified as 'highly deprived' (e.g. Wheeler et al., 2006), where individuals are more likely to be struggling financially and looking for ways to ease their financial burden. In this case, it has been argued that their anxiety or worry is a consequence of gambling, not the cause (Blaszczynski & Nower, 2002).

Linked to this concept are the associated risk factors of unemployment and job type that have been linked to problem gambling. Martinez-Pina et al. (1991) found that problem gamblers have been found more likely than control subjects to lack work, with unemployment subsequently and consistently being found to be a risk factor for PG (BGPS, 2010; Clarke et al., 2006; Feigelman et al., 1995; Hall et al., 2000). Indeed, individuals living on social welfare have demonstrated similar associations (Rönnberg et al., 1999; Volberg et al., 2001). A possible antecedent to this occupational situation is that lower academic achievement has been associated with more PG in adolescents (Shead et al., 2010; Winters et al., 2002), college students (Winters et al., 1998) and adults (Scherrer et al., 2007; Yip et al., 2011), which may impact on the individual's ability to find suitable employment.

Criminality

General criminality and an increasing amount of arrests have been associated with problem gambling (Feigelman et al., 1995; Hall et al., 2000; McConaghy, 1980; Welte et al., 2004). It has been hypothesised that perhaps crime is committed by individuals in efforts to pay debts (Ashley & Boehlke, 2012) after a study by Nower (2003) found that 21% to 85% of problem gamblers had committed crimes ranging from fraud, theft and embezzlement to robbery, assault and blackmail. Anecdotal evidence from treatment services in the UK and the author's clinical experience suggest a significant proportion of problem and pathological gamblers engaged in criminal behaviour to fund their gambling habits after they had developed a gambling problem.

Arguably there could exist a potential circular causality in this argument when considering the pathways model of problem gambling, where criminal behaviour might precede or occur simultaneously in the context of the 'Antisocial Impulsivist' group, whereas with the 'Behaviourally Conditioned' and 'Emotionally Vulnerable' groups, criminal behaviour would most likely be a 'last resort' to recover gambling losses. To the knowledge of Blaszczynski and Nower (2002), research has not yet been conducted to establish such a connection.

Ethnicity

Non-Caucasian ethnicities have been associated as having a higher risk of problem gambling (Abbott & Volberg, 1999; Welte et al., 2006). For example, those with Asian/Asian-British and Black/Black-British ethnicity were over-represented in problem gamblers compared to those with White ethnicity (2.8%, 1.5% and 0.8% respectively, BGPS, 2010), replicating findings of Welte et al. (2004), who found an over-representation of African-American, Asian and Hispanic ethnicity amongst problem gamblers. This research does appear to support the popular notion of gambling being culturally more acceptable within the Chinese community specifically.

Parental gambling

The perceived presence of problem gambling in a family member has been associated with self-perceived gambling problems (Cronce, et al., 2007), and actual defined parental problem gambling or regularity of gambling has been correlated to subsequent problem gambling in their offspring (BGPS, 2010; Winters et al., 2002). Interestingly, Clarke and Clarkson (2009) also found that the amount parents had gambled was significantly related to problem gambling in older adults and this was specifically in relation to where they thought their parents had gambled too much.

Pathways model of problem gambling

In order to introduce a logical structure to this debate we will use Blaszcynski and Nower's (2002) 'Pathways Model of Problem Gambling' as a framework for the discussion and as a way of organising the varied research material on the topic.

The pathways model proposes three types or groups of problem gambler – the Behavioural Conditioned, Emotionally Vulnerable and Antisocial Impulsivist. Each of these groups has certain distinct characteristics (Table 4.1), and in terms of risk factors and demographic information we shall take each of these groups in turn.

The 'Behavioural Conditioned' group

The Behavioural Conditioned are those problem gamblers who have been 'conditioned' (as in behavioural psychology/behaviourist) via their environment (pro- or gambling-positive), a big (and often early) win, social gambling (where friends, colleagues and family are engaged), and a family history of gambling or problem gambling, to be problematic, pathological or excessive gamblers.

Table 4.1 A Pathway model of problem gambling

Pathway of problem gambler[1]	Conditions
Behavioural Conditioned	• Environment • Big win • Social gambling • Family history
Emotionally Vulnerable	• Depression • Anxiety • PTSD
Antisocial Impulsivist	• Antisocial personality disorder • Borderline personality disorder

The 'Emotionally Vulnerable group'

The Emotionally Vulnerable group gamble to an excessive or pathological extent in order to compensate, distract or alleviate (or 'self-medicate') for another, pre-existing emotional problem, usually depression, anxiety or post-traumatic stress disorder (PTSD). Indeed, suppression and reactive coping styles have been found in problem gamblers, as well as lower scores on reflective coping styles (Getty et al., 2000).

Depression and anxiety

Depression and anxiety have been associated with greater likelihood of PG (Blaszczynski, 1995; Ibáñez et al., 2001; Scherrer et al., 2007; Shead et al., 2010; Yip et al., 2011) both in treatment and at follow-up (Smith et al., 2011). Dussault et al. (2011) conducted a longitudinal study of over 1000 males to explore the directionality of the links between depression and problem gambling. The authors found that impulsivity at age 14 predicted depression and problem gambling by age 17, and that this in turn increased depressive symptoms between the ages of 17 to 23. Also of note, however, is that depressive symptoms at 17 also predicted an increase in problem gambling in early adulthood, highlighting a mutual and potentially complex relationship between problem gambling and depression and one for further exploration. Higher anxiety levels have been found in those with PG (Coman et al., 1997; Ibáñez et al., 2001; Shead et al., 2010) and higher intensity of OCD symptoms in PG (Frost et al., 2001; Johansson et al., 2009).

Post-traumatic stress disorder

Ledgerwood and Petry (2006) found 34% of individuals seeking treatment for PG had high levels of PTSD (assessed through self-report measures), appearing to corroborate earlier findings where PGs were found to have experienced major traumatic life events (Kausch et al., 2006; Taber et al., 1987). Indeed, the overall occurrence of PTSD in PG has been estimated at from 12.5% to 29% (Ledgerwood

& Petry, 2006) and has highlighted a pattern of worse functioning and higher pathology in PG with PTSD compared to those without (Najavits et al., 2010).

Substance misuse

Higher alcohol use has been associated with gambling (Feigelman et al., 1995; Ladouceur et al., 1999) and dependence on alcohol has been identified as a risk factor for problem gambling (Welte et al., 2006). An association between substance use and PG has been found in adolescence (Delfabbro et al., 2006; Shead et al., 2010; Winters et al., 2002) and substance abuse disorders in adults (Hodgins et al., 2005; Petry et al., 2005; Welte et al., 2004; Yip et al., 2011) with drug dependence associated with past-year PG (Scherrer et al., 2007) and methadone treatment correlated to higher gambling rates too (Feigelman et al., 1995).

The 'Antisocial Impulsivist' group

The Antisocial Impulsivist group is that group that has a pre-existing borderline or antisocial personality disorder, and gambling happens to be one of (sometimes many) other forms of impulsive behaviour.

Indeed, higher incidence of personality disorders have been found in problem gamblers (Ibáñez et al., 2001; Petry et al., 2005), particularly antisocial personality disorder (McConaghy, 1980; Scherrer et al., 2007; Slutske et al., 2001). This second finding is consistent with such a group's disregard for risk-taking in the context of showing less regard and respect for the social values around money and the requirement to repay debts.

Impulsivity

Greater-rated PG severity has been associated with higher rates of impulsivity (Vitaro et al., 1997; Shead et al., 2010). Indeed, Shenassa et al. (2012) conducted a 30-year prospective community-based study and found that those individuals who were exhibiting impulsive behaviours at age seven were 3.09 (95% CI: 1.40–6.82) times more likely to report problem gambling in later years. Further to this, Grall-Bronnec et al. (2011) found that within problem gambling high impulsivity levels or a history of anxiety disorders were a co-morbid risk factor with ADHD. Furthermore, Dussault et al. (2011) also found that impulsivity at age 14 predicted depressive symptoms and gambling problems at age 17. Evidence has, however, been found to the contrary, where no relationship was found between impulsivity and gambling in a sample of male adolescents aged between 16 and 18 years (Gerdner & Svensson, 2003). There is also the suggestion that there might be a neurological component within this impulsive group.[2]

Conclusion

As a note of caution, the literature investigating psychiatric co-morbidity and PG should be considered with the caveat of association rather than causation. There may well be multiple interactions of variables placing an individual at higher risk of PG, making causality very difficult to determine (Ashley & Boehlke, 2012). Indeed, when analysed singularly, risk factors may well correlate to PG, but when combined in simultaneous prediction models many effects can be nullified, suggesting careful consideration of the literature. Indeed, Jackson et al. (2008) noted this very point in their study where the number of risk factors for gambling in adolescence significantly reduced when entered into simultaneous prediction.

Problem gambling is a relatively newly identified disorder which has aspects of a pure behavioural addiction, co-morbidity with existing mental disorders and neurological aspects, and is a complex, multifaceted and emerging field. Whilst the causal connection between problem gambling and co-morbid disorders/ conditions has not been established, we should be mindful that the definition and aetiology so far are embryonic, so to begin to view it from a bio-psycho-social perspective seems to be a usefully broad position to take.

Pathological gambling is one of the few disorders that seems to sit more comfortably and convincingly within a behavioural explanation of its aetiology and cause at present. Currently the most pragmatic, effective and evidence-based way of treating the problem (and getting good results) is the behavioural and cognitive-behavioural approach, but it might not fully explain the aetiology of the problem. Variables such as mental co-morbidity and neuropathology are very likely linked to this behaviour and need to be incorporated in the explanation of the condition in the future.

Notes

1 Based on the pathways model of problem and pathological gambling developed by Blaszczynski and Nower (2002).
2 See R. B. Dewey (2010), Pathological gambling in PD: did the devil make me do it? *Neurology* 9(75):1668–9.

References

Abbott, M. W. & Volberg, R. A. (1999). *Gambling and problem gambling in the community: An international overview and critique*. Wellington: Department of Internal Affairs.

Abbott, M., McKenna, B. G. & Giles, L. C. (2000). *Gambling and problem gambling among recently sentenced males in four New Zealand prisons*. Wellington: Department of Internal Affairs.

Abbott, M. W, Volberg, R. A. & Rönnberg, S. (2004). Comparing the New Zealand and Swedish National Surveys of Gambling and Problem Gambling. *Journal of Gambling Studies*, 20(3): 237–58.

Ashley, L. L. & Boehlke, K. K. (2012). Pathological gambling: a general overview. *Journal of Psychoactive Drugs*, 44(1):27–37.

Australian Productivity Commission (1999). Australia's gambling industries. Canberra, ACT: Productivity Commission.

Blaszczynski, A. P. (1995). Workshop on the assessment and treatment of pathological gambling, Australian and New Zealand Association of Psychiatry, Psychology and the Law Conference, Melbourne, May.

Blaszczynski, A. & Nower, L. (2002). A pathways model of problem and pathological gambling. *Addiction*, 97(5):487–99.

Bondolfi, G., Osiek, C. & Ferrero, F. (2000). Prevalence estimates of pathological gambling in Switzerland. *Acta Psychiatrica Scandinavica*, 10: 473–5.

British Gambling Prevalence Survey (2010). London: The Stationery Office.

Burge, A. N., Pietrzak, R. H. & Petry, N. M. (2006). Pre/early adolescent onset of gambling and psychosocial problems in treatment-seeking pathological gamblers. *Journal of Gambling Studies*, 22(3):263–74.

Chalmers, H. & Willoughby, T. (2006). Do predictors of gambling involvement differ across male and female adolescents? *Journal of Gambling Studies*, 22(4):373–92.

Clarke, D. & Clarkson J. (2009). A preliminary investigation into motivational factors associated with older adults' problem gambling. *International Journal of Mental Health & Addiction*, 7(1):12–28.

Clarke, D., Abbott, M., Tse, S., Townsend, S., Kingi, P. & Manaia, W. (2006). Gender, age, ethnic and occupational associations with pathological gambling in a New Zealand urban sample. *New Zealand Journal of Psychology*, 35(2):84–91.

Coman, G. J., Burrows, G. D. & Evans, B. J. (1997). Stress and anxiety as factors in the onset of problem gambling: implications for treatment. *Stress Medicine*, 13(4):235–44.

Cronce, J. M., Corbin, W. R., Steinberg, M.A. & Potenza, M. N. (2007). Self-perception of gambling problems among adolescents identified as at-risk or problem gamblers. *Journal of Gambling Studies*, 23(4):363–75.

Delfabbro, P., Lahn, J. & Grabosky, P. (2006). Psychosocial correlates of problem gambling in Australian students. *Australian and New Zealand Journal of Psychiatry*, 40(6–7):587–95.

Desai, R. A., Maciejewski, P. K., Dausey, D. J., Caldarone, B. J. & Potenza, M. N. (2004). Health correlates of recreational gambling in older adults. *American Journal of Psychiatry*, 161:1672–9.

Dussault, F., Brendgen, M., Vitaro, F., Wanner, B. & Tremblay, R. E. (2011). Longitudinal links between impulsivity, gambling problems and depressive symptoms: a transactional model from adolescence to early adulthood. *Journal of Child Psychology & Psychiatry*, 52(2):130–8.

Feigelman, W., Kleinman, P., Lesieur, H., Millman, R. & Lesser, M. (1995). Pathological gambling among methadone patients. *Drug and Alcohol Dependence*, 39:75–81.

Frost, R., Meagher, B. & Riskand, J. (2001). Obsessive compulsive features in pathological lottery and scratch-ticket gamblers. *Journal of Gambling Studies*, 17:5–19.

Gerdner, A. & Svensson, K. (2003). Predictors of gambling problems among male adolescents. *International Journal of Social Welfare*, 12(3):182–92.

Getty, H., Watson, J. & Frisch, G. (2000). A comparison of depression and styles of coping in male and female GA members and controls. *Journal of Gambling Studies*, 16:377–91.

Goudriaan, A., Oosterlaan, J., de Beurs, E. & Van den Brink, W. (2004). Pathological gambling: a comprehensive review of biobehavioral findings. *Neuroscience and Biobehavioral Reviews*, 28(2):123–41.

Govoni, R., Rupcich, N. & Frisch, G. (1996). Gambling behaviour of adolescents. *Journal of Gambling Studies*, 12(3):1–10.

Grall-Bronnec, M., Wainstein, L., Augy, J., Bouju, G. L., Feuillet, F. & Vénisse, J. L. (2011). Attention Deficit Hyperactivity Disorder among pathological and at-risk gamblers seeking treatment: a hidden disorder. *European Addiction Research*, 17(5):231–40.

Hall, G., Carriero, N., Takushi, R., Montoya, I., Preston, K. & Gorelick, D. (2000). Pathological gambling among cocaine-dependent outpatients. *American Journal of Psychiatry*, 157:1127–33.

Harris, C. R., Jenkins, M. & Glaser, D. (2006). Gender differences in risk assessment: why do women take fewer risks than men? *Judgment and Decision Making*, 1(1):48–63.

Hodgins, S., Tiihonen, J. & Ross, D. (2005). The consequences of conduct disorder for males who develop schizophrenia: associations with criminality, aggressive behaviour, substance use, and psychiatric services. *Schizophrenia Research*, 78(2): 323–35.

Ibáñez, A., Blanco, C., Donahue, E., Lesieur, H., Pérez de Castro, L., Fernández-Piqueras, J. & Sáiz-Ruiz, J. (2001). Psychiatric comorbidity in pathological gamblers seeking treatment. *American Journal of Psychiatry*, 158:1733–5.

Jackson, A. C., Dowling, N., Thomas, S. A., Bond, L. & Patton, G. (2008). Adolescent gambling behaviour and attitudes: a prevalence study and correlates in an Australian population. *International Journal of Mental Health & Addiction*, 6(3):325–52.

Johansson, A., Grant, J. E., Won Kim, S., Odlaug, B. L. & Götestam, K. G. (2009). Risk factors for problematic gambling: a critical literature review. *Journal of Gambling Studies*, 25(1):67–92.

Kalyoncu, Ö., Pektaş, Ö. & Mirsal, H. (2003). Pathological gambling: biopsychosocial approach. *Journal of Dependence*, 4 (2):76–80.

Kausch, O., Rugle, L. & Rowland, D. Y. (2006). Lifetime histories of trauma among pathological gamblers. *American Journal on Addictions*, 15:35–43.

Ladouceur, R., Boudreault, N., Jacques, C. & Vitaro, F. (1999). Pathological gambling and related problems among adolescents. *Journal of Child and Adolescent Substance Abuse*, 8:55–68.

Ledgerwood, D. M. & Petry, N. M. (2006). Posttraumatic stress disorder symptoms in treatment-seeking pathological gamblers. *Journal of Traumatic Stress*, 19:411–16.

Martínez-Pina, A., Guirao de Parga, J. L., Vallverdu, R. F., Planas, X. S., Mateo, M. M. & Aguado, V. M. (1991). The Catalonian Survey: personality and intelligence structure in a sample of compulsive gamblers. *Journal of Gambling Studies*. 4: 275–99.

McConaghy, N. (1980). Behaviour completion mechanisms rather than primary drives maintain behavioural patterns. *Activitas Nervosa Superior (Praha)*, 22:138–51.

McLellan, T., Luborsky, L., O'Brien, C. P. & Woody, G. E. (1980). An improved diagnostic instrument for substance abuse patients: the Addiction Severity Index. *Journal of Nervous & Mental Diseases*, 168:26–33.

Moreyra, P., Ibáñez, A., Saiz-Ruiz, J., Nissenson, K. & Blanco, C. (2000). Review of the phenomenology, etiology and treatment of pathological gambling. *German Journal of Psychiatry*, 3(2):37–52.

Morgan Research (2000). Seventh survey of community gambling patterns and perceptions. Project report. Prepared for Victorian Casino and Gaming Authority. Retrieved 21 February 2007 from http://vcgr.vic.gov.au/CA256F800017E8D4/Statistics.

Najavits, L. M., Meyer, T., Johnson, K. M. & Korn, D. (2010). Pathological gambling and posttraumatic stress disorder: a study of the co-morbidity versus each alone. *Journal of Gambling Studies*, doi:10.1007/s10899-010-9230-0.

Nower, L. (2003). Pathological gamblers in the workplace: a primer for employers. *Employee Assistance Quarterly*, 18(4):55–72.

Petry, N. M., Weinstock, J., Ledgerwood, D. M. & Morasco, B. (2005). A randomized trial of brief interventions for problem and pathological gamblers. *Journal of Consulting and Clinical Psychology*, 76(2):318–28.

Raylu, N. & Oei, T. P. (2002). Pathological gambling: a comprehensive review. *Clinical Psychology Review*, 22(7):1009–61.

Rönnberg, S., Volberg, R., Abbott, M., Moore, L., Andrén, A., Munck, I., Jonsson, J., Nilsson, T. & Svensson, O. (1999). Gambling and pathological gambling in Sweden: report no. 1–3 in NIPH series on problem gambling. Stockholm, Folkhälsoinstitutet (National Institute of Public Health, NIPH).

Scherrer, J. F., Xian, H., Kapp, J. M., Waterman, B., Shah, K. R., Volberg, R. & Eisen, S. A. (2007). Association between exposure to childhood and lifetime traumatic events and lifetime pathological gambling in a twin cohort. *Journal of Nervous and Mental Disease*, 195(1):72–8.

Shaffer, H. J. & Hall, M. N. (1996). Estimating the prevalence of adolescent gambling disorders: a quantitative synthesis and guide toward standard gambling nomenclature. *Journal of Gambling Studies*, 12(2):193–214.

Shead, N. W., Derevensky, J. L. & Gupta, R. (2010). Risk and protective factors associated with youth problem gambling. *International Journal of Adolescent Medicine & Health*, 22(1):39–58.

Shenassa, E. D., Paradis, A. D., Dolan, S. L., Wilhelm. C. S. & Buka, S. L. (2012). Childhood impulsive behaviour and problem gambling by adulthood: a 30-year prospective community based study. *Addiction*, 107(1):160–8.

Slutske, W., Eisen, S., Xian, H., True, W., Lyons, M., Goldberg, J. & Tsung, M. (2001). A twin study of the association between pathological gambling and antisocial personality disorder. *Journal of Abnormal Psychology*, 110:297–308.

Smith, N., Kitchenham, N. & Bowden-Jones, H. (2011). Pathological gambling and the treatment of psychosis with aripiprazole: case reports. *The British Journal of Psychiatry*, 199(2):158–9.

Taber, J. I., McCormick, R. A. & Ramirez, L. F. (1987). The prevalence and impact of major life stressors among pathological gamblers. *International Journal of the Addictions*, 22:71–9.

Vitaro, F., Arsenault, L. & Tremblay, R. (1997). Dispositional predictors of problem gambling in male adolescents. *American Journal of Psychiatry*, 154:1769–70.

Volberg, R. A., Abbott, M. W., Rönnberg, S. & Munck, I. M. E. (2001). Prevalence and risks of pathological gambling in Sweden. *Acta Psychiatrica Scandinavica*, 104(4):250–6.

Welte, J. W., Barnes, G. M., Wieczorek, W. F., Tidwell, M.-C. O. & Parker, J. C. (2004). Risk factors for pathological gambling. *Addictive Behaviours*, 29(2):323–35.

Welte, J. W., Wieczorek, W. F., Barnes, G. M., Tidwell, M.-C. O. (2006). Multiple risk factors for frequent and problem gambling: individual, social, and ecological. *Journal of Applied Social Psychology*, 36(6):1548–68.

Wheeler, B. W., Rigby, J. E. & Huriwai, T. (2006). Pokies and poverty: problem gambling risk factor geography in New Zealand. *Health & Place*, 12(1):86–96.

Wilber, M. K. & Potenza, M. N. (2006). Adolescent gambling: research and clinical implications. *Psychiatry (Edgmont)*, 3(10):40–8.

Winters, K. C., Bengston, P., Door, D. & Stinchfield, R. (1998). Prevalence and risk factors of problem gambling among college students. *Psychology of Addictive Behaviours*, 12(2):127–35.

Winters, K. C., Stinchfield, R. D., Botzet, A. & Anderson, N. (2002). A prospective study of youth gambling behaviours. *Psychology of Addictive Behaviours*, 16(1):3–9.

Yip, S. W., Desai, R. A., Steinberg, M. A., Rugle, L., Cavallo, D. A. & Krishnan-Sarin, S. (2011). Health/functioning characteristics, gambling behaviours, and gambling-related motivations in adolescents stratified by gambling problem severity: findings from a high school survey. *American Journal on Addictions*, 20(6):495–508.

Chapter 5

Cognitive-behavioural models of problem gambling

Neil Smith and Snehal Shah

Aim

I To summarise the existing literature on behavioural and cognitive-behavioural accounts and models of the development and maintenance of problem gambling.

Introduction

There are several different models that attempt to explain the development and maintenance of problem gambling in individuals. This chapter will focus on the cognitive and behavioural models of problem gambling and a further chapter will describe the neurological underpinnings.

Behavioural accounts

Early theoretical accounts attempting to explain the development and maintenance of problem gambling were mainly behaviourist in nature. Gambling was conceptualised as an operant behaviour, with gambling behaviour dictated to by the individual's previous reinforcement history.

Early on in gambling behaviour an individual may learn to associate gambling with pleasurable feelings and, over time, any reminder of gambling, such as the sight of money or gambling premises, becomes associated with pleasure. A gambler might rationalise losses in the early days by attributing them to lack of experience or using the wrong strategy. During this period, an individual would repeatedly expose themselves to gambling, emphasising the rewarding aspects of it, playing down the losses and speeding up the behavioural conditioning process.

This theory also tries to explain why gambling continues beyond the point at which it is helpful, and also why cravings endure once gambling has stopped. Skinner (1953), through investigating learned behavioural patterns in rats and pigeons, claimed that early success with gambling would increase the chances of gambling behaviour continuing, even if the reinforcement ratio decreased – i.e. the person was winning less often. Thus the individual would continue to gamble in the hope of experiencing that big win again, given that it had happened at least once.

Behavioural accounts emphasise the role of intermittent rewards in producing greater persistence in problem gambling behaviour, despite there being very little reinforcement – i.e. when gamblers lose much more than they win. Reinforcement schedules that pay off only intermittently (like gambling) are known to produce a greater persistence in the behaviour after the reward is stopped (Petry, 2005). This is known as partial reinforcement and is thought to enhance conditioning learning. Intermittent rewards help to promote the belief that persevering with the behaviour through losses is necessary to receive a reward. Losses are just a necessary step on the way to a win and can be discounted, as they will be recouped when the win comes. When the reward does finally come it may also be experienced with a greater degree of relief and enjoyment due to the degree of anticipation. Thus persistence to gamble, even after many losses, is strengthened, because the gambler will eventually experience a win if he or she continues to gamble, and also because of the possibly greater increase in relief and enjoyment.

Arousal

Arousal has been suggested to be the primary reinforcer of gambling behaviour. There is evidence supporting the association between autonomic arousal and numerous forms of gambling, including casino gambling (Anderson & Brown, 1984), horse race betting (e.g. Blaszczynski et al., 1986), and poker-machine gambling (Leary & Dickerson, 1985; Sharpe et al., 1995). It has been suggested individuals have different psychophysiological arousal needs, and for some, gambling is used to regulate their arousal needs (Brown, 1987). According to Brown (1987), some individuals experience higher levels of boredom and therefore pursue a greater intensity in stimulation to achieve the optimal level of arousal. However, sensation seeking as a trait is not thought to be elevated in problem gamblers (MacLaren et al., 2011).

Arousal may be a determinant of type of gambling though: horse-racing gamblers are more prone to sensation-seeking gambling, whereas poker-machine players are not, and this may be a function of the perception of skill, as opposed to luck or chance, that the game entails (Cocco et al., 1995). Sharpe (2002) argues that through using gambling as a way of escape, the negative arousal associated with stress can be re-interpreted as positive arousal (e.g. as excitement) in the gambling venue, thereby negatively reinforcing the gambling.

While there is some evidence for the association between the role of arousal and gambling behaviour, the theory is limited in terms of being able to explain fully why some individuals persist with gambling, despite devastating consequences on various aspects of their lives. Sharpe and Tarrier (1993) propose that initially gambling is maintained by operant conditioning, as arousal and rewards encourage further gambling. If gambling continues, they propose that cognitive processes become more important. Arousal and cognition have been linked by the association between heart rate and irrational verbalisations (Coulombe et al., 1992). Sharpe and Tarrier (1993) also found that when usual cognitive associations with the task were prevented through asking participants to count wins, arousal responses were prevented. This showed that the role of arousal may be mediated by cognitive events.

Cognitive-behavioural accounts

Cognitive-behavioural accounts attempt to merge together cognitive and behavioural accounts with the aim of providing an explanation for both the development and maintenance of problem gambling. Three models will be described here: Orford and colleagues, 1996; Sharpe and Tarrier, 1993; Sharpe, 2002.

Orford, Morison and Somers

Orford, Morison and Somers (1996) developed a model of 'attachment' to gambling that involved cognitive and behavioural factors. Their model suggested that primary, secondary and tertiary factors promote the development of attachment. The primary factor involved positive experiences with gambling, leading to initiation of difficulties, with arousal states and winning money as examples. Secondary factors included a newly developed drive to obtain money, the chasing of losses, secrecy of the habit from others and 'cognitive defences'. The latter relate to the minimising of losses or harms associated with gambling. Tertiary factors in the model relate to negative consequences – such as debt, loss of job or low self-esteem – that might further drive the person to wish to gamble. Orford and colleagues' model was devised from interviews and surveys with alcohol users and problem gamblers; they notably failed to find any concepts of tolerance or withdrawal in the gamblers' responses, differing from the experience of alcohol misuse.

Sharpe and Tarrier

The Sharpe and Tarrier model suggested that individuals are likely to have some vulnerability to developing problem gambling. A variety of situations may trigger the temptation to gamble, including gambling-related stimuli and stress, which the authors argue may stimulate arousal which is similar to that associated with gambling. The interaction of vulnerability with the format of gambling games is thought to generate associations between arousal and cognitive biases to produce a pattern of persistence with gambling, whether the gambler is winning or losing.

Control over gambling is mediated by a set of coping skills, which are thought to protect individuals from developing problems with gambling. These include:

- control over autonomic arousal;
- the ability to challenge cognitions;
- problem-solving skills;
- the ability to delay reinforcement.

Sharpe and Tarrier (1993) add that the consequences of continued losses may further undermine such coping skills, leading to the creation of a vicious cycle. These consequences might include:

- low-self esteem;
- alcohol use;
- financial difficulties;
- stress.

Sharpe and Tarrier's (1993) model was speculative and was developed to provide a theoretical framework to elicit testable hypotheses to guide future research and treatment (Sharpe, 2002). Sharpe developed a reformulated cognitive-behavioural model of problem gambling, which is empirically based and builds on the earlier (1993) model.

Sharpe

The Sharpe (2002) model (Figure 5.1) proposes that individuals are likely to have a genetic vulnerability to problem gambling, although the specific phenotype is not known. They suggest that the genetic vulnerability could be due to biological changes in neurotransmitters: dopamine, noradrenaline and serotonin. A variety of early childhood experiences also seem to predispose an individual towards developing future problem gambling. These include impulsivity, poor problem-solving skills, and positive family attitudes towards gambling. Easy access to and availability of gambling opportunities also increases the risk of future gambling problems.

Sharpe (2002) emphasised the importance of early gambling history. Early big wins or a series of relatively small wins may lead to the development of beliefs around gambling, such as the 'gambler's fallacy' (runs of 'bad luck' must be followed by good luck), and an illusion of control over gambling. Cognitive biases which lead individuals to attend more to wins than losses could lead to individuals overestimating their chances of winning. Furthermore, the early wins and nearly winning become associated with arousal. As gambling behaviour becomes more frequent, the interaction of arousal, gambling beliefs and biases becomes more automatic and less effortful, increasing the risk for gambling behaviour to go out of control.

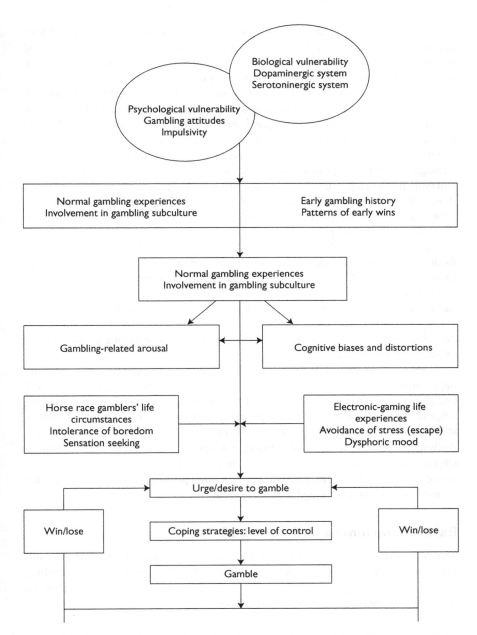

Figure 5.1 A bio-psycho-social model of pathological gambling (Sharpe, 2002).

Life events also formed part of this model. The relevance of the life event may depend on the form of gambling; for example, those who play electronic gaming machines may use gambling as an escape from their problems, as the arousal associated with stress can be reinterpreted as excitement.

As gambling is used more and more to accomplish different functions, it becomes more reinforcing and therefore more entrenched. Internal cues (stress or boredom) and external triggers (gambling-related stimuli) interact to activate arousal associated with gambling and gambling cognitions (urges).

The likelihood of acting on these urges depends on the available coping strategies. Those with poor coping strategies would find it hard to resist the urge, and end up engaging in gambling behaviour. Whether the individual loses or wins, those with high levels of arousal (positive or negative), powerful expectancies related to winning and poor available coping strategies are likely to continue with the gambling behaviour.

The consequences related to the gambling (e.g. job loss, relationship breakdown) further perpetuate the gambling behaviour, as individuals gamble to escape from these. Also the mounting consequences make the significance of the win as a solution to the problems so huge, that losing further seems negligible. Furthermore, the stress associated with the mounting consequences may diminish available coping strategies. The more these patterns become entrenched, the more self-perpetuating they become, and gambling becomes all-consuming at the expense of other aspects of life.

In terms of treatment implications, it is important in the short term to limit opportunities to gamble and break associations between gambling-related stimuli and gambling behaviour. Also, interventions at reducing impulsivity and learning helpful coping strategies such as problem solving can be helpful. Cognitive strategies to challenge irrational beliefs and mindfulness may also be useful. Activities that offer a sense of pleasure/mastery to alleviate boredom or relieve stress, as well as physical exercise to generate endorphins and offer a sense of mastery can also be useful. Finally, any relational problems as well as significant co-morbidity should be attended to.

Early experiences and core beliefs

The cognitive models described thus far provide little detail on the mechanisms via which early experiences lead to the development of problem gambling. Following are two approaches to explain this factor: the cognitive-developmental model of substance misuse and schema theory.

The cognitive developmental model of substance abuse

Liese and Franz (1996) have proposed a developmental model of substance abuse, which though designed for substance misuse can be adapted easily to problem gambling populations. The Liese and Franz model draws on Beck's (1996) cognitive models, suggesting that early life experiences lead to the development of negative core beliefs which, on exposure to an addictive substance, lead to the development of positive drug-related beliefs and on to continued usage of the substance.

Liese and Franz argue that it is specifically negative events that lead to schemas and beliefs that make individuals vulnerable to problems with addictions. Examples of early life experiences could include parents who are critical or invalidating. Positive early life experiences (e.g. secure interpersonal relationships) could lead to the development of resilience against developing problems with addictive behaviours.

Liese and Franz categorise early core beliefs by two domains: lovability and adequacy. Lovability schemas include basic beliefs about connectedness, self-worth and intimacy. Adequacy schemas involve beliefs about competence, success and autonomy. Examples of maladaptive schemas and basic beliefs include: 'I am bad', 'I am unlovable', 'if you don't have money you are a nobody', 'the world is not for me'. Initially, the beliefs are not specifically related to gambling. However, as individuals begin to use gambling as a coping strategy, they develop gambling-related beliefs that become associated with maladaptive basic beliefs. For example, 'I can't stand being bored' becomes 'gambling gives me the buzz and is great for getting rid of boredom'. Conditional beliefs may also develop; for example, 'if I win at gambling, people will like me'.

The development of problem gambling requires exposure to and experimentation with gambling. Some problem gamblers may have started gambling at any age, and exposure may have been through chance, family members or peer groups, whereas the decision to engage in gambling for those with more dysfunctional schemas and beliefs might be more intentional. Early positive experiences contribute to the individual's development of beliefs around gambling. This may be a monetary win at gambling, positive reinforcement from a peer group or a sense of community from gambling premises. Here standard cognitive distortions such as the gambler's fallacy or the illusion of control may develop. These cognitions feed into the individual's desire to return to the behaviour.

Schema theory and problem gambling

The second part of this chapter will describe a more detailed approach to understanding problem gambling, drawing on schema theory. The elements of schema theory in this section of the chapter are drawn from Jeffery Young's 1999 text and from his website (http://www.schematherapy.com).

'Chasing' in gambling behaviour

A win at gambling very much follows theorised reactions to substances, as seen in the cognitive-developmental model above. The person holds negative beliefs about self, resulting in negative emotions. Upon exposure to gambling, a gambling win specifically, negative beliefs about self are challenged and the individual experiences an improvement in mood, leading to the reinforcement of positive beliefs about the index activity that make future use more likely. In this model it is easy to see why individuals might 'chase' wins.

Winning at gambling challenges failure core beliefs, and, therefore, gambling can become a strategy via which the individual copes with the core belief, or copes with times when the core belief has been activated. In the Beck cognitive-conceptualisation diagram, gambling may appear in two areas. It may become a general compensatory strategy, employed as a means of enabling a rule/assumption that the individual must be successful. Alternatively, it may be a behaviour that appears as a consequence of a situation or scenario that activates the core belief and associated negative emotions.

The alternate side of the equation in gambling – the experience of losing – shares less with the substance misuse arena and is less immediately explicable by existing cognitive models of substance misuse. When the problem gambler experiences a loss at gambling, the individual's mood worsens and negative emotions are experienced. However, as the literature shows, this leads not to cessation of the behaviour in the problem gambler, but increased usage, and often more reckless, dangerous and damaging use. It is difficult to see this experience occurring with other addictive behaviours: an immediate aversive reaction to a drug, leading to distressing emotions, would not logically lead to greater and more urgent usage as a consequence. It appears paradoxical; indeed many clients present in treatment in a state of confusion, and with the belief that gambling is a form of self-harm or sabotage.

Schema theory

Schema theory can provide an explanation for this apparently paradoxical behaviour in the form of Early Maladaptive Schemas (EMS). Schema theory developed from Beck's early work on belief structures in depression. He postulated that schemas were stable cognitive structures for evaluating stimuli in the individual's environment (Beck, 1967). Jeffery Young's development of cognitive therapy, termed schema therapy, further developed these stable constructs and detailed different types that commonly occur (Young, 1999). In Young's theory, schemas are 'stable and enduring themes that develop during childhood, are elaborated during adulthood and are generally dysfunctional'. Young developed 18 different EMS following his experience of long-term psychotherapy with clients using CBT techniques. Young provided names for these schemas, listed definitions for each one in terms of beliefs, and detailed common family origin experiences. These 18 schemas fell under five separate domains, relating to the developmental needs of a child. These domains and schemas are summarised in Table 5.1.

Table 5.1 List of schema domains and Early Maladaptive Schemas (EMS)

Disconnection/rejection

Expectation that one's needs for security, safety, stability, nurturance, empathy, sharing of feelings, acceptance and respect will not be met in a predictable manner.

Individual EMS are termed 'Abandonment/instability', 'Mistrust/abuse', 'Emotional deprivation', 'Defectiveness/shame' and 'Social isolation/alienation'.

Impaired autonomy and performance

Expectations about oneself and the environment that interfere with one's perceived ability to separate, survive, function independently or perform successfully.

Individual EMS are termed 'Dependence/incompetence', 'Vulnerability to harm/illness', 'Enmeshment/undeveloped self' and 'Failure'.

Impaired limits

Deficiency in internal limits, responsibility to others, or long-term goal orientation. Leads to difficulty in respecting the rights of others, cooperating with others, making commitments, or setting and meeting realistic personal goals. Individual EMS are termed 'Entitlement/grandiosity' and 'Insufficient self-control/self-discipline'.

Other-directedness

An excessive focus on the desires, feelings and responses of others, at the expense of one's own needs – in order to gain love and approval, maintain one's sense of connection, or avoid retaliation. Usually involves suppression and lack of awareness regarding one's own anger and natural inclinations. Individual EMS are termed 'Subjugation', 'Self-sacrifice' and 'Approval-seeking/recognition-seeking'.

Over-vigiliance and inhibition

Excessive emphasis on suppressing one's spontaneous feelings, impulses, and choices or on meeting rigid, internalized rules and expectations about performance and ethical behaviour – often at the expense of happiness, self-expression, relaxation, close relationships or health.

Individual EMS are termed 'Negativity/pessimism', 'Emotional inhibition', 'Unrelenting standards/hypercriticalness', and 'Punitiveness'.

Schema theory, EMS and problem gambling

There are two key parts of schema theory in terms explaining the phenomena of loss or win chasing: affective arousal and schema processes.

Affective arousal

Schema theory is built on the understanding in cognitive theory of the relationship between affect and deeply held beliefs. The theory and practice of cognitive therapy involves the identification of 'hot cognitions' in therapy. These cognitions are identified on the basis of their link with emotion; in the cognitive-conceptualisation diagram the automatic thought is relevant because of its link to the core belief and the associated emotions that result. Early schema theory placed more emphasis on this link, stipulating that strong emotional reactions that appear disproportionate can be a sign that an EMS has been activated. The EMS is said to 'erupt', leading to intense emotions and efforts to ameliorate these emotions. Young noted that EMS related to failure are 'usually accompanied by a high level of affective arousal, in this case anxiety'. He also noted that depending on circumstances and particular EMS 'the individual might experience other emotions such as sadness, shame, guilt or anger' (1999, p. 11).

The model of loss chasing presented here suggests that the intense arousal associated with winning or losing, which is characteristic of the compulsive or pathological gambler, may indeed be as a result of the activation of the dysfunctional EMS.

Figure 5.2 displays a how a typical cognitive formulation, using Beck's cognitive conceptualisation diagram, might try to explain chasing losses.

Here we have a situation – the loss – that has led to automatic thoughts that cause negative emotions because of the connection with a deeply held core belief, such as failure.

However, the link between the negative emotion and the coping behaviour, returning to what caused the negative emotion, does not make sense in this formulation. Gambling in this model might be the last thing the individual would do in reaction to the emotions caused by gambling. In this way the standard cognitive conceptualisation is not an adequate explanation for chasing losses.

Figure 5.3 provides a more complete model of the development and maintenance of gambling problems based on schema theory.

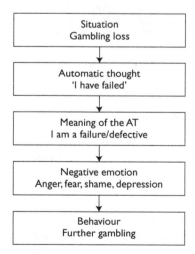

Figure 5.2 A cognitive-conceptualisation diagram of gambling loss-chasing behaviour.

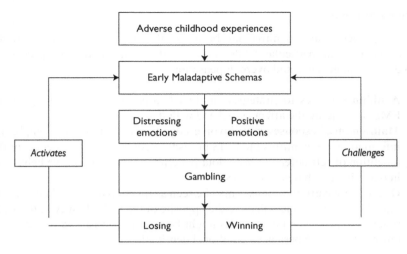

Figure 5.3 Schema-drive theory of gambling loss-chasing behaviour.

As with the standard Beck cognitive model, it shows how early adverse experiences lead to the development of dysfunctional beliefs, EMS in this model. However, here exposure to gambling has a bi-directional effect on the EMS, both of which lead to further gambling: gambling wins challenge the EMS, and gambling losses activate it. This makes gambling extremely attractive to an individual with dysfunctional EMS. Gambling is not just an escape behaviour, as seen in the Beck formulation, but an active coping strategy to deal with the negative core beliefs activated by gambling.

When a vulnerable individual has been exposed to gambling wins, as most problem gamblers are at some point in their early playing career, thoughts and feelings that are the opposite of their particular EMS will have resulted. When gambling losses occur, the EMS is activated and negative feelings associated with it are felt intensely. Therefore, in this scenario it would be entirely rational for the individual to seek to redress those reoccurring thoughts and feelings with something that has helped in the past – i.e. winning at gambling. If the standard cognitive distortions seen in problem gambling (e.g. gambler's fallacy) exist, then these can then be used to facilitate further gambling, in a seemingly rational attempt to reduce negative emotions.

A behaviourist might suggest that the variable ratio reinforcement seen in gambling, with wins/rewards provided at random points, is sufficient to explain this pattern. But the behaviourist model does not fully explain the reason for the presence of distressing emotions seen in loss chasing. The frustration of a simple stimulus–response, or operant conditioning, relationship does not provide the 'good fit' explanation for these negative emotions in the way that schema theory can. Schema theory as described here may also provide a cognitive explanation for the strength of response to apparent reward.

Schema processes

Schema processes are cognitive and behavioural responses or reactions by the individual to their particular EMS. Young (1997) identified three processes: avoidance, maintenance and overcompensation.

1   **Avoidance** relates to strategies employed to prevent the triggering of the EMS or avoiding the affect associated with it.
2   **Maintenance** responses may involve cognitive distortions that emphasise information that confirms the EMS or dismiss contradictory evidence, or the repetition of self-defeating behaviour patterns, such as submissive behaviour in one with a 'subjugation' EMS.
3   **Overcompensation** responses may be seen as functional in that they relate to thoughts and behaviours that are the opposite of the EMS; however, these are often rigid and overemployed, as might be seen in narcissistic responses to those who have experienced emotional deprivation.

The reaction of further gambling as a response to substantial gambling losses, as seen in the compulsive or problem gambler, could be explained by each of the processes:

•   The person trying to gamble to be successful may be compensating for feelings of failure.
•   The individual repeatedly gambling and losing may well be maintaining feelings of defectiveness.
•   The individual may be adopting avoidant coping of the reality of gambling losses.

Research has suggested that gamblers are most likely to adopt avoidant coping strategies to cope with life stressors (e.g. McCormick, 1994) and to cope with gambling losses (Shepherd & Dickerson, 2001). Further, Yi and Kanetkar (2011) identified avoidant coping strategies in gamblers and found positive correlations between avoidant coping and gambling severity, and between shame-related emotions and avoidant coping. As noted above, shame is an emotion that is often seen on activation of an EMS.

The only study that has investigated the prevalence of EMS in pathological gamblers compared 167 problem gamblers with matched controls (Estevez & Calvete, 2007). The authors found the most substantial and significant differences in EMS scores in the domains of 'Disconnection/rejection' and 'Impaired autonomy and performance'. The EMS in these domains include 'failure', 'defectiveness' and 'alienation' – EMS that Young suggests would result in feelings of shame.

The avoidance seen in problem gamblers by gambling again is most likely a form of cognitive distortion: avoiding the reality of the loss by convincing the self that a win is imminent. Yi and Kanetkar (2011) investigated distortion of loss as an avoidant coping strategy. This related to thoughts that losses are a necessary part of winning, and to those who dismissed the importance of the monies lost. Distortion of loss was associated with both the severity of the gambling problem and emotions of shame.

Conclusion

Schema theory provides a more detailed explanation than standard cognitive conceptualisations for the phenomena of chasing losses and wins, as found in the behaviour of problem gamblers. The schema-drive model suggests an affective arousal hypothesis for the emotionally driven and reckless gambling that problem gamblers report when loss chasing. Schema theory further provides a conceptual framework whereby therapists can conceptualise loss chasing in terms of an individual's particular reaction to deeply held EMS.

Schema theory suggests that exposure to gambling may be particularly problematic for individuals with adverse early upbringings and the resulting Early Maladaptive Schemas. There are multiple studies linking early adverse experiences with the development of problem gambling: the pathways model of problem gambling (Blaszczynski & Nower, 2002) provides an excellent summary of the evidence collected in this area and suggests it relates to increasing severity of gambling problems. The schema chasing model presented here, and schema theory, adds to that picture by explaining the cognitive and affective mechanisms behind those links.

References

Anderson, G. & Brown, R. J. F. (1984). Real and laboratory gambling, sensation-seeking and arousal. *British Journal of Psychiatry*, 75:401–10.

Beck, A. T. (1967). *Depression: Clinical, Experimental, and Theoretical Aspects*. New York: Hoeber.

Beck, J. S. (1996). *Cognitive Therapy: Basics and Beyond*. New York: Guilford Press.

Blaszczynski, A., & Nower, L. (2002). A pathways model of problem and pathological gambling. *Addiction*, 97:487–99.

Blaszczynski, A. P., Wilson, A. C. & McConaghy, N. (1986). Sensation seeking and pathological gambling. *British Journal of Addiction*, 81:113–17.

Brown, R. (1987). Gambling addictions, arousal, and an affective/decision-making explanation of behavioural reversions or relapses. *International Journal of the Addictions*, 22:1053–67.

Cocco, N., Sharpe, L. & Blaszczynski, A. (1995). Differences in preferred level of arousal in two sub-groups of problem gamblers: a preliminary study. *Journal of Gambling Studies*, 11:221–30.

Coulombe, A., Ladouceur, R. & Desharnais, R. (1992). Erroneous perceptions and arousal among regular and occasional video poker players. *Journal of Gambling Studies*, 8:235–44.

Estevez, A. Y. & Calvete, E. (2007). Cognitive schemata in people suffering from pathological gambling and their relationships with parenting. *Clínica y Salud*, 18:23–43.

Leary, K. & Dickerson, M. G. (1985). Levels of arousal in high and low frequency gamblers. *Behavioural Research and Therapy*, 23:635–40.

Liese, B. S. & Franz, R. A. (1996). Treating substance use disorders with cognitive therapy: lessons learned and implications for the future. In P. M. Salkovskis (ed.), *Frontiers of Cognitive Therapy*, pp. 470–508. New York: Guilford Press.

MacLaren, V., Fugelsang, J. & Harrigan, K. (2011). The personality of pathological gamblers: a meta-analysis. *Clinical Psychology Review*, 31:1057–67.

McCormick, R. A. (1994). The importance of coping skill enhancement in the treatment of the pathological gambler. *Journal of Gambling Studies*, 10:77–86.

Orford, J., Morison, V. & Somers, M. (1996). Drinking and gambling: a comparison with implications for theories of addiction. *Drug & Alcohol Review*, 15:47–56.

Petry, N. (2005). *Pathological Gambling: Etiology, Comorbidity, and Treatment*. Washington, DC: American Psychological Association.

Sharpe, L. (2002). A reformulated cognitive-behavioural model of problem gambling: a biopsychosocial perspective. *Clinical Psychology Review*, 22:1–25.

Sharpe, L. & Tarrier, N. (1993). Towards a cognitive and behavioural model of problem gambling. *British Journal of Psychiatry*, 162:407–12.

Sharpe, L., Tarrier, N., Schotte, D. & Spence, S. H. (1995). The role of autonomic gambling arousal in problem gambling. *Addiction*, 90:1529–40.

Shepherd, L. & Dickerson, M. (2001). Situational coping with loss and control over gambling in regular poker machine players. *Australian Journal of Psychology*, 53:160–9.

Skinner, B. F. (1953). *Science and Human Behaviour*. New York: Macmillan.

Yi, S. & Kanetkar, V. (2011). Coping with guilt and shame following gambling loss. *Journal of Gambling Studies*, 27:371–87.

Young, J. E. (1999). *Cognitive Therapy for Personality Disorders: A Schema-Focused Approach (3rd edn)*. Sarasota: Professional Resource Press.

Chapter 6

Neurobiology of pathological gambling

Luke Clark

Aims

1   To give the reader an understanding of pathological gambling from a neurobiological perspective. To outline the concept of pathological gambling as a disorder of decision making.
2   To make the reader aware of the latest scientific research in the area of disordered gambling. To outline the neurochemistry involved in the illness.
3   To list the cognitive distortions most commonly seen in pathological gamblers, and their impact on gambling.
4   To outline the differences between pathological gambling and other addictions.

Introduction

Research on the neurobiological substrates of gambling has unquestionably seen the greatest expansion over the past decade. Two phenomena make a compelling case for a neurobiological level of explanation for disordered gambling. The first, is the effect of brain injury to a specific sector of the frontal lobe, the ventromedial prefrontal cortex (vmPFC). The resulting lesion syndrome is characterised by changes in personality, emotion and judgment, at the core of which lies disturbed decision making (Clark & Manes, 2004; Damasio, 1994). These patients make incoherent decisions that are often based on immediate and superficial gains, without regard for the longer-term repercussions, such as for their finances, physical wellbeing or family relationships. The model translates well to disordered gambling where the gambler continues to pursue their harmful behaviour, in the face of clear evidence and knowledge that this action will only serve to increase their difficulties (Bechara & Damasio, 2002; Bickel & Marsch, 2001). The second, is seen in Parkinson's Disease (PD), an illness characterised by a degeneration of dopamine cells in the basal ganglia. Some dopaminergic medications used to treat PD, by either increasing dopamine synthesis or stimulating dopamine receptors, elicit spontaneous disordered gambling in some patients (Voon et al., 2007; Weintraub et al., 2010). Many of these patients have negligible prior involvement in gambling, and the gambling rapidly dissipates as the medication is withdrawn. Hence it is hard to refute a conclusion that elevated dopamine transmission is somehow triggering an endogenous bias towards a specific form of risky decision making.

These two examples highlight a conceptualisation of disordered gambling as a disorder of decision making (Clark, 2010; Studer et al., 2012). And so, the neural systems that support decisional processing are thus the main focus of this chapter.

As an activity, gambling is a decision (or typically a series of decisions) to risk a monetary bet on the uncertain prospect of a larger financial gain. In pathological gamblers, this decision is made repeatedly ('compulsively') in the face of mounting debt and other negative consequences (e.g. relationship problems, criminal activity to support gambling). Within a psychological framework, a single gamble can then be deconstructed into several stages. The initial period (henceforth 'selection') involves the placing of the bet, and this may involve a complex decision between many alternatives, as in a horse race, or may be as simple as pressing the spin button on a slot machine. (It is worth noting that many slot-machine gamblers nevertheless engage in careful deliberation over which machine to play, believing that some machines are 'hot', and hence there is often a decisional component). Subsequent to selection, there is a delay (henceforth 'anticipation'), which is typically an exciting period: the horse race itself, or the spin of the roulette wheel or slot-machine reels. This period varies in length across different games, from just a few seconds (slot machine) to a few minutes (horse race) or several days (lottery). Finally, the 'outcome' is revealed, and the gambler discovers whether they have won or lost.

The emergent field on the neurobiology of disordered gambling has utilised a number of convergence neuroscience techniques. Studies using neuropsychological probes like the Iowa Gambling Task or Wisconsin Card Sort Test have been complemented by functional neuroimaging investigations, mainly using functional Magnetic Resonance Imaging (fMRI) during cognitive activation tasks. Structural changes have been measured with voxel-based morphometry and white-matter tractography, using fMRI. Positron Emission Tomography (PET) studies have used radiotracers with selective neurotransmitter targets such as the dopamine D2 receptor (the [11C] raclopride tracer), to dissect neurochemistry relevant to disordered gambling, and these will be discussed later.

As a note on research design, the vast majority of studies to date have been cross-sectional, comparing a group with disordered gambling against a control group who are typically healthy non-gamblers, but may occasionally be recreational players with gambling experience but no symptoms (e.g. Miedl et al., 2010). The term *pathological gambling* refers to a relatively severe group who meet stringent DSM diagnostic criteria and/or threshold scores on screening instruments such as the South Oaks Gambling Screen (Lesieur & Blume, 1987) or, increasingly, the Canadian Problem Gambling Index (Ferris & Wynne, 2001).

The term *problem gambler* refers to a less severe group who meet lower thresholds on these screening tools, and hence display some symptoms but may not reach clinical diagnostic criteria (see Toce-Gerstein et al., 2003). In the discussion that follows, the term *disordered gambling* is used to refer to groups with pathological and/or problem gambling, collectively, and this term is likely to be adopted in the DSM-5 (Mitzner et al., 2011). A roughly equal number of studies to date have recruited treatment-seeking gamblers through clinical referral routes, or recruited disordered gamblers through community advertisement. Of course, the latter group are typically not seeking treatment and may have limited awareness of their gambling severity. This carries some implications for their psychological state, which has not been explored in the research to date. It should be borne in mind that cross-sectional designs can shed light on the neurobiological factors associated with the current state of being a problem gambler, but provide no direct insight into the aetiological processes by which that state arose. While there are some longitudinal and prospective designs of trait influences in problem gambling (Slutske et al., 2005, Vitaro et al., 1999), usually from the epidemiological perspective, these designs have not been utilised as yet in neurobiological research.

Neuropsychology and behavioural economic approaches

The traditional neuropsychological approach applies behavioural tasks that have established sensitivity to focal brain damage, either in computerised or pencil-and-paper format, to characterise pathophysiology in neuropsychiatric illnesses. This pathophysiology is likely to occur at the level of brain systems rather than focal lesions, and is likely to be of gradual and developmental origin rather than a circumscribed insult (Clark et al., 2012a).

The handful of broad-brush neuropsychological studies that were conducted prior to 2000 (reviewed in Goudriaan et al., 2004) indicated that several cognitive domains were basically intact in pathological gamblers, including sensory processing, language, motor function and memory. Subsequent research over the past decade has honed in on higher-level functions associated with the prefrontal cortex, namely decision making, and the 'executive functions' that include working memory, planning and inhibition of automatic responses. It is now well established that pathological gamblers perform abnormally on tests of risk-based decision making (Clark, 2010; Leeman & Potenza, 2012), and this finding points to dysregulation in the vmPFC that can be tested more directly with fMRI (described later in this chapter).

The Iowa Gambling Task (Bechara et al., 1994) is the most well-known probe of decision making, placing the participant in an uncertain learning environment (four decks of cards) and requiring them to make a series of choices with hypothetical financial outcomes. Healthy volunteers realise that the two of the card decks that appear superficially rewarding in fact harbour large occasional penalties, and they opt instead for the safe decks that accrue a gradual profit.

Pathological gamblers fail to learn this advantageous strategy (see e.g. Cavedini et al., 2002; Forbush et al., 2008; Goudriaan et al., 2006), resembling the profile seen in lesion cases with damage to the vmPFC.

The resemblance to vmPFC damage was substantiated in a study using the Cambridge Gambling Task (Rogers et al., 1999) in a group of community-recruited problem gamblers and a group with alcohol dependence (Lawrence et al., 2009; see also Grant et al., 2011). The strength of the Cambridge Gambling Task is that it removes the learning demands from the Iowa Gambling Task, allowing a clearer assessment of risk preference: both the problem gamblers and alcoholics placed higher wagers on simple probability decisions than did demographically matched healthy controls. The same effect was observed in lesion patients with focal vmPFC damage due predominantly to anterior aneurysms (Clark et al., 2008).

At least two of the experiments on decision making have found dissociations from measures of executive function. In Cavedini et al. (2002), pathological gamblers were impaired on the Iowa Gambling Task but did not differ from controls on the Wisconsin Card Sort Test. In Lawrence et al. (2009), problem gamblers (and individuals with alcohol dependence) placed elevated bets on the Cambridge Gambling Task, but only the alcohol-dependent group were impaired on a test of spatial working memory. Nevertheless, executive impairments have been indicated in some other studies (Leiserson & Pihl, 2007; Regard et al., 2003; Rugle & Melamed, 1993) and it is likely that such impairments are either restricted to a subgroup of gamblers (e.g. Blaszczynski and Nower's (2002) 'antisocial impulsivists') or are simply of smaller effect than the decision making/vmPFC abnormalities. There are some separable components of executive function (e.g. Miyake et al., 2000), and inhibitory control may be most relevant to disordered gambling, as the neuropsychological corollary of impulsivity, a trait that is reliably increased in disordered gambling (Michalczuk et al., 2011) and predictive of later gambling in youth cohorts (Slutske et al., 2005; Vitaro et al., 1999). Disordered gamblers commit more false responses on Go–No–Go tasks (Fuentes et al., 2006), have slower stop-signal reaction times (Odlaug et al., 2011), make more prepotent Stroop errors (Kertzman et al., 2006), make more non-reflective errors on the Matching Familiar Figures Test (Kertzman et al., 2010), and sample less information on another measure of 'reflection impulsivity' (Lawrence et al., 2009). The extent to which these changes tap a common resource or neural system remains unclear.

A further probe of impulsivity has been derived from behavioural economics. In a *delay discounting* scenario, the participant must choose between a small reward available now or a larger reward available in the future (Bickel & Marsch, 2001). This is typically performed with monetary rewards, and the delays need not be experienced firsthand (e.g. 'Would you prefer £15 now or £40 in one month?'). The tendency to choose the smaller but immediate reward (or 'discount' the larger later reward) is considered an impulsive choice, similar to children's inability to 'delay gratification' when given analogous decisions involving sweets (Mischel et al., 1989). Rates of discounting may be described by mathematical models that assume an underlying hyperbolic function (Reynolds, 2006) or disproportionately weight immediate outcomes (McClure et al., 2004). Pathological gamblers show steeper rates of delay discounting compared to healthy subjects (Dixon et al., 2003; Michalczuk et al., 2011; Petry, 2001), mimicking the effect seen in various substance-addicted groups. A lesion study has confirmed the same effect in cases with damage to the orbitofrontal cortex (an area that largely overlaps the vmPFC) (Sellitto et al., 2010). Within gamblers, discounting correlates with gambling severity (Alessi & Petry, 2003), drug addiction co-morbidities (Petry & Casarella, 1999) and gambling-related beliefs and cognitive distortions (Michalczuk et al., 2011).

The delay scenario can also be converted into a probability format: 'Would you prefer £15 for certain or a 50% chance of winning £40?' Here, gamblers' preferences reverse; they prefer *uncertain* larger rewards and hence display *lower* discounting rates (Madden et al., 2009). It remains unclear to what extent probabilities and delays are handled by common or distinct neural systems (Peters & Buchel, 2009).

Gambling research has recently seen other fruitful advances from the injection of measures from behavioural economics and Judgment and Decision Making (JDM). In a procedure for assessing overconfidence by Goodie (2005), subjects answered general knowledge questions (e.g. 'Which state has the larger population, Indiana or Utah?') and gave confidence estimates on their answers. Bets were then constructed for each item ('Win 133 points if Indiana is correct, or zero if incorrect'). The bets were titrated from the confidence estimate such that the bet amounts would be unfavourable for overconfident responses. Problem gamblers were seen to be overconfident relative to non-problem gamblers, and accepted a higher number of unfavourable bets.

A related experiment modelled the probability weighting function within Prospect Theory: as the objective probability of an outcome varies across the range 0 to 1, the perceived probability follows a S-shaped curve, with low-probability events (such as gambling wins) considered more likely, and high-probability events considered less likely, than their true values. Ligneul et al. (2013) examined this non-linearity in problem gamblers, but the findings in fact indicated an overall upward shift in perceived probability, such that uncertain outcomes were considered more likely across the full range. This echoes the increased betting seen on the Cambridge Gambling Task, where problem gamblers bet high, but adjusted their bets to the odds to the same extent as controls (Lawrence et al., 2009).

These findings imply the judgment system in disordered gamblers may be adequately 'calibrated' but that either the overall 'risk appetite' or confidence at a given level of risk is elevated.

Functional neuroimaging

The initial wave of imaging studies in pathological gamblers began with the dual fMRI experiments by Potenza and colleagues in 2003 (2003a, 2003b), and applied cognitive tasks that had established sensitivity in drug addiction. Using the Stroop test to measure inhibitory control, and a cue-reactivity task involving autobiographical scripts and a gambling video, a small group of male pathological gamblers showed reduced activation of the vmPFC region on both procedures (Potenza et al., 2003a; Potenza et al., 2003b). This finding not only converged with the neuropsychological evidence of vmPFC involvement (as discussed earlier), but concurrent work from the same group found similar effects in cocaine addicts (Potenza, 2008).

A similar design scanned the Iowa Gambling Task in substance-dependent individuals with and without problem gambling; both groups showed reduced vmPFC compared to healthy controls (Tanabe et al., 2007). A further line of studies by De Ruiter and colleagues used a three-group design comparing pathological gamblers with heavy smokers and healthy controls, scanning impulsivity-related tests of reversal learning and stop-signal inhibition. The picture from these studies is that multiple sectors of prefrontal cortex may be underactive across both gamblers and smokers, including lateral PFC underactivity to positive and negative feedback, and dorsomedial PFC during response inhibition (de Ruiter et al., 2012; de Ruiter et al., 2009).

Cue reactivity has become a popular experimental paradigm in gambling research (Ashrafioun & Rosenberg, 2012), driven in part by behavioural evidence of attentional biases to gambling stimuli in problem gamblers (Boyer & Dickerson, 2003; McCusker & Gettings, 1997) and data in drug addiction showing that attentional biases predict treatment relapse in heroin users (Marissen et al., 2006), and neural activity to drug cues is responsive to treatment in alcoholics (Myrick et al., 2008). At the current time, the fMRI studies of cue reactivity in disordered gambling yield a confusing picture. The initial study indicated vmPFC hypoactivity (Potenza et al., 2003b), but subsequent work has shown hyperactivity in problem gamblers in the dorsolateral PFC (Crockford et al., 2005), striatum and hippocampus (Goudriaan et al., 2010). An EEG study also reported an elevated late positivity to gambling cues, similar to that following positive and negative (non-gambling) emotional pictures (Wolfling et al., 2011). This hyper-reactivity may constitute the mnemonic or sensory signatures of the conditioned cue-associations, and/or the craving itself. Given the likely time courses of these effects, procedural details in the scanner will be critical. These include cue duration (e.g. a 5-second still photo versus a 30-second scripted video) and amount of repetition, as well as the degree of tailoring of the stimulus to the preferred game of the gambler: for a smoker, a simple cigarette photo serves as a powerful cue, whereas for a sports gambler, an image of a slot machine may have negligible impact. These methodological issues have received scant attention so far.

A similar story has emerged in the burgeoning literature on reinforcement processing in PG. The seminal study here used a two-choice card-guessing task in fMRI in 15 pathological gamblers and 15 healthy controls (Reuter et al., 2005). On each trial, participants made their guess and then either won or lost one euro. The fMRI contrast of wins and losses detected robust signal increases to wins in ventral striatum and vmPFC, areas that are well-established nodes in the brain 'reward circuit' and respond to many other kinds of reinforcer (Delgado, 2007). These outcome responses were attenuated in the pathological gamblers, and the vmPFC signal was also negatively correlated with gambling severity. The timings of the card-guessing game only allowed Reuter et al. to model the *outcome*-related brain activity, but a recent study by Balodis et al. (2012) used a different monetary incentive task to fully disambiguate brain responses to the anticipation of winning (or losing), and the win/loss outcome itself. Consistent with Reuter et al., the pathological gamblers displayed reduced activity in VS and vmPFC to both the anticipation and receipt of wins; similar hypoactivity was also observed in the loss conditions.

However, a conceptually similar experiment by van Holst et al. (2012b) tells a different story. Here, pathological gamblers played a wheel of fortune game where they either expected to win or lose, and this outcome could be of high (five euros) or low (one euro) magnitude. The pathological gamblers showed *elevated* anticipation signals in the (dorsal) striatum and ventral prefrontal cortex as function of the gain expectancy, and *elevated* signal in (dorsal) striatum to the high versus low win conditions. Using a realistic blackjack task that involved decisions to 'hit' on either high-risk hands (15 or 16 points) or low-risk hands (12 or 13 points), pathological gamblers showed *greater* brain activity to high-risk hands in the lateral prefrontal cortex and thalamus (Miedl et al., 2010). In this study, the ventral striatum was responsive to the winning hands in both pathological gamblers and occasional gamblers, but this response did not differ between groups.

Two EEG studies also reported *increased* feedback-related negativities in problem gamblers in a blackjack game (wins after high-risk hit decisions) (Hewig et al., 2010) and the Iowa Gambling Task (Oberg et al., 2011). A later study by Miedl et al. (2012) used the delay-discounting and probability-discounting procedures, where gamblers discount delayed rewards but prefer uncertain rewards (see earlier). Testing for brain regions where selection-related activity was correlated with the subjective value of the delayed or uncertain option that was chosen, pathological gamblers showed *stronger* correlations in the ventral striatum with the value of delayed outcomes, coupled with weaker correlations in ventral striatum for the value of uncertain outcomes.

Clearly, there are groups of experiments that illustrate either *hyper*activity or *hypo*activity of brain reward circuitry during reinforcement-based tasks. There is a pressing need for reconciliation of these two sets of findings, as either result has theoretical significance. Hypoactivity supports the *reward deficiency* hypothesis of addiction vulnerability (Bowirrat & Oscar-Berman, 2005; Comings & Blum, 2000), which proposes that certain individuals are drawn to highly rewarding or stimulating activities to compensate for a genetic insensitivity to natural reinforcers (see also section on neurochemistry). Conversely, the evidence of hyperactivity supports the *incentive salience* hypothesis (Robinson & Berridge, 2003), that drugs of abuse (or gambling) come to sensitise the neural response to drugs and their associated cues, so that drug-taking gradually monopolises behaviour.

At present, the design differences between the experiments are manifold. Certainly, it is vital to consider at which point in the trial sequence neural activity has been modelled (i.e. selection, anticipation, outcome), and the extent to which the trial timings permit the disambiguation of these stages (Hommer et al., 2011). First, for example, without adequate temporal separation ('jitter'), it is possible that apparent outcome responses may in fact be driven by risk-taking during selection, or changes in anticipatory processing. Second, while all these experiments involve financial gains and losses, it should be borne in mind that some tasks bear a reasonably strong resemblance to actual gambling (Miedl et al., 2010; van Holst et al., 2012b), whereas other tasks have virtually none (Balodis et al., 2012; Miedl et al., 2012). As realistic tasks involve gambling-associated cues (e.g. coins, playing cards), the incentive effects will become intertwined with the cue-reactivity effects.

Neurochemistry

Much of the psychopharmacological research on problem gambling has focused on the dopamine system, given the established role of this neurotransmitter in signalling reward (Schultz, 2006) and in drug addiction (Wise, 2004). There are several lines of support for dopamine dysregulation in problem gamblers. As well as the observation that dopamine agonist medications can induce disordered gambling in some patients with Parkinson's Disease (Voon et al., 2007; Weintraub et al., 2010), early studies reported altered peripheral levels of dopamine metabolites (Bergh et al., 1997) and altered rates of certain dopamine gene polymorphisms (Lobo & Kennedy, 2009) in pathological gamblers. Studies by Zack and Poulos (2004; 2007) also described increases in gambling urges and gambling-induced arousal in pathological gamblers following a dopamine manipulation: either amphetamine (an indirect agonist) or haloperidol (a D2 receptor antagonist that may up regulate dopamine transmission under single low doses). The most direct method of quantifying central dopamine function in humans is via PET imaging with dopaminergic ligands – 11C-raclopride ligand, a D2/D3 receptor antagonist that binds predominantly in the striatum. A programme of work in drug addiction by Volkow and colleagues (e.g.Volkow et al., 1996; 1997; 2001) used the 11C-raclopride ligand, a D2/D3 receptor antagonist that binds predominantly in the striatum. These studies indicated reduced striatal D2/D3 receptor binding across drug users dependent upon several different substances, including cocaine, heroin and alcohol (see also Heinz et al., 2004; Martinez et al., 2004). This reduction in D2 levels could arise as a consequence of prolonged drug use, or could alternatively pre-date the addiction as a marker of vulnerability. The latter account has dominated, on the basis of evidence that in healthy volunteers, raclopride binding was negatively correlated with the hedonic response to methylphenidate (Volkow et al., 1999), and in drug users, the reduction in raclopride binding showed limited recovery with prolonged abstinence (Volkow et al., 1993; Volkow et al., 2002).

The raclopride data generated a strong prediction in pathological gamblers, that D2 levels would also be reduced as a manifestation of the common addiction liability. Yet of five studies to date that have compared dopamine binding in pathological gamblers and controls (Clark et al., 2012c; Joutsa et al., 2012; Linnet et al., 2011) or in Parkinson's Disease patients with and without the medication syndrome (O'Sullivan et al., 2011; Steeves et al., 2009), only one of these studies has detected difference (Steeves et al., 2009). In our own study (Clark et al., 2012c), raclopride binding did not differ between nine male pathological gamblers and nine healthy controls, but we did detect a strong negative correlation in the gamblers between raclopride binding and a facet of impulsivity called 'urgency' (mood-related impulsivity), which has also been seen in the drug addictions literature (Lee et al., 2009).

Some of the studies have utilised dynamic PET designs, comparing the change in raclopride binding between a baseline scan and a task scan, in order to estimate task-induced dopamine release (see Koepp et al. (1998) for the pioneering study of this technique with a video game). Here, there are some provocative indications of changes in dopamine release. For example, Steeves et al. (2009) scanned Parkinson's Disease patients with and without pathological gambling on two occasions, where one session involved a guessing task with monetary reward. The subjects with pathological gambling showed a greater reduction in raclopride binding on the gambling session (14% versus 8%). Two studies in primary pathological gambling found no *overall* group differences, but gambling-induced dopamine release was *positively* correlated with subjective excitement (on the Iowa Gambling Task) (Linnet et al., 2011) and gambling severity (using a realistic slot machine) (Joutsa et al., 2012). These findings are interesting in juxtaposition to drug addiction, where *blunted* dopamine release has been reported following controlled stimulant administration (Martinez et al., 2007; Volkow et al., 1997). Studies with alternative PET ligands will shed further light on different sources of neurotransmitter dysfunction in pathological gambling. The [18F]fallypride and [11C]PHNO tracers are better able to quantify extra-striatal D2/D3 receptor binding, particularly in the midbrain, and PHNO has a much higher affinity for D3 receptors; these ligands have shown promise in relation to impulsivity (Buckholtz et al., 2010) and drug addiction (Boileau et al., 2012) but have not been utilised in disordered gambling at present. Parkinson's Disease cases with pathological gambling displayed reduced dopamine transporter binding in the ventral striatum, using the [123-I] FP-CIT tracer (Cilia et al., 2010). Presynaptic mechanisms may also contribute to the increase in (task-related) extra-cellular dopamine suggested above. Dopamine synthesis would also be a fruitful target with the F-DOPA ligand (Heinz et al., 2005).

Beyond dopamine, the endogenous opioid system is a key target for study based on the clinical data of naltrexone efficacy in pathological gambling, and similar rationales can be created for measuring serotonin, glutamate, GABA and noradrenaline transmission (see Leeman & Potenza, 2012 for review).

Cognitive distortions

The cognitive tasks that have been applied to disordered gambling in the neuroimaging studies to date have largely derived from the neuropsychological approach outlined above. While neuropsychological tests of decision making (e.g. the Iowa Gambling Task) capture the basic processes involved in gambling (i.e. selection, anticipation and outcome), these tasks have limited ecological validity to real gambling play. Cognitive approaches to gambling have instead highlighted the complex array of *distortions* that gamblers experience during play.

These were initially detected using the 'think aloud' procedure wherein gamblers verbalise a high rate of faulty, irrational cognitions during brief periods of real play (Ladouceur & Walker, 1996). Subsequent research has developed psychometric scales for measuring a range of gambling biases and distorted beliefs, such as the Gambling Related Cognitions Scale (Raylu & Oei, 2004) and the Gambling Beliefs Questionnaire (Steenbergh et al., 2002). It is evident that higher levels of distortions in pathological gamblers predicts future relapse (Oei & Gordon, 2008) and may be a useful target for cognitive interventions (Fortune & Goodie, 2012). By developing more realistic gambling tasks, it is possible to elicit these distortions in the laboratory or brain scanner, and compare these neural signatures in problem gamblers and controls. This works at an early stage, as it involves a substantial investment in novel task development. In our own work, we have developed a simplified slot-machine game that delivers real monetary wins (Chase & Clark, 2010; Clark et al., 2009), but where the non-win events can be further divided into *near*-misses and *full*-misses. These events are objectively equivalent, but gamblers appear to experience near-misses as salient events that increase gambling persistence (Kassinove & Schare, 2001). By taking subjective ratings on our simulated game, it is clear that near-misses are unpleasant, but simultaneously increase the motivation to play (Clark et al., 2009; Qi et al., 2011). Using psychophysiological monitoring, near-misses elicit greater signs of arousal (skin conductance, heart rate changes) than full-misses (Clark et al., 2012b). Using fMRI, we have seen that near-misses recruit parts of brain reward circuitry (ventral striatum, insula) that also respond to monetary wins (Clark et al., 2009). Insula activation by near-misses was correlated with the trait susceptibility to gambling distortions.

In a follow-up study in regular gamblers, the brain response to near-misses in the dopaminergic midbrain (approximately substantia nigra) was predicted (positively) by gambling-symptom severity (Chase & Clark, 2010).

One account of these effects is that gamblers interpret near-miss outcomes as evidence that they're improving their skills (Reid, 1986); such an inference has some validity in skilful situations such as sports, but the logic does not hold in games of chance. Other factors associated with this 'illusion of control' also modulate striatal reward responses. For example, striatal responses to financial gains were greater when subjects chose one of two gambles, compared to when their choice was forced by the computer (Coricelli et al., 2005). The dorsal striatum responded more to gains that were contingent upon a rapid motor response than equivalent gains that were delivered non-contingently (Tricomi et al., 2004). Choice and instrumentality (or involvements) are key determinants of illusory control (Langer, 1975; Martinez et al., 2009). Other distortions occur in the processing of event sequences, underpinned by a failure to appreciate the statistical independence of turns.

In the gambler's fallacy, if a player observes a run of one outcome (e.g. consecutive heads in a coin-toss), he predicts that the other outcome (tails) is more likely to occur next (Oskarsson et al., 2009). In the 'hot hand' belief, players predict that their winning streaks will continue because they are 'in the zone' (Ayton & Fischer, 2004). Functional imaging studies have examined how reward-related responses vary as function of the recent outcome history. Ventral striatum, at the core of the reward circuitry, is perhaps surprisingly insensitive to the sequential nature of outcome streaks (Akitsuki et al., 2003; Xue et al., 2012). Rather, prefrontal regions seem more attuned to detecting this higher-order structure of the task, and the integration of recent outcomes to inform ongoing choice (Rushworth & Behrens, 2008).

For example, the rostral part of the anterior cingulate cortex (within the vmPFC region) showed greater response on the fourth win or loss of a streak, compared to the first win or loss, respectively (Akitsuki et al., 2003; Elliott et al., 2000). The lateral prefrontal cortex is sensitive to *violation* of outcome runs (e.g. XXXXXXO or XOXOXOO) (Huettel et al., 2002) and lateral PFC activity also predicted a switch of choice (indicative of gambler's fallacy) following long outcome runs (Xue et al., 2012). Hence, in addition to the striatal mechanisms implicated in the sensitivity to illusory control, studies of sequential processing also implicated prefrontal sectors in the erroneous detection of streaks and streak violations in sequences that are, in fact, random. A multitude of specific gambling distortions have been identified, and their overarching taxonomy is not well characterised (Toneatto et al., 1997).

Other biases include superstitious conditioning (e.g. gambling rituals or lucky charms) and the 'explaining away' of loss outcomes *(hindsight bias)*; these have received virtually no attention from a neurobiological perspective to date. One net consequence of these distortions seems to be a willingness to *chase losses*, one of the cardinal symptoms of disordered gambling. Campbell-Meiklejohn, Rogers and colleagues have studied the brain systems involved in these chase decisions, using a 'double or quits' game where the participant can sustain a small loss, or increase their stake to take a chance of recovering the loss (Campbell-Meiklejohn et al., 2008; 2011). There is a sequential structure to this task, and the decision to loss-chase may change as the stakes get higher through a sequence. Chasing behaviour on this task correlated with a psychometric measure of chasing tendencies in real-life gambling. In an fMRI study, decisions to chase a loss were associated with greater activity in vmPFC reward regions, whereas decisions to quit were associated with greater activity in regions linked to conflict processing (dorsal anterior cingulate cortex), particularly following loss trials (Campbell-Meiklejohn et al., 2008). The authors speculated that in pathological gamblers, the balance between these two systems may be altered, predisposing the tendency to loss-chase. Subsequent work with the task has used pharmacological manipulations in healthy volunteers to converge with the neurochemical studies in disordered gambling described above: a serotonin manipulation (dietary tryptophan depletion) increased chasing tendencies, whereas the dopamine agonist pramipexole, which is linked to the Parkinsonian syndrome, increased the sensitivity to the chased amount (Campbell-Meiklejohn et al., 2011).

Conclusion

Studies of neuropsychological performance and functional neuroimaging in disordered gambling have pointed to robust abnormalities in risky and impulsive decision making (e.g. Iowa Gambling Task, delay discounting) and activation of brain reward circuitry focused around the ventral striatum and vmPFC.

These abnormalities closely resemble the changes reported in drug-addicted populations, and indeed a number of studies using three-group designs have reported common effects across groups with disordered gambling and drug addiction (de Ruiter et al., 2009; Petry, 2001; Tanabe et al., 2007). This evidence has been pivotal in supporting the proposed reclassification of pathological gambling into the Addictions and Related Disorders category in the DSM-5 (Bowden-Jones & Clark, 2011; Mitzner et al., 2011). From my discussions with various stakeholders, the reclassification would be endorsed and viewed as a positive development by most parties, including clients with gambling problems, the clinicians and counsellors involved in treatment, and researchers of gambling behaviour. However, we must be cautious, so as to not overlook potentially meaningful differences between disordered gambling and drug addiction. Preliminary PET data measuring aspects of dopamine transmission in pathological gamblers has failed to detect the reduction in baseline D2/D3 receptor availability that is a replicated finding in drug users. In addition, gambling-induced dopamine release appears to be elevated in pathological gamblers compared to controls (at least in a subset of gamblers) (Joutsa et al., 2012; Linnet et al., 2011), whereas drug-induced dopamine release is attenuated in drug users (Martinez et al., 2007; Volkow et al., 1997). While many of these experiments involved small samples that were only powered to detect large effects, one implication is that the observed dopaminergic effects in drug users may reflect neuroadaptive changes precipitated by chronic drug consumption, rather than core aetiological processes in addictive disorders.

Much of the attention on pathological gambling within the addiction arisen from this vulnerability model, based upon a logic that the ne consequences of drugs of abuse may be absent in gamblers (Verdejo-Garcia et a., 2008). Thus, any behavioural or neural effects in pathological gamblers may be associated with the liability to addiction-spectrum disorders, rather than a consequence of the compulsive behaviour. This approach has been fruitful in neuropsychological studies, where disordered gamblers and drug users display shared deficits in decision making (putatively linked to vulnerability), but the drug users display additional impairments in working memory (presumed a neurotoxic consequence) (Albein-Urios et al., 2012; Lawrence et al., 2009). While the logic here is attractive, the intimate relationship between brain function and brain structure is increasingly recognised, and it is likely that the cycle of monetary winning and (predominantly) losing experienced by the gambler could also be sufficient to trigger structural reconfigurations, in the same way that practising a novel motor skill like juggling causes rapid structural plasticity in the motor system (Draganski & May, 2008). The first structural fMRI investigations in pathological gambling have begun to be published. While two studies have detected no significant grey-matter differences between problem gamblers and controls using voxel-based morphometry (Joutsa et al., 2011; van Holst et al., 2012a), diffusion tensor imaging indicated reduced white-matter integrity in multiple tracts, similar to that seen in studies of drug addiction (Joutsa et al., 2011). A further difference between pathological gambling and drug addiction may exist in the cognitive distortions that occur during gambling play. Gambling distortions have received no empirical attention with drug addiction, and it is unclear whether effects like loss chasing or illusory control have analogues in the phenomenology of drug addiction.

Research on the brain basis of gambling distortions has begun to integrate the basic work from human neuropsychology and the neuroscience of decision making, with our understanding of thought processes during real gambling that is derived from social and cognitive psychology. It is evident that gambling distortions can be elicited in controlled laboratory environments, providing the tasks are carefully designed to maintain ecological validity, for example by using engaging displays and real monetary reinforcement. The brain areas that are sensitive to gambling distortions (near-misses, illusory control, streak effects) are largely the same areas that ordinarily process natural reinforcers like food and drink, associative learning and skill acquisition (Clark, 2010). Of course, it may not be accidental that these games of chance harness brain systems that evolved to predict probabilistically-determined events in the world, and fine motor-skill learning. These appetitive regions interact during gambling, with higher-order structures involved in planning, conflict detection and self-control, and the transition into disordered gambling will likely be accompanied (and possibly predisposed) by a shift in the balance between these systems. Future studies exploring the neurobiological substrates in this area need to look at longitudinal and prospective designs of trait influences in problem gambling.

At the time of writing, no studies have scanned groups with pathological gambling on these more realistic tasks that capture gambling-related cognitive distortions. There is also a paucity of prospective studies in gambling research, which are needed to adjudicate whether gambling distortions comprise a separate part of the variance from the general liability that is shared across the addictive disorders.

Key points

1   PG is conceptualised as an impaired decision-making process caused by the neural subsystem that supports the decisional processing.
2   The vast majority of research studies on PG have been cross-sectional.
3   PGs perform abnormally on tests of risk-based decision making and this finding points to dysregulation in the ventromedial prefrontal cortex.
4   Dopamine dysregulation is present in PGs according to several research studies.
5   Cognitive distortions are experienced by PGs during play.

References

Akitsuki, Y., Sugiura, M., Watanabe, J., Yamashita, K., Sassa, Y., Awata, S., Matsuoka, H., Maeda, Y., Fukuda, H. & Kawashima, R. (2003). Context-dependent cortical activation in response to financial reward and penalty: an event-related fMRI study. *Neuroimage*, 19:1674–85.

Albein-Urios, N., Martinez-Gonzalez, J. M., Lozano, O., Clark, L. & Verdejo-Garcia, A. (2012). Comparison of impulsivity and working memory in cocaine addiction and pathological gambling: implications for cocaine-induced neurotoxicity. *Drug and Alcohol Dependence*, 126:1–6.

Alessi, S. M. & Petry, N. M. (2003). Pathological gambling severity is associated with impulsivity in a delay discounting procedure. *Behav Processes*, 64:345–54.

Ashrafioun, L. & Rosenberg, H. (2012). Methods of assessing craving to gamble: a narrative review. *Psychol Addict Behav*, 26(3):536–49.

Ayton, P. & Fischer, I. (2004). The hot hand fallacy and the gambler's fallacy: two faces of subjective randomness? *MemCognit*, 32:1369–78.

Balodis, I. M., Kober, H., Worhunsky, P. D., Stevens, M. C., Pearlson, G. D. & Potenza, M. N. (2012). Diminished frontostriatal activity during processing of monetary rewards and losses in pathological gambling. *Biological Psychiatry*, 71:749–57.

Bechara, A., Damasio, A. R., Damasio, H. & Anderson, S. W. (1994). Insensitivity to future consequences following damage to human prefrontal cortex. *Cognition*, 50:7–15.

Bechara, A. & Damasio, H. (2002). Decision-making and addiction (part I): impaired activation of somatic states in substance dependent individuals when pondering decisions with negative future consequences. *Neuropsychologia*, 40:1675–89.

Bergh, C., Eklund, T., Sodersten, P. & Nordin, C. (1997). Altered dopamine function in pathological gambling. *Psychol Med*, 27:473–5.

Bickel, W. K. & Marsch, L. A. (2001). Toward a behavioral economic understanding of drug dependence: delay discounting processes. *Addiction*, 96:73–86.

Blaszczynski, A. & Nower, L. (2002). A pathways model of problem and pathological gambling. *Addiction*, 97:487–99.

Boileau, I., Payer, D., Houle, S., Behzadi, A., Rusjan, P. M., Tong, J., Wilkins, D., Selby, P., George, T. P., Zack, M., Furukawa, Y., McCluskey, T., Wilson, A. A. & Kish, S. J. (2012). Higher binding of the dopamine D3 receptor-preferring ligand [11C]-(+)-propyl-hexahydronaphtho-oxazin in methamphetamine polydrug users: a positron emission tomography study. *Journal of Neuroscience*, 32:1353–9.

Bowden-Jones, H. & Clark, L. (2011). Pathological gambling: a neurobiological and clinical update. *British Journal of Psychiatry*, 199:87–9.

Bowirrat, A. & Oscar-Berman, M. (2005). Relationship between dopaminergic neurotransmission, alcoholism, and Reward Deficiency syndrome. *Am J Med Genet B Neuropsychiatr Genet*, 132:29–37.

Boyer, M. & Dickerson, M. (2003). Attentional bias and addictive behaviour: automaticity in a gambling-specific modified Stroop task. *Addiction*, 98:61–70.

Buckholtz, J. W., Treadway, M. T., Cowan, R. L., Woodward, N. D., Li, R., Ansari, M. S., Baldwin, R. M., Schwartzman, A. N., Shelby, E. S., Smith, C. E., Kessler, R. M. & Zald, D. H. (2010). Dopaminergic network differences in human impulsivity. *Science*, 329:532.

Campbell-Meiklejohn, D. K., Woolrich, M. W., Passingham, R. E. & Rogers, R. D. (2008). Knowing when to stop: the brain mechanisms of chasing losses. *Biological Psychiatry*, 63:293–300.

Campbell-Meiklejohn, D., Wakeley, J., Herbert, V., Cook, J., Scollo, P., Ray, M. K., Selvaraj, S., Passingham, R. E., Cowen, P. & Rogers, R. D. (2011). Serotonin and dopamine play complementary roles in gambling to recover losses. *Neuropsychopharmacology*, 36:402–10.

Cavedini, P., Riboldi, G., Keller, R., D'anucci, A. & Bellodi, L. (2002). Frontal lobe dysfunction in pathological gambling patients. *Biol Psychiatry*, 51:334–41.

Chase, H. W. & Clark, L. (2010). Gambling severity predicts midbrain response to near-miss outcomes. *Journal of Neuroscience*, 30:6180–7.

Cilia, R., Ko, J. H., Cho, S. S., Van Eimeren, T., Marotta, G., Pellecchia, G., Pezzoli, G., Antonni, A. & Strafella, A. P. (2010). Reduced dopamine transporter density in the ventral striatum of patients with Parkinson's Disease and pathological gambling. *Neurobiology of Disease*, 39:98–104.

Clark, L. (2010). Decision-making during gambling: an integration of cognitive and psychobiological approaches. *Philosophical Transactions of the Royal Society of London. Series B, Biological Sciences*, 365:319–30.

Clark, L., Bechara, A., Damasio, H., Aitken, M. R., Sahakian, B. J. & Robbins, T. W. (2008). Differential effects of insular and ventromedial prefrontal cortex lesions on risky decisionmaking. *Brain,* 131:1311–22.

Clark, L., Lawrence, A. J., Astley-Jones, F. & Gray, N. (2009). Gambling near-misses enhance motivation to gamble and recruit win-related brain circuitry. *Neuron*, 61:481–90.

Clark, L., Boxer, O., Sahakian, J. & Bilder, R. M. (2012a). Research methods: cognitive neuropsychological methods. *Handbook of Clinical Neurology*, 106:75–87.

Clark, L., Crooks, B., Clarke, R., Aitken, M. R. & Dunn, B. D. (2012b). Physiological responses to near-miss outcomes and personal control during simulated gambling. *Journal of Gambling Studies*, 28:123–37.

Clark, L. & Manes, F. (2004). Social and emotional decision-making following frontal lobe injury. *Neurocase*, 10:398–403.

Clark, L., Stokes, P. R., Wu, K., Michalczuk, R., Benecke, A., Watson, B. J., Egerton, A., Piccini, P., Nutt, D. J., Bowden-Jones, H. & Lingford-Hughes, A. R. (2012c). Striatal dopamine D2/D3 receptor binding in pathological gambling is correlated with mood-related impulsivity. *NeuroImage*, 63:40–6.

Comings, D. E. & Blum, K. (2000). Reward deficiency syndrome: genetic aspects of behavioural disorders. *Progress in Brain Research*, 126:325–41.

Coricelli, G., Critchley, H. D., Joffily, M., O'Doherty, J. P., Sirigu, A. & Dolan, R. J. (2005). Regret and its avoidance: a neuroimaging study of choice behaviour. *Nat Neurosci*, 8:1255–62.

Crockford, D. N., Goodyear, B., Edwards, J., Quickfall, J. & El-Guebaly, N. (2005). Cue-induced brain activity in pathological gamblers. *Biol Psychiatry*, 58:787–95.

Damasio, A. R. (1994). *Descartes' Error: Emotion, Reason and the Human Brain*. New York: G. P. Putnam.

Delgado, M. R. (2007). Reward-related responses in the human striatum. *Ann N Y AcadSci*, 1104:70–88.

De Ruiter, M. B., Veltman, D. J., Goudriaan, J., Sjoerds, Z. & Van Den Brink, W. (2009). Response perseveration and ventral prefrontal sensitivity to reward and punishment in male problem gamblers and smokers. *Neuropsychopharmacology*, 34:1027–38.

De Ruiter, M. B., Oosterlaan, J., Veltman, D., Van Den Brink, W. & Goudriaan, A. E. (2012). Similar hyporesponsiveness of the dorsomedial prefrontal cortex in problem gamblers and heavy smokers during an inhibitory control task. *Drug and Alcohol Dependence*, 121:81–9.

Dixon, M. R., Marley, J. & Jacobs, E. A. (2003). Delay discounting by pathological gamblers. *J Appl Behav Anal*, 36:449–58.

Draganski, B. & May, A. (2008). Training-induced structural changes in the adult human brain. *Behavioural Brain Research*, 192:137–42.

Elliott, R., Friston, K. J. & Dolan, R. J. (2000). Dissociable neural responses in human reward systems. *Journal of Neuroscience*, 20:6159–65.

Ferris, J. & Wynne, H. (2001). Canadian Problem Gambling Index. Ottawa, Ontario: Canadian Centre on Substance Abuse.

Forbush, K. T., Shaw, M., Graeber, M. A., Hovick, L., Meyer, V. J., Moser, D. J., Bayless, J., Watson, D. & Black, D. W. (2008). Neuropsychological characteristics and personality traits in pathological gambling. *CNS Spectrums*, 13:306–15.

Fortune, E. E. & Goodie, A. S. (2012). Cognitive distortions as a component and treatment focus of pathological gambling: a review. *Psychology of Addictive Behaviors*, 26:298–310.

Fuentes, D., Tavares, H., Artes, R. & Gorenstein, C. (2006). Self-reported and neuropsychological measures of impulsivity in pathological gambling. *Journal of the International Neuropsychological Society*, 12:907–12.

Goodie, A. S. (2005). The role of perceived control and overconfidence in pathological gambling. *Journal of Gambling Studies*, 2:481–502.

Goudriaan, A. E., Oosterlaan, J., De Beurs, E. & Van Den Brink, W. (2004). Pathological gambling: a comprehensive review of biobehavioral findings. *Neurosci Biobehav Rev*, 28:23–41.

Goudriaan, A. E., Oosterlaan, J., De Beurs, E. & Van Den Brink, W. (2006). Neurocognitive functions in pathological gambling: a comparison with alcohol dependence, Tourette syndrome and normal controls. *Addiction*, 101:534–47.

Goudriaan, A. E., De Ruiter, M. B., Van Den Brink, W., Oosterlaan, J. & Veltman, D. J. (2010). Brain activation patterns associated with cue reactivity and craving in abstinent problem gamblers, heavy smokers and healthy controls: an fMRI study. *Addiction Biology*, 15:491–503.

Grant, J. E., Chamberlain, S. R., Schreiber, L. R., Odlaug, B. L. & Kin, S. W. (2011). Selective decision-making deficits in at-risk gamblers. *Psychiatry Research*, 189:115–20.

Heinz, A., Siessmeier, T., Wrase, J., Buchholz, H. G., Grunder, G., Kumakura, Y., Cumming, P., Schreckeberger, M., Smolka, M. N., Rosch, F., Mann, K. & Bartenstein, P. (2005). Correlation of alcohol craving with striatal dopamine synthesis capacity and D2/3 receptor availability: a combined [18F]DOPA and [18F]DMFP PET study in detoxified alcoholic patients. *American Journal of Psychiatry*, 162:1515–20.

Heinz, A., Siessmeier, T., Wrase, J., Hermann, D., Klein, S., Grusser, S. M., Flor, H., Braus, D. F., Buchholz, H. G., Grunder, G., Schreckenberger, M., Smolka, M. N., Rosch, F., Mann, K. & Bartenstein, P. (2004). Correlation between dopamine D(2) receptors in the ventral striatum and central processing of alcohol cues and craving. *American Journal of Psychiatry*, 161:1783–9.

Hewig, J., Kretschmer, N., Trippe, R. H., Hecht, H., Coles, M. G., Holroyd, C. B. & Miltner, W. H. (2010). Hypersensitivity to reward in problem gamblers. *Biological Psychiatry*, 67:781–3.

Hommer, D. W., Bjork, J. M. & Gilman, J. M. (2011). Imaging brain response to reward in addictive disorders. *Annals of the New York Academy of Sciences*, 1216:50–61.

Huettel, S. A., Mack, P. B. & McCrathy, G. (2002). Perceiving patterns in random series: dynamic processing of sequence in prefrontal cortex. *Nature Neuroscience*, 5:485–90.

Joutsa, J., Saunavaara, J., Parkkola, R., Niemela, S. & Kaasinen, V. (2011). Extensive abnormality of brain white matter integrity in pathological gambling. *Psychiatry Research*, 194:340–6.

Joutsa, J., Johansson, J., Niemela, S., Ollikainen, A., Hironen, M. M., Piepponen, P., Arponen, E., Alho, H., Voon, V., Rinne, J. O., Hietala, A. J. & Kaasinen, V. (2012). Mesolimbic dopamine release is linked to symptom severity in pathological gambling. *NeuroImage*, 60:1992–9.

Kassinove, J. I. & Schare, M. L. (2001). Effects of the 'near miss' and the 'big win' on persistence at slot machine gambling. *Psychology of Addictive Behaviors*, 15:155–8.

Kertzman, S., Lowengrub, K., Aizer, A., Nahum, Z. B., Kotler, M. & Dannon, P. N. (2006). Stroop performance in pathological gamblers. *Psychiatry Research*, 142:1–10.

Kertzman, S., Vainder, M., Vishne, T., Aizer, A., Kotler, M. & Dannon, P. N. (2010). Speedaccuracy trade off in decision-making performance among pathological gamblers. *European Addiction Research*, 16:23–30.

Koepp, M. J., Gunn, R. N., Lawrence, A. D., Cunningham, V. J., Dagher, A., Jones, T., Brooks, D. J., Bench, C. J. & Grasby, P. M. (1998). Evidence for striatal dopamine release during a video game. *Nature*, 393:266–8.

Ladouceur, R. & Walker, M. (1996). A cognitive perspective on gambling. In: Salkovskis, P. M. (ed.), *Trends in Cognitive and Behavioural Therapies*. Chichester: Wiley & Sons.

Langer, E. J. (1975). The illusion of control. *Journal of Personality and Social Psychology*, 32:311–28.

Lawrence, A. J., Luty, J., Bodgan, N. A., Sahakian, B. J. & Clark, L. (2009). Problem gamblers share deficits in impulsive decision-making with alcohol-dependent individuals. *Addiction*,104:006–15.

Lee, B., London, E. D., Poldrack, R. A., Farahi, J., Nacca, A., Monterosso, J. R., Mumford, J. A., Bokarius, A. V., Dahlbom, M., Mukehrjee, J., Bilder, R. M., Brody, A. L. & Mandelkern, M. A. (2009). Striatal dopamine d2/d3 receptor availability is reduced in methamphetamine dependence and is linked to impulsivity. *Journal of Neuroscience*, 29:14734–40.

Leeman, R. F. & Potenza, M. N. (2012). Similarities and differences between pathological gambling and substance use disorders: a focus on impulsivity and compulsivity. *Psychopharmacology (Berlin)*, 219:469–90.

Leiserson, V., Pihl, R. O. (2007). Reward-sensitivity, inhibition of reward-seeking, and dorsolateral prefrontal working memory function in problem gamblers not in treatment. *J Gambl Stud*, 23:435–55.

Lesieur, H. R. & Blume, S. B. (1987). The South Oaks Gambling Screen (SOGS): a new instrument for the identification of pathological gamblers. *American Journal of Psychiatry*, 144:1184–8.

Ligneul, R., Sescousse, G., Barbalat, G., Domenech, P. & Dreher, J. C. (2013). Shifted risk preferences in pathological gambling. *Psychological Medicine*, 43:1059–68.

Linnet, J., Moller, A., Peterson, E., Gjedde, A. & Doudet, D. (2011). Dopamine release in ventral striatum during Iowa Gambling Task performance is associated with increased excitement levels in pathological gambling. *Addiction*, 106:383–90.

Lobo, D. S. & Kennedy, J. L. (2009). Genetic aspects of pathological gambling: a complex disorder with shared genetic vulnerabilities. *Addiction*, 104:1454–65.

Madden, G. J., Petry, N. M. & Johnson, P. S. (2009). Pathological gamblers discount probabilistic rewards less steeply than matched controls. *Experimental and Clinical Psychopharmacology*,17:283–90.

Marissen, M. A., Franken, I. H., Waters, A. J., Blanken, P., Van Den Brink, W. & Hendriks, V. M. (2006). Attentional bias predicts heroin relapse following treatment. *Addiction*, 101:1306–12.

Martinez, D., Broft, A., Foltin, R. W., Slifstein, M., Hwang, D. R., Huang, Y., Perez, A., Frankle, W. G., Cooper, T., Kleber, H. D., Fischman, N. M. & Laruelle, M. (2004). Cocaine dependence and d2 receptor availability in the functional subdivisions of the striatum: relationship with cocaine-seeking behaviour. *Neuropsychopharmacology*, 29:1190–202.

Martinez, D., Narendran, R., Foltin, R. W., Slifstein, M., Hwang, D. R., Broft, A., Huang, Y., Cooper, T. B., Fischman, M. W., Kleber, H. D. & Laruelle, M. (2007). Amphetamine induced dopamine release: markedly blunted in cocaine dependence and predictive of the choice to self-administer cocaine. *American Journal of Psychiatry*, 164:622–9.

Martinez, F., Bonnefon, J. F. & Hoskens, J. (2009). Active involvement, not illusory control, increases risk taking in a gambling game. *Quarterly Journal of Experimental Psychology*, 62:1063–71.

McClure, S. M., Laibson, D. I., Loewenstein, G. & Cohen, J. D. (2004). Separate neural systems value immediate and delayed monetary rewards. *Science*, 306:503–7.

McCusker, C. G. & Gettings, B. (1997). Automaticity of cognitive biases in addictive behaviours: further evidence with gamblers. *Br J Clin Psychol,* 36 (Pt 4):543–54.

Michalczuk, R., Bowden-Jones, H., Verdejo-Garcia, A. & Clark L. (2011). Impulsivity and cognitive distortions in pathological gamblers attending the UK National Problem Gambling Clinic: a preliminary report. *Psychological Medicine,* 41:2625–35.

Miedl, S. F., Fehr, T., Meyer, G. & Herrmann, M. (2010). Neurobiological correlates of problem gambling in a quasi-realistic blackjack scenario as revealed by fMRI. *Psychiatry Research,* 181:165–73.

Miedl, S. F., Peters, J., Buchel, C. (2012). Altered neural reward representations in pathological gamblers revealed by delay and probability discounting. *Archives of General Psychiatry,* 69:177–86.

Mischel, W., Shoda, Y. & Rodriguez, M. I. (1989). Delay of gratification in children. *Science,* 244:933–8.

Mitzner, G. B., Whelan, J. P. & Meyers, A. W. (2011). Comments from the trenches: proposed changes to the DSM-V classification of pathological gambling. *Journal of Gambling Studies,* 27(3):517–21.

Miyake, A., Friedman, N. P., Emerson, M. J., Witzki, A. H., Howerter, A. & Wager, T. D. (2000). The unity and diversity of executive functions and their contributions to complex 'Frontal Lobe' tasks: a latent variable analysis. *Cognit Psychol,* 4:49–100.

Myrick, H., Anton, R. F., Li, X., Henderson, S., Randall, P. K. & Voronin, K. (2008). Effect of naltrexone and ondansetron on alcohol cue-induced activation of the ventral striatum in alcohol-dependent people. *Archives of General Psychiatry,* 65:466–75.

Oberg, S. A., Christie, G. J. & Tata, M. S. (2011). Problem gamblers exhibit reward hypersensitivity in medial frontal cortex during gambling. *Neuropsychologia,* 49:3768–75.

Odlaug, B. L., Chamberlain, S. R., Kim, S. W., Schreiber, L. R. & Grant, J. E. (2011). A neurocognitive comparison of cognitive flexibility and response inhibition in gamblers with varying degrees of clinical severity. *Psychological Medicine,* 41:111–9.

Oei, T. P. & Gordon, L. M. (2008). Psychosocial factors related to gambling abstinence and relapse in members of Gamblers Anonymous. *Journal of Gambling Studies,* 24:91–105.

Oskarsson, A. T., Van Boven, L., McClelland, G. H. & Hastie, R. (2009). What's next? Judging sequences of binary events. *Psychological Bulletin,* 135:262–85.

O'Sullivan, S. S., Wu, K., Politis, M., Lawrence, A. D., Evans, A. H., Bose, S. K., Djamshidian, A., Lees, A. J. & Piccini, P. (2011). Cue-induced striatal dopamine release in Parkinson's Disease-associated impulsive-compulsive behaviours. *Brain,* 134:969–78.

Peters, J. & Buchel, C. (2009). Overlapping and distinct neural systems code for subjective value during intertemporal and risky decision making. *Journal of Neuroscience,* 29:15727–34.

Petry, N. M. (2001). Pathological gamblers, with and without substance use disorders, discount delayed rewards at high rates. *J Abnorm Psychol,* 110:482–7.

Petry, N. M. & Casarella, T. (1999). Excessive discounting of delayed rewards in substance abusers with gambling problems. *Drug Alcohol Depend,* 56:25–32.

Potenza, M. N. (2008). The neurobiology of pathological gambling and drug addiction: an overview and new findings. *Philos Trans R SocLond B BiolSci,* 363:3181–9.

Potenza, M. N., Leung, H. C., Blumberg, H. P., Peterson, B. S., Fulbright, R. K., Lacadie, C. M., Skudlarski, P. & Gore, J. C. (2003a). An FMRI Stroop task study of ventromedial prefrontal cortical function in pathological gamblers. *American Journal of Psychiatry*, 160:1990–4.

Potenza, M. N., Steinberg, M. A., Skudlarski, P., Fulbright, R. K., Lacadie, C. M., Wilber, M. K., Rounsaville, B. J., Gore, J. C. & Wexler, B. E. (2003b). Gambling urges in pathological gambling: a functional magnetic resonance imaging study. *Archives of General Psychiatry*, 60:828–36.

Qi, S., Ding, C., Song, Y. & Yang, D. (2011). Neural correlates of near-misses effect in gambling. *Neuroscience Letters*, 493:80–5.

Raylu, N. & Oei, T. P. (2004). The Gambling Related Cognitions Scale (GRCS): development, confirmatory factor validation and psychometric properties. *Addiction*, 99:757–69.

Regard, M., Knoch, D., Gutling, E. & Landis, T. (2003). Brain damage and addictive behaviour: a neuropsychological and electroencephalogram investigation with pathologic gamblers. *Cogn Behav Neurol*, 16:47–53.

Reid, R. L. (1986). The psychology of the near miss. *Journal of Gambling Behaviour*, 2:32–9.

Reuter, J., Raedler, T,. Rose, M., Hand, I., Glascher, J. & Buchel, C. (2005). Pathological gambling is linked to reduced activation of the mesolimbic reward system. *Nat Neurosci*, 8:147–8.

Reynolds, B. (2006). A review of delay-discounting research with humans: relations to drug use and gambling. *Behav Pharmacol*, 17:651–67.

Robinson, T. E. & Berridge, K. C. (2003). Addiction. *Annual Review of Psychology*, 54:25–53.

Rogers, R. D., Everitt, B. J., Baldacchino, A., Blackshaw, A. J., Swainson, R., Wynne, K., Baker, N. B., Hunter, J., Carthy, T., Booker, E., London, M., Deakin, J. F., Sahakian, B. J. & Robbins, T. W. (1999). Dissociable deficits in the decision-making cognition of chronic amphetamine abusers, opiate abusers, patients with focal damage to prefrontal cortex, and tryptophan-depleted normal volunteers: evidence for monoaminergic mechanisms. *Neuropsychopharmacology*, 20:322–39.

Rugle, L. & Melamed, L. (1993). Neuropsychological assessment of attention problems in pathological gamblers. *J Nerv Ment Dis*, 181:107–12.

Rushworth, M. F. & Behrens, T. E. (2008). Choice, uncertainty and value in prefrontal and cingulate cortex. *Nature Neuroscience*, 11:389–97.

Schultz, W. (2006). Behavioral theories and the neurophysiology of reward. *Annu Rev Psychol*, 57:87–115.

Sellitto, M., Ciaramelli, E. & Di Pellegrino, G. 2010. Myopic discounting of future rewards after medial orbitofrontal damage in humans. *Journal of Neuroscience*, 30:16429–36.

Slutske, W. S., Caspi, A., Moffitt, T. E. & Poulton, R. (2005). Personality and problem gambling: a prospective study of a birth cohort of young adults. *Arch Gen Psychiatry*, 62:769–75.

Steenbergh, T. A., Meyers, A. W., May, R. K. & Whelan, J. P. (2002). Development and validation of the Gamblers' Beliefs Questionnaire. *Psychology of Addictive Behaviors*, 16:143–9.

Steeves, T. D., Miyasaki, J., Zurowski, M., Lang, A. E., Pellecchia, G., Van Eimeren, T., Rusjan, P., Houle, S. & Strafella, A. P. (2009). Increased striatal dopamine release in Parkinsonian patients with pathological gambling: a [11C] raclopride PET study. *Brain*, 132:1376–85.

Studer, B., Apergis-Schoute, A. M., Robbins, T. W. & Clark, L. (2012). What are the odds? The neural correlates of active choice during gambling. *Front Neurosci*, 6:46.

Tanabe, J., Thompson, L., Claus, E., Dalwani, M., Hutchison, K, &. Banich, M. T. (2007). Prefrontal cortex activity is reduced in gambling and non-gambling substance users during decision-making. *Hum Brain Mapp*, 28:1276–86.

Toce-Gerstein, M., Gerstein, D. R. & Volberg, R. A. (2003). A hierarchy of gambling disorders in the community. *Addiction*, 98:1661–72.

Toneatto, T., Blitz-Miller, T., Calderwood, K., Dragonetti, R. & Tsanos, A. (1997). Cognitive distortions in heavy gambling. *J Gambl Stud*, 13:253–66.

Tricomi, E. M., Delgano, M. R. & Fiez, J. A. (2004). Modulation of caudate activity by action contingency. *Neuron*, 41:281–92.

Van Holst, R. J., de Ruiter, M. B., Van Den Brink ,W,. Veltman, D. J. & Goudriann, A. E. (2012a). A voxel-based morphometry study comparing problem gamblers, alcohol abusers, and healthy controls. *Drug and Alcohol Dependence*, 124:142–8.

Van Holst, R. J., Veltman, D. J., Buchel, C., Van Den Brink, W. & Goudriaan, A. E. (2012b). Distorted expectancy coding in problem gambling: is the addictive in the anticipation? *Biological Psychiatry*, 71:741–8.

Verdejo-Garcia, A., Lawrence, A. J. & Clark, L. 2008. Impulsivity as a vulnerability marker for substance-use disorders: review of findings from high-risk research, problem gamblers and genetic association studies. *Neurosci Biobehav Rev*, 32:777–810.

Vitaro, F., Arseneault, L. & Tremblay, R. E. (1999). Impulsivity predicts problem gambling in low SES adolescent males. *Addiction*, 94:565–75.

Volkow, N. D., Fowler, J. S., Wang, G. J., Hitzemann, R., Logan, J., Schyler, D. J., Dewey, S. L. & Wolf, A. P. (1993). Decreased dopamine D2 receptor availability is associated with reduced frontal metabolism in cocaine abusers. *Synapse*, 14:169–77.

Volkow, N. D., Wang, G. J., Fowler, J. S., Logan, J., Hitzemann, R., Ding, Y. S., Pappas, N., Shea, C. & Piscani, K. (1996). Decreases in dopamine receptors but not in dopamine transporters in alcoholics. *Alcohol ClinExp Res*, 20:1594–8.

Volkow, N. D., Wang, G. J., Fowler, J. S., Logan, J., Gatley, S. J., Hitzemann, R., Chen, A. D., Dewey, S. L. & Pappas, N. (1997). Decreased striatal dopaminergic responsiveness in detoxified cocaine–dependent subjects. *Nature*, 386:830–3.

Volkow, N. D., Wang, G. J., Fowler, J. S., Logan, J., Gatley, S. J., Gifford, A., Hitzemann, R., Ding, Y. S. & Pappas, N. (1999). Prediction of reinforcing responses to psychostimulants in humans by brain dopamine D2 receptor levels. *Am J Psychiatry*, 156:1440–3.

Volkow, N. D., Chang, L., Wang, G. J., Fowler, J. S., Ding, Y. S., Sedler, M., Logan, J., Franceshi, D., Gatley, J., Hitzemann, R., Gifford, A., Wong, C. & Pappas, N. (2001). Low level of brain dopamine D2 receptors in methamphetamine abusers: association with metabolism in the orbitofrontal cortex. *American Journal of Psychiatry*, 158:2015–21.

Volkow, N. D., Wang, G. J., Maynard, L., Fowler, J. S., Jayne, B., Telang, F., Logan, J., Ding, Y. S., Gatley, S. J., Hitzemann, R., Wong, C. & Pappas, N. (2002). Effects of alcohol detoxification on dopamine D2 receptors in alcoholics: a preliminary study. *Psychiatry Research*, 116:163–72.

Voon, V., Thomsen, T., Miyasaki, J. M., Desouza, M., Shafro, A., Fox, S. H., Duff-Canning, S., Lang, A. E. & Zurowski, M. (2007). Factors associated with dopaminergic drug-related pathological gambling in Parkinson disease. *Arch Neurol*, 64:212–16.

Weintraub, D., Koester, J., Potenza, M. N., Siderowf, A. D., Stacy, M., Voon, V., Whetteckey, J., Wunderlich, G. R. & Lang, A. E. (2010). Impulse control disorders in Parkinson disease: a cross-sectional study of 3090 patients. *Archives of Neurology*, 67:589–95.

Wise, R. A. (2004). Dopamine, learning and motivation. *Nat Rev Neurosci*, 5:483–94.

Wolfling, K., Morsen, C. P., Duven, E., Alberecht, U., Grusser, S. M. & Flor, H. (2011). To gamble or not to gamble: at risk for craving and relapse – learned motivated attention in pathological gambling. *Biological Psychology*, 87:275–81.

Xue, G., Juan, C. H., Chang, C. F., Lu, Z. L. & Dong, Q. (2012). Lateral prefrontal cortex contributes to maladaptive decisions. *Proc Natl Acad Sci USA*, 109:401–6.

Zack, M. & Poulos, C. X. (2004). Amphetamine primes motivation to gamble and gambling-related semantic networks in problem gamblers. *Neuropsychopharmacology*, 29:195–207.

Zack, M. & Poulos, C. X. (2007). A D2 antagonist enhances the rewarding and priming effects of a gambling episode in pathological gamblers. *Neuropsychopharmacology*, 32:1678–86.

Chapter 7

Psychiatric co-morbidity in gambling

Romina Lopez Gaston

Aims

1   To discuss the common psychiatric disorders which are co-morbid with pathological gambling.
2   To explore key issues in the assessment and treatment of such co-morbidity.

Introduction

Co-morbidity, in this context, is used to describe the co-occurrence of two or more disorders; each disorder can occur independently or concurrently (Petry, 2002). Existing studies focusing on psychiatric co-morbidity associated with pathological gambling (PG) suggest that psychiatric co-morbidity appears to be the rule rather than the exception (Petry et al., 2005; Ibáñez et al., 2001).

Individuals with gambling problems have high rates of psychopathology, especially substance misuse disorders (Specker et al., 1996). Addiction to gambling is also associated with psychosocial impairment and suicide (Black & Moyer, 1998; Petry & Kiluk, 2002), and social distress in the form of occupational, financial, legal and marital disruption (Shaw et al., 2007), all of which lead to a significant impairment of the quality of life (Black, et al., 2003; Zimmerman et al., 2006). It is suggested that the identification and treatment of co-morbid conditions is likely to improve treatment outcomes in pathological gamblers (Najavits et al., 2011; Specker et al., 1996).

This chapter will focus on the most common psychiatric disorders that are co-morbid with pathological gambling and explore key issues in the assessment and treatment of such co-morbidity. Although the term problem gambling is preferred in the UK, as most of the research discussed in this chapter is from the United States (USA), the term pathological gambling will be used here.

Pathological gambling and psychiatric co-morbidity

In this section, I will first briefly look at the co-morbidity of pathological gambling among patients with psychiatric disorders, and then discuss the co-existence of psychiatric disorders among pathological gamblers.

Rates of pathological gambling in patients with psychiatric disorders

Zimmerman et al. (2006) examined the current and lifetime prevalence of pathological gambling in 1709 psychiatric outpatients, interviewed with a semi-structured questionnaire, attending a private practice in the USA. Approximately 2.3% of the patients had a lifetime history of DSM-IV pathological gambling, all of whom had at least one other DSM-IV Axis I disorder. Pathological gambling was *rarely the principal reason patients presented for treatment*. The authors concluded that pathological gamblers had significantly higher rates of bipolar disorder, social phobia, panic disorder with agoraphobia, alcohol use disorder and other impulse control disorders.

McIntyre et al. (2007) cross-referenced information from the Canadian Community Health Survey, and reported that pathological gambling was highly prevalent amongst patients with bipolar disorder (6.3% versus 2% general population). Further, this risk was increased in those with addiction to alcohol and illicit substances.

When looking at psychiatric inpatients, Lesieur and Blume (1990) found that the risk for pathological gambling was *two to five* times that of the general population. A recent study found that gambling difficulties were experienced by 3% of mentally healthy inpatients compared with 9% of psychiatric inpatients. The same study pointed out that gambling was significantly more prevalent in those individuals with psychotic disorders (Aragay et al., 2012).

There is scarce systematic data on gambling behaviour and psychotic disorders. Desai and Potenza (2009) interviewed a sample of 337 outpatients diagnosed with schizophrenia/schizoaffective disorder to establish the rate of problem and pathological gamblers compared to non-gamblers. Of the cohort, 9.5% met the criteria for problem gambling and 9.8% for pathological gambling. This study also highlighted that patients dually diagnosed were more prone to suffer substance misuse problems and mood disorders, with an increased rate in the use of mental health services.

Rates of psychiatric conditions in pathological gamblers compared to the general population

Illicit drug use

Petry et al. (2005) found that 38.1% of lifetime pathological gamblers had a psychiatric disorder with one or more other substances, the rate in non-gamblers was only 8.8%. Three national epidemiological studies conducted in the USA (Gerstein et al., 1999; Petry et al., 2005; Welte et al., 2001) suggest that pathological gambling is a disorder that rarely occurs in isolation, and Bland et al. (1993) in Canada and Petry et al. (2005) in the USA identified that pathological gamblers have an approximate 4% to 4.4% increase in the risk of illicit drug use. Some authors suggest that pathological gambling acts as a 'predicting factor' in the development of substance misuse (Kessler et al., 2008).

In treatment-seeking pathological gamblers, Stinchfield and Winters (2001) found that 35% had a lifetime diagnosis of substance use disorders and Ibáñez et al. (2001) described 11% of this population having marijuana abuse or dependence. Differences emerged when comparing treatment-seeking pathological gamblers with a history of substance misuse with those without one (Ladd & Petry, 2003). The former presented with greater psychiatric distress, more frequent gambling, and more years of disordered gambling. They were also more likely to be engaged with mental health services (Ladd & Petry, 2003).

Studies looking at individuals seeking treatment for substance misuse disorders (Cunningham-Williams et al., 2000; Langenbucher et al., 2001; McCormick, 1993) found rates of pathological gambling ranging from 10% to 13% (Smith et al., 2007).

Alcohol abuse/dependence

In studies conducted by Gerstein (1999), Welte (2001) and Petry (2005), approximately 25% of pathological gamblers presented with alcohol dependence, compared with 1.4% of controls. In addition, the lifetime rate of alcohol abuse/ dependence was 73.2% among those identified as lifetime pathological gamblers against 25% in controls. Bland et al. (1993) found that the lifetime rate of alcohol abuse or dependence was almost four times higher in pathological gamblers compared with controls (Smith et al., 2007).

In a Spanish study of treatment-seeking pathological gamblers (Ibáñez et al., 2001), 35% had a history of alcohol use disorders and 23% reported current alcohol use disorders, rates that appear higher compared to the general population.

Some studies suggest that pathological gambling and alcoholism converge on a shared neurobiological pathway mediating systems controlling 'urges and rewards' (Winters & Kushner, 2003). Grant and Kim (2002) stressed that both conditions might be mediated by impulse-control locations that involve the central processing of appetitive stimuli in the brain (i.e. the ventral tegmental area– nucleus accumbens orbital frontal cortex circuit). Naltrexone has shown a positive treatment outcome in both disorders and this could support the hypothesis of a shared neuropathophysiology (Blum et al., 1996).

Mood disorders

Three general population surveys have looked into the association of pathological gambling and psychiatric co-morbidities including bipolar affective disorder (BAD), major depressive disorder (MDD), dysthymia and rates of suicidality. Bland et al. (1993) found that PGs presented with approximately double rates of mood disorders compared with controls. In a population of pathological gamblers, Petry et al. (2005) found that approximately half of this cohort was suffering from a mood disorder. When studying treatment-seeking populations, Stinchfield and Winters (2001) reported that 12% of the cohort of pathological gamblers suffered from a current mood disorder.

Taking this into consideration, it is almost 'mandatory' to rule out BAD *prior* to considering the diagnosis of PG, as manic patients may gamble excessively when unwell. In this group, the patient's overspending is episodic (rather than chronic and ongoing), and occurs in the context of additional signs and symptoms compatible with BAD (ICD-10) such as euphoric mood, grandiosity, unrealistic plans, etc. Two general population surveys (Bland et al., 1993; Cunningham-Williams & Cottler, 2001) did not find a significant association between pathological gambling and mania, whilst more recently, Petry et al. (2005) reported that the likelihood of suffering from BAD was eight times higher in pathological gamblers compared to the general population.

Cunningham-Williams et al. (1998) reported higher rates of major depressive disorder (MDD) and dysthymia in PGs, whilst Petry et al. (2005) identified an odds ratio of 3.3 for these disorders and 1.8 for hypomania among pathological gamblers. In a more recent review, Won Kim et al. (2006) highlighted that 'depressive symptoms' associated with the consequences of gambling are more prevalent than primary depression.

Personality disorders

The prevalence rates of personality disorders among pathological gamblers tend to vary according to the assessment tool used. Studies that employ self-report instruments consistently yield higher rates of personality disorder (87%–93%) than those that use semi-structured interviews (25%–61%) (Bagby et al., 2008). Bagby et al. (2008) found that only those patients with borderline personality disorder (BPD) had consistently high and significant prevalence rates across both types of measures (Blaszczynski & Nower, 2002).

Fernández-Montalvo and Echeburúa (2004) also used a structured clinical interview in their study of 50 non-treatment-seeking pathological gamblers. BPD was the most prevalent personality disorder at a rate of 16%; this was followed by antisocial, paranoid, narcissistic and no specified disorder, which were each observed in 8% of patients. The authors also found that the presence of a personality disorder is associated with greater gambling severity and more severe anxiety, depression and alcohol abuse.

In a general population survey (Petry et al., 2005) a robust association was found between pathological gambling and all the personality disorders studied. The odds of having any personality disorder if one also has gambling disorder were 8.3 times greater than for the general population. In the same sample, the OR (odds ratio) of having histrionic personality disorder was 6.9; avoidant personality disorder was 6.5l; paranoid personality disorder was 6.1; antisocial personality disorder (ASPD) was 6.0; dependent personality disorder was 5.5; schizoid personality disorder was 5.0; and obsessive-compulsive personality disorder was 4.6. Borderline, narcissistic and schizotypal types were not assessed in the study.

ASPD occurs at relatively high rates among those with pathological gambling disorder. Slutske et al. (2001) found that the odds of a lifetime diagnosis of ASPD were 6.4 times greater among people with a lifetime history of PG. Fifteen per cent of their sample of pathological gamblers also had ASPD compared with 2% of controls.

Pietrzak and Petry (2005) compared treatment-seeking PGs with and without ASPD. Those with ASPD had more severe gambling and more medical and drug-related problems; they scored higher on symptom measures of somatisation, paranoid ideation and phobic anxiety. They were also more likely to be younger, male, less educated, divorced or separated, and to have had a history of substance abuse treatment than their non-ASPD counterparts.

When dimensional personality traits in PG were measured with the Temperament and Character Inventory (TCI) (Cloninger et al., 1994), those with PG scored higher on novelty seeking and harm avoidance, and lower on self-directedness, suggesting that PGs are less responsible, purposeful and self-acceptant, and have less impulse control (Forbush et al., 2008; Nordin & Nylander, 2007).

Anxiety disorders

In The National Co-morbidity Survey replication, Kessler et al. (2008) found that 60.3% of the cohort of PGs had an anxiety disorder: 52.2% had phobias, 21.9% had panic disorder, 16.6% had generalised anxiety disorder and 14.8% had post-traumatic stress disorder. Likewise, Bland and co-workers (1993), Petry et al. (2005) and Cunningham-Williams et al. (1998) also found higher levels of anxiety disorder compared to the general population.

Lifetime prevalence of anxiety disorders in PGs differs among studies; for instance, whilst Ibáñez, et al. (2001) found a lifetime rate of GAD = 7.2%, Specker et al. (1996) found rates of 37.5% and Black and Moyer (1998) reported the disorder in up to 40% of their sample. The latter also found rates for panic disorder and OCD equal to 10% each, whilst Specker (1996) and colleagues reported rates of 20% and 2.5% respectively.

In a cross-sectional study, Najavits and colleagues (2011) compared community samples of patients suffering with PG, PTSD and both disorders. The former presented with higher index of co-morbid conditions, suicidality and poor levels of functioning.

Attention Deficit Hyperactivity Disorder (ADHD)

In a general population survey, Kessler et al. (2008) found that 13.4% of people with PG also had ADHD. Clinical data support a substantial overlap between both disorders and suggest that they could act as a mutual risk factor.

A cohort of 33 PGs was compared with 33 controls (Rugle & Melamed, 1993) on 9 attention measures and childhood-behaviour questionnaires. PGs performed significantly worse than controls on higher-order attentional measures and exhibited more childhood behaviours consistent with ADHD. Specker and colleagues (1995) reported that 8 of 40 (20%) patients with PG met criteria for ADHD, and another 7 (17.5%) had symptoms that were considered 'sub-threshold'. Studies (Castellani & Rugle, 1995; DeCaria et al., 1996) have shown that patients with PG scored significantly higher than alcoholics and cocaine abusers on measures of impulsivity: such as coming to quick decisions, moving quickly from impulse to action, and lack of future planning. These authors hypothesised that ADHD and associated behaviours may predispose to substance abuse or PG, and that gamblers with attention deficits might choose gambling activities that do not require sustained attention or concentration.

Impulse control disorders

Pathological gambling and its co-morbidity with other impulse-control disorders has not been studied as thoroughly as other Axis I disorders, although rates of impulse-control disorders appear higher in persons with pathological gambling than in the general population. Investigators have reported rates ranging from 18% to 43% for one or more impulse-control disorder (Black & Moyer, 1998; Grant & Kim, 2001; Specker et al., 1995).

Specker and colleagues (1995) examined rates of ICDs in a treatment-seeking sample and found increased levels of compulsive shopping and sexual behaviours, intermittent explosive disorder and kleptomania. Black and Moyer (1998) found high rates of compulsive buying (23%), compulsive sexual behaviour (17%) and intermittent explosive disorder (13%) in their sample. Grant and Kim (2001) found lower rates of these behaviours in a larger sample with rates of 8%, 9% and 2% for each of the former disorders respectively.

Studies suggest that individuals with one impulse-control disorder, such as pathological gambling, appear more likely to have a second impulse-control disorder (Black et al., 1997; McElroy et al., 1994; Schlosser et al., 1994).

Obsessive compulsive disorder

Some researchers suggest that PG could fall within the obsessive compulsive spectrum guided by the persistent thoughts and urges followed by repetitive behaviours. However, others challenge this view, as the OCD constellation of symptoms is generally resisted by the individual, while gambling is perceived as pleasurable. Co-morbidity studies suggest that from 2.5% to 20% of persons with pathological gambling also have OCD (Linden et al., 1986; Specker et al., 1996). But in two family studies of OCD that also looked at pathological gambling, there were few data to support the existence of a relationship between these disorders (Black et al., 1994).

Methodological limitations of studies investigating co-morbidity

Both community- and hospital-based studies suggest that substance use disorders, mood, anxiety disorders and personality disorders are highly prevalent in persons with PG (Argo & Black, 2004). However, when examining outcomes of available studies, attention should be placed on methodological biases that have hampered research of addiction gambling and co-morbid psychiatric conditions, some of which are discussed later.

The terminology used in gambling research has included 'problem gambling', 'pathological gambling' and 'compulsive gambling'. These terms are used distinctively by some authors and interchangeably by others. Svetieva and Walker (2008) described this as a 'conceptual muddle' that has prevented the recognition of concepts and paradigms associated with each term. Terminological inaccuracies can also raise doubts as to whether the population selected in research studies is homogeneous and therefore comparable.

Additional methodological problems include studies that are mostly unsystematic, samples often small in number, and those at reach – often treatment-seeking individuals – are likely to present with higher rates of co-morbid psychopathology and perhaps not represent accurately the wider population (Winters & Kushner, 2003). All of these factors can confound study results.

Another potential pitfall in the available evidence is the reliability and validity of the assessment tools used, which can impact on the interpretation of research findings (Smith, et al., 2007). For instance, the presence or absence of a disorder can be affected by the psychometric properties of the instrument used in each study, leading to different diagnosis. This process could become even more complex if we add cultural or ethnic issues into the equation (Smith et al., 2007).

Another important factor to consider is the sample size and statistical significance. Variations in significance levels may reflect problems associated with the gap between the sample that needs to be recruited (power of the study) and that which has actually taken part. Studies without enough power can mislead conclusions related to relationship or significance across cohorts (Smith et al., 2007).

The nature and direction of the temporal relationship between pathological gambling and other psychiatric conditions is difficult to establish with the available evidence. Research cannot accurately tell us whether people with mental disorders are more likely to suffer from pathological gambling or whether pathological gambling increases the propensity of developing psychiatric co-morbidity (Smith et al., 2007; Winters & Kushner, 2003). This is primarily due to the cross-sectional nature of the available evidence. Most studies on pathological gambling focus on current rates of gambling and co-morbid conditions (cross-sectional relationship). This confounds the interpretation of the results, as it estimates pathology at a specific point in time, relying on retrospective reports (Smith et al., 2007; Winters & Kushner, 2003). Although longitudinal studies that focus on the lifetime prevalence of pathological gambling (longitudinal association) could potentially address the question of directionality, these studies are scarce, as they are costly, lengthy and difficult to conduct due to the low base rate of this disorder (Winters & Kushner, 2003).

In summary, available data cannot address accurately the issue of co-morbidity in PG. There are still gaps in understanding the interplay of shared and specific risk factors over time in these conditions (Smith et al., 2007; Winters & Kushner, 2003); it is therefore essential to examine the existing evidence with a critical eye when interpreting outcomes.

Assessment of psychiatric co-morbidity in pathological gamblers

The psychiatric history should be carefully explored when assessing a patient with PG. The relationship between the gambling behaviour and co-morbid disorders becomes clinically relevant to determine to which extent they influence each other. To date, the most commonly used diagnostic instruments for psychiatric disorders are the ICD-10 (WHO, 1992) and DSM-IV (APA, 1994).

When taking a psychiatric history, we encourage patients to tell us what they see as *their* main concern (chief complaint). The discordance between the patient's views (i.e. low mood/suicide) and what the referrer or significant other believes is the main issue (i.e. gambling), sometimes reflects the degree of insight that patients have into their problems.

Presenting complaints and reasons for referral bring together a combination of symptoms that can later on be clustered into psychiatric disorders. For instance, a chief complaint of 'sadness' will take the interviewer through the ICD-10 criteria of mood disorders; if the patient has 'odd thoughts' or perceptual disturbances, then the ICD-10 will be helpful to rule out psychotic disorders; if anxiety is the primary concern, neurotic disorders are the pathway to follow, etc. Given the high rates of co-morbidity with PG, substance misuse disorders should be addressed and extensively narrowed down to distinguish between harmful use and dependence on one or multiple substances. There are structured interviews that can aid clinicians to explore psychiatric symptomatology (Figure 7.1).

- SCID – Structural Clinical Interview for DSM-IV Axis I & II disorders (First et al., 1997)
- SCAN – Schedules for Clinical Assessment in Neuropsychiatry (Wing et al., 1990)
- Brief Psychiatric Rating Scale (Overall & Gorham, 1962)
- Becks Depression Inventory (Beck et al., 1961) and Becks Anxiety Inventory (Beck & Steer, 1993)
- Hamilton Rating Scale for Depression (Hamilton, 1960)
- Hamilton Rating Scale for Anxiety (Hamilton, 1959)
- PANS – Positive and Negative Syndrome Scale (Kay, 1991)

Figure 7.1 Structured interviews that can be used as guidance to apply the ICD-10/DSM-IV criteria.

Once the cluster of symptoms is established, the interviewer should determine the severity and impact on day-to-day activities. The gap between the patient's pre-morbid level of functioning and current one is a good indicator of how ill/impaired the patient has been. In addition, and depending on the severity, disorders tend to impact on the patient's psychosocial circumstances (financial, relationship, forensic, etc.), which reflects the wide-reaching consequences of the illness.

The risk assessment is an essential part of the psychiatric history and the one that will dictate the level of urgency to act. We have briefly discussed the constellation of psychosocial complications (marital, financial, etc.) that patients with PG present with; these can act as triggering factors that can drive patients to desperation. Risks include those of self-harm, harm to others and self-neglect. An empathetic approach is necessary to disentangle the patient's thought process and level of intent. The more tangible the plans to harm, the riskier the patient has become. Equally, lack of drive to self-care and keep basic survival needs (food, self-care, shelter) suggests neglect as a potential complication.

Based on the above, the history will result – more often than not – in a combination of disorders. The temporal relationship among these will determine whether they run alongside each other or will have in some ways developed in a sequential manner. In patients with chronic disorders, it can become problematic to make this distinction as symptoms blend with each other over time.

The ICD-10 criteria (WHO, 1992) aid interviewers to focus their attention on clusters and allow in most cases, for them to reach diagnostic categories towards the end of the assessment. Diagnoses are necessary to offer patients a direction of treatment in the framework of a management plan.

Gathering information with the patient's consent, from a relative or close friend, tends to be enlightening at times, particularly if the patient's insight is poor and there is an underestimation of the negative consequences of the problems in their life. Also, eliciting whether there is a family history of psychiatric or substance misuse disorders will enhance the interviewer's attention towards intergenerational vulnerabilities.

The patient's history of physical illness, surgeries, drug allergies and medical treatment can help to rule out medical illnesses that could be influencing the clinical presentation (e.g. mass lesions, endocrinological problems, etc.); they may also identify conditions that contraindicate the use of certain medications prescribed to treat the disorder. An example of this could be the prescription of high doses of naltrexone for PG in patients known to suffer chronic pain and in need of opiate-based painkillers. The interviewer should also obtain the medication being prescribed to the patient, so interactions can be kept in mind if psychotropics were to be introduced at a later stage.

Treatment issues

Looking at available research studies, Winters and Kushner (2003) identified some obstacles in the treatment outcomes in patients suffering from pathological gambling and co-morbid psychiatric disorders. Most studies have not addressed co-morbidity as a variable, and in those that have, none reported if treatment outcomes were impacted by it. This absence of data raises questions as to how treatment can be best tailored for these individuals.

In clinical practice the first step is to disentangle whether the patient is suffering from isolated symptoms (anxiety, depressive, etc.), or whether those symptoms amount to a primary disorder (as per ICD-10 or DSM-IV criteria). If the clinician encounters the former, these symptoms could be associated with the consequences of pathological gambling; hence its treatment becomes a priority. However, if the latter is the case, one needs to conceptualise the patient as suffering from two or more distinct disorders, all of which need treatment in their own right (dual diagnosis).

Despite existing National Guidelines (DOH, 2002; NICE, 2010), there still exist some reservations in the management of dually diagnosed patients (Winters & Kushner, 2003). For instance, it is not uncommon for treatment services to prevent patients from entering treatment unless either their psychiatric or addictive disorder is treated first by the relevant service (mental health services or addiction services). This 'sequential' approach has not been found as successful as treating disorders 'concurrently'. Indeed, maximal efficacy for treating pathological gamblers with co-morbid disorders would involve adjusting interventions for specific concomitant psychiatric disorders as an adjunct to the core treatment of pathological gambling. In these cases, the patient should be usually treated for the index psychiatric disorder while the addictive behaviour is managed simultaneously through a process of psychoeducation, behavioural contracting and psycho-pharmacology (DOH, 2002; Winters & Kushner, 2003). Mindful of this process, a fluent collaborative relationship should be built up among mental health and addiction treatment services.

Conclusion

In summary, evidence suggests that co-morbidity appears to be the rule rather than the exception in pathological gambling. Therefore increased awareness and comprehensive routine assessments aiming to identify co-morbidity are needed. Axis I and II disorders have been described as more prevalent in pathological gamblers, particularly addictive behaviours, neurotic and affective disorders, ADHD and personality disorders. Mechanisms underlying the interplay between these disorders remain unclear and this is the result of methodological biases coupled with the scarce number of longitudinal studies conducted in this field.

The treatment pathway for patients suffering with pathological gambling and co-morbid disorders is still not completely understood. Patients with addictive behaviours and mental illness should be treated collaboratively by mental health and addiction services. Disorders should be addressed concurrently without either of them becoming an obstacle to enter treatment at any point in time.

Key points

1   Psychiatric co-morbidity is more the norm than the exception among pathological gamblers.
2   The most common psychiatric disorders found to be co-morbid with pathological gambling are substance misuse, mood disorders and personality disorders.
3   Much more needs to be done at assessment and treatment levels to ensure that these dually diagnosed patients get the help they need.

References

American Psychiatric Association (APA) (1994). *DSM–IV. Diagnostic and Statistical Manual of Mental Disorders*. Washington, DC: American Psychiatric Association Publishing.

Aragay, N., Roca, A., Garcia, B., Marqueta, C., Guijarro, C., Delgado, L., Garolera, M., Albemi, J. & Valles, V. (2012). Pathological Gambling in a psychiatric sample, *Comprehensive Psychiatry*, 53:9–14.

Argo, T. & Black, D. W. (2004). The characteristics of pathological gambling. In J. Grant and M. Potenza (eds), *Understanding and Treating Pathological Gambling*. Washington, DC: American Psychiatric Publishing, Inc., 39–53.

Bagby, R. M., Vachon, D. D., Bulmash, E. & Quilty, L. C. (2008). Personality disorders and pathological gambling: a review and re-examination of prevalence rates. *J Personal Disord*, 22:191–207.

Beck, A. T. & Steer, R. A. (1993). *Beck Anxiety Inventory Manual*. San Antonio: Company Publishers.

Beck, A. T., Ward, C. H., Mendelson, M., Mock, J. & Erbaugh, J. (1961). An inventory for measuring depression. *Arch. Gen. Psychiatry*, 4(6): 561–71. doi: 10.1001/archpsyc.1961.01710120031004.

Black D. W. & Moyer, T. (1998). Clinical features and psychiatric comorbidity of subjects with pathological gambling behaviour. *Psychiatr Serv*, 49:1434–9.

Black, D. W., Moyer, T. & Schlosser, S. (2003). Quality of life and family history in pathological gambling. *J Nerv Ment Dis*, 191:124–6.

Black, D. W., Goldstein, R. B., Noyes, R. Jr. & Blum, N. (1994). Compulsive behaviors and obsessive-compulsive disorder (OCD): lack of a relationship between OCD, eating disorders, and gambling. *Compr Psychiatry*, 35:145–8.

Black, D. W., Kehrberg, L. L., Flumerfelt, D. L. & Schlosser, S. S. (1997). Characteristics of 36 subjects reporting compulsive sexual behaviour. *Am J Psychiatry*, 154:243–9.

Bland, R. C., Newman, S. C., Orn, H. & Stebelsky, G. (1993). Epidemiology of pathological gambling in Edmonton. *Can J Psychiatry*, 38:108–12.

Blaszczynski, A. & Nower, L. (2002): A pathways model of problem and pathological gambling. *Addiction*, 97:487–99.

Blum, K., Sheridan, P. J., Wood, R. C., Braverman, E. R., Chen, T. J., Cull, J. G. & Comings, D. E. (1996). The D2 dopamine receptor gene as a determinant of reward deficiency syndrome. *J R Soc Med*, 89(7):396–400.

Castellani, B. & Rugle, L. (1995). A comparison of pathological gamblers to alcoholics and cocaine misusers on impulsivity, sensation seeking, and craving. *Int J Addict*, 30:275–89.

Cloninger, C. R., Przybeck, T. R., Svrakic, D. M. & Wetzel, R. D. (1994). *The Temperament and Character Inventory (TCI): A Guide to its Development and Use*. St Louis: Center for Psychobiology of Personality, Washington University.

Cunningham-Williams, R. M. & Cottler, L. B. (2001). The epidemiology of pathological gambling. *Semin Clin Neuropsychiatry*, 6:155–66.

Cunningham-Williams, R. M., Cottler, L. B., Compton, W. M. III & Spitznagel, E. L. (1998). Taking chances: problem gamblers and mental health disorders—results from the St Louis Epidemiologic Catchment Area Study. *Am J Public Health*, 88:1093–6.

Cunningham-Williams, R. M., Cottler, L. B., Compton, W. M., Spitznagel, E. L. & Ben-Abdallah, A. (2000). Problem gambling and comorbid psychiatric and substance use disorders among drug users recruited from drug treatment and community settings. *Journal of Gambling Studies*, 16(4):347–75.

DeCaria, C. M., Hollander, E., Grossman, R. et al. (1996). Diagnosis, neurobiology, and treatment of pathological gambling. *J Clin Psychiatry*, 57(suppl 8):80–4.

Department of Health (DOH) (2002). *Dual diagnosis – good practice guidance*. London: DOH.

Desai, R. A. & Potenza, M. N. (2009). A cross sectional study of problem and pathological gambling in patients with schizophrenia/schizoaffective disorders. *J Clin Psychiatry*, 70(9):1250–7.

DSM–IV (1994). *Diagnostic and Statistical Manual of Mental Disorders*. Washington, US: American Psychiatric Association.

Fernández-Montalvo, J. & Echeburúa, E. (2004). Pathological gambling and personality disorders: an exploratory study with the IPDE. *J Personal Disord*, 18:500–5.

First, M. B., Spitzer, R. L., Gibbon, M. & Williams, J. B. W. (1997). SCID-I Structured Clinical Interview for DSM-IV® Axis I Disorders, Clinician Version, User's Guide. Biometrics Research at Columbia University. www.scid4.org.

Forbush, K. T., Shaw, M., Graeber, M. A. et al. (2008). Neuro-psychological characteristics and personality traits in pathological gambling. *CNS Spectr*, 13:306–15.

Gerstein, D. R., Volberg, R. A., Toce, M. T. et al. (1999). Gambling Impact and Behaviour Study: report to the National Gambling Impact Study Commission. Chicago: National Opinion Research Center.

Grant, J. E. & Kim, S. W. (2001). Demographic and clinical features of 131 adult pathological gamblers. *J Clin Psychiatry*, 62:957–62.

Grant, J. E. & Kim, S. W. (2002). Gender differences in pathological gamblers seeking medical treatment. *Compr Psychiatry*, 43:56–62.

Hamilton, M. (1959). The assessment of anxiety states by rating. *Br J Med Psychol* 32:50–5. Retreived on 10 October 2014 from: http://dcf.psychiatry.ufl.edu/files/2011/05/HAMILTON-ANXIETY.pdf.

Hamilton, M. (1960). A rating scale for depression. *Journal of Neurology, Neurosurgery and Psychiatry*, 23:56–62. Online resources: doi:10.1136/jnnp.23.1.56PMID 14399272. Retreived on 10 October 2014 from: http://healthnet.umassmed.edu/mhealth/HAMD.pdf.

Ibáñez, A., Blanco, C., Donahue, E., et al. (2001). Psychiatric comorbidity in pathological gamblers seeking treatment. *Am J Psychiatry*, 158:1733–5.

Kay, S. R. (1991). *Positive and Negative Syndromes in Schizophrenia*. Oxford: Routledge Mental Health, 33–6.

Kessler, R. C., Hwang, I., LaBrie, R. et al. (2008). *DSM-IV Pathological Gambling in the National Comorbidity Survey Replication. Psychological Medicine*. Cambridge: Cambridge University Press.

Ladd, G. T. & Petry, N. M. (2003). A comparison of pathological gamblers with and without substance abuse treatment histories. *Exp Clin Psychopharmacol*, 11: 202–9.

Langenbucher, J., Bavly, L., Labouvie, E., Sanjuan, P. M. & Martin, C. S. (2001). Clinical features of pathological gambling in an addictions treatment cohort. *Psychology of Addictive Behaviors*,15(1):77–9.

Lesieur, H. R. & Blume, S. B. (1990). Characteristics of pathological gamblers identified among patients on a psychiatric admission service. *Hospital and Community Psychiatry*, 41:1009–12.

Linden, R. D., Pope, H. D. Jr & Jonas, J. M. (1986). Pathological gambling and major affective disorder: preliminary findings. *J Clin Psychiatry*, 47:201–3.

McCormick, R. A. (1993). Disinhibition and negative affectivity in substance abusers with and without a gambling problem. *Addictive Behaviors*, 18(3):331–6.

McElroy, S. L., Keck, P. E. Jr, Pope, H. G. Jr et al. (1994). Compulsive buying: a report of 20 cases. *J Clin Psychiatry*, 55:242–8.

McIntyre, R. S., McElroy, S. L., Knorski, J. Z. et al. (2007). Problem gambling in bipolar disorder: results from the Canadian Community Health Survey. *J Affect Disord*, 102(1–3):27–34.

Najavits, L. M., Meyer, T., Johnson, K. M. & Korn, D. (2011). Pathological gambling and Posttraumatic Stress Disorder: a study of co-morbidity versus each alone. *J Gambl Stud*, 27(4).

National Institute for Clinical Excellence (NICE) (2010). *Psychosis and Substance Misuse*. London: NICE.

Nordin, C. & Nylander, P. O. (2007). Temperament and character in pathological gambling. *J Gambl Stud*, 23:113–20.

Overall, J. E. & Gorham, D. R. (1962). The brief psychiatric rating scale. *Psychological Reports*, 10:799–812.

Petry, N. (2002). *Pathological Gambling: Etiology, Co-morbidity andTtreatment (1st edn)*. Washington, DC: American Psychological Association, 85.

Petry, N. M. & Kiluk, B. D. (2002). Suicidal ideation and suicide attempts in treatment-seeking pathological gamblers. *J Nerv Ment Dis*, 190:462–9.

Petry, N. M., Stinson, F. S. & Grant, B. F. (2005). Co-morbidity of DSM-IV pathological gambling and other psychiatric disorders: results from the National Epidemiologic Survey on Alcohol and Related Conditions. *J Clin Psychiatry*, 66:564–74.

Pietrzak, R. H. & Petry, N. M. (2005). Antisocial personality disorder is associated with increased severity of gambling, medical, drug and psychiatric problems among treatment-seeking pathological gamblers. *Addiction*, 100:1183–93.

Rugle, L. & Melamed, L. (1993). Neuropsychological assessment of attention problems in pathological gamblers. *J Nerv Ment Dis*, 181:107–12.

Schlosser, S., Black, D. W., Repertinger, S. & Freet, D. (1994). Compulsive buying: demography, phenomenology, and comorbidity in 46 subjects. *Gen Hosp Psychiatry*, 16:205–12.

Shaw, M. C., Forbush, K. T., Schlinder, J., Rosenman, E. & Black, D. W. (2007). The effect of pathological gambling on families, marriages and children. *CNS Spectrum: The International Journal of Neuropsychiatric Medicines*, 12:615–22.

Slutske, W. S., Eisen, S., Xian, H. et al. (2001). A twin study of the association between pathological gambling and antisocial personality disorder. *J Abnorm Psychol*, 110:297–308.

Smith, G., Hodgins, D. & Williams, R. (2007). Research and measurement issues in gambling studies. In N. M. Petry and J. Weinstock, *Comorbidity and Mental Illness*. London: Elsevier.

Specker, S. M., Carlson, G. A., Christenson, G. A. & Marcotte, M. (1995). Impulse control disorders and attention deficit disorder in pathological gamblers. *Ann Clin Psychiatry*, 7:175–9.

Specker, S. M., Carlson, G. A., Edmonson, K. M. et al. (1996). Psychopathology in pathological gamblers seeking treatment. *J Gambl Stud*, 12:67–81.

Stinchfield, R. & Winters, K. C. (2001). Outcome of Minnesota's gambling treatment programs. *J Gambl Stud*, 17:217–45.

Svetieva, E. & Walker, M. (2008). Inconsistency between concept and measurement: The Canadian Problem Gambling Index (CPGI). *Journal of Gambling*, 22.

Welte, J., Barnes, G., Wieczorek, W., Tidwell, M. C. & Parker, J. (2001). Alcohol and gambling pathology among U.S. adults: prevalence, demographic patterns and comorbidity. *J Stud Alcohol*, Sep. 62(5):706–12.

Wing, J. K. et al. (1990). SCAN. Schedules for Clinical Assessment in Neuropsychiatry. *Arch Gen Psychiatry*, 47(6):589–93.

Winters, K. C. & Kushner, M. G. (2003). Treatment issues pertaining to pathological gamblers with comorbid disorders. *Journal of Gambling Studies*, 19(3):261.

Won Kim, S., Grant, J. E., Eckert, E. D. et al. (2006). Pathological gambling and mood disorders: clinical associations and treatment implications. *J Affect Disord*, 92:109–12.

World Health Organization (WHO) (1992). ICD-10. *Classification of Mental and Behavioural Disorders*. Geneva: World Health Organization.
Zimmerman, M., Chelminski, I. & Young, D. (2006). Prevalence and diagnostic correlates of DSM-IV pathological gambling in psychiatric outpatients. *J Gambl Stud*, 22:255–62.

Chapter 8

Effects of gambling on the family

Richard Velleman, Jennifer Cousins and Jim Orford

Aim

| | To describe the effects of problem gambling on families, including children. |

Introduction

In discussions about problem gambling – and the same has been true in the case of problem alcohol and drug use – there has been an unfortunate tendency to neglect the majority of individuals who experience the problem at first hand. We refer here to the close family members – parents, partners, children and others – who live under the same roof as, or whose lives are otherwise very closely bound up with, someone who is personally suffering from the addiction. As one commentator from the USA put it, family members of problem gamblers are 'a group with no ... voice' (Castellani, 2000, p. 177). There are a lot of these 'affected others': the report of the Australian Productivity Commission (1999), in its comprehensive assessment of the costs and benefits of gambling to Australian society, concluded, on the basis of a survey of clients in counselling, that on average a single gambling problem adversely affected seven other people. The 2010 British Gambling Prevalence Survey included the question: *In the last 12 months, has any close relative of yours (including partner) had a gambling problem?* In that representative British sample, 3.8% answered that question in the affirmative (previously unpublished data), which is equivalent to over one million people, and is roughly four to five times the percentage who in the same survey were themselves identified as people with gambling problems according to their answers to screening questions (Wardle et al., 2011).

The effects of problem gambling on adult family members and friends

Early impressions

One of the earliest clinical accounts of compulsive gambling from the 1960s cited the following wife: 'Over the last few years we have had a monster living with our family – a monster in the shape of a "fruit-machine". Practically every penny my husband earned went into that machine and while it consumed, we starved. He was obsessed by it. Frequently we were without food, fuel and light' (Barker & Miller, 1968, pp. 287–8). An early series of studies of wives of male problem gamblers in the USA in the 1980s gave ample evidence of the stress that they were under as a result. Wives commonly reported feelings of anger and resentment, depression, loneliness or isolation from their husbands. Feelings of helplessness and confusion were common, as were physical symptoms of stress such as severe headaches, bowel irregularities, feelings of faintness or dizziness, hypertension and breathing irregularities. Wives reported unsatisfactory sexual relationships during the worst of their spouses' gambling and nearly all had considered separation from their gambling husbands (Lorenz & Yaffe, 1988). Particularly sad is the guilt that many spouses described because they thought they might be the reason for their partners' gambling problems and/or because, despite their efforts, they were unable to do anything to stop the behaviour. One of the modern classics of the problem gambling literature, entitled *When Luck Runs Out*, had a chapter on compulsive gambling and the family, which included the following statement: 'It is the nature of emotional disorders that when one member of the family is afflicted, the effects are felt by all the others. There are few, however, in which the impact is felt with such severity as in the case of compulsive gambling' (Custer & Milt, 1985, pp. 122–3).

Recent research and clinical experience

Recent research exploring the impact of problem gambling on family members has focused on spouses, with lesser attention to the impact on parents, and occasional papers focusing on other family members (Kalischuk et al., 2006). Furthermore, although one recent piece of research (Kalischuk, 2010) was based on fairly equal numbers of male and female respondents, that remains the exception, and the following is based heavily on the experiences of adult women affected by their male relatives' gambling.

One feature of a gambling problem, compared to other addictive behaviour problems, is the absence of obvious physical signs and symptoms, rendering it relatively easy to hide from family members. Even if family members notice changes in their relatives (such as irritability, decrease in sleep, less time at home), without full information, changes may be attributed to other difficulties such as stress at work, a possible affair, or recent life events such as a bereavement. A feature of problem gambling is that the person struggling often lies about his or her increasing difficulties. Additionally, the general population may still be relatively unfamiliar with the nature and extent of gambling problems. All of these factors combine to make it much more likely that the disclosure or discovery of a gambling problem is 'sudden, devastating and traumatic' for a family member (McComb et al., 2009). Krishnan and Orford (2002), focusing on the dilemmas partners and parents faced in deciding how to cope, found that once the problem is recognised it is still quite unclear to family members what they should do about it. One of the first things family members try is to discuss the matter openly, but family members often explained that they were unable to do so because the gambling relative was rarely at home or because, when they tried to discuss the problem, the relative denied that there was any problem at all, refused to talk about the subject or simply reacted angrily to any mention of his or her gambling.

There is evidence of co-morbidity of problem gambling with other addiction problems and with depression (Weinstock, 2007), so family members may additionally have to cope with the impact of these other difficulties that their gambling relatives may be experiencing, as well as, in our experience, occasionally gambling combined with a psychotic condition or a learning disability. Hence multiple professional systems may be involved. To the authors' knowledge no research has been completed on how these additional complications impact on family members and how they cope.

Concurring with our experience, McComb et al. (2009) identified the following main areas in which research indicates that family members are affected: financial, relational, and emotional and physical health.

The financial impact

Although there can be severe negative financial consequences for family members affected by other forms of addiction, in the case of problem gambling this is a much more common and central part of their experience. Nor is it always a matter of debts accumulating over a period of time, since the loss of very large sums of money can happen in a matter of minutes when gambling. Many authors have commented on the financial impact that gambling problems can have on family members in the short, medium and long term. One of the very earliest interview studies of 'compulsive gamblers' in the USA included a focus on what the author referred to as an 'exploitative' financial relationship with the gambler's family. This included using money earmarked for family needs, 'borrowing' from relations, lying about the true extent of his (all of the gamblers in that study were men) earnings, and selling or pawning his own or family members' possessions (Lesieur, 1984). Family members may be put at serious financial risk (Leseiur, 1998). They may have to cope with large credit card debt, loans (both illegal and legal and money owed to other family members) as well as loss of mortgage and rent funds. In a case known to one of us, a new mother had found out that all the money saved for her maternity leave had been spent on gambling.

When they have a close relative with a gambling problem, partners and others, such as parents, face uncertainty about how to cope. These 'coping dilemmas' (Orford, 2012) are very similar to those described by family members whose relatives have other types of addiction, but those revolving around money are prominent. Family members may have to decide whether to cut back on their spending, which would impact on their usual lifestyle, including social life. Additionally, family members frequently make the difficult decision to take up the role of managing family finances and controlling their relative's access to money in order to either help the relative or to gain as much oversight as possible to aid their family's financial recovery (Valentine & Hughes, 2010). This can add considerable stress if this way of working, either for the person or family, is not familiar to them or goes outside usual cultural and/or gender expectations. In one study (Krishnan & Orford, 2002), parents of sons or daughters with gambling problems who took part talked about watching money very carefully. Those who had been advised by Gamblers Anonymous, or who had attended Gam-Anon – for family members or friends of compulsive gamblers – knew that the recommendation was not to give gamblers money under any circumstances. But these parents worried that their offspring would suffer as a result, perhaps even starve, or that they would start stealing and getting into trouble. Some had therefore lent their gambling children money although they believed there was little chance of being repaid. Some had covered their children's debts or rent, sometimes to the tune of several thousand pounds. Some had successfully taken over their children's finances, only handing out money for what were thought to be reasonable expenses.

In the medium to long term, family members have to cope with the often lengthy process of paying back debts and with the pay-day anxiety that pay may trigger a return to gambling behaviour. A family member may question whether the relative has different values regarding money and how this might affect the future of the relationship. Family members may have to return to work, sell property and items that can no longer be afforded and/or arrange changes in childcare and education to reflect changes in the financial situation.

The relational impact

Loss of trust is a significant factor within relationships affected by problem gambling (Dickson-Swift et al., 2005), particularly, in the authors' experience, for those family members in close contact with their gambling relatives. Loss of trust can stay just within the area of gambling (family members do not trust what their relatives say about their gambling, whether they have stopped, etc.) or can affect all aspects of the relationship (e.g. in relation to parental decisions the relative makes, or regarding emotional and physical intimacy) so that every aspect of the relationship feels uncertain or on shaky ground. This can be particularly felt when family members are coming to terms with what has happened and are beginning to realise how the problem gambling is linked to behaviours such as secrecy, misleading, lying, and blaming comments made by their relative, and arguments between the family member and the relative. Family members frequently describe feeling as though their relatives are distant, uninterested or argumentative, and as a result family members may respond by 'treading carefully', not wanting to 'cause' further gambling behaviour. Family members often describe their relatives as neglecting family roles and responsibilities and communicating poorly. Higher rates of domestic abuse (verbal and physical violence) have been reported in families affected by excessive gambling (Muelleman et al., 2002). Lesieur (1989) reported that 87% of problem gamblers ridiculed, insulted, embarrassed or belittled their wives in front of their children, and 43% of Lorenz and Shuttleworth's (1983) respondents reported verbal and/or physical abuse.

In working with an affected family member, questions may be raised regarding whether the relative can overcome the gambling difficulty, and how this may affect their future relationship. One outcome is a repairing of the damage that has been done to the relationship and the restoration of closeness. But another is the establishment of a more distant relationship, or separation or divorce in the case of couples. In fact Shaw et al. (2007) reported much higher rates of divorce among couples affected by problem/pathological gambling than in the general population (between 39% and 53% in comparison to 18%).

Family members may describe a change in other relationships too, as a consequence of not being able to go out as much (due to reduced finances), or because of worries about talking about the relative's difficulties (either due to a feeling that others will not understand or that others may think badly of the relative), and sometimes due to tension arising out of the different ways people respond to the relative (for example, another family member or friend may have a different view of how active to be in helping the relative, or about how 'understanding' as opposed to 'confrontational' it is appropriate to be) (Orford, 2012).

The emotional and physical health impact

Family members who are experiencing problem gambling within their families often describe high levels of anxiety, low mood, fear and isolation. Family members also describe themselves as feeling angry, frustrated, irritable and very shocked about the position their relatives have put them in (Dickson-Swift et al., 2005; Lorenz & Yaffe, 1988). They often feel guilty, believing that they may have in some way caused or contributed to the problem gambling (Dickson-Swift et al., 2005). This may be more pronounced if the family member has ever gone gambling with the relative or encouraged it in the early stages through accepting gifts or by being hopeful of a win. There may also be feelings of grief and resentment on account of a loss of 'the future' that the family member thought had been planned and agreed upon, or had hoped for, but which is now found not to be possible, perhaps at least in the immediate term, nor possibly in the long term either.

Typically family members describe a lot of pressure and stress that contributes to a feeling of being on high alert, watching their relatives and trying to ascertain whether gambling has continued, all of which leads them to feeling exhausted and overwrought. They describe sleeping problems, blood pressure problems, changes in eating patterns (either loss of appetite or an increase in appetite), an increase in alcohol or drug use, loss of concentration, and stomach problems or pain (Lorenz & Yaffe, 1988). It is common in our experience for family members to ask whether long-term illnesses they may have might have been exacerbated by their relatives' problem gambling.

The effects of problem gambling on children

Immediate impact on children

The effects are well documented of growing up in a family where one or both parents or other close relative (step-parent, sibling, etc.) has an alcohol or drug problem (Cleaver et al., 2011; Kroll & Taylor, 2003; Velleman & Templeton, 2007). The question of how parental *gambling* problems affect children has been far less extensively examined. Darbyshire et al. (2001) undertook a review which explored children's experiences of living with a parent with a gambling problem. They concluded that there was almost no recognition of the experiences of children who live in problem gambling families within the gambling and child health literatures. They cited a finding of the Productivity Commission in Australia (1999) that there are statistically '0.6 children (under the age of 15 years) living with the average problem gambler' (Productivity Commission 1999, v.1, 7.31–7.33), which suggests that there may be about 175,000 Australian children living within a problem gambling family in Australia. They also cite (p. 287) Jacobs et al.'s estimate in 1989 that, in the USA, 'the most conservative estimate of the prevalence of young people affected is 2.5 million'.

There is a great deal of anecdotal evidence showing that the effects on children of a parental gambling problem are very similar to those found in the children of parents with other addiction problems. However, unlike alcohol and drug misuse (which are widely recognised as being severely problematic for children and other family members), gambling is less widely recognised as such, and so children and other family members may find it more difficult to access sympathetic help. Clinical observation (e.g. Franklin & Thoms, 1989) has suggested that children of 'pathological gamblers' often experience role conflicts, including taking on the role of peacemaker, being caught in the middle of family tensions, serving as scapegoat and/or taking the blame for family difficulties stemming from the problem gambling, and often experience disappointment due to broken promises. Lorenz (1987, p. 83) observed:

> Children of the pathological gambler are probably the most victimized by the illness. Usually underage, emotionally and financially dependent upon the gambler during the worst of the illness, it is the children who are the most helpless. They hear the arguments, recriminations, apologies, broken

promises, insults, lies, and fights. They hear their mother arguing with their father about not having money for food, clothes, or school items for the children... The children of pathological gamblers, growing up in an atmosphere of emotional deprivation, isolation, parental abuse, rejection, poor role modelling, and emphasis on money, are very likely to have equally problem-ridden lives.

These strongly expressed clinical observations have received some support from empirical research. For example, Jacobs et al. (1989) took the self-rating measures of 52 children in the ninth through twelfth grades in the USA who described one or both of their parents as having 'compulsive gambling problems' and compared them to a group of students who reported no gambling problems among their parents. Their findings suggested that the former were at much greater risk for health-threatening behaviours, such as smoking and alcohol or drug use; psychosocial problems, such as an unhappy childhood, or having a 'broken home'; educational difficulties; and emotional disorders, including depression, dysphoria and suicidal behaviour.

Lesieur and Rothschild (1989) surveyed via questionnaire 105 children of married GA members throughout the USA and Canada. They found that, when compared with nationally normed samples from intact families, the GA children were more likely to have been subjected to parental physical violence and abuse. When asked about their feelings concerning their parents' gambling, two thirds reported feeling sad, over half emotionally hurt, depressed, confused, with between a quarter and a half feeling angry most or all of the time, pity for their parents' gambling, hateful, shameful, helpless, isolated, abandoned and guilty.

The US National Gambling Impact Study Commission (1999) reported: 'Children of compulsive gamblers are often prone to suffer abuse, as well as neglect, as a result of parental problem or pathological gambling' (NGISC, Ch. 7, p. 28) and they cite two studies indicating that between 10% and 17% of children of compulsive gamblers had been abused. Media and other informal reports in the USA have given an indication of some of the problems that can occur. For example, in Indiana a review of the state's gaming commission records revealed that 72 children were found abandoned on casino premises during a 14-month period (e.g. Grace Schneider, 'Children Being Left Alone While Parents Gamble', [Louisville] *Courier-Journal*, July 18, 2000). It is also documented in the National Gambling Impact Study Commission Report that a number of children have died as a direct result of adult gambling problems. As examples, they cite cases in Louisiana and South Carolina where children died after being locked in hot cars for hours while their caretakers gambled; and an Illinois mother was sentenced to prison for suffocating her infant daughter in order to collect insurance money to continue gambling. Cases of child abandonment at Foxwoods, the nation's largest casino, in Ledyard, Connecticut, became so commonplace that authorities were forced to post signs in the casino's parking lots warning parents not to leave children in cars unattended (NGISC, 1999).

Vitaro et al. (2008) compared offspring of problem gamblers with offspring of parents without gambling problems, and found that the former reported more depressive feelings and more conduct problems at mid-adolescence than children of parents without gambling problems. They also experienced an increase in depressive symptoms from mid-adolescence to early adulthood. Importantly (and again in line with the findings from other areas of substance misuse), ineffective parenting mediated almost all the links between parental problem gambling and children's adjustment problems.

What these limited studies of the children of compulsive gamblers suggest is that the effects on children of living in an environment where one or both parents have significant problems controlling their gambling behaviour are very similar to the effects seen in the children of parents with other addictive problems. This implies (as Lesieur and Rothschild (1989) argue) that we should be cautious and not overgeneralise, because with children whose parents have other addictive problems, whilst there are often many significant deleterious effects, it is also the case that a substantial proportion of these children do manage *not* to be negatively affected by these experiences – they do manage to remain resilient (Velleman & Templeton, 2007).

Does gambling run in families?

Evidence that problem gambling is associated with parental gambling comes from both clinical and community studies, and from several countries. In an early clinical study in the USA, of 83 patients questioned by Gambino et al. (1993), for example, 24% reported that a parent (more often father than mother) had a gambling problem. Such studies alone provide rather weak evidence since the samples are highly selective. They are supported, however, by survey data such as that collected for the Australian Productivity Commission (1999), who reported a parental problem gambling rate of 2.3% amongst those who themselves had gambling problems in the previous year, compared to a rate of 0.4% amongst those without such problems; a Swedish survey by Rönnberg et al. (1999) who also found a significantly higher (6%) rate of reported parental gambling problems amongst those who scored as problem gamblers themselves in the Swedish prevalence survey; and each of the three British Gambling Prevalence Surveys carried out to date, in the latest of which 5% of respondents who reported that a parent had had problems with gambling scored as having gambling problems themselves, compared with 1% who did not (Wardle et al., 2011). The influence of parents is also highlighted in British studies of adolescent gambling. Wood and Griffiths (1998), who gave questionnaires to over 1000 11–15-year-olds in nine schools, reported significant positive correlations between adolescent and parental (as reported by the adolescents) participation on both the National Lottery and scratch cards. Dowling et al. (2010) concluded from their research and review that children of parents with a gambling problem are at least ten times more likely than their peers to develop gambling problems later in life. Their research involved national surveys across Australia with nearly 4000 adults, over 600 secondary students and more than 800 students aged between 18 and 25. They estimated that the children of fathers with gambling problems were 13.5 times more likely to develop a gambling problem than their peers, and the children of mothers with gambling problems 10.6 times more likely.

Black and colleagues have undertaken a number of related studies into family histories (see Shaw et al.'s review, 2007) and they concluded that the prevalence of both pathological and problem gambling combined was significantly greater in the relatives of those with pathological gambling than in comparison relatives (12.4% versus 3.5%). The few twin studies that have been carried out suggest a role for genetic influence. A study of over 3000 male–male twin pairs in which both twins served in the US military during the Vietnam era (Eisen et al., 1998) suggested that inherited factors (plus shared environmental experiences) might explain between 46% and 55% of the variance in reports of pathological gambling symptoms (depending upon the exact criterion used). A much smaller study involved 155 young adult twin pairs identified from state birth records in Minnesota, USA (Winters & Rich, 1998). That study is interesting because of its suggestion that the role of genetics might be very different for men and women, for different types of gambling activity, and for different gambling criteria. Differences between MZ and DZ twins emerged mostly for men and not for women (gambling machines being an exception), and for frequency of gambling. Walters' (2001) preliminary meta-analysis of the available gambling studies concluded that both family and twin studies showed a significant familial effect, which was stronger for the sons of problem gambling fathers than for the daughters of problem gambling mothers and for more severe forms of problem gambling.

It is generally agreed in the addiction field that family transmission processes, whatever the combination of heritable and environmental factors and their interaction, may in part be specific to an individual type of substance or activity, but are more likely to be general to a variety of types and/or to overlap with general forms of vulnerability (Agrawal et al., 2012). In the case of gambling, this is supported by some of the findings of family studies. For example, Black and colleagues found a significantly increased lifetime prevalence of alcohol disorders, drug-use disorders, major depression, generalised anxiety disorder, and 'any psychiatric disorder' among relatives of those with pathological gambling than among control relatives (Black et al. 2003; 2006). Schreiber et al. (2009) compared the characteristics of over 500 adult 'pathological gamblers' with and without a problem gambling parent. The former were also more likely to have a father with an alcohol abuse/dependence problem and themselves to report daily nicotine use.

The greatest weight of existing research on transmission falls not in the area of genetics, but rather in the domains of family environmental factors such as parental monitoring and modelling and encouragements to gambling. For example, Vachon et al. (2004) explored the possible links between family risk factors (parent gambling and parenting practices) and adolescent gambling in a community sample of nearly 1000 adolescents, using standardised questionnaire assessments. Adolescent gambling frequency was related to both parents' gambling frequency and problems. However, adolescent gambling problems were linked only to fathers' severity of gambling problems. Low levels of parental monitoring enhanced adolescents' risk of getting involved in gambling activities and developing related problems. A higher level of inadequate disciplinary practices was also related to greater gambling problems in youth. These links were significant after controlling for socio-economic status, gender, and impulsivity-hyperactivity problems. Similar findings relating parental monitoring and parental consequences to young people's use and misuse of alcohol have also been reported (reviewed in Velleman, 2009).

In an interview study of men and women who had been identified as people with gambling problems in the 1999 British Gambling Prevalence Survey, a number emphasised the key role played by 'other people' in influencing their early gambling experiences (White et al., 2001). Some felt that growing up in an environment where parents or other family members gambled regularly had influenced them to try gambling, particularly where a positive image of gambling had been conveyed or when seeing the interest of family members in gambling created the impression that gambling was an acceptable and 'natural' activity.

Dowling et al. (2010) in their final Report on Children at Risk of Developing Problem Gambling, suggest that

> children raised in problem gambling families are more likely to develop gambling problems because they start gambling at a younger age; and that many problem gamblers think that the gambling behaviour of their family members directly influenced their own gambling behaviour by becoming a social norm or a way to interact with their parents. These findings support the proposition that parental problem gambling can affect offspring gambling problems through observation of parental gambling, exposure to gambling role models (including parents, parents' friends, other relatives), increased access to gambling opportunities, and peer influence... [and] by influencing child problem gambling through gambling expectancies and motives (p. 193).

Arguing that their research showed that the effect of parental problem gambling on children is much greater than previously understood, they called for urgent government action. Among their ideas is the utilisation of methods found useful in the alcohol-prevention area in Australia, such as the Kids Absorb Your Drinking mass-media campaign.

Conclusion

There is no doubt that gambling problems cause major difficulties for family members. This chapter has briefly reviewed the major impacts that such problems have both on adult family members and on children, and has summarised some of the evidence suggesting that gambling problems may be transmitted through the generations. There are strong similarities with the effects that other addictive problems (such as alcohol and drug problems) have on families, and some suggestion that problems in some areas may be even worse for families of those with gambling problems, due to the even more hidden nature of gambling disorders and the general ignorance on the part of the general public as to the existence of such problems. Also not in doubt is the conclusion that adult and child family members require help with the difficulties they face. It is vital that major treatment and prevention initiatives are undertaken to help deal with this great and growing problem.

Key points

1   Research indicates that family members of problem gamblers are affected in the following main areas: financial, relational, and emotional and physical health.
2   The effects of parental problem gambling on children include role conflicts, such as taking on the role of peacemaker, being caught in the middle of family tensions, serving as scapegoat and/or taking the blame for family difficulties stemming from the problem gambling, and they often experience disappointment due to broken promises.
3   Evidence suggests that children raised in problem gambling families are more likely to develop gambling problems.
4   Gambling treatment services need to take note of the needs of families affected by their loved one's problem gambling.

References

Agrawal, A., Budney, A. J. & Lynskey, M. T. (2012). The co-occurring use and misuse of cannabis and tobacco: a review. *Addiction*, 107:1221–33.

Barker, J. & Miller, M. (1968). Aversion therapy for compulsive gambling. *Journal of Nervous and Mental Disease*, 146:285–302.

Barnard, M. & McKeganey, N. (2004). The impact of parental problem drug use on children: what is the problem and what can be done to help? *Addiction*, 99:552–9.

Black, D., Moyer, T. & Schlosser, S. (2003). Quality of life and family history in pathological gambling. *Journal of Nervous and Mental Disorders*, 191:124–6.

Black, D., Monahan, P., Temkit, M. & Shaw, M. (2006). A family study of pathological gambling. *Psychiatry Research*, 141:295–303.

Castellani, B. (2000). *Pathological Gambling: The Making of a Medical Problem.* New York: State University of New York Press.

Cleaver, H., Unell, I. & Aldgate, J. (2011). *Children's Needs – Parenting Capacity (2nd edn).* London: The Stationery Office.

Cotton, N. (1979). The familial incidence of alcoholism: a review. *Journal of Studies on Alcohol*, 40:89–116.

Custer, R. & Milt, H. (1985). *When Luck Runs Out: Help for Compulsive Gamblers and their Families*. New York: Facts on File Publications.

Darbyshire, P., Oster, C. & Carrig, H. (2001). Children of parent(s) who have a gambling problem: a review of the literature and commentary on research approaches. *Health Soc Care Community*, 9, 185–93.

Dickson-Swift, V. A., James, E. L. & Kippen, S. (2005). The experience of living with a problem gambler: spouses and partners speak out. *Journal of Gambling Issues*, 13:1–22.

Dowling, N., Jackson, A., Thomas, S. & Frydenberg, E. (2010). *Children at Risk of Developing Problem Gambling*. A report to Gambling Research Australia in fulfilment of Tender 103/06. Final report. Melbourne: Victoria Government.

Eisen, S. A., Lin, N., Lyons, M. J., Scherrer, J. F., Griffith, K., True, W. R., Goldberg, J. & Tsuang, M. T. (1998). Familial influences on gambling behaviour: an analysis of 3359 twin pairs. *Addiction*, 93:1375–84.

Franklin, J. & Thoms, D. (1989). Clinical observations of family members of compulsive gamblers. In H. Shaffer, S. Gambino & T. Cummings (eds), *Compulsive Gambling: Theory, Research and Practice*. Toronto: Lexington Books, pp. 135–46.

Gambino, B., Fitzgerald, R., Shaffer, H., Renner, J. & Courtnage, P. (1993). Perceived family history of problem gambling and scores on SOGS. *Journal of Gambling Studies*, 9:169–84.

Jacobs, D., Marston, A., Singer, R., Widsman, K., Little, T. & Veizades. J. (1989). Children of problem gamblers. *Journal of Gambling Behaviours*, 5:261–8.

Kalischuk, R. G. (2010). Cocreating life pathways: problem gambling and its impact on families. *The Family Journal*, 18:7.

Kalischuk, R. G., Nowatzki, N., Cardwell, K., Klien, K. & Solowoniuk, J. (2006). Problem gambling and its impact on families: a literature review. *International Gambling Studies*, 6:31–60.

Krishnan, M. & Orford, J. (2002). Gambling and the family from the stress-coping-support perspective. *International Gambling Studies*, 2:61–83.

Kroll, B. & Taylor, A. (2003). *Parental Substance Misuse and Child Welfare*. London: Jessica Kingsley.

Lesieur, H. R. (1984). *The Chase: The Career of the Compulsive Gambler*. Rochester, Vermont: Schenkman.

Lesieur, H. (1989). Current research into pathological gambling and gaps in the literature. In H. J. Shaffer, S. A. Gambino & T. M. Cummings (eds), *Compulsive Gambling: Theory, Research, and Practice*. Toronto: Lexington Books, pp. 225–48.

Lesieur, H. (1998). Costs and treatment of pathological gambling. *The Annals of the American Academy of Political & Social Sciences*, 556:153–71.

Lesieur, H. & Rothschild, J. (1989). Children of Gamblers Anonymous members. *Journal of Gambling Behaviour*, 5:269–81.

Lorenz, V. (1987). Family dynamics of pathological gamblers. In T. Galski (ed.), *The Handbook of Pathological Gambling*. Springfield, IL: Charles C. Thomas, pp. 83–4.

Lorenz, V. C. & Shuttleworth, D. E (1983). The impact of pathological gambling on the spouse of the gambler. *Journal of Community Psychology*, 11:67–76.

Lorenz, V. C. & Yaffe, R. A. (1988). Pathological gambling: psychosomatic, emotional and marital difficulties as reported by the spouse. *Journal of Gambling Behaviour*, 4:13–26.

McComb, J. L., Lee, B. K. & Sprenkle, D. H. (2009). Conceptualizing and treating problem gambling as a family issue. *Journal of Marital and Family Therapy*, 35:415–31.

Muelleman, R. L., DenOtter, T., Wadman, M. C., Tran, T. P. & Anderson, J. (2002). Problem gambling in the partner of the emergency department patient as a risk factor for intimate partner violence. *Journal of Emergency Medicine*, 23:307–12.

National Gambling Impact Study Commission Final Report (1999). (http://govinfo.library. unt.edu/ngisc/reports/7.pdf), p. 7–28 (accessed 24 April 2012).

Orford, J. (2012). *Addiction Dilemmas: Family Experiences in Literature and Research and their Lessons for Practice*. Chichester: Wiley-Blackwell.

Productivity Commission (1999). *Australia's Gambling Industries*. Report No. 10, AusInfo, Canberra, Australia. Volume 1, Part C. http://www.pc.gov.au/projects/inquiry/ gambling/docs/finalreport (accessed 24 April 2012).

Rönnberg, S., Volberg, R. A., Abbott, M. W., Moore, W. L., Andrén, A., Munck, I., Jonsson, J., Nilsson,T. & Svensson, O. (1999). *Gambling and Problem Gambling in Sweden*. Report no. 2 of the National Institute of Public Health Series on Gambling.

Schreiber, L., Odlaug, B., Kim, K. & Grant, J. (2009). Characteristics of pathological gamblers with a problem gambling parent. *The American Journal on Addictions*, 18:462–9.

Shaw, M. C., Forbush, K. T., Schlinder, J., Rosenman, E. & Black, D. W. (2007). The effect of pathological gambling on families, marriages and children. *CNS Spectrum: The International Journal of Neuropsychiatric Medicines*, 12:615–22.

Vachon, J., Vitaro, F., Wanner, B. & Tremblay, R. (2004). Adolescent gambling: relationships with parent gambling and parenting practices. *Psychology of Addictive Behaviors*, 18(4):398–401.

Valentine, G. & Hughes, K. (2010). Ripples in the pond: the disclosure to, and management of, Internet problem gambling with/in the family. *Community, Work, & Family*, 13(3):273–90.

Velleman, R. (2009). *Influences on how children and young people learn about and behave towards alcohol: a review of the literature*. York: Joseph Rowntree Foundation. Available online from http://www.jrf.org.uk/sites/files/jrf/children-alcohol-use-partone. pdf (accessed 5 October 2014).

Velleman, R. & Templeton, L. (2007). Understanding and modifying the impact of parents' substance misuse on children. *Advances in Psychiatric Treatment*, 13:79–89.

Vitaro, F., Wanner, B., Brendgen, M. & Tremblay, R. (2008). Offspring of parents with gambling problems: adjustment problems and explanatory mechanisms. *Journal of Gambling Studies*, 24(4):535–53.

Walters, G. (2001). Behaviour genetic research on gambling and problem gambling – a preliminary meta-analysis of available data. *Journal of Gambling Studies*, 17 (4):255–71.

Wardle, H., Moody, A., Spence, S., Orford, J., Volberg, R., Jotangia, D., Griffiths, M., Hussey, D. & Dobbie, F. (2011). British Gambling Prevalence Survey 2010. National Centre for Social Research/Gambling Commission. London: The Stationery Office.

Weinstock, J. (2007). Comorbidity and mental illness. In G. Smith, D. Hodgins & R. Williams (eds), *Research and Measurement Issues in Gambling Studies*. San Diego: Academic Press, pp. 305–25.

White, C., Mitchell, L. & Orford, J. (2001). *Exploring Gambling Behaviour In-Depth: A Qualitative Study*. London: National Centre for Social Research.

Winters, K. C. & Rich, T. (1998). A twin study of adult gambling behaviour. *Journal of Gambling Studies*, 14:213–25.

Wood, T. A. & Griffiths, M. D. (1998). The acquisition, development and maintenance of lottery and scratch card gambling in adolescence. *Journal of Adolescence*, 21:265–73.

Chapter 9

Pathological gambling
Screening, diagnosis and assessment

Phoebe Kaspar

Aim

> l   To discuss key issues in the screening, diagnosis and assessment of pathological gambling.

Introduction

This chapter is divided into three sections. Section one will discuss some of the commonly used screening tools along with their merits and disadvantages, section two will discuss the diagnostic criteria for pathological gambling, and section three will focus on how to carry out an assessment of a person's gambling.

Screening

Screening of a potential problem or pathological gambler is typically the initial stage in the process of engaging a patient in treatment. If a patient is identified as a potential problem gambler, the clinician will determine whether they meet sufficient criteria to warrant a diagnosis. The patient then undergoes a detailed clinical assessment in order to effectively plan the treatment that will prove most beneficial to the patient. In practice, however, these stages do not necessarily follow this sequence; the diagnostic decision and assessment process may well occur together, and a patient may self-refer to services, meaning screening does not take place, or may form part of the assessment.

Purpose

The purpose of a screening tool for problem gambling is to identify individuals who are an 'at risk' or 'probable' problem gambler. It is vital that clinicians utilise effective screening tools that enable them to detect a potential gambling problem, so that the patient may be encouraged to address the problem and an appropriate referral can be made. It is also beneficial to be able to detect a potential gambling problem in its early stages, as this limits the opportunity for severe consequences to occur and optimises the chances of a successful outcome following treatment (Hodgins et al., 2007).

I. Tools

There are at least 25 screening tools that have been used in research into problem gambling. The Problem Gambling Research and Treatment Centre (PGRTC) (2011) evaluated the brevity, sensitivity, validity and reliability of 16 of the better-known problem gambling screening tools in order to develop a shortlist of seven 'recommended' tools, discussed in more detail below:

a) Short

Shorter screening tools are clinically useful as they can be rapidly and routinely administered to high-risk populations to identify those cases where a more lengthy assessment would be justified. Shorter gambling screening tools aim to include a subset of items that highlight individuals who would score positively for problem gambling on a lengthier standardised tool. The PGRTC shortlist includes three 'Brief' screening tools, defined as those with fewer than three items:

i) BRIEF BIO-SOCIAL GAMBLING SCREEN (BBGS)

Gebauer et al.'s (2010) BBGS was recently developed from analysing data from the 2001–2 National Epidemiological Survey on Alcohol and Related Conditions (NESARC), completed by 43,093 individuals from a general household population. The BBGS includes three 'past year' items to which the respondent has to answer at least one in the affirmative to be identified as a potential problem gambler. Item one establishes whether the person has experienced withdrawals: 'During the past 12 months, have you become restless, irritable or anxious when trying to stop/cut down on gambling?' Item two investigates deception: 'During the past 12 months, have you tried to keep your family or friends from knowing how much you gambled?' The final item questions bailout: 'During the past 12 months, did you have such financial trouble that you had to get help with living expenses from family, friends or welfare?' The tool demonstrates excellent sensitivity (the ability to accurately classify a problem gambler as a problem gambler) and specificity (the ability to accurately classify a non-problem gambler as a non-problem gambler) compared to scores obtained from the longer DSM-IV-based tool developed for use in the NESARC. The past-year time frame is a strength of the tool, as it is more likely to give an indication of the current behaviour than those using lifetime time frames. However, the limited published information relating to the lengthier DSM-IV-based tool's reliability and validity has been criticised (see Volberg & Williams, 2011) and therefore its value in being used as a benchmark is questionable without further research.

ii) NODS-CLiP

The NODS-CLiP (Toce-Gerstein et al., 2009) is a second three-item screening tool on the Monash University shortlist. This tool is a subset of items taken from the 17-item NODS (NORC Diagnostic Screen for Gambling Disorders), a DSM-IV-based screening tool. Three lifetime time-frame items relevant to control, lying and preoccupation (hence CLiP) were found to reliably identify problem and pathological gamblers from a large community sample. Item one investigates the clients' control of their gambling: 'Have you ever tried to stop, cut down, or control your gambling?' Similarly to the BBGS, item two also focuses on lying: 'Have you ever lied to family members, friends or others about how much you gamble or how much money you lost on gambling?' The third item investigates the person's preoccupation with gambling: 'Have there been periods lasting two weeks or longer when you spent a lot of time thinking about your gambling experiences, or planning out future gambling ventures or bets?' Toce-Gerstein et al. (2009) report excellent specificity, but moderate sensitivity, recommending respondents who endorse one or more of the three items complete the remaining NODS items, rather than this tool being used as a 'stand-alone' screen. However, as stated by the Monash University Guidelines, the NODS appears to be a more stringent measure of problem gambling than the DSM-IV criteria from which it was derived, and a large-scale validation study is required to further investigate the issue. Furthermore, the lifetime time frame means results may not accurately reflect the person's current gambling behaviour, a concern for professionals aiming to rapidly and straightforwardly identify those at risk of *current* problem gambling.

iii) LIE-BET QUESTIONNAIRE

The Lie-Bet questionnaire (Johnson et al., 1997) is a screening tool made up of only two items derived from a questionnaire based on the ten DSM-IV diagnostic criteria. The researchers found these two lifetime time-frame items reliably distinguished between a sample of Gamblers Anonymous members and a control group who did not exhibit any problem gambling traits. The first item again focuses on lying: 'Have you ever had to lie to people important to you about how much you gambled?' While the second investigates the client's experience of tolerance: 'Have you ever felt the need to bet more and more money?' Because of its brevity, this screening tool is particularly clinically practical and requires no training to administer – a positive answer to at least one of the questions identifies a potential problem gambler. The original researchers found good sensitivity, specificity and predictive value using this tool, but were criticised for using a male-only sample. A follow-up study which included women (Johnson et al., 1998) has verified its merit as a useful brief screening tool appropriate for determining whether the client should complete a lengthier, more extensively standardised tool, such as the Problem Gambling Severity Index (see p. 107).

b) Medium

i) PROBLEM GAMBLING SEVERITY INDEX (PGSI)

The widely used PGSI (Ferris & Wynne, 2001) is a nine-question screening tool that is part of the larger Canadian Problem Gambling Index (CPGI). The PGSI recognises a continuum of problem gambling by distinguishing between 'Non-Problem Gamblers', 'Low Risk Gamblers', 'Moderate Risk Gamblers' and 'Problem Gamblers', who must score at least 8 out of a total score of 27. Rather than a dichotomous yes/no answer to items, respondents can choose from 'never', 'sometimes', 'most of the time' and 'almost always'. Unlike many other tools, the PGSI was developed with both a clinical and general population sample and has the benefit of being an easy and relatively brief tool that requires no training to administer. The tool scored more favourably than two longer tools on the PGRTC shortlist, the South Oaks Gambling Screen and the Victorian Gambling Screen, in terms of measurement properties (McMillan & Wensel, 2006). However, it has been criticised for including items that suggest an outdated view of pathological gambling, rather than the harm-orientated approach reflected in the current definition of problem gambling (see Svetieva & Walker, 2008). It has also been suggested that some items may benefit from being weighted, to better distinguish between different severities of problem gambling (McCready & Adlaf, 2006). Despite this, the PGSI is becoming the favoured tool to screen for problem gambling, having been widely utilised in international research and treatment centres.

c) Long

i) SOUTH OAKS GAMBLING SCREEN (SOGS)

Lesieur and Blume's (1987) SOGS is the most widely used screening tool in the field of problem gambling. The SOGS is a 20-item self-administered questionnaire, based on the original DSM-III diagnostic criteria, with input from interviews with problem gamblers, their families and their counsellors. Whilst this is a lengthier tool, it is straightforward to score by summing the number of items endorsed out of a possible 20. The researchers recommend a score of 5 or above indicates a 'Probable Problem Gambler'. The original SOGS investigates lifetime problem gambling, but subsequent versions have been developed that assess gambling over the past year and past three and six months (Wulfert et al., 2005; Lesieur & Blume, 1993; Stinchfield & Winters, 1996), which can be of particular value when assessing change after therapeutic intervention. Intended for use in a clinical setting, the SOGS has good validity, reliability and accuracy amongst clinical samples (Lesieur & Blume, 1987; Stinchfield, 2002). However, the accuracy of the tool compared to the DSM-IV criteria decreases when used in a general population sample, with Stinchfield (2002) reporting a 50% false positive rate.

The tool is criticised as placing too much emphasis on financial problems, as ten items are specifically related to this (Volberg & Wray, 2007), and a concern is that this may produce false positives in lower socio-economic groups (Young & Stevens, 2008). The tool has also been criticised as being outdated, as it was not revised to account for the newer DSM-IV diagnostic criteria, a major reason for its now waning popularity (Hodgins & Stinchfield, 2008, cited in PGRTC, 2011).

ii) VICTORIAN GAMBLING SCREEN (VGS)

The development of the VGS (Ben-Tovim et al., 2001) was commissioned by the Victorian Casino and Gaming Authority with the aim of developing a tool that, unlike the SOGS, would be appropriate for use in community as well as in clinical samples. The result was a 21-item tool with three subscales: 'Harm to Self', 'Harm to Partner' and 'Enjoyment of Gambling'. Ben-Tovim et al.'s (2001) validation of the scale used a sample that included participants from gambling treatment centres as well as random door-to-door surveys and gaming venues. Validation indicated only the 'Harm to Self' scale could be used to identify problem gambling, and a score of 21 or above was identified as indicating a 'Problem Gambler'. Tolchard and Battersby (2010) investigated the reliability and validity of the VGS in a clinical sample, reporting good reliability and 'satisfactory' convergent validity with the SOGS. However, the scale needs to be extensively validated using a full-scale population sample before it can be recommended for general use. Its test–retest reliability must also be confirmed before it can be dependably used and employed as a tool able to assess change over time (Ben-Tovim et al., 2001).

iii) PROBLEM AND PATHOLOGICAL GAMBLING MEASURE (PPGM)

Williams is currently developing the PPGM tool in response to the weaknesses and criticisms made of existing problem gambling screening tools. It uses a past-year time frame and has similar benefits to those described for the PGSI. It acknowledges a continuum of problem gambling by having four categories: 'Recreational Gambler', 'At Risk Gambler', 'Problem Gambler' and 'Pathological Gambler'. The PPGM was also developed with both community and clinical samples. It is a 14-item tool organised into three sections: 'Problems', 'Impaired Control' and 'Other Issues'. A unique strength of the tool is that at least one item from the 'Problems' and 'Impaired Control' categories must be endorsed for the respondent to be classified as a 'Problem Gambler'. Endorsement of several items from these categories will typically indicate a 'Pathological Gambler'. This overcomes a criticism of many older tools, where simply meeting a certain number of the available items is sufficient for classification, despite some being more serious and indicative of problem gambling than others (Williams & Volberg, 2010). Another advantage is the tool's potential to identify problem gamblers in denial or with little insight into their gambling behaviour. For instance it asks whether *other people* would say the respondent has significant problems due to problem gambling and/or difficulty controlling the behaviour. This new tool has excellent specificity and sensitivity, although due to its novelty, statistics are only available from the validation study data and more research is required to evaluate its psychometric properties, specificity and sensitivity further.

2. Who should be screened?

Pride, shame and denial are factors that non-treatment-seeking problem gamblers identify as barriers against them seeking treatment (Bondolfi et al., 2002; Pulford et al., 2009). This contributes towards making the disorder hugely challenging for health care professionals to identify, as the person may be unlikely to disclose their gambling problems voluntarily. However, certain patient groups are known to have elevated rates of problem gambling and health care professionals can therefore be educated to routinely screen these individuals when they encounter them.

a) Depression and anxiety

Major depression and anxiety are frequently linked to problem gambling (Blaszczynski & McConaghy, 1989; Cunningham-Williams, et al., 1998) and problem gamblers have been found to present to their general practitioner (GP) with these co-morbidities without disclosing their underlying gambling problem (Sullivan et al., 1998). Therefore clinicians should be mindful of problem gambling when encountering an individual with non-specific anxiety and/or depression who may either be reluctant to expose their underlying addiction or unable to recognise the link between them.

b) Substance misuse

Sufficient research has been conducted to urge clinicians to screen for problem gambling when encountering other addictions. Literature has consistently found elevated levels of alcohol dependence in those who gamble problematically, compared to the general population (Cunningham-Williams et al., 2005; Kausch, 2003; Maccallum & Blaszczynski, 2002). Those who use alcohol are more likely to experience gambling-related problems (Welte et al., 2001; 2004) and, importantly, the number of these problems increases in proportion to the average amount of alcohol consumed (French, et al., 2008). Hence, patients presenting with alcohol misuse problems may be considered an 'at risk' population especially when consumption is particularly high. Non-alcohol-related substance misuse must also be considered: rates of problem gambling in samples of substance users are dramatically higher than those observed in the general population (Rupcich et al., 1997; Toneatto & Brennan, 2002). Up to 21% of methadone maintenance patients have been found to have co-morbid problem gambling (Spunt et al.,

1996). Reported figures are even higher for cannabis users, at up to 24% (Toneatto & Brennan, 2002), and cocaine users at up to 30% (Blume & Lesieur, 1987).

c) Domestic violence

Research has linked problem gambling with an increased risk of Intimate Partner Violence (IPV). Muelleman et al. (2002) interviewed women admitted to a hospital emergency department and identified a significant association between problem gambling and IPV: women who reported their partner was a problem gambler were significantly more at risk of experiencing IPV than those without a partner who problematically gambled. Afifi et al. (2010) found dating and marital violence as well as child maltreatment were associated with problem gambling, with the severity of the violence increasing in line with the severity of the PG. Those who commit violence in the home may therefore be considered an 'at risk' client group eligible for automatic screening for problem gambling.

Diagnosis

1. Definitions and DSM update

The American Psychiatric Association (APA) defines Pathological Gambling in the DSM-IV as 'persistent and recurrent maladaptive gambling behaviour that disrupts personal, family or vocational pursuits'. Importantly, a diagnosis cannot be made if the presentation is 'better accounted for by a Manic Episode'. Pathological Gambling is currently listed as an 'Impulse Control Disorder, Not Otherwise Classified.' However, with the upcoming release of the DSM-5, the APA proposes to reclassify it under 'Substance Related Disorders', which in turn will be renamed 'Addiction and Related Disorders' (American Psychiatric Association, 2010). The current ten DSM-IV criteria for Pathological Gambling make up the main instrument used by trained professionals to diagnose problem gambling. A person who concurrently meets three or four of the criteria is classified as a 'Problem Gambler', whilst a score of five or more indicates a probable 'Pathological Gambler'.

2. The DSM-IV criteria in practice

This diagnostic tool is not without its weaknesses. For instance, the criteria are responded to in a dichotomous 'yes/no' format. This fails to reflect the true complexity and diversity of presentations found in assessment of potential problem gamblers and can cause the clinician uncertainty when trying to decipher how many criteria should be met. Most importantly, the DSM-IV does not state a time frame to be used as a reference, and therefore the clinician is presented with a dilemma as to whether to use a lifetime or more recent time frame. Of course this can result in dramatically different diagnoses depending on the decision. Those who carry out assessments of problem gamblers advise that the final number of DSM-IV criteria met should be based on the behaviour as it presents most recently. This will ensure that if a clinical diagnosis is made, it will be current and relevant, rather than highlighting behaviour that was problematic in the past but ceases to be now. This advice clarifies use of the criteria to an extent, but some ambiguity remains where a degree of clinical judgement must be relied upon.

3. DSM-IV criteria for Pathological Gambling:

1. *The gambler is preoccupied with gambling (e.g. preoccupied with reliving past gambling experiences, handicapping or planning the next venture, or thinking of ways to get money with which to gamble).*

The majority of gamblers attending for assessment will meet the first criterion. They describe thinking almost constantly about gambling, which is often a source of guilt, as they feel unable to commit to other important aspects of their life, for instance their partner or children. As suggested by the above description, preoccupation can take a variety of forms. Problem gamblers describe a range of behaviours such as extensive research to inform their next bet, intricate planning of excuses to enable more gambling and forming schemes to put in place next time ('if I only bet even numbers...').

2. *The gambler needs to gamble with increasing amounts of money in order to achieve the desired excitement.*

The second criterion refers to tolerance. In a similar way that someone who uses a substance builds tolerance and requires larger intake to sustain the desired effect, problem gamblers often report increasing the amount of money gambled in order to achieve the desired arousal or 'buzz'. This can be done during one gambling episode or more gradually over time, but the clinician must consider recent examples when informing their decision in regards to whether the client meets this criterion.

3. *The gambler has had repeated unsuccessful efforts to control, cut back, or stop gambling.*

Again, the majority of clients attending assessment will meet this criterion. Often, treatment is sought after a variety of failed attempts by the gambler to stop or control the behaviour; perhaps they have agreed limits with themselves that they failed to keep or have tried relying on willpower unsuccessfully. Clients may have made some treatment attempts in the past that were successful for a time but ultimately ended in lapse.

4. *The gambler is restless or irritable when attempting to cut back or stop gambling.*

The fourth criterion refers to withdrawal symptoms. Problem gamblers often report uncomfortable physiological symptoms when access to gambling is restricted, which may subside for a time if they continue to gamble. As well as restlessness and irritability, problem gamblers commonly report sweating, nausea, and 'butterflies', which can trigger a gambling episode as a short-term relief from this discomfort.

5.   *The gambler gambles as a way of escaping from problems or of relieving dysphoric mood (e.g. feelings of helplessness, guilt, anxiety, depression).*

The fifth criterion can be investigated by asking the client the context in which they gamble. Some gamblers report an increase in gambling during stressful periods at work or home; in some cases an episode may be triggered by a particular negative event such as an argument. Problem gamblers report an experience of 'tunnel vision' when gambling, which enables short-lived relief from the reality of a difficult or stressful situation.

6.   *After losing money gambling, the gambler often returns another day to get even (i.e. 'chasing' one's losses).*

This is another criterion that is likely to be met by the majority of problem gamblers. Whereas the 'professional' gambler has strict limits that are rigorously followed, the problem gambler struggles to exert such control, and continues to gamble in the face of mounting debts. If unable to continue a gambling episode immediately, problem gamblers describe becoming fixated on acquiring enough money to continue gambling and win back losses the next day. This 'chasing' also applies to wins: often the problem gambler fails to walk away with winnings but rather continues gambling, which unfortunately ends in losses either immediately or on another day.

7.   *The gambler lies to family members, their therapist, or others to conceal the extent of involvement with gambling.*

The seventh criterion is a common component of problem gambling, which contributes to the disastrous consequences of the behaviour. Trying to conceal the behaviour from family, friends, colleagues and even their therapist can become a considerable source of anxiety for the client as they become involved with intricate lies. Shame contributes significantly to a gambler concealing their behaviour, and as adverse consequences accumulate, problem gamblers report feeling less able to ask for help and more likely to try and repair the damage themselves through continued gambling.

8.   *The gambler has committed illegal acts such as forgery, fraud, theft, or embezzlement to finance gambling.*

Whilst this is a straightforward criterion to answer in a dichotomous yes/no format, it is more difficult to decide whether an individual who committed a crime many years ago to fund their gambling should satisfy this criteria currently. It is advisable to consider whether the client is *currently* committing or at risk of committing an illegal act to fund their gambling. If the individual did so many years ago but has since ceased illegal activity, then it is recommended that they would not satisfy this criterion.

9. *The gambler has jeopardised or lost a significant relationship, job, or educational or career opportunity because of gambling.*
The ninth criterion refers to the broad range of adverse consequences that are reported by problem gamblers. Clients articulate their struggle to maintain important relationship and work commitments as their preoccupation with gambling consumes their energy. As with the eighth criterion, the clinician must determine whether these adverse consequences are of current relevance to the client. Even if a job or relationship was lost or jeopardised in the past, the criterion could still be met if the client continues to be affected by the consequences.

10. *The gambler relies on others to provide money to relieve a desperate financial situation caused by gambling.*
Whilst some gamblers report only using their own salary or benefits to gamble with, the majority will have at some point taken loans from friends, family, colleagues, banks or loan sharks. Again, clinical judgement must determine whether the client has financially relied on others recently in order to conclude whether or not this criterion is satisfied.

Although the DSM-IV criteria for pathological gambling is the one that is more widely used, I will still briefly mention the ICD-10 criteria.
    ICD-10 uses the term 'pathological gambling' and classifies this disorder under 'habit and impulse control disorders'. It describes the key feature of pathological gambling as 'persistently repeated gambling, which continues and often increases despite adverse social consequences such as impoverishment, impaired family relationships, and disruption of personal life'.

Assessment

1. Purpose

The purpose of an assessment of a potential problem gambler is to arrive at a definitive diagnosis that enables the clinician to develop a comprehensive treatment care plan aimed at meeting the specific needs of the individual.

2. Interviewing style

It is worth noting that assessment is an extremely important opportunity to engage the person. The initial assessment may be the first occasion where the person has spoken to a health care professional about their gambling, and they are likely to be feeling nervous, reluctant and ashamed. A warm manner and non-judgmental, empathic approach will be useful in reassuring the client and encouraging engagement with treatment.

3. Core content

a) Gambling

i) CURRENT GAMBLING BEHAVIOUR

The assessor should aim to gather as much information as possible about the current gambling behaviour. It is useful to use an open questioning style and begin the assessment for instance by asking, 'Could you start by telling me about how your gambling is at the moment?' The assessor should be looking to note the type and frequency of gambling as well as the severity in terms of money spent per day (relative to income) and disruption to other activities. Also of interest are current attempts at controlling the behaviour, for instance whether the client has self-excluded from bookmakers, or blocked online gambling sites. This may give an early indicator of the client's motivation to change their gambling.

ii) DEVELOPMENT OF GAMBLING BEHAVIOUR

During assessment, detailed information should be collected about the development of the problem behaviour. The assessor should spend time focusing on a history of their gambling, encouraging the client to report events chronologically, thus producing a 'time line' of significant events. An exploration of any previous attempts to stop gambling will offer insights that may be constructive in therapeutic application. Factors that contributed towards abstinence, as well as those that were associated with lapse, should be explored. Commonly reported triggers include negative emotional states, a need to make money, giving in to cravings and boredom (Hodgins & el-Guebaly, 2004). Past experiences of treatment successes and failures will again provide a basis for developing an appropriate care plan for the individual.

iii) MOTIVATION

During assessment of PG, it is essential to ascertain the client's motivation to engage in treatment. A client can attend assessment for a variety of reasons, and someone who has been coerced into attending, for instance by an ultimatum from a partner, family member or employer, or mandated through probation, may benefit from help to explore their ambivalence. By asking the client open questions such as 'What are you hoping to achieve from treatment?', 'Why do you think you need treatment?' and 'Why have you decided to seek treatment now?', the therapist is able to gauge the client's ambivalence about change. Hodgins et al. (2009) report that the strength of commitment talk is predictive of treatment outcome at a one-year follow-up: participants expressing greater commitment to reducing their gambling behaviour were most likely to be successful in fulfilling their goals. Assessing motivation is therefore important in developing an appropriate care plan, perhaps including some sessions of Motivational Interviewing, which is tailored to the individual's needs and more likely to reduce the gambling behaviour.

b) Co-morbidity

i) AXIS I

The assessor must examine in detail the client's psychiatric history. Research suggests psychiatric co-morbidity is high in problem gambling, with personality disorders and substance abuse being among the more commonly reported (Blaszczynzski & Steel, 1998; Ibáñez et al., 2001). Black & Moyer (1998) investigated the presence of Axis 1 co-morbidity in a sample of 30 problem gamblers. Findings revealed that lifetime rates of Axis 1 co-morbidity were significantly higher than would be expected in the general population. Substance use disorders were the most common, with 63% meeting these criteria. Rates of anxiety disorders were also excessive, with 40% of the sample satisfying the lifetime criteria. Consistent with Kausch (2003), rates of impulse-control disorders were significantly elevated: 23% of the sample were classified as compulsive buyers and 17% showed compulsive sexual behaviour, as indicated by the Minnesota Impulsive Disorders Interview.

ii) DEPRESSION AND SUICIDALITY

Three quarters of problem gamblers suffer from symptoms of depression (Blaszczynski & McConaghy, 1989), meaning it warrants particular attention during assessment. The assessor must be mindful of anchoring some questions around the biological symptoms of depression such as anhedonia, poor concentration and changes in sleep patterns and appetite. If depression is detected, the assessor should sensitively explore suicidal ideation, ascertaining whether intent is present and what protective factors the individual may have, such as children. Problem gamblers are more likely to attempt suicide than non-problem gamblers (Bland et al., 1993), and over 50% have been found to have thoughts of suicide (Beaudoin & Cox, 1999). As a group, problem gamblers are less likely to seek professional help for suicidality than non-problem gamblers (Seguin et al., 2010), making this an especially important opportunity to address this topic. Those with co-morbidities such as personality disorders are at increased risk of completed suicide (Seguin et al., 2010), meaning assessors should be particularly mindful of suicide risk when such co-morbidity is detected. If appropriate, a crisis plan should be developed, and the assessor may consider asking the client's permission to communicate their concerns to their GP.

iii) AXIS 2

Axis 2 co-morbidity has also been found to be significantly elevated amongst problem gamblers. Black & Moyer (1998) report that 87% of their sample met criteria for a Personality Disorder. The most frequent Personality Disorders were Avoidant, Obsessive Compulsive, Schizoid and Schizotypal, although Narcissistic and Anti-social Personality Disorders were also common.

iv) CO-MORBIDITY AND TREATMENT

The presence of co-morbidity may negatively impact the client's ability to engage with and benefit from treatment. Leblond et al. (2003) linked impulsivity to treatment failure, whilst substance abuse has been associated with lapse following treatment (Echeburua et al., 2001). It is important the assessor gathers enough information to determine the appropriate course of action when co-morbidity is detected. For instance, if substance use is present, the assessor should question the extent to which this co-occurs with the gambling behaviour, and gather as much information as possible about levels of intake and types of substances. It might just be that special attention should be paid to this during treatment, but in some cases an appropriate referral may need to be made to a substance misuse service before gambling treatment commences. The assessor should consider whether the co-morbidity would make the client unsuitable for group intervention. Whilst this may be a quicker way of accessing treatment, co-morbidity may be difficult to manage in a group environment and can be associated with elevated risk. A comprehensive examination of Axis 1 and 2 co-morbidity at assessment will contribute towards ensuring co-morbidities are detected and addressed effectively in the individual's care plan.

c) Consequences of problem gambling

By the time a problem gambler presents for assessment, it is unlikely that the consequences of the behaviour are limited to the individual, and the assessor must be mindful of this. By gathering information about the extent to which other aspects of their life have been negatively impacted, not only will some indicator of severity be gained, but the individual can be supported in addressing the damage.

i) FAMILIAL

In discussion about the consequences of a client's gambling, the assessor is encouraged to consider the impact of the behaviour on the client's loved ones. Useful questions may include 'Who has been most impacted by your gambling?', 'How has your relationship changed?' Research is limited in this area, but studies have shown that Concerned Significant Others (CSOs) are at increased risk of suffering from anxiety and depression (Shaw et al., 2007) and experience significant distress, particularly when living with the gambler (Hodgins, Shead & Makarchuk, 2007). Even 'minimal' interventions such as a self-help workbook have been found to significantly reduce relationship and personal distress, as reported by CSOs (Hodgins et al., 2007). Research suggests that significant others may also have a valuable influence on treatment outcomes: problem gamblers with family members who are engaged in the treatment process have improved treatment outcomes and remain in treatment longer than those without involved significant others (Ingle et al., 2008). However, the assessor must be mindful of safeguarding issues; research indicates Intimate Partner Violence and/or child maltreatment are significantly more common in relationships where one partner problematically gambles (Afifi et al., 2010; Korman et al., 2008), meaning CSO involvement must be approached sensitively and cautiously.

ii) CRIMINAL

More than half of individuals attending Gamblers Anonymous have admitted to past criminal activity in order to fund their gambling (Meyer & Fabian, 1992). Problem gamblers who turn to crime to fund their gambling tend to exhibit more severe gambling behaviours, abuse substances, suffer from suicidality and have larger debts than problem gamblers who have not committed crimes (Meyer & Fabian, 1992; Potenza et al., 2000). Of problem gamblers who commit crimes, two thirds describe doing so as a direct result of their gambling (Blazsczynski et al., 1989). Clinicians should be mindful of potential criminal consequences of their clients gambling, as well as the shame that is likely to be associated with admitting to these. If a client admits to illegal acts, the assessor should tactfully try to find out more information, such as whether they are due in court, and if so, what sentence they are expecting and whether this may disrupt their ability to engage in treatment. The assessor might consider whether they can be of assistance in terms of a letter verifying the client is seeking treatment, for example.

iii) FINANCIAL

A delicate discussion about the client's current financial situation will help to identify those who may benefit from financial advice as part of treatment. The assessor should explore whether the client has already put strategies in place to repay debts or control their access to money, for instance by allowing a family member to keep their credit cards, or whether they still could access significant amounts of money. The assessor may investigate whether the client is able to pay living expenses, such as food and bills, and whether they are financially responsible for others, for instance children. By asking the client their overall monetary losses and current debts, a tentative indicator of severity may be given, when considered in relation to earnings. However, answers should not be assumed reliable: gamblers have been found to substantially under- and overestimate expenditure

(Abbott & Volberg, 2000). Gaining enough information at this stage of assessment will give the best likelihood that financial concerns can be addressed, and limit the extent to which they contribute to a continuation of the gambling behaviour.

iv) VOCATIONAL

Problem gambling can have serious implications in the workplace and this should be investigated during the assessment: 69–76% of problem gamblers have missed work because of gambling, while 21–36% of treatment-seeking problem gamblers admit to actually losing a job as a consequence of their gambling (Ladouceur et al., 1994; Lesieur & Anderson, 1995; Meyer et al., 1995; Thompson et al., 1996, cited in Lesieur, 1998). The assessor should determine the extent to which the client's job has been jeopardised, for instance through absences or loss of productivity, whether fellow employees have an awareness of the problem gambling, and if so, what their response has been. If the client works within the gambling industry or handles significant sums of money, then certain aspects of treatment, for example trigger management, may be particularly important and require special consideration.

d) Personal history

Towards the end of the assessment, the assessor should aim to develop an understanding of the person's personal history. Areas of interest include the circumstances in which they were brought up, relationships with family members, experiences at school, including academic ability and friendships, and experiences of abuse or trauma of any description. Information gained here can be important in determining an appropriate treatment plan. It may be that there was a specific context in which the behaviour initially arose and the client could therefore benefit from formulation work as part of treatment to understand the underlying issues that produced and maintain their problem.

Conclusion

There is a wide range of screening tools available to the clinician, and factors such as brevity, sensitivity and specificity are important in informing this choice. Screening is only the first step in the assessment of a problem/pathological gambler. A comprehensive assessment will inform the formulation of a treatment plan.

Key points

1 Screening tools for problem/pathological gambling vary in length, specificity and sensitivity.
2 DSM-IV is the most commonly used diagnostic criteria in both clinical practice and research in the field of problem gambling.
3 Assessment of the adverse consequences and psychiatric co-morbidity of gambling are key components of the assessment of a problem/pathological gambler.

References

Abbott, M. W. & Volberg, R. A. (2000). *Taking the pulse on gambling and problem gambling in New Zealand: a report on phase one of the 1999 National Prevalence Survey. New Zealand.* Department of Internal Affairs, Government of New Zealand.

Afifi, T. O., Brownridge, D. A., MacMillan, H. et al. (2010). The relationship of gambling to intimate partner violence and child maltreatment in a nationally representative sample. *Journal of Psychiatric Research*, 44:331–7.

American Psychiatric Association (APA) (2010). Pathological gambling. In proposed draft revisions to DSM Disorders and Criteria, pp. 312–31. Arlington, VA: American Psychiatric Association.

Beaudoin, C. M. & Cox B. J. (1999). Characteristics of problem gambling in a Canadian context: a preliminary study using a DSM-IV-based questionnaire. *Canadian Journal of Psychiatry*, 44:483–7.

Ben-Tovim, D., Esterman, A., Tolchard, B., et al. (2001). *The Victorian Gambling Screen: Project Report.* Melbourne: Victorian Research Panel.

Black, D. W. & Moyer, T. (1998). Clinical features and psychiatric comorbidity of subjects with pathological gambling behaviour. *Psychiatric Services*, 48:1434–9.

Bland, R. C., Newman, S. C., Om, H. et al. (1993). Epidemiology of pathological gambling in Edmonton. *Canadian Journal of Psychiatry*, 38:108–12.

Blaszczynski, A. & McConaghy, N. (1989). Anxiety and/or depression in the pathogenesis of pathological gambling. *International Journal of the Addictions*, 24:337–50.

Blaszczynzski, A. & Steel, Z. (1998). Personality disorders among pathological gamblers. *Journal of Gambling Studies*, 14:51–71.

Blazsczynzski, A., McConaghy, N. & Frankova, A. (1989). Crime, antisocial personality and pathological gambling. *Journal of Gambling Studies*, 5:137–52.

Blume, S. B. & Lesieur, H. R. (1987). *Cocaine: A Clinician's Handbook.* A. M. Washington, & M. S. Gold (eds), pp. 208–13. New York: The Guilford Press.

Bondolfi, G., Osiek, C. & Ferrer, F. (2002). Pathological gambling: an increasing and underestimated disorder. *Schweizer Archiv für Neurologie und Psychiatrie*, 153:116–22.

Cunningham-Williams, R. M., Cottler, L. B., Compton, W. M. et al. (1998). Taking chances: problem gamblers and mental health disorders – results from the St. Louis epidemiologic catchment area study. *American Journal of Public Health*, 88:1093–6.

Cunningham-Williams, R. M., Grucza, R. A., Cottler, L. B. et al. (2005). Prevalence and predictors of pathological gambling: results from the St. Louis personality, health and lifestyle (SLPHL) study. *Journal of Psychiatric Research*, 39:377–90.

Echeburua, E., Fernandez-Montalvo, J. & Baez, C. (2001). Predictors of therapeutic failure in slot-machine pathological gamblers following behavioural treatment. *Behavioural and Cognitive Psychotherapy*, 29:379–83.

Ferris, J. & Wynne, H. (2001). *The Canadian Problem Gambling Index: Final report.* Ottawa: Canadian Centre on Substance Abuse.

French, M. T., Maclean, J. C. & Ettner, S. L. (2008). Drinkers and bettors: investigating the complementarity of alcohol consumption and problem gambling. *Drug and Alcohol Dependence*, 96:155–64.

Gebauer, L., LaBrie, R. A. & Shaffer, H. J. (2010). Optimizing DSM-IV-TR classification accuracy: a brief bio-social screen for detecting current gambling disorders among gamblers in the general household population. *Canadian Journal of Psychiatry*, 55:82–90.

Hodgins, D. C. & el-Guebaly, N. (2004). Retrospective and prospective reports of precipitants to relapse in pathological gambling. *Journal of Consulting and Clinical Psychology*, 27:72–80.

Hodgins, D. & Stinchfield, R. (eds) (2008). *Gambling Disorders*. Oxford: New York. Cited in Problem Gambling Research and Treatment Centre (PGRTC) (2011), *Guidelines for Screening, Assessment and Treatment in Problem Gambling*. Clayton: Monash University.

Hodgins, D. C., Shead, N. & Makarchuk, K. (2007). Relationship satisfaction and psychological distress among concerned significant others of pathological gamblers. *Journal of Nervous and Mental Disease*, 195:65–71.

Hodgins, D., Toneatto, T., Makarchuk, K. et al. (2007). Minimal treatment approaches for concerned significant others of problem gamblers: a randomised controlled trial. *Journal of Gambling Studies*, 23:215–30.

Hodgins, D. C., Ching, L. E. & McEwe, J. (2009). Strength of commitment language in motivational interviewing and gambling outcomes. *Psychology of Addictive Behaviours,* 23:122–13.

Ibáñez, A., Blanco, C., Donahue, E. et al. (2001). Psychiatric comorbidity in pathological gamblers seeking treatment. *American Journal of Psychiatry*, 158:1733–5.

Ingle, P. J., Marotta, J., McMillan, G. et al. (2008). Significant others and gambling treatment outcomes. *Journal of Gambling Studies*, 24:381–92.

Johnson, E. E., Hamer, R., Nora, R. M. et al. (1997). The lie/bet questionnaire for screening pathological gamblers. *Psychological Reports*, 80:83–8.

Johnson, E. E., Hamer, R. M. & Nora, R. M. (1998). The lie/bet questionnaire for screening pathological gamblers: a follow-up study. *Psychological Reports*, 83:1219–24.

Kausch, O. (2003). Patterns of substance abuse among treatment seeking pathological gamblers. *Journal of Substance Abuse Treatment*, 25:263–70.

Korman, L. M., Collins, J., Dutton, D. et al. (2008). Problem gambling and intimate partner violence. *Journal of Gambling Studies*, 24:13–23.

Ladouceur, R., Boisvert, J., Pepin, M. et al. (1994). Social cost of pathological gambling. *Journal of Gambling Studies*, 10:399–409. Cited in H. R. Lesieur (1998), Costs and treatment of pathological gambling. *Annals of the American Academy of Political and Social Science*, 556:153–71.

Leblond, J., Ladouceur, R. & Blaszczynski, A. (2003). Which pathological gamblers will complete treatment? *British Journal of Clinical Psychology*, 42:205–9.

Lesieur, H. R. (1998). Costs and treatment of pathological gambling. *Annals of the American Academy of Political and Social Science*, 556:153–71.

Lesieur, H. R. & Anderson, C. (1995). Results of a survey of Gamblers Anonymous members in Illinois. Illinois: Illinois Council on Problem and Compulsive Gambling. Cited in H. R. Lesieur (1998), Costs and treatment of pathological gambling. *Annals of the American Academy of Political and Social Science*, 556:153–71.

Lesieur, H. R. & Blume, S. B. (1987). The South Oaks Gambling Screen (SOGS): a new instrument for the identification of pathological gamblers. *American Journal of Psychiatry*, 144:1184–8.

Lesieur, H. R. & Blume, S. B. (1993). Revising the South Oaks Gambling Screen in different settings. *Journal of Gambling Studies*, 9:213–23.

Maccallum, F. & Blaszczynski, A. (2002). Pathological gambling and comorbid substance use. *Australian and New Zealand Journal of Psychiatry*, 36(3):411–15.

McCready, J. & Adlaf, E. (2006). *Performance and enhancement of the Canadian Problem Gambling Index (CPGI): report and recommendations*. Ottawa, Canadian Centre on Substance Abuse.

McMillen, J. & Wenzel, M. (2006). Measuring problem gambling: assessment of three prevalence screens. *International Gambling Studies*, 6:147–74.

Meyer, G. & Fabian, T. (1992). Delinquency among pathological gamblers: a causal approach. *Journal of Gambling Studies*, 8:61–77.

Meyer, G., Fabian, T. & Peter, W. (1995). The social costs of pathological gambling. Paper presented to the First European Conference on Gambling Studies and Policy Issues. Cambridge, England. Cited in H. R. Lesieur (1998), Costs and treatment of pathological gambling. *Annals of the American Academy of Political and Social Science*, 556:153–71.

Muelleman, R., DenOtter, T., Wadman, M. C. et al. (2002). Problem gambling in the partner of the emergency department patient as a risk factor for intimate partner violence. *Journal of Emergency Medicine*, 23:307–12.

Potenza, M. N., Steinberg, M. A., McLaughlin, S. D., Rounsaville, B. J. & O'Malley, S. S. (2000). Illegal behaviors in problem gambling: analysis of data from a gambling helpline. *Journal of the American Academy of Psychiatry and the Law Online*, 28(4)389–403.

Problem Gambling Research and Treatment Centre (PGRTC) (2011). Guideline for screening, assessment and treatment in problem gambling. Clayton: Monash University.

Pulford, J., Bellringer, M., Abbott, M. et al. (2009). Reasons for seeking help for a gambling problem: the experiences of gamblers who have sought specialist assistance and the perceptions of those who have not. *Journal of Gambling Studies*, 25:33–48.

Rupcich, N., Frisch, G. R. & Govoni, R. (1997). Comorbidity of pathological gambling in addiction treatment facilities. *Journal of Substance Abuse Treatment*, 14:573–4.

Seguin, M., Boyer, R. & Lesage, A. (2010). Suicide and gambling: psychopathology and treatment–seeking. *Psychology of Addictive Behaviors*, 24:541–7.

Shaw, M. C., Forbush, K. T., Schlinder, J. et al. (2007). The effect of pathological gambling on families, marriages and children. *CNS Spectrums*, 12:615–22.

Spunt, B., Lesieur, H., Liberty, H. J. & Hunt, D. (1996). Pathological gamblers in methadone treatment. A comparison between men and women. *Journal of Gambling Studies*, 12:431–49.

Stinchfield, R. (2002). Reliability, validity, and classification accuracy of the South Oaks Gambling Screen (SOGS). *Addictive Behaviors*, 27:1–19.

Stinchfield, R. D. & Winters, K. C. (1996). *Treatment Effectiveness of Six State-supported Compulsive Gambling Treatment Programs in Minnesota*. Minneapolis, MN: Department of Psychiatry, University of Minnesota.

Sullivan, S., Arroll, B., Coster, G. & Abbott, M. (1998). Problem gamblers: a challenge for GPs. *New Zealand Family Physician*, 25:37–42.

Svetieva, E. & Walker, M. (2008). Inconsistency between concept and measurement: the Canadian Problem Gambling Index (CPGI). *Journal of Gambling Issues*, 22:157–73.

Thompson, W. N., Gazel, R. & Rickman, D. (1996). The social costs of gambling in Wisconsin. *Wisconsin Policy Research Institute Report*, 9:1–44. Cited in H. R. Lesieur (1998), Costs and treatment of pathological gambling. *Annals of the American Academy of Political and Social Science*, 556:153–71.

Toce-Gerstein, M., Gerstein, D. R. & Volberg, R. A. (2009). The NODS-CLiP: a rapid screen for adult pathological and problem gambling. *Journal of Gambling Studies*, 25:541–55.

Tolchard, B. & Battersby, M. W. (2010). The Victorian Gambling Screen: reliability and validation in a clinical population. *Journal of Gambling Studies*, 26:623–38.

Toneatto, T. & Brennan, J. (2002). Pathological gambling in treatment-seeking substance abusers. *Addictive Behaviors*, 27(3):465–9.

Volberg, R. A. & Williams, R. J. (2011). *Developing a Brief Problem Gambling Screen Using Clinically Validated Samples of At-risk, Problem and Pathological Gamblers*. Edmonton: Alberta Gaming Research Institute.

Volberg, R. & Wray, M. (2007). Legal gambling and problem gambling as mechanisms of social domination? Some considerations for future research. *American Behavioural Science*, 51:56–85.

Welte, J. W., Barnes, G. M., Wieczorek, W. F. et al. (2001). Alcohol and gambling pathology among US adults. Prevalence, demographic patterns and co-morbidity. *Journal of Studies on Alcohol*, 62:706–12.

Welte, J. W., Barnes, G. M., Wieczorek, W. F. et al. (2004). Risk factors for pathological gambling. *Addictive Behaviours*, 29:323–3.

Williams, R. J. & Volberg, R. A. (2010). Best Practices in the Population Assessment of Problem Gambling. Report prepared for the Ontario Problem Gambling Research Centre. Guelph, Ontario, Canada.

Wulfert, E., Hartley, J., Lee, M. et al. (2005). Gambling screens: does shortening the time frame affect their psychometric properties? *Journal of Gambling Studies*, 21:521–36.

Young, M. & Stevens, M. (2008). SOGS and CPGI: parallel comparison on a diverse population. *Journal of Gambling Studies*, 24:337–56.

Chapter 10

Psychosocial treatments for problem and pathological gambling

Nancy M. Petry

Aims

1 To review psychosocial treatment approaches for gambling problems, including their evidence base.

2 To identify strengths and limitations of the studies in this field and suggest areas for future research in the psychosocial treatment of gambling.

Introduction

Individuals have gambled since the beginning of recorded history, and problems with gambling transcend generations and cultures. Only in the past few decades, however, has excessive gambling been recognised as a psychiatric disorder, and research on its diagnosis, origins and treatment has proliferated in the last several years.

In the United States, as well as many countries throughout the world, this psychiatric diagnosis is classified by criteria set forth in the Diagnostic and Statistical Manual for Mental Disorders (DSM). In the fourth revision of the DSM-IV (1994), pathological gambling is diagnosed when an individual meets five of ten criteria. The criteria include: preoccupation with gambling; tolerance; repeated unsuccessful efforts to stop or control gambling; withdrawal symptoms (restlessness, irritability) when attempting to reduce or stop gambling; gambling as a method of escaping from problems or relieving dysphoric mood; chasing losses; lying to others about one's gambling; committing illegal acts to finance gambling; impaired relationship, career or education due to gambling; and relying on others for money to relieve a desperate financial situation caused by gambling.

In the fifth version of the DSM, published in 2013, the number of criteria and threshold for a diagnosis have been reduced to nine. The proposal is that meeting four of nine criteria will result in a diagnosis for pathological gambling (Petry, 2010). This lower threshold improves diagnostic accuracy (Jiménez-Murcia et al., 2009; Stinchfield 2003; Stinchfield et al., 2005). The committing illegal acts criterion is recommended for deletion because it is rarely endorsed in the absence of meeting many other criteria (Blanco et al., 2006; McBride et al., 2010; Orford et al., 2003; Toce-Geretein et al., 2003), and it adds little to diagnostic accuracy (Zimmerman et al., 2006).

Although meeting criteria for a diagnosis may be less strict in DSM-5 relative to earlier versions, many individuals endorse fewer criteria, yet still experience some degree of gambling problems. These individuals are often termed 'problem gamblers'. For the purposes of this chapter, the term 'pathological gambler' will be reserved for those meeting DSM-IV diagnostic criteria, and 'problem gamblers' will be used to describe those meeting fewer than five criteria.

The vast majority of problem and pathological gamblers never seek treatment. Data reveal that fewer than 10% of pathological gamblers access formal gambling treatment services, and almost no problem gamblers seek treatment (Hodgins et al., 1999; Slutske, 2006). Furthermore, cross-sectional and longitudinal analyses suggest that a significant proportion of problem and pathological gamblers recover without treatment (Hodgins et al., 1999; Slutske, 2006).

Although many problem and pathological gamblers recover on their own, interventions may improve the rapidity with which gambling problems dissipate or the proportion of individuals who experience reductions in gambling problems. A number of psychosocial treatments have been developed and evaluated for treating gambling problems. This chapter will review psychosocial treatment approaches. It will also identify strengths and limitations of the prior studies and suggest areas for future research in the treatment of gambling.

Gamblers Anonymous

Among gamblers who seek treatment, Gamblers Anonymous (GA) is the most commonly accessed intervention in the United States, and GA chapters exist throughout many countries in the world as well. GA is modelled after the 12-step approach of Alcoholics Anonymous. Despite its popularity, few empirical studies have evaluated the effectiveness of 12-step intervention. In a report from Scotland of 232 individuals who attended at least one GA meeting (Stewart & Brown, 1988), only 8% remained engaged in the fellowship and maintained gambling abstinence for one year. More positive outcomes for GA have been noted when this modality is encouraged in conjunction with professional gambling treatment. In a study of 342 pathological gamblers enrolled in professional treatment (Petry, 2003), 48% of patients who also attended GA were abstinent from gambling for at least two months, but only 36% of patients who attended professional gambling treatment alone maintained this period of gambling abstinence. Although suggestive of benefits of participating in GA, this study was not randomised, and self-selection biases may have impacted results. Individuals who are more motivated for change may be more likely to attend both GA and professional treatment and thereby realise greater beneficial outcomes.

Cognitive-behavioral therapy

Cognitive-behavioral therapies (CBT) are the most widely researched treatments for pathological gambling. Petry (2005) developed an eight-session manualised CBT for gamblers that focuses on building skills towards relapse prevention, problem solving, and development of alternative behaviours. The intervention consists of eight topics: identification of triggers, functional analysis of triggers and consequences of gambling, engaging in alternative activities, self-management of triggers, coping with urges to gamble, gambling-refusal skills, cognitive distortions related to gambling, and relapse prevention. The sessions are described in detail in Petry (2005), and specific instructions and hand-outs are included.

In a randomised study evaluating the efficacy of this CBT approach (Petry et al., 2006), 235 pathological gamblers were randomised to one of three conditions. All were referred to and encouraged to attend GA, and about two-thirds of the participants also received CBT, either delivered by a counsellor in once-weekly individual sessions, or completed by the patient in a workbook format. Both conditions were compared to referral to GA alone. Gambling was assessed at baseline, and one, two (post-treatment), six, and twelve months later. Collateral informants provided independent assessments of participants' gambling. Outcomes included reductions in pathological gambling symptoms, frequency of gambling episodes, and amount of money wagered. Using an intent-to-treat analysis that included all patients randomly assigned to conditions, participants assigned to the individual CBT plus GA referral group had significantly greater reductions in gambling and related problems than participants assigned to GA referral alone, and they also improved more than participants assigned to the CBT workbook condition on some indices. Furthermore, some benefits were maintained throughout the 12-month follow-up period.

Participants in all groups were equally likely to attend GA sessions, such that GA involvement was not responsible for the differential effects of interventions on outcomes. The counsellor-delivered CBT condition, however, resulted in better outcomes than the CBT workbook condition because of differential compliance. Sixty-one per cent of those assigned to the counsellor-delivered CBT attended all or most all of the sessions, while only 37% of those assigned to the workbook condition completed the bulk of the chapters. Number of sessions attended or chapters completed was significantly associated with outcomes. Not surprisingly, therapists engage patients in treatment better than workbooks, and beneficial effects of interventions will not be realised when patients do not access or engage in them.

A secondary analysis of the outcome data from the above study (Petry et al., 2007) found that short-term treatment benefits of the CBT were mediated by the development of new coping skills. These data provide support for the hypothesised mechanism of action in CBT; as patients develop better coping skills while receiving CBT, their gambling decreases. A detailed description of the common internal and external precipitants to gambling, and how patients typically respond to them, is provided by Morasco et al. (2007).

Others have also evaluated CBT for treating gambling. In Sweden, Carlbring et al. (2008) randomised 66 pathological gamblers, without severe co-morbid depression, to eight weeks of Internet-based CBT or a waitlist control condition. In the CBT condition, therapist contact occurred via email and weekly telephone calls (about four hours in total). The Internet-based CBT resulted in greater reductions in gambling than the no-treatment control condition during the eight-week study period. Post-treatment evaluations, conducted only for those assigned to the CBT condition, found reductions in gambling appeared to be maintained throughout 36 months, but there was no comparator condition during the follow-up period, because patients initially assigned to the waitlist condition were offered the CBT after eight weeks. Thus, the long-term effects of Internet-based CBT are unknown.

In another study of this approach, Carlbring et al. (2012) applied Internet-delivered CBT to 316 pathological gamblers, without exclusionary criteria for depression. Participants were assessed for 36 months after initiating treatment. Again, reductions in gambling were noted over time, along with improvements in psychiatric symptoms and social functioning, but whether these effects were related to the intervention itself or reflective of participant characteristics could not be determined because no control condition was included in this study design. Further, as in the Petry et al. (2006) study, engagement in non-professionally delivered treatment was relatively low. Only 44% enrolled participants completed the treatment. Together, data from these studies appear to suggest that therapist-delivered CBT may engender better engagement and outcomes than self-directed treatment.

Other researchers have likewise attempted to modify the format of CBT delivery to determine if delivery format impacts outcomes. In particular, group-delivered therapy is less costly to administer than individual therapy. Dowling et al. (2007) randomised 56 female pathological gamblers to a 12-session CBT intervention delivered in either individual or group format or a waitlist control condition. As in other studies, the CBT consisted of financial limit setting, alternative activity planning, cognitive correction, problem solving, communication training, relapse prevention, and imaginal desensitisation. Individual and group CBT formats produced comparable gambling outcomes, but group treatment failed to produce superior outcomes to the control condition with respect psychological functioning. Further, at the follow-up, 92% of the gamblers who had earlier received individual CBT no longer met criteria for pathological gambling compared with only 60% of those who had received group CBT. Thus, this study found that CBT delivered in an individual format was more efficacious than CBT delivered in a group format.

Korman et al. (2008) evaluated an integrated treatment for co-morbid problem gambling, anger, and substance use, which also contained many elements of CBT. Problem gamblers with co-morbid anger and substance use problems were randomised to either a 14-week integrated treatment targeting anger and addictions (i.e. both gambling and substance use) using dialectical behaviour therapy, which also incorporated many features central to CBT, or to treatment as usual for gambling and substance use, consisting of an eclectic, non-manualised CBT. Participants were assessed at baseline, post-treatment and at a 6-month follow-up. Relative to the treatment as usual condition, participants in the integrated anger and addictions treatment reported significantly less gambling at post-treatment and follow-up, as well as less trait anger and substance use at the follow-up evaluation. The relatively poorer outcomes noted with the treatment-as-usual intervention in this study may relate to therapists not appropriately delivering CBT as treatment was not manualised, and therapists were not trained or specifically monitored in that condition. In sum, the vast majority of studies utilising CBT did find improvements relative to control or waitlist conditions.

Cognitive therapy

Many of the above studies of CBT included one or more sessions directed toward dispelling cognitive illusions related to gambling. More strictly cognitive-based therapies have also been applied to the treatment of pathological gambling. The premise behind this approach is that gamblers may suffer from cognitive illusions about winning in gambling; by effectively challenging these illusions, gambling may decrease.

Three studies have evaluated cognitive therapy. Sylvain et al. (1997) randomly assigned 40 pathological gamblers to cognitive therapy available immediately or a waitlist control condition. Of those assigned to the immediate treatment condition, 64% attended sessions, and treatment was delivered until the patient ceased gambling. Average number of sessions attended was about 17, but it ranged up to 30. Significant benefits of the cognitive therapy were reported in terms of number of DSM criteria endorsed, and perceived control over gambling and desire to gamble.

In a second study, Ladouceur et al. (2001) randomised 59 pathological gamblers to cognitive therapy or a waitlist control condition. Of the patients assigned to the cognitive therapy condition, 59% completed treatment, which involved up to 20 sessions, or until the patient stopped gambling. The cognitive therapy focused on correcting inappropriate cognitions about randomness and assessing erroneous cognitions associated with high-risk gambling situations. As in the earlier study, the cognitive therapy appeared to be successful relative to the waitlist condition in reducing gambling.

In a third study of this approach, Ladouceur et al. (2003) evaluated the efficacy of this same cognitive therapy when applied in a group format. Seventy-one pathological gamblers were randomly assigned to a group cognitive therapy condition available immediately or a waitlist control condition, and as in the earlier study of individual cognitive therapy, benefits in reducing gambling were noted in the short term. However, with waitlist control designs, long-term efficacy cannot be established.

Brief and motivational interventions

The above studies, especially of cognitive therapy, involved fairly intensive treatment, up to 20 sessions. Given the relatively low rates of engagement in therapy in general, other research has been directed at minimal interventions for treating gamblers. Motivational Interviewing (MI), and Motivational Enhancement Therapy (MET), was originally designed as minimal interventions for treating substance use disorders, and these approaches have also been adapted for treating problem and pathological gambling. In several studies of CBT, motivational interventions have been delivered prior to or in conjunction with CBT.

For example, Hodgins and colleagues (2001) randomly assigned 102 problem and pathological gamblers to one of three conditions: a waitlist control, a workbook containing CBT exercises, or an MI session with the CBT workbook. The CBT workbook alone did not lead to greater reductions in gambling than the waitlist condition. However, the CBT workbook combined with MI resulted in significant reductions in gambling. Follow-up assessments, restricted to patients in the active treatment conditions, found that some benefits of the MI were apparent long after the intervention period relative to the workbook-alone condition.

In a follow-up study, Hodgins et al. (2009) randomised 314 problem and pathological gamblers to one of two motivational interventions, a workbook-only control condition or a six-week waitlist control condition. One brief motivational treatment involved a telephone motivational interview and a mailed CBT workbook. The second motivation intervention used this same approach and added six booster telephone calls over a nine-month period. Both brief motivational interventions resulted in less gambling at week six relative to the control groups. However, the CBT-workbook-only participants were as likely as the brief MI participants to have significantly reduced their losses over the year and to have not met criteria for pathological gambling. Further, the booster phone calls did not yield any improvements relative to the MI and workbook-alone condition. These results provide further support for the value of brief treatments for pathological gambling, but they also indicate that more treatment does not necessarily confer greater benefits.

Grant et al. (2009) evaluated the efficacy of the Petry et al. (2006) CBT intervention in conjunction with a motivational session versus referral to GA. Sixty-eight pathological gamblers were assigned to the two conditions, and those who received the motivational session plus the CBT demonstrated greater reductions in gambling than those assigned to GA referral.

Oei et al. (2010) randomised 102 pathological gamblers to MI+CBT delivered in an individual format, MI+CBT delivered in a group format, or a six-week waitlist control condition. At week six, significant improvements were noted in both MI+CBT conditions relative to the waitlist control, with no differences noted between the individually delivered and group-delivered treatment conditions. In contrast to the findings of Dowling et al. (2007), the results from this study indicated group versus individually delivered treatments were equally effective.

The above studies combined motivational techniques with CBT, but several studies have evaluated motivational treatments alone. Petry et al. (2009) randomised 117 problem and pathological gambling college students to one of four conditions: an assessment-only control, ten minutes of brief advice about gambling that included personal feedback and concrete suggestions for reducing gambling, one 50-minute session of MI, or one session of MI plus three sessions of CBT. Gambling was assessed at baseline, week six, and month nine. Compared to the control condition, students who received any of the active interventions displayed significant reductions in some problem gambling indices, but outcomes were not systematically impacted by all treatments. Only the MI-alone condition significantly increased the odds of a clinically significant reduction in gambling at the nine-month follow-up.

In a study with a similar design, Petry et al. (2008) screened individuals in waiting rooms at medical clinics and substance abuse treatment clinics. Those who screened positive for problem or pathological gambling (N = 180) were asked to participate in a brief intervention study. Again, participants were randomly assigned to a no-treatment control condition, ten minutes of brief advice, one 50-minute motivational session, or one session of MI plus three additional sessions of CBT. Those assigned to the ten-minute brief advice condition evidenced significant reductions in gambling and gambling problems relative to the no-treatment control condition in the six-week period following study initiation, and this was the only intervention associated with a clinically significant reduction in gambling nine months later in this study. Again, the other interventions had effects on some, but not all, outcome measures.

In the above two studies, the brief advice included the following recommendations: 1) gamble for fun, not to make money; 2) gamble only what you can afford to lose (pay monthly bills first); 3) set a dollar limit each time you gamble; 4) set a time limit each time you gamble; 5) leave checks, credit cards and ATM cards at home; 6) take your winnings home; and 7) remember the odds are always in favour of the house (or casinos and lotteries would not be in business). These brief advice recommendations are consistent with a harm-reduction approach and may be particularly palatable for patients who do not wish to abstain entirely from gambling.

The MI consisted of a 50-minute individual session, in which participants received personalised feedback about their gambling in relation to national data. With the therapist, participants explored positive and negative consequences of gambling and discussed how gambling impacted their life goals. Participants also completed a change-plan worksheet, which involved discussing changes that could be made, reasons to make them, steps to be taken and potential support persons. Those in the MI+CBT condition received the MI as above, plus individually tailored CBT exercises selected from personally relevant sessions from the eight-session CBT intervention described earlier (2006).

The results from these studies indicate that single-session interventions can be efficacious in reducing gambling problems, although the exact format and duration of the intervention with the most pronounced effects on outcomes varied across studies and populations. Data from these studies were consistent, nevertheless, in indicating that more extensive treatments (e.g. MI+CBT) did not appear to further improve outcomes beyond single-session interventions in non-treatment-seeking populations.

In a study evaluating more extensive brief interventions, Carlbring et al. (2010) randomised 150 problem and pathological gamblers to four individual sessions of MET, eight sessions of CBT delivered in a group format, or a no-treatment waitlist control. Both the MET and CBT interventions demonstrated improvements relative to the waitlist condition, with no differences noted between the two interventions. Thus, similarly to the Petry et al. (2009, 2008) studies, more treatment did not translate to greater reductions in gambling.

Three studies from Canada also revealed benefits of single-session motivational interventions. Cunningham et al. (2009) randomly assigned 61 problem and pathological gamblers to a personalised feedback summary intervention or to a waitlist control condition. At a three-month evaluation, gamblers assigned to the feedback condition displayed some evidence that they were spending less money on gambling than those in the waitlist condition. Diskin and Hodgins (2009) randomised 81 gamblers to MI, delivered in the context of a single face-to-face interview, or a control intervention consisting of administration of a structured psychiatric interview. At the 12-month follow-up, participants in the MI condition spent significantly less money gambling, wagered on fewer days, and reported less distress than participants in the control condition. In the third study, Cunningham et al. (2012) randomised 209 problem and pathological gamblers to one of three conditions. Two conditions involved feedback, with one integrating full personalised normative feedback, and the other was similar but did not include comparisons to general-population gambling norms. Another condition was a waitlist control. Contrary to expectations, reductions in days gambled occurred among patients assigned to the partial-feedback condition, but no differences were noted between the full-feedback intervention and the control condition. These results, similarly to Petry et al. (2009, 2008), suggest that a single motivational session may be sufficient to reduce gambling at least in a subset of gamblers, but the exact content of the most efficacious brief intervention remains to be determined, as well as the populations for whom brief interventions are best suited.

Conclusion

In sum, psychosocial treatments are efficacious in reducing gambling problems in the short term, but the specific types of treatment(s) most efficacious remain to be determined. Cognitive and cognitive-behavioral interventions, along with brief and motivational treatments, have all been shown to reduce gambling behaviours during and soon after treatment ends. Few trials, however, have included control conditions. Instead, many studies conducted to date have employed waitlist control conditions, which impact expectancy effects and obviate the ability to assess long-term outcomes. Because many problem and pathological gamblers recover without formal interventions, and many others substantially decrease gambling once they decide to initiate treatment, it is imperative that future studies evaluate the long-term efficacy of potentially promising interventions.

The studies conducted thus far have generally found that interventions are efficacious when patients access them, but Internet-based and workbook-delivered treatments tend to suffer from fairly low rates of engagement, potentially limiting their effectiveness. Identification of patient factors associated with compliance in and benefits from self-directed interventions would allow for resources associated with more intensive interventions to be directed towards patients who really need them.

A concern across studies is that no generally accepted standard exists with respect to determining gambling outcomes. Some studies have relied on self-reports of urges or desires to gamble, others report upon actual days of gambling or amounts wagered, and still others use DSM symptom counts. Rarely have independent evaluations of gambling problems been conducted (e.g. collateral information about gambling).

Some studies have suffered from low rates of participation in follow-up interviews, which can bias reporting of outcomes. Patients who do not participate in follow-up evaluations may differ in important ways from those who do. Only a handful of studies have utilised sophisticated statistical techniques to account for missing data.

Further, few studies have systematically measured therapist adherence and competence in therapy delivery. Therapies not delivered as intended are unlikely to impact outcomes. Moreover, few studies have examined how the therapies exert their effects on gambling outcomes, i.e. mechanisms of action. Therapeutic alliance is a strong and consistent factor associated with outcomes across forms of psychotherapies and psychiatric conditions. Its effects may overshadow those of specific interventions and should also be considered in the design and evaluation of subsequent studies.

Although this field is far advanced relative to a decade ago, future research into psychotherapies for problem and pathological gambling is needed to identify the most promising interventions and how these interventions impact their effects. Additionally, greater attention is needed with respect to the long-term effects of interventions and the specific populations who may benefit most from them.

Key points

1	Psychosocial interventions such as Gamblers Anonymous, cognitive-behaviour therapies, and brief and motivational interventions have been applied to reduce gambling problems.
2	Future studies need to evaluate the long-term efficacy of potentially promising interventions.

References

American Psychiatric Association (1994). *Diagnostic and Statistical Manual of Mental Disorders (4th edn)*. Washington, DC: American Psychiatric Association.

Blanco, C., Hasin, D. S., Petry, N., Stinson, F. S. & Grant, B. F. (2006). Sex differences in subclinical and DSM-IV pathological gambling: results from the National Epidemiologic Survey on Alcohol and Related Conditions. *Psychol Med*, 36:943–53.

Carlbring, P. & Smit, F. (2008). Randomized trial of Internet-delivered self-help with telephone support for pathological gamblers. *J Consult Clin Psychol*, 76(6):1090–4.

Carlbring, P., Jonsson, J., Josephson, H. & Forsberg, L. (2010). Motivational interviewing versus cognitive behavioral group therapy in the treatment of problem and pathological gambling: a randomized controlled trial. *Cogn Behav Ther*, 39(2):92–103.

Carlbring, P., Degerman, N., Jonsson, J. & Andersson, G. (2012). Internet-based treatment of pathological gambling with a three-year follow-up. *Cogn Behav Ther*, 41:1–14.

Cunningham, J. A., Hodgins, D. C., Toneatto, T., Rai, A. & Cordingley, J. (2009). Pilot study of a personalized feedback intervention for problem gamblers. *Behav Ther*, 40(3):219–24.

Cunningham, J. A., Hodgins, D. C., Toneatto, T. & Murphy, M. A. (2012). Randomized controlled trial of a personalized feedback intervention for problem gamblers. *PloS One*, 7(2):e31586. Doi: 10.1371/journal.pone.0031586.

Diskin, K. M. & Hodgins, D. C. (2009). A randomized controlled trial of a single session motivational intervention for concerned gamblers. *Behav Res Ther*, 47:382–8.

Dowling, N., Smith, D. & Thomas, T. (2007). A comparison of individual and group cognitive–behavioural treatment for female pathological gambling. *Behav Res Ther*, 45:2192–202.

Grant, J. E., Donahue, C. B., Odlaug, B. L., Kim, S. W., Miller, M. J. & Petry, N. M. (2009). Imaginal desensitisation plus motivational interviewing for pathological gambling: randomised controlled trial. *Brit J Psychiatry*, 195:266–7.

Hodgins, D. C., Wynne, H. & Makarchuk, K. (1999). Pathways to recovery from gambling problems: follow-up from a general population survey. *J Gambl Stud*, 15:93–104.

Hodgins, D. C., Currie, S. R. & el-Guebaly, N. (2001). Motivational enhancement and self-help treatments for problem gambling. *J Consult Clin Psychol*, 69(1):50–7.

Hodgins, D. C., Currie, S. R., Currie, G. & Fick G. H. (2009). Randomized trial of brief motivational treatments for pathological gamblers: more is not necessarily better. *J Consult Clin Psychol*, 77(5):950–60.

Jiménez-Murcia, S., Stinchfield, R., Alvarez-Moya, E., Jaurrieta, N., Bueno, B., Granero, R. et al. (2009). Reliability, validity, and classification accuracy of a Spanish translation of a measure of DSM-IV diagnostic criteria for pathological gambling. *J Gambl Stud*, 25:93–104.

Korman, L., Collins, J., Littman-Sharp, N., Skinner, W., McMain, S. & Mercado, V. (2008). Randomized control trial of an integrated therapy for comorbid anger and gambling. *Psychother Res*, 18(4):454–65.

Ladouceur, R., Sylvain, C., Boutin, C., Lachance, S., Doucet, C., Leblond, J. et al. (2001). Cognitive treatment of pathological gambling. *J Nerv Ment Dis*, 189:774–80.

Ladouceur, R., Sylvain, C., Boutin, C., Lachance, S., Doucet, C. & Leblond, J. (2003). Group therapy for pathological gamblers: a cognitive approach. *Behav Res Ther*, 41:587–96.

McBride, O., Adamson, G. & Shevlin, M. (2010). A latent class analysis of DSM-IV pathological gambling criteria in a nationally representative British sample. *Psychiatry Res*, 178:401–7.

Morasco, B. J., Weinstock, J., Ledgerwood, D. M. & Petry, N. M. (2007). Psychological factors that promote and inhibit pathological gambling. *Cogn Behav Pract*, 14:208–17.

Oei, T. P. S., Raylu, N. & Casey, L. M. (2010). Effectiveness of group and individual formats of a combined motivational interviewing and cognitive behavioral treatment program for problem gambling: a randomized controlled trial. *Behav Cogn Psychother*, 38:233–8.

Orford, J., Sposton, K. & Erens, B. (2003). SOGS and DSMIV in the British Gambling Prevalence Survey: reliability and facture structure. *International Gambl Stud*, 3:53–65.

Petry, N. M. (2003). Patterns and correlates of Gamblers Anonymous attendance in pathological gamblers seeking professional treatment. *Addict Behav*, Aug. 28(6):1049–62.

Petry, N. M. (2005). *Pathological Gambling: Etiology, Comorbidity, and Treatment.* Washington, DC: American Psychological Association Press.

Petry, N. M. (2010). Pathological gambling and the DSM-V. *International Gamb Stud*, 10:113–15.

Petry, N. M., Ammerman, Y., Bohl, J., Doersch, A., Gay, H., Kadden, R., et al. (2006). Cognitive-behavioral therapy for pathological gamblers. *J Consult Clin Psychol*, 74(3):555–67.

Petry, N. M., Litt, M. D., Kadden, R. & Ledgerwood, D. M. (2007). Do coping skills mediate the relationship between cognitive-behavioral therapy and reductions in gambling in pathological gamblers? *Addiction*, 102(8):1280–91.

Petry, N. M., Weinstock, J., Ledgerwood, D. M. & Morasco, B. (2008). A randomized trial of brief interventions for problem and pathological gamblers. *J Consult Clin Psychol*, 76(2):318–28.

Petry, N. M., Weinstock, J., Morasco, B. J. & Ledgerwood, D. M. (2009). Brief motivational interventions for college student problem gamblers. *Addiction*, 104:1569–78.

Slutske, W. S. (2006). Natural recovery and treatment-seeking in pathological gambling: results of two U.S. national surveys. *Am J Psychiatry*, 163(2):297–302.

Stewart, R. M. & Brown, R. I. (1998). An outcome study of Gamblers Anonymous. *Br J Psychiatry*, 152:284–8.

Stinchfield, R. (2003). Reliability, validity, and classification accuracy of a measure of DSM–IV diagnostic criteria for pathological gambling. *Am J Psychiatry*, 160:180–2.

Stinchfield, R., Govoni, R. & Frisch, G. R. (2005). DSM-IV diagnostic criteria for pathological gambling: reliability, validity, and classification accuracy. *Am J Addict*, 14:73–82.

Sylvain, C., Ladouceur, R. & Boisvert, J. M. (1997). Cognitive and behavioral treatment of pathological gambling: a controlled study. *J Consult Clin Psychol*, 65(5):727–32.

Toce-Geretein, M., Gerstein, D. R. & Volberg, R. A. (2003). A hierarchy of gambling disorders in the community. *Addiction*, 98:1661–72.

Zimmerman, M., Chelminski, I. & Young, D. (2006). A psychometric evaluation of the DSM-IV pathological gambling diagnostic criteria. *J Gambl Stud*, 22:329–37.

Chapter 11

Pharmacological treatments

Scott Bullock and Marc N. Potenza

Aim

1   To look at the various pharmacotherapies that have been tried in treatment of pathological gambling, with the main focus on results from placebo-controlled randomised clinical trials (RCTs) conducted to date.

Introduction

Pathological gambling (PG) affects about 0.6% of adults in the UK (Wardle et al., 2007). This number has remained relatively steady since the first survey was conducted in 1999, despite the increase in gambling venues and the decrease in respondents stating they have gambled in the past year from 72% of the population to 68%. PG represents an important public-health concern due to financial, interpersonal, mental and physical health impacts and subsyndromal levels of exhibiting elevated co-occurrences with substance use (e.g. tobacco and alcohol) and other psychiatric disorders (Aragay et al., 2012; Petry, 2007; Petry et al., 2005; Wareham & Potenza, 2010). Thus, PG and subsyndromal gambling are important to understand within a public-health framework.

PG shares diagnostic criteria and neurobiological features with those for substance use disorders (SUDs), and these similarities have guided some pharmacological trials for PG. In the upcoming DSM-5, proposals have been made to categorise PG as an addiction in the same category with SUDs (Holden, 2010). Similarities also exist in the biologies of the disorders: non-substance ('behavioral') and substance addictions involve motivational-neural-pathway differences involving such structures as the ventral striatum and ventromedial prefrontal cortex and dopaminergic, noradrenergic, serotonergic and glutamatergic neurochemical systems (Brewer & Potenza, 2008; Petry 2007; Wareham & Potenza, 2010). Brain-imaging modalities (e.g. functional magnetic resonance imaging (fMRI) and positron emission tomography (PET)) have been used to develop a better understanding of the pathophysiology of PG. In the past decade, there have been significant advances in understanding the biological underpinnings of PG, and this increased understanding of the neural correlates of PG has led to the testing of novel treatment options in clinical trials. In this chapter, we will discuss these trials, with a main focus on results from placebo-controlled randomised clinical trials (RCTs) conducted to date. There may be additional knowledge that can be gained from the open-label case studies that have been conducted, but one should be cautious about interpreting the results from these studies due to placebo effects noted in RCTs for PG. For this reason, open-label studies will be mentioned briefly along with a more detailed description of RCT findings.

Pharmacotherapies

Pharmacological interventions have been based on the currently understood neurobiological underpinnings of PG. Pharmacotherapies efficacious in the treatment of substance addictions and other psychiatric disorders that co-occur with PG have also guided the evaluation of potential new treatments for PG. Many medications investigated for their efficacies and tolerabilities in the treatment of PG have focused on the neurochemical pathways believed to be involved in PG. These include opioid antagonists, mood stabilisers, serotonin reuptake inhibitors (SRIs) and glutamatergic drugs. Reviews of pharmacological trials will be separated into the system that the medications purportedly target.

Serotonin

Clomipramine

SRIs and selective SRIs (SSRIs) have been shown to be efficacious in treating obsessive-compulsive disorder, and a role for serotonin in PG has been suggested through cerebrospinal fluid, pharmacological challenge and other biological studies. These data provided a rationale for clinical trials investigating SRIs and SSRIs in the treatment of PG. The SRI clomipramine showed promise in an early case study (Hollander et al., 1992). A single patient was treated for ten weeks with placebo and ten weeks with clomipramine (titrated from 25mg/day to 150mg/day with a final study dose of 125mg/day due to irritability at the 150mg/day dose) in a double-blinded fashion. The clomipramine appeared to be more efficacious than placebo as the patient abstained from gambling during the ten-week period on active medication. Furthermore, the patient maintained abstinence (with one brief relapse) for an additional 28 weeks on open-label clomipramine treatment.

Fluvoxamine

The promising results seen in the clomipramine study led to larger studies of SSRIs. SSRIs may have fewer adverse side effects than SRIs like clomipramine (e.g. with respect to sedation). In one pilot study, 16 PG subjects were recruited for a single-blind, placebo lead-in study with the SSRI fluvoxamine. The ten patients who remained in the study throughout the placebo lead-in and the fluvoxamine phase of the study ended with a mean fluvoxamine dose of 220mg/day (SD = 79, minimum 100 mg/day for four weeks). It was noted that treatment responders tended to have lower mean doses (207mg/day) than non-responders (250mg/day). Treatment responders were defined as having Clinical Global Impressions (CGI) scores of 1 (very much improved) or 2 (much improved), along with a greater than 25% reduction in Yale Brown Obsessive Compulsive Scale adapted for Pathological Gambling (PG-YBOCS) scores. By this definition, seven of the ten patients were considered treatment responders. Of the three 'non-responders', relapse of gambling behaviour may have been related to co-morbid cyclothymia being exacerbated by the higher dose of 250mg/day (Hollander et al., 1998).

The success from this pilot study led to a subsequent double-blind randomised study with all subjects entering a single-blind, placebo lead-in, followed by randomised assignment to either eight weeks of fluvoxamine treatment followed by eight weeks of placebo (or the reverse order) (Hollander et al., 2000). Fifteen subjects were recruited and ten subjects completed the study. Of these ten subjects, six received placebo first followed by fluvoxamine; the remaining subjects received fluvoxamine first followed by placebo. The one-week placebo lead-in assessed medication compliance and early placebo response. Dosing began at 50mg/day, was then titrated up in 50mg/day increments over the next five weeks with a maximum dose of 250mg/day. The mean dose at the end of study was 195 ± 50mg/day. Treatment response was based on significant improvement on the PG-CGI scale. Based on this, fluvoxamine (40.6%) treatment had a greater response than placebo (16.6%). Improvement in PG-YBOCS scores was not as significant (33.4% improvement for those on fluvoxamine versus 28% placebo). As has been noted in other trials involving the treatment of PG, an early placebo response was observed. Post-hoc analysis revealed a significant phase-by-drug interaction relating to a difference in fluvoxamine versus placebo in the second phase but not the first.

In a concurrent double-blind study of fluvoxamine, 32 people with PG were enrolled with 15 randomly assigned to a fluvoxamine arm and 17 to a placebo arm (Blanco et al., 2002). Treatment lasted for six months with a dose of 100mg/day for the first two weeks, titrated up to 200mg/day for the remainder of the trial. Outcome measures were average amount of money spent gambling (primary) and time spent gambling (secondary). Although improvement across both outcome measures was noted, those on fluvoxamine showed faster improvement than those on placebo. Of note in this trial of fluvoxamine was the high placebo response rate of 59%.

A case study from Singapore reported on a female PG who presented for her compulsive gambling (Lim, 2001). Despite the negative consequences her gambling was having on her family, she continued gambling. She was started on psychotherapeutic methods, but after several relapses, fluvoxamine at 150mg was initiated. Sustained abstinence was achieved after several additional relapses. It should be noted this trial of fluvoxamine combined behavioral therapy with pharmacotherapy and there was no placebo condition; thus the results cannot be attributed to one component.

A clinical trial comparing topiramate to fluvoxamine was conducted with 31 PG patients (Dannon et al., 2005). Topiramate has pro-GABAergic (GABA = gamma-amino-butyric acid) properties. Patients were randomly assigned to one of two groups (15 to topiramate and 16 to fluvoxamine). Although the study subjects and physicians were not blinded to the assignment, the raters were. Topiramate and fluvoxamine were both titrated to a study dose of 200mg/day in 50mg/day increments. Twelve of 15 patients from the topiramate group were considered completers compared with 8 out of 16 from the fluvoxamine group. Those assigned to fluvoxamine often reported adverse side effects that led to non-completion. In the topiramate group, nine reported full remission, three reported partial remission, and CGI scores were significantly improved in the entire group. In the fluvoxamine group, six reported full remission and two reported partial remission. Although this trial aimed to compare treatment across two different medications, findings suggested that each medication may help in the treatment of PG. However, results should be interpreted cautiously given the small sample, lack of a placebo control and absence of double-blinding.

In a long-term follow-up study of clinical trials, 43 male PG patients responded fully to one of four medications (Dannon et al., 2007). Eighteen patients were treated with bupropion SR, nine with topiramate, ten with naltrexone, and six with fluvoxamine. To be included in this long-term follow-up, all patients had to have responded fully to their prospective medication during their original trial. At the end of each of those trials, responders were selected and followed for an additional six months once they completed their medication regime. Relapses were noted in three of the six individuals from the fluvoxamine group, three of the nine from the topiramate group, seven of the eighteen from the bupropion SR group, and four of the ten from the naltrexone group.

A factor in determining the mechanism underlying the efficacy of pharmacological treatments for PG involves linking treatment outcome to neurobiological measures. One study involved a 36-year-old man with PG who underwent fMRI prior to and following treatment with fluvoxamine. The patient's gambling behaviour improved, with a decrease in desire to gamble and abstinence from gambling during the follow-up period. Decreased activation in previously activated areas – left frontal (Brodmann's area 6), right parietal (Brodmann's areas 7, 40) and left parietal (Brodmann's areas 7, 19 and 40) – were reported when the patient was exposed to gambling images (Chung et al., 2009). As this was a single case study (with single subject fMRI data being of questionable relevance) and was open-label, caution should be taken when interpreting the results.

Sertraline

One RCT and two case studies have been reported involving sertraline. In the only RCT to date, Saiz-Ruiz et al. (2005) conducted a double-blind, flexible-dose, placebo-controlled study of 66 PG subjects. Of the 66 randomly assigned to the 24-week trial, 60 were included in the analysis – 31 in the sertraline group and 29 in the placebo group. Dosage was started at 50mg/day during the first week, increased up to 100 mg/day by the fourth week, and then, depending on clinical response, a final increase to 150 mg/day was made by the end of the eighth week. If the subject showed a response to a lower dose, or if he/she reported adverse effects, increasing the dose was halted. By the end of the study, the mean dose across all subjects in the sertraline group was 95mg/day. The study's primary outcome measure was the Criteria for Control of Pathological Gambling Questionnaire (CCPGQ). Secondary measures included visual analog scales, frequency of gambling behaviour, CGI scores and amount of money spent gambling. No statistically significant differences were found between placebo and sertraline.

The two case studies involving sertraline – Meroni et al. (2004) and Milovanovic et al. (2006) – did report success in treating with sertraline single patients presenting with PG and co-occurring Obsessive Compulsive Disorder (OCD). As with any study lacking a placebo and involving single subjects, results should be interpreted cautiously.

Citalopram

PG often presents with co-occurring disorders. As SRIs are effective in treating anxiety and depression, they might be particularly helpful for individuals with these co-occurring conditions. An open-label study investigated the effectiveness of citalopram in treating PG with or without co-occurring major depressive disorder (MDD) (Zimmerman et al., 2002). Fifteen PG patients were administered citalopram for up to 12 weeks. Significant improvements were observed in gambling measures such as amount of money lost, amount of time spent gambling, gambling urges and preoccupation with gambling. Thirteen (86.7%) of the patients showed improvement in scores of the CGI for gambling. Eight of the patients had co-occurring MDD while seven did not. Both groups showed approximately the same level of improvement.

Escitalopram

The efficacy and tolerability of escitalopram in treating PG with co-occurring anxiety disorders was subsequently investigated (Grant & Potenza, 2006). The study involved initial open-label treatment with responders (>30% reduction on the PG-YBOCS) invited to an eight-week double-blind discontinuation phase. Significant improvement in outcome measures in individuals with PG and co-occurring anxiety disorders were found during the first phase. Thirteen subjects were enrolled. All subjects began with a one-week placebo lead-in followed by eleven weeks of open-label escitalopram. Nine of thirteen subjects enrolled completed the open-label phase of the study. Of these nine, eight were considered responders, with four moving into the discontinuation phase. From the first open-label phase, the PG-YBOCS scores improved by 46.8% from baseline. In addition, anxiety as measured by the Hamilton Anxiety Scale (HAM-A) improved by 82.8% from baseline. Of the four who underwent double-blind discontinuation phase, assignment to placebo was associated with worsening of gambling and anxiety, while assignment to active drug was associated with sustained improvement in both areas.

Escitalopram has also been studied as adjunctive therapy with a behavioral therapy platform. In a randomised trial involving two parallel treatment arms, 30 subjects were enrolled (Myrseth et al., 2011). The first arm consisted of CBT alone; the second arm consisted of eight weeks of escitalopram only followed by an additional eight weeks of escitalopram combined with CBT. Primary outcome measures were self-report scales (Gambling Symptom Assessment Scale (G-SAS) and PG 100-mm Visual Analogue Craving Scale (PG-VAC)), which were administered by a clinician blinded to treatment condition. There were no significant between-group differences but the authors found that both treatment groups improved over time. In this study, escitalopram did not appear to provide any additional benefit to CBT treatment.

Paroxetine

To date, there have been two RCTs investigating the efficacy of paroxetine in the treatment of PG. In the first study, 53 individuals with PG were enrolled in an eight-week double-blind, placebo-controlled, parallel-arm, flexible-dosing trial (Kim et al., 2002). These subjects were diagnosed with PG but without additional Axis 1 disorders. All subjects began the trial with a one-week placebo lead-in followed by eight weeks of double-blinded treatment with paroxetine. Dosing was titrated from 20mg up to 60mg (in 10mg increments per week) with dosing incrementation stopped if response was noted or if adverse effects developed. The mean dose at study end was 51.7 ± 13.1mg/day. Primary outcome measures were scored on the CGI and G-SAS. Forty-five subjects from those enrolled continued on to the medication phases. Six subjects showed response to the placebo during the one-week lead-in and two additional subjects dropped out. Those in the paroxetine arm had a greater reduction in G-SAS scores than the placebo arm (52% versus 23%). A greater improvement was also noted on the CGI for paroxetine versus placebo (47.8% versus 4.5%).

The second trial investigating paroxetine was a multi-centre RCT performed at five study sites across two countries (Grant et al., 2003). As with the previous trial of paroxetine, subjects with other Axis I disorders were excluded. All subjects began with a one-week placebo lead-in and those responding to the placebo were dropped. The primary outcome measure was the PG-CGI. Secondary measures included the PG-YBOCS and G-SAS. Eighty-three patients were enrolled, with seven of those discontinued due to response to placebo (placebo response was defined as 30% or greater reduction in PG-YBOCS score). Twenty-one patients assigned to paroxetine and 24 patients assigned to placebo completed all study visits. Dosing started at 10mg/day for week one and was subsequently increased in weekly increments of 10mg/day up to 60mg/day depending on tolerability and response. Paroxetine was not statistically better than placebo, with both placebo and paroxetine groups showing improvements in scores across all measures.

Nefazodone

Only one clinical trial (eight-week open-label) has been conducted evaluating nefazodone in the treatment of PG (Pallanti et al., 2002). Nefazodone differs from SSRIs in that it has a primarily antagonistic activity on the serotonin 5-HT$_2$ receptors. The primary outcome measures were the PG-YBOCS and the PG-CGI. Fourteen subjects were enrolled in the study, with two dropping out before finishing all study visits. Nefazodone was started at 50mg and titrated up to 500mg depending on efficacy and tolerability, with all patients having a minimum dose of 100mg per day. Nine of the 12 subjects who completed the trial were considered responders. Response criteria included scoring a 1 or 2 on the PG-CGI as well as having significant improvement in PG-YBOCS scores (there was a 37% reduction from baseline). In addition, there was significant improvement noted on self-report measures of how much time was spent gambling, number of times gambled and how much money lost to gambling over the course of the study.

Fluoxetine

There has been only one report of a trial involving fluoxetine (De la Gandara et al., 1999). The author presented findings from a six-month comparison study looking at fluoxetine plus psychotherapy and psychotherapy alone. Fluoxetine was given at 20mg/day in conjunction with psychotherapy. Outcome measures were the Ludo-Cage test, PG-CGI, and adherence to treatment. Those in the fluoxetine plus psychotherapy group showed greater improvement in the PG-CGI and Ludo-Cage scores. In addition, they had higher rates of adherence to treatment than those in the psychotherapy-only group. This study was presented only as a conference abstract; thus, additional information is limited.

Dopamine

Bupropion

Bupropion, a dopamine and norepinephrine reuptake inhibitor, has been tested in the treatment of PG (Black, 2004). Ten subjects were enrolled in the open-label study. Subjects had a three-week titration phase followed by a five-week maintenance phase; all subjects were tapered off the drug unless they wished to continue on the medication. The initial dose was 100mg/day and could be increased by up to 100mg/week before the five-week maintenance phase. All subjects were given baseline assessments including the PG-YBOCS, Attention Deficit Hyperactivity Disorder (ADHD) checklist, Mini International Neuropsychiatric Interview (MINI) and Hamilton Depression Rating Scale (HDRS). The primary outcome was measured by improvement on the PG-YBOCS, CGI and Sheehan Disability Scale (SDS). Scores on the PG-YBOCS decreased significantly and seven subjects achieved a score of 1 (very much improved) or 2 (much improved) on the CGI.

A subsequent trial compared bupropion to naltrexone in a blind-rater study comparing 19 PG subjects taking naltrexone and 17 PG subjects taking bupropion (Dannon et al., 2005). The trial ran in a parallel fashion over a 12-week period. Bupropion SR dosing started at 150mg/day for the first week, increased to 300mg/day for three weeks, and increased again to 450mg/day if no response or only a partial response was seen at lower doses. Naltrexone dosing began at 25mg/day for the first four days, increased to 100mg/day (50mg b.i.d.) for three weeks, and increased again to 150mg/day if no response or only a partial response was seen at lower doses. Twelve out of 17 participants in the bupropion group completed the study compared to 13 out of 19 in the naltrexone group. Nine out of the 12 individuals in the bupropion group were considered full responders (defined as absence of gambling behaviour for two weeks and improvement on the CGI) as compared to 10 out of the 13 in the naltrexone group. The remaining participants from both groups were all considered partial responders (defined as a decrease in the frequency of gambling behavior and amount of money spent gambling). To achieve results, those in the bupropion group typically took the highest dose, while those taking naltrexone often responded to more moderate doses. A major limitation of this (and many psychopharmacology studies done on PG) is the exclusion of other Axis I or II disorders, which limits the ability to apply these findings to the greater population of PG subjects, many of whom have co-occurring disorders.

A case study of bupropion treatment involving a 61-year-old male with a 40-year history of PG has also been reported (Padala et al., 2007). The patient had unsuccessfully sought treatment through behavioral therapies in the past. Though obtaining abstinence during his treatments, he would relapse within a month or two following his release. After completing a 30-day outpatient treatment programme, the patient was started on bupropion SR. He maintained abstinence for eight months, and only after his medications ran out, did he begin to feel the urge to gamble return. He was started back on the medication and reported a decrease in urges to gamble.

An RCT examined bupropion in a 12-week, double-blind, placebo-controlled study involving non-depressed PG subjects (Black et al., 2007). A two-week observation period was conducted before beginning the medication phase. Dosing started at 75mg/day and could be titrated up to 375mg/day in increments of 150mg per week. In order to be included in the study, subjects needed to maintain a minimum dose of 150mg/day. The average dose by study end was 324mg/day. Subject evaluations were performed at one, three and six months with additional assessments of efficacy and tolerability at multiple time-points. Outcome measures included the PG-YBOCS (primary) along with the G-SAS and CGI (secondary). Thirty-nine subjects (18 bupropion, 21 placebo) were randomised into the study with 22 completing (8 bupropion, 14 placebo). Eight subjects dropped before a post-baseline assessment could be obtained, with an additional 17 subjects withdrawing during the trial. Reasons for discontinuation varied and there were no significant between-treatment-group differences found. Across multiple measures (CGI, HDRS, G-SAS and ADHD) those assigned to placebo and those assigned to active medication were balanced with respect to baseline severity of scores. Both groups showed improvement on their PG-YBOCS scores, and no statistically significant difference was observed between groups (the final scores on the PG-YBOCS for the bupropion group decreased by 9.2 points while those on placebo showed a decrease of 9.7 points). In addition, both groups showed similar improvements across the secondary measures.

Modafinil

Modafinil, a stimulant drug with pro-dopaminergic and pro-noradrenergic properties, has been studied in regards to PG in only one study to date. Due to reports of its efficacy in targeting impulsivity in subjects with attention deficit/hyperactivity disorder (ADHD) and cocaine dependence, a double-blind, placebo-controlled study on PG subjects with high impulsivity (HI) versus PG subjects with low impulsivity (LI) was performed (Zack & Poulos, 2009). The authors hypothesised that a 200mg dose of modafinil would decrease the priming and reinforcing effect of a slot machine. They further predicted that this effect would be more pronounced in HI versus LI subjects. Multiple measures were used to assess outcome, including betting behaviour, physiological responses to gambling, and self-reports on the pleasurable effects of gambling experienced and desires to gamble. A secondary, behavioral measure (performance on the Stop-Signal Task (SST)) was used to assess post-game inhibitory control. All subjects gambled on an electronic machine in a mock-bar setting after being explicitly informed that this was not a treatment study. The Eysenck Impulsivity Questionnaire (EIQ) was used to separate the 20 subjects enrolled into HI and LI groups. A score of <9 was considered LI and a score ≥9 was considered HI. Each subject participated in two slot-machine-playing days. On one day they would receive placebo before gambling and on the other day they would receive modafinil before gambling. The assignment to placebo or modafinil was done in a random-order double-blinded fashion. The results suggested that modafinil decreased motivations to gamble, decreased risky decision making and improved inhibitory control in HI subjects but had an opposite effect on LI subjects. Across both groups, modafinil did not affect self-reported pleasure during gambling but did significantly decrease the mean bet size in a similar manner in both HI and LI subjects. As with many of the studies in this chapter, the exclusion of co-morbidities reduces the generalisability of the findings to the population as a whole. Furthermore, the findings suggest that heterogeneity in PG may influence choices of effective pharmacotherapies.

Individual differences also warrant consideration with other pro-dopaminergic medications and PG. Dopamine replacement therapies (e.g. pramipexole, ropinirole and levo-dopa, amongst others) have been associated with PG and other Impulse Control Disorders (ICDs) in Parkinson's Disease (Leeman & Potenza, 2011; 2012). Case reports have also been reported for other conditions including restless legs syndrome. One case study involving modafinil and the onset of PG has been reported (Tarrant et al., 2010). The patient was a 39-year-old male who presented with narcolepsy. He was taking modafinil 300mg daily (150mg b.i.d.), was reported to be developing a tolerance to this dosage, and when an increased dosage was discussed, he expressed some reservations due to a problem with gambling. A two-month period of withholding modafinil saw a return of his narcoleptic symptoms and decreased gambling. The patient was prescribed clomipramine, which appeared to help with the narcolepsy and gambling. As with other case studies, findings should be interpreted cautiously.

Disulfiram

Disulfiram can influence the function of dopamine beta-hydroxylase, an enzyme facilitating the conversion of dopamine to norepinephrine, thereby leading to lower levels of norepinephrine in the brain. There have been no RCTs utilising disulfiram as of this date. Disulfiram has shown effectiveness in treating alcohol dependence (AD) and cocaine dependence (CD). Due to the similarities between these substance addictions and behavioral addictions such as PG, it has been hypothesised that disulfiram may prove effective in treating PG (Mutschler et al., 2010). The authors presented a case report of a subject with AD and co-morbid PG (Mutschler et al., 2010). This patient developed AD about 25 years prior to this report, and around the same time also developed PG. Though he sought treatment for his AD over the past 25 years, he did not seek treatment specific for his PG. After his last inpatient treatment for AD, he remained abstinent from alcohol for six to seven months, but continued to gamble. He presented for AD treatment, was treated inpatient for five weeks and then continued outpatient treatment for another 12 months. Treatment included disulfiram (500mg, three days a week) and psychotherapy. Though being treated specifically for AD, the patient was able to maintain abstinence from alcohol and gambling for a period of 12 months. In his previous detoxifications, his gambling was not affected, so the authors theorised that the disulfiram targeted both AD and PG.

An additional two cases of PG patients treated with disulfiram have been reported (Muller et al., 2011). Their first patient was a 44-year-old male with PG who was started on outpatient cognitive behavioral therapy and offered pharmacological treatment in conjunction. He did not want to be treated with

SSRIs so he chose to take disulfiram and was started on 200mg per day. After one week of therapy, his PG-YBOCS went from 17 to 13. He experienced sedation and an increase in hours slept per day. Before his next visit he relapsed and discontinued the medication himself, but began again prior to his visit. He continued with the medication but kept experiencing sedation. A reduction to 100mg per day did not alleviate the sedation so the patient chose to discontinue the medications. His last follow-up showed a complete remission of sedative effects, and at that time his PG-YBOCS was 8.

The second patient was a 56-year-old male with PG who had had previous psychiatric treatment for depressive episodes. He had intermittent periods of abstinence from gambling but experienced continued gambling problems. His therapy initially involved CBT, and due to his lack of responses to previous treatments with citalopram and venlafaxine, he was offered disulfiram. His initial PG-YBOCS score was 22. The patient tolerated the medication well in the beginning, but there was no significant impact on his gambling. Soon after starting the disulfiram, the patient developed psychotic syndromes necessitating admission to an inpatient unit. Disulfiram was discontinued and his symptoms remitted. Three weeks after discharge from the unit, he had relapsed and his PG-YBOCS score was now 25.

Taken together, there is limited support for the use of disulfiram in the treatment of PG.

Olanzapine

Olanzapine, an atypical antipsychotic used frequently in treating schizophrenia, acts antagonistically at dopamine and serotonin receptors. In treating PG it has been tested in two RCTs. The first trial was a 12-week double-blind, placebo-controlled, flexible-dose study (McElroy et al., 2008). The study began with a placebo treatment, with responders to placebo (defined as 50% or greater reduction in PG-YBOCS score) excluded. Thereafter, olanzapine was started at 2.5mg per day, titrated up by 2.5mg/day every week, to a maximum dose of 15mg/day unless response to a lower dose was noted or adverse effects emerged. The mean dose at study end was 8.9mg/day. Forty-two subjects were randomised. Forty subjects had at least one post-randomisation measure, with 25 completing all phases (15 placebo, 10 olanzapine). Reasons for discontinuation were varied with no significant between-group differences noted. The results showed no significant difference between olanzapine and placebo on the primary outcome measure (PG-YBOCS) or secondary measures (frequency of gambling episodes, time spent gambling and CGI scores). While no difference was found between the two groups, all subjects showed improvement on all measures.

The only other RCT involving olanzapine investigated its efficacy and tolerability in treating PG among video-poker gamblers (Fong et al., 2008). The double-blind, placebo-controlled, seven-week trial involved 23 participants who enrolled and 21 who completed. Dosage began at 2.5mg/day, was titrated up in increments of 2.5mg/day every week until the final dose of 10mg/day was reached and maintained for the last four weeks. In addition to meeting with the study team weekly, all subjects were also encouraged to attend GA. Outcome measures included self-report measures of craving on the Brecksville Gambling Craving Scale (BGCS) and Desire to Gamble Scale (DGS) and gambling-related improvement on the CGI-PG. As with the first RCT of olanzapine, the investigators found no significant differences between those on placebo and those on olanzapine across all measures. They too noted reductions in gambling behaviours in both groups over time. The study had multiple limitations including small size, short-term treatment, possible influences of meeting weekly with a clinician and enrolment solely of patients who reported video poker as their main problem.

These trials do not support olanzapine in the treatment of PG.

Haloperidol

Haloperidol, a D2-like dopamine receptor antagonist, has not been tested for its efficacy in treating PG, but has been tested for its effects on slot-machine gambling (Zack & Poulos, 2007). Thirty-eight subjects (20 non-treatment-seeking PG subjects and 18 healthy controls) attended two sessions of slot-machine gambling, one week apart. Sessions were randomised in a double-blind fashion with one session involving administration of haloperidol (3mg) and one placebo. Once the drug was administered, subjects would wait 2.75 hours before gambling in a mock-bar setting. Subjects gambled for 15 minutes or until they exhausted their $200 in credits. To assess the effects of haloperidol, the Addiction Research Center Inventory (ARCI) and short form of the Profile of Mood States (POMS) were administered at two separate times – before drug administration and again immediately before they gambled. In addition, to measure subjective ratings of pleasure, a visual analogue scale was used before drug administration, again immediately before they gambled, and immediately after the gambling episode. Additional measures included the Lexical Salience Task (LST) given right after the slot-machine episode and blood pressure taken every 30 minutes. Haloperidol in PG subjects was associated with an increase in enjoyment and excitement, increased gambling and stronger motivations to gamble. Control subjects, on the other hand, displayed no such effects. There was a rise in blood pressure in both groups under both conditions while gambling. Haloperidol augmented this rise in blood pressure in both groups. In addition, among the PG subjects, salience to gambling words appeared enhanced during the haloperidol sessions relative to neutral words. This was not seen in the control subjects and suggests Dompamine (DA) antagonists may exacerbate/initiate gambling-related thoughts and behaviours in people with PG.

Risperidone

Risperidone is an atypical antipsychotic drug. In a case PG associated with dopamine agonist treatment in Parkinson's Disease (PD), a 59-year-old woman was treated with 1mg daily risperidone in addition to her usual PD medications

(Seedat et al., 2000; Stein & Grant, 2005). This addition appeared to lead to reductions in gambling but also worsened her PD, which was improved with adjuvant low-dose levodopa/carbidopa treatment.

Quetiapine

Two additional case reports of PD patients who developed PG after beginning treatment on dopamine agonists involve additional medications (Kurlan, 2004). Gambling in one case appeared not to respond to citalopram but rather to Gamblers Anonymous (GA) attendance. He began GA sessions, which led to a significant reduction and finally abstinence in his gambling behaviour. Another case involved a 42-year-old male who was admitted to inpatient treatment for gambling problems and jealous delusions six months after beginning 3.5mg/day pergolide treatment for PD (Sevincok et al., 2007). He was started on 100mg per day of quetiapine and increased to 700mg per day within four weeks. After ten weeks he was free of PG behaviour and his delusional behaviour was also significantly improved. There were no adverse effects on his PD.

Clozapine

Three cases of PD patients who developed PG after beginning dopamine agonist treatments have been described (Rotondo et al., 2010). All three individuals had past histories of depression and alcohol abuse. In all three cases, SSRIs were tried first to alleviate PG without success. Clozapine was initiated, and in two of the three, PG remitted.

These cases and others suggest that dopamine function may contribute to PG in complex manners. Many of the data come from uncontrolled studies, and RCTs indicate no advantage of dopaminergic therapies for PG. Currently there does not appear to be indications for dopamine agonists or antagonists in the treatment of PG.

Glutamate

N-Acetyl Cysteine

N-Acetyl Cysteine (NAC) is a nutraceutical with glutamatergic properties and through glutamatergic modulation is thought to influence reward-reinforcement pathways in the brain. Due to its classification as a nutraceutical, it can be purchased over the counter in health-food stores, and thus some individuals who may be hesitant to take medications may be more willing to take NAC. To date, one study has investigated NAC in PG (Grant et al., 2007). Twenty-seven subjects began an eight-week open-label period with 'responders' (defined as a $\geq$ 30% reduction in PG-YBOCS total score) then randomised to a six-week, double-blind, placebo-controlled trial. Dosage began at 600mg/day for two weeks, was titrated to 1200mg/day for another two weeks, and was further titrated to 1800mg/day for the last four weeks, depending on tolerability and clinical improvement. The mean dosage at the end of the eight-week open-label period was 1476.9 ± 311.3mg/day. Responders from this open-label period were randomised to placebo-controlled double-blind discontinuation over a six-week period. Twenty-seven subjects were enrolled in the open-label phase of the study with 23 completing this phase. Those 23 subjects showed an average decrease on the PG-YBOCS of 41.9%, with 16 subjects meeting the *a priori* definition of a 'responder'. Thirteen of those 16 (NAC n = 6, placebo n = 7) agreed to continue into the randomised six-week double-blind, placebo-controlled discontinuation phase. Five non-responders from the open-label phase were concurrently on a psychotropic medication (their participation was allowed as they were stable on the medication for three months prior to enrolment, and agreed to make no changes to their current medication schedule while participating in this study), and they showed no response to the open-label NAC. In the RCT phase of the study, treatment outcome remained based on PG-YBOCS scores. NAC was found to be significantly better than placebo, with 83.3% versus 28.6% meeting responder criteria by the end of the double-blind phase.

Memantine

Memantine is a noncompetitive antagonist of N-methyl D-aspartate (NMDA) glutamate receptors. It has been used primarily in treating cognitive decline in Alzheimer's disease. Given that memantine has also shown efficacy in treating alcoholism, it has been investigated in PG in a ten-week, open-label treatment study (Grant, Chamberlain et al., 2010). Twenty-nine subjects were enrolled with a starting dose of 10mg/day. The dose was subsequently increased to 20mg/day after two weeks and up to 30mg/day after four weeks, depending on tolerability and clinical improvement. The primary outcome measure was the PG-YBOCS, with secondary measures including the G-SAS and CGI. Twenty subjects completed the entire study. PG-YBOCS scores showed an average of 59.17% reduction from baseline. Eighteen subjects met the criteria of >35% reduction in PG-YBOCS and CGI score of 1 or 2 to be considered 'responders'. The mean effective dose at study end was 23.4 ± 8.1mg/day. In addition to improvement on gambling measures, the authors noted an increase in cognitive flexibility among responders.

Topiramate

Topiramate is a glutamatergic antagonist and pro-GABAergic drug. It has shown some promise in treating disorders characterised by impulsivity and cravings/urges. Topiramate has been evaluated in the treatment of PG in a 14-week double-blinded, placebo-controlled trial (Berlin et al., 2011). Dosing was titrated to 300mg/day over the first six-week period, with titration ending if intolerable side effects were noted or effects were seen at a lower dose. Subjects were then maintained on their final dosage for the second period of seven weeks. Subjects were tapered off the medication over a one-week period at study end. In order to remain in the study, subjects had to maintain a minimum dose of 50mg/day. Mean dose at study end was 222.50mg/day. Changes in the obsessions subscale of the PG-YBOCS were used as the primary outcome measure with secondary measures including the full PG-YBOCS score. Subjects were randomised to topiramate (n = 20) or placebo (n = 22) with 27 participants completing the study (14 from the topiramate group and 13 from the placebo group). There were no outcome differences seen between those on topiramate versus placebo. The only measure that suggested a between-group difference involved scores on the Barratt Impulsiveness Scale (BIS-11), where topiramate showed trends towards a greater reduction in the total score along with reductions in the motor and non-planning subscales. Significant decreases in PG-YBOCS scores (total and obsessions subscale) and improvement on the CGI were noted in both groups. Exclusionary criteria included those with non-PG Axis I disorders, thereby limiting the generalisability of the study.

A case study described a 57-year-old woman with a history of Bipolar Disorder II and PG (Nicolato et al., 2007). She experienced hypomania at the initial visit and was started on lithium up to 900mg/day. Her affective state improved but there was no improvement in her gambling behaviour. As such, topiramate was added and titrated up to 200mg/day with reported improvement in her gambling behaviour. After two months of combined treatment, she demonstrated abstinence from gambling that persisted at long-term follow-up. Two additional studies involving topiramate have been discussed under the section on serotonergic mechanisms of action (Dannon, Lowengrub and Gonopolski et al., 2005; Dannon et al., 2007).

Amantadine

A trial examining in PG the efficacy and tolerability of amantadine, an NMDA antagonist with anticholinergic properties that is used in the treatment of PD, was undertaken amongst individuals with PD (Thomas et al., 2010). Seventeen patients who developed PG in the past ten months were selected. These subjects were selected from over a thousand patients with PD at their clinic. In addition, their gambling behaviour could not have already responded to reductions in dopamine-replacement medications or a behavioral therapy. The trial was a 17-week double-blind, placebo-controlled, crossover open extension study. Four weeks of baseline were followed by eight weeks of amantadine/placebo crossover with one week of discontinuation and four weeks of follow-up. Amantadine was given as part of their ongoing treatment for PD. The dosage schedule was titrated from 50mg/b.i.d. to 100mg/b.i.d. over a 16-day period. The primary outcome measures were the G-SAS and PG-YBOCS. In all, five patients dropped out of the study. Of the remaining subjects, seven had full remission of gambling behavior, with the remaining five showing reduced scores on the G-SAS and PG-YBOCS. G-SAS and PG-YBOCS scores showed significant reduction (80%) after two weeks of treatment with amantadine, whereas no changes were seen during treatment with placebo.

Following up their study assessing the prevalence of ICDs in PD patients, Weintraub, Koester et al. (2010) analysed the data from that study comparing the use of amantadine versus no amantadine in those with and without ICDs (Weintraub, Sohr et al., 2010). They found that the use of amantadine was associated with ICDs (17.6% versus 12.4%) and specifically with problem/pathological gambling (7.4% versus 4.2%), which persisted after controlling for variables such as dopamine agonist use and levodopa use. These studies highlight the need for caution in using amantadine to treat PG in PD patients, and further investigation is needed to determine the efficacy and safety of its use in psychopharmacological treatments geared towards those with PG and without PD.

Acamprosate

Acamprosate, an NMDA antagonist with pro-GABAergic properties, has been used in the treatment of PG in a 50-year-old woman with a long history of depression who presented for treatment of depressive symptoms (Raj, 2010). She was also noted to have both AD and PG. Her depression medications were switched to duloxetine (to which she had previously responded), and she subsequently presented for a follow-up visit just prior to entering an alcohol treatment program, stating she could no longer control her drinking or gambling on her own. At this time, she was only looking for treatment for her AD. She was treated with 666mg/day of acamprosate for AD and venlafaxine for her depressive symptoms. Four months later, the patient was reporting partial remission of her AD, but full remission of her PG. At one point her medications ran out and she returned to gambling, but upon resuming the medications she again stopped gambling entirely.

Mood stabilisers

Lithium

In this first study of lithium in treating PG, Moksowitz et al. conducted an open-label study of three individuals with PG and co-morbid bipolar disorder who were treated with lithium (Moskowitz, 1980). All three patients reportedly responded to the treatment. In the first placebo-controlled medication trial for PG with co-occurring bipolar disorder (Bipolar II, Bipolar Disorder Not Otherwise Specified, or cyclothymia, with Bipolar I being excluded), sustained-release lithium carbonate was examined in a ten-week randomised, double-blind, placebo-controlled study (Hollander et al., 2005). Dosing began at 300mg/day for the first four days, 600mg/day for the next four days, and then 900mg/day thereafter unless intolerable side effects developed or efficacy was reached at a lower dose. Serum levels of lithium were obtained to target blood level in the range of 0.6–1.2 meq/liter. Primary outcome measures were the CGI and PG-YBOCS. Forty subjects (lithium n = 18, placebo n = 22) enrolled in the study, with 12 from the lithium group and 17 from the placebo group completing. Ten subjects from the lithium-treated group were considered responders (defined as a >35% reduction in PG-YBOCS score and an end score of 1 or 2 on the CGI) compared to just 5 from the placebo group. The improvement in PG-YBOCS scores was also significantly higher for those in the lithium group (68.8% reduction) than for those in the placebo group (32.2% reduction). Across multiple other outcome measures (CGI, and gambling urges/behaviour) the lithium group showed greater improvement from baseline than the placebo group. Mania ratings also improved to a greater extent in the lithium-treated group as compared to the placebo-treated one.

Data investigating lithium treatment in PG were also examined with respect to brain function (Hollander et al., 2008; Pallanti et al., 2010). Twenty-one patients with PG and co-morbid bipolar-spectrum disorder and a comparison group of 21 comparison subjects participated in a Positron Emission Tomography (PET) scan. Sixteen of the patients with PG and bipolar disorder were subsequently enrolled in the RCT trial of lithium described in the paragraph above. Responders were defined as a 50% or greater reduction in PG-YBOCS scores from baseline. Four out of the five assigned to the lithium group and three out of 11 assigned to the placebo group were responders. A second PET scan was conducted on the original 16 patients after ten weeks of treatment. The authors found an increased relative glucose metabolic rate (rGMR) in the ventral caudate but no change in rGMR in the putamen and thalamus. Baseline PET scan revealed a lower rGMR among PG patients than controls. Treatment with lithium appeared to raise rGMR in PG patients to levels more closely matched to the controls at baseline. This may indicate that elevating the rGMR in the caudate nucleus through the use of lithium may help to alleviate some PG symptoms. As each of the patients in this study had co-occurring bipolar disorder, the findings may not extend to the general population of PG patients. Additionally, findings should be viewed cautiously given the limited number of participants (particularly the small sample sizes within the groups receiving either lithium or placebo).

A 14-week trial compared lithium to valproate in the treatment of PG (Pallanti et al., 2002). Forty-two patients (lithium n = 23, valproate n = 19) were enrolled, with 15 from the lithium group and 16 from the valproate group completing the study. Dosing for the lithium group began at 600mg/day for the first four days, was titrated to 900mg/day for the next five days, and then increased to 1200mg/day if tolerated. Dosing for the valproate group began at 600mg/day for the first five days and was then titrated up to 1500mg/day as tolerated. Both groups were monitored weekly for blood levels of their respective medications. Those in the lithium group were monitored to ensure levels below 1meq/liter while those in the valproate group were kept at a level between 50 and 100mg/ml. The mean dose at study end for lithium was 795.6 ± 261.5mg/day and for valproate was 873.7 ± 280.1mg/day. The primary outcome measures were the PG-YBOCS and CGI.

Secondary measures included the Hamilton Rating Scale for Depression (HAM-D) and Mania Rating Scale (MRS). Improvements in both groups were seen at the end of the first week of treatment; however, further improvement was not seen until after the fourth week of treatment. CGI scores were significantly reduced in both groups at the end of the study compared to baseline, with 14 from the lithium group and 13 from the valproate group considered responders (defined as a score of very much or much improved on the CGI). Similar improvement was seen in both groups on the PG-YBOCS scores, with improvement of on average 30.1% for those on lithium and 35.9% for those on valproate.

In a case study, a 30-year-old woman presented with severe PG and cyclothymia (Dell'Osso & Hollander, 2005). She reported gambling to help relieve her depressed mood. Her gambling escalated and she was started on 300mg/day lithium, and was titrated up to 1200mg/day over a ten-week period without apparent adverse effects. Her condition improved significantly as determined by her scores on the PG-YBOCS and CGI. After ten weeks, the patient reported no gambling behaviour. Her improvement in PG coincided with improvement in her affective stability.

Carbamazepine

An open-label treatment study of extended-release carbamazepine in the treatment of PG has been reported (Black et al., 2008). Eight subjects were enrolled in the 12-week study and had at least one visit after baseline (one dropped after the first week, one after five, and one after eight weeks). Five subjects completed the entire study. All subjects had a two-week observation period prior to starting the medications. Dosage was started at 200mg twice daily for seven days and then titrated to 800mg/day divided into two doses. The final dosage was determined by response to medication and emergence of adverse effects. The primary outcome measure was the PG-YBOCS and secondary measures included the CGI, G-SAS and SDS. By the final two weeks of the study, five subjects were abstinent from gambling. In addition, there was significant improvement across all measures, including an average weekly decrease on the PG-YBOCS of 1.44 points. The average PG-YBOCS at baseline was 22.5 and at the final visit it was 8. There were several side effects among seven of the eight subjects, with somnolence being the most common. Limitations to this study include the small sample size, lack of placebo control, exclusion of co-morbiditie, and short length of trial.

In a case study using carbamazepine, positive results were described when treating a single patient who failed to respond to conventional treatment (behaviour therapy, psychoanalysis, GA) (Haller & Hinterhuber, 1994). The patient was started on 600mg/day carbamazepine and achieved abstinence within two weeks, maintaining that abstinence over a 30-month period of treatment.

Opioid antagonists/agonists

Naltrexone

Naltrexone acts as an antagonist at mu and kappa opioid receptors. These receptors are considered part of a system that processes pleasure in the brain and thus implicated in addictive disorders. Multiple RCTs demonstrate the efficacy of naltrexone in treating substance addictions such as alcohol and opioid dependence. Though not approved by the FDA for treating behavioral addictions such as PG, several recent RCTs suggest it is also efficacious in treating PG. Naltrexone has exhibited dose-dependent hepatotoxicity that is generally reversible upon drug discontinuation.

A case study of a 49-year-old male with AD and PG involved treatment with 50mg/day naltrexone for a four-week period (Crockford & el-Guebaly, 1998). By the end of the first 48 hours, he reported a cessation in his craving for alcohol and gambling. No relapses were noted during the four-week period he was on naltrexone.

In a second case report, a 55-year-old male with severe PG and compulsive shopping was started on 50mg/day naltrexone for two weeks with no improvement (Kim, 1998). His dosage was increased to 100mg/day and by his second visit he had improved significantly and maintained abstinence during a nine-month period.

An open-label trial of naltrexone further explored its efficacy and tolerability in PG (Kim & Grant, 2001). Seventeen patients were enrolled into a six-week, open-label, flexible-dose trial of naltrexone. Primary outcome measures were the CGI-PT (patient rated), CGI-MD (clinician rated) and G-SAS. Dosing started at 25mg/day for two days, followed by 50mg/day for the rest of the first week. After the first week, the dosage was titrated up by 50mg/week until improvement was noted, significant side effects emerged, or a maximum dose of 250mg/day was reached. Fourteen patients completed the study with 17 included in an intent-to-treat (ITT) analysis. The average dose at the end of the study was 157mg/day. Side effects included nausea, diarrhoea, drowsiness and insomnia. Significant improvement on all measures was noted across all subjects, with the therapeutic effects emerging between one to four weeks. Limitations include the open-label nature of the study, short duration of the trial, small sample size, and potential hepatotoxicity, particularly with dosages above 50mg/day.

Naltrexone was subsequently investigated in an 11-week, double-blind, placebo-controlled trial beginning with a one-week single-blind placebo lead-in (Kim et al., 2001). The primary outcome measures were the G-SAS, the CGI-PT (patient rated) and CGI-MD (clinician rated). During the placebo lead-in, responders (defined as an improvement of 50% or more on the G-SAS) were excluded from continuing. Dosing began at 25mg/day for the first two days, increased to 50mg/day for the remainder of the first week, and then further titrated up until improvement was seen or 250mg/day was reached. For safety reasons, the rate of increase was limited to at most 50mg/week. Eighty-three subjects enrolled in the trial with 38 subjects terminated from the study prior to receiving a minimum of 100mg/day naltrexone for a two-week period. Of the 38 subjects, 22 were dropped after the placebo lead-in for being placebo responders, five had abnormal hepatic transaminase levels, and the rest gave varying reasons for not wishing to continue. Forty-five subjects remained (25 assigned to placebo), of which 36 completed all study visits, with the final nine subjects having completed at least six visits (and thus were included in analyses). Across all study measures, naltrexone was more effective than placebo. CGI results for those assigned to the naltrexone group showed 55% very much improved and 20% much improved, compared to only 12% on both categories for placebo. The mean study dose of naltrexone at study end was 188mg/day, with a portion (over 20%) developing elevated liver transaminase levels (particularly in those taking concurrent non-steroidal anti-inflammatory drugs). Adverse effects were common to both groups, and with the exception of decreased libido, dry mouth and vivid dreams, no significant between-group differences were found.

The next RCT investigating naltrexone was an 18-week, double-blind, placebo-controlled trial involving four conditions – placebo, naltrexone at 50mg/day, 100mg/day and 150mg/day (Grant, Kim and Hartman, 2008). This study built on the promising findings from the above trial, and similar to that study, included a one-week placebo lead-in. Co-occurring disorders (except for bipolar, substance abuse and psychotic disorders) were not exclusionary criteria, which allow for the results to be more broadly generalised to the PG population. One of the main side effects of naltrexone is nausea, so to ensure subjects would not be able to determine if they were in the placebo or medication group, all subjects were given ondansetron (4mg/day) for the first three days to guard against nausea developing. In addition, an investigator who would not have contact with study subjects at any other visit conducted the week-two visit to assess adverse effects and improvement. The PG-YBOCS was the primary outcome measure with the G-SAS and CGI being secondary outcome measures. Eighty-three subjects enrolled in the study with all subjects beginning with the one-week placebo lead-in. Of those 83 subjects, 6 were considered responders (greater than 50% reduction on the G-SAS), with the remaining 77 randomised into one of the four groups for 17 weeks of treatment (placebo, N = 19, naltrexone, N = 58). Dosing for naltrexone or placebo started at 25mg/day for two days, and was then titrated up to 50mg/day. Those assigned to the 100mg or 150mg/day groups were titrated up to their respective dosage at week three. Adverse events included nausea, diarrhoea, insomnia, dry mouth and constipation, with no significant differences between groups. Subjects assigned to one of the naltrexone groups were similar in baseline characteristic and showed no differences in terms of their compliance during the study, so all three groups were collapsed into one at study end and compared to the placebo group. Six subjects from the placebo group and 22 from the naltrexone group dropped prior to completing all their study visits; however, there were no significant between-group differences in the reasons given for discontinuing. Statistically significant between-group differences were seen on the PG-YBOCS and the G-SAS, especially on the urge and behaviour subscales. Total scores on the PG-YBOCS decreased, on average, 43% for those assigned to naltrexone, while those on placebo experienced an average decrease of 31%.

Psychiatric disorders commonly co-occur with PG and many trials exclude such individuals. One trial combined naltrexone and behavioral therapy in treating individuals with co-occurring AD and PG (Toneatto et al., 2009). Fifty-two subjects were enrolled in the trial and all subjects began with a one-week placebo lead-in. Those who responded to placebo (n = 1, defined as a 50% or greater reduction in gambling behaviour or alcohol consumption) were dropped, with those remaining entering an 11-week double-blind, placebo-controlled trial of naltrexone with concurrent CBT. Twenty-five subjects were randomly assigned to placebo with the remaining 27 assigned to naltrexone. Naltrexone dosing began at 25mg/day for three days, was titrated up to 50mg/day for 11 days, and was maintained at that level unless no therapeutic effect was seen, in which case a further titration in increments of 50mg/day was done until therapeutic effect was noted. Titration would occur every two weeks up to a maximum dose of 250mg/day. The mean dose by study end was 100 mg ± 59.4mg. Adverse effects included nausea, dry mouth, fatigue and headaches. As part of the study, concurrent to the medication regime, all subjects received up to seven sessions of cognitive behavioral therapy (CBT) for both their AD and PG. The primary outcome measures included the amount of money spent gambling and/or number of drinks on days they engaged in the respective behavior, as well as the overall number of days drinking and/or gambling. To be considered a completer, subjects had to attend a 12-month follow-up assessment. Nineteen subjects from each group completed the study, with one subject dropping during the medication portion and the remaining seven subjects from the naltrexone group and six subjects from the placebo group failing to attend the 12-month follow-up. Across all behavioral measures, no between-group differences were found. No clinician-rated assessments of improvement (i.e. PG-YBOCS, G-SAS, etc.) were used in this study. Additional limitations to this study include a predominantly male sample (93%). Additionally, the fact that all subjects received CBT concurrent with medication makes it not possible to attribute behavioral improvement to the medication or to the counselling.

A targeted use of naltrexone with one session of motivational brief intervention has been described in PG (Lahti et al., 2010). In most clinical trials, subjects take the medication or placebo on a daily basis. This study sought to replicate promising findings from alcohol studies that taking the medication (50mg of naltrexone) before a gambling episode, or as soon as an urge was felt, may prove beneficial without potential adverse effects of daily naltrexone. The brief intervention with the clinician was to provide patients with means to practise healthy alternative behaviours when they are not gambling. The primary outcome measure was the PG-YBOCS with secondary measures including the alcohol use disorders identification test (AUDIT), EuroQuol Five Dimension quality of life survey (EQ-5D) and the Beck depression inventory (BDI). Thirty-nine subjects were enrolled, with the instructions to take 50mg of naltrexone upon feeling an urge to gamble or immediately before engaging in gambling activities. Subjects reported significant decreases in gambling-related thoughts and behaviours as well as depressive symptoms. In addition, subjects reported an increase in their quality of life during the study. These findings are preliminary and require replication with a larger sample to determine if this type of pharmacological intervention may be efficacious in treating PG.

Three cases of patients with PD and PG treated with naltrexone have been reported (Bosco et al., 2012). Each patient was recruited and followed for a two-year period. All three patients reported the development of PG symptoms within months of beginning DA agonist treatment for their PD. All three patients reported no improvement of gambling behavior after discontinuing DA therapy, so SRIs were begun with no apparent benefit. Naltrexone was prescribed to all three with remission of PG symptoms occurring within weeks of beginning treatment. In addition, two of the patients were able to maintain remission of symptoms after discounting naltrexone therapy, while the third patient refused to discontinue the medication.

Nalmefene

Nalmefene is similar to naltrexone in that both antagonise mu, delta and kappa opioid receptors, albeit with different specificities. However, nalmefene is not hepatotoxic like naltrexone and thus may represent a safer alternative. Nalmefene has shown some promising results in the treatment of substance addictions such as AD. The first RCT investigating nalmefene treatment of PG was in a 16-week, randomised, double-blind, placebo-controlled trial conducted at 15 sites throughout the United States (Grant et al., 2006). A total of 207 subjects were enrolled. The primary outcome measure was the total score on the PG-YBOCS. Secondary measures included the G-SAS, Sheehan Disability Scale (SDS), and CGI. Subjects were randomly assigned to one of four groups – placebo (n = 51), nalmefene at 25mg/day (n = 52), 50mg/day (n = 52) and 100mg/day (n = 52). Dosage for nalmefene or placebo equivalent began at 25mg/day for the first week, with those assigned to the 50mg or 100mg/day group increasing to their respective dose in week two. There were high numbers of drop-outs (placebo dropouts n = 27, nalmefene dropouts n = 107) from all groups in this study, with significantly more subjects discontinuing among the 50mg and 100mg nalmefene groups compared to the placebo group. In addition, those subjects assigned to the higher dosage of nalmefene discontinued earlier in the study compared to those in the placebo or the 25mg/day nalmefene groups. The subjects assigned to the 25mg/day nalmefene group did not differ significantly from the placebo group in numbers or reasons for discontinuing. The primary reasons for withdrawal among the nalmefene group included adverse events (47%) and loss to follow-up (31%). Adverse events were mild to moderate in nature and occurred primarily in the first week of treatment. Data from the three nalmefene groups did not differ significantly, so these data were combined and compared as a group against the placebo group. Nalmefene proved superior to placebo in reducing PG-YBOCS scores (placebo – 18.9% reduction, nalmefene – 36.3% reduction). Responders were defined by scoring 1 'very much improved' or 2 'much improved' on the CGI at the last evaluation point. Nalmefene again proved more effective than placebo on this measure, with those assigned to the 25mg/day nalmefene group having 59% defined as responders compared to 34% on placebo. Though not significantly different from the placebo group, those assigned to the 50mg and 100mg group also had high rates of responders (48% and 42% respectively).

A second randomised, double-blind treatment study of nalmefene with a single-blind placebo lead-in phase was conducted (Grant et al., 2010). Two hundred and thirty-three participants from 25 outpatient centres throughout the United States were enrolled. Placebo responders (defined as a reduction on their PG-YBOCS to a score under 15) were dropped, with those remaining being randomised into one of three groups for the double-blind phase – nalmefene at 20mg/day (n = 77), nalmefene at 40mg/day (n = 82) or placebo (n = 74). Dosing began at 5mg/day nalmefene or placebo-equivalent and was then titrated up to 20mg/day for week two, with those assigned to the 40mg/day group having a final titration at week three to bring them to 40mg/day. The total score on the PG-YBOCS served as the primary outcome measure with the subscales serving as a secondary outcome measure. Additional secondary measures included the G-SAS and SDS. In an Intent to Treat (ITT) analysis, no statistically significant between-group differences were found on any measure. Responders (defined as decrease of 35% or greater on the PG-YBOCS total score) were high across all groups, with 59.5% of those on placebo, 46.8% of those on 20mg/day and 56.1% of those on 40mg/day being considered responders. However, further analyses showed that in the ITT group, there were 43 participants who did not receive a full titration of the active medication for at least a week. When removing those subjects from analyses, it was shown that those assigned to the 40mg/day group had a significant difference in mean PG-YBOCS scores compared to the placebo group, especially in urges associated with PG.

Given the heterogeneity of PG, there are certain factors that associate with treatment outcome. To investigate, data from several placebo-controlled RCTs of naltrexone and nalmefene were analyzed to identify factors associated with treatment outcome (Grant et al., 2010; Monterosso et al., 2001; O'Brien, 2005). In treating AD with opiate antagonists such as naltrexone or nalmefene, positive outcomes are often found in those with a family history of alcoholism and who display strong cravings for alcohol. This same phenomenon was observed in trials involving naltrexone or nalmefene treatment for PG. A family history of alcoholism and strong gambling urges at treatment onset were associated with better treatment response, especially amongst those receiving higher doses of opioid antagonist (nalmefene 50 or 100mg, naltrexone 100 or 150mg). On the other hand, placebo response (for which PG trials have a high occurrence) was most strongly associated with younger age.

Multi-pharmacotherapy chart review

A chart review has been reported of 50 adult patients seen clinically for PG (Grant & Kim, 2002). These patients were not part of a treatment study and received either monotherapy with naltrexone (minimal effective dose of 100mg/day), one of the SSRIs (minimal effective daily doses of fluoxetine 60mg, paroxetine 40mg, sertraline 200mg, citalopram 40mg) or treatment with one of the previous medications plus augmentation with any of the following (olanzapine 5mg, lamotrigine 200mg, gabapentin 1800mg and topiramate 200mg) if no response to monotherapy was achieved. Choice of medication was based on how the patient presented to the clinic. If reasons for gambling were primarily to relieve dysphoric mood, an SSRI was used. If the primary reason for gambling related to urges or cravings, naltrexone was used. The primary outcome assessments were the Clinical Global Impressions Scale for PG (PG-CGI), Gambling Symptom Assessment Scale (G-SAS), Global Assessment of Functioning (GAF), and Yale-Brown Obsessive Compulsive Scale Modified for Pathological Gambling (PG-YBOCS). The 50 subjects (25 female) were followed for an average of 360 days. Seventy-eight per cent were considered responders (PG-CGI score of 1 'very much improved' or 2 'much improved') with an average time between starting the medication and responding being 105 days. Of the 39 responders, 36 maintained their response beyond a 60-day period. A main limitation is the open-label nature of the study, particularly as frequent placebo responses have been observed in many studies. Another limitation is the heterogeneity of treatments, further complicated by the offering of CBT to all subjects, with eight subjects receiving some CBT. A follow-up chart review of 14 older PG subjects was reported; it similarly involved heterogeneous treatments and an open-label structure, thus limiting conclusions that could be drawn (Grant & Grosz, 2004).

Conclusions

Although no drugs have been approved with an indication for PG, placebo-controlled, double-blind RCTs suggest the efficacy and tolerability of several classes of medications in the treatment of PG. Arguably the most robust data exist for opioid antagonists (naltrexone, nalmefene), particularly for individuals with a familial history of alcoholism and/or strong gambling urges at treatment onset. Data also suggest that SSRIs and mood stabilisers, particularly lithium, are helpful in certain groups of people with PG. As most pharmacotherapy trials have examined only short-term outcomes, additional research is needed to determine the extent to which specific therapies are associated with long-term improvements. Additionally, the extent to which pharmacotherapies might be used in conjunction with behavioral therapies in the treatment of PG also warrants additional investigation.

Key points

1   Medications investigated for their efficacies and tolerabilities in the treatment of pathological gambling have focused on the neurochemical pathways believed to be involved: these have included opioid antagonists, mood stabilisers, serotonin reuptake inhibitors (SRIs) and glutamatergic drugs.
2   Although no drug is licensed for treatment of pathological gambling, all the above class of drugs have been shown to be beneficial, with opioid antagonists showing most promise.
3   Further studies are required, which are methodologically more robust and look at the benefits of combined pharmacotherapy and psychotherapies.

References

Aragay, N., Roca, A., Garcia, B., Marqueta, C., Guijarro, S., Delgado, L. et al. (2012). Pathological gambling in a psychiatric sample. *Compr Psychiatry*, 53(1):9–14.

Berlin, H. A., Braun, A., Simeon, D., Koran, L. M., Potenza, M. N., McElroy, S. L. et al. (2011). A double-blind, placebo-controlled trial of topiramate for pathological gambling. *World J Biol Psychiatry*, 14:121–8.

Black, D. W. (2004). An open-label trial of bupropion in the treatment of pathologic gambling. *J Clin Psychopharmacol*, 24(1):108–10.

Black, D. W., Arndt, S., Coryell, W. H., Argo, T., Forbush, K. T., Shaw, M. C. et al. (2007). Bupropion in the treatment of pathological gambling: a randomised, double-blind, placebo-controlled, flexible-dose study. *J Clin Psychopharmacol*, 27(2):143–50.

Black, D. W., Shaw, M. C. & Allen, J. (2008). Extended release carbamazepine in the treatment of pathological gambling: an open-label study. Prog Neuropsychopharmacol. *Biol Psychiatry*, 32(5):1191–4.

Blanco, C., Petkova,E., Ibáñez, A. & Saiz-Ruiz, J. (2002). A pilot placebo-controlled study of fluvoxamine for pathological gambling. *Ann Clin Psychiatry*, 14(1):9–15.

Bosco, D., Plastino, M., Colica, C., Bosco, F., Arianna, S., Vecchio, A. et al. (2012). Opioid antagonist naltrexone for the treatment of pathological gambling in Parkinson disease. *Clin Neuropharmacol*, 35(3):118–20.

Brewer, J. A. & Potenza, M. N. (2008). The neurobiology and genetics of impulse control disorders: relationships to drug addictions. *Biochem Pharmacol*, 75(1):63–75.

Chung, S. K., You, I. H., Cho, G. H., Chung, G. H., Shin, Y. C., Kim, D. J. et al. (2009). Changes of functional MRI findings in a patient whose pathological gambling improved with fluvoxamine. *Yonsei Med J*, 50(3):441–4.

Crockford, D. N. & el-Guebaly, N. (1998). Naltrexone in the treatment of pathological gambling and alcohol dependence. *Can J Psychiatry*, 43(1):86.

Dannon, P. N., Lowengrub, K., Gonopolski, Y., Musin, E. & Kotler, M. (2005). Topiramate versus fluvoxamine in the treatment of pathological gambling: a randomized, blind-rater comparison study. *Clin Neuropharmacol*, 28(1):6–10.

Dannon, P. N., Lowengrub, K., Musin, E., Gonopolski, Y. & Kotler, M. (2005). Sustained-release bupropion versus naltrexone in the treatment of pathological gambling: a preliminary blind-rater study. *J Clin Psychopharmacol*, 25(6):593–6.

Dannon, P. N., Lowengrub, K., Musin, E., Gonopolsky, Y. & Kotler, M. (2007). 12-month follow-up study of drug treatment in pathological gamblers: a primary outcome study. *J Clin Psychopharmacol*, 27(6):620–4.

De la Gandara, J., Sanz, O. & Gilaberte, I. (1999). Fluoxetine: open-trial in pathological gambling. 152nd Annual Meeting of the American Psychiatric Association, May 16–211999, Washington, DC.

Dell'Osso, B. & Hollander, E. (2005). The impact of comorbidity on the management of pathological gambling. *CNS Spectr*, 10(8):619–21.

Fong, T., Kalechstein, A., Bernhard, B., Rosenthal, R. & Rugle, L. (2008). A double-blind, placebo-controlled trial of olanzapine for the treatment of video poker pathological gamblers. *Pharmacol Biochem Behav*, 89(3):298–303.

Grant, J. E. & Grosz, R. (2004). Pharmacotherapy outcome in older pathological gamblers: a preliminary investigation. *J Geriatr Psychiatry Neurol*, 17(1):9–12.

Grant, J. E. & Kim, S. W. (2002). Effectiveness of pharmacotherapy for pathological gambling: a chart review. *Ann Clin Psychiatry*, 14(3):155–61.

Grant, J. E. & Potenza, M. N. (2006). Escitalopram treatment of pathological gambling with co-occurring anxiety: an open-label pilot study with double-blind discontinuation. *Int Clin Psychopharmacol*, 21(4):203–9.

Grant, J. E., Kim, S. W., Potenza, M. N., Blanco, C., Ibáñez, A., Stevens, L. et al. (2003). Paroxetine treatment of pathological gambling: a multi-centre randomized controlled trial. *Int Clin Psychopharmacol*, 18(4):243–9.

Grant, J. E., Potenza, M. N., Hollander, E., Cunningham-Williams, R., Nurminen, T., Smits, G. et al. (2006). Multicenter investigation of the opioid antagonist nalmefene in the treatment of pathological gambling. *Am J Psychiatry*, 163(2):303–12.

Grant, J. E., Kim, S. W. & Odlaug, B. L. (2007). N-acetyl cysteine, a glutamate-modulating agent, in the treatment of pathological gambling: a pilot study. *Biol Psychiatry*, 62(6):652–7.

Grant, J. E., Kim, S. W. & Hartman, B. K. (2008). A double-blind, placebo-controlled study of the opiate antagonist naltrexone in the treatment of pathological gambling urges. *J Clin Psychiatry*, 69(5):783–9.

Grant, J. E., Kim, S. W., Hollander, E. & Potenza, M. N. (2008). Predicting response to opiate antagonists and placebo in the treatment of pathological gambling. *Psychopharmacology (Berl)*, 200(4):521–7.

Grant, J. E., Chamberlain, S. R., Odlaug, B. L., Potenza, M. N. & Kim, S. W. (2010). Memantine shows promise in reducing gambling severity and cognitive inflexibility in pathological gambling: a pilot study. *Psychopharmacology (Berl)*, 212(4):603–12.

Grant, J. E., Odlaug, B. L., Potenza, M. N., Hollander, E. & Kim, S. W. (2010). Nalmefene in the treatment of pathological gambling: multicentre, double-blind, placebo-controlled study. *Br J Psychiatry*, 197(4):330–1.

Haller, R. & Hinterhuber, H. (1994). Treatment of pathological gambling with carbamazepine. *Pharmacopsychiatry*, 27(3):129.

Holden, C. (2010). Psychiatry. Behavioral addictions debut in proposed DSM-V. *Science*, 327(5968):935.

Hollander, E., Frenkel, M., DeCaria, C., Trungold, S. & Stein, D. J. (1992). Treatment of pathological gambling with clomipramine. *Am J Psychiatry*, 149(5):710–1.

Hollander, E., DeCaria, C. M., Mari, E., Wong, C. M., Mosovich, S., Grossman, R. et al. (1998). Short-term single-blind fluvoxamine treatment of pathological gambling. *Am J Psychiatry*, 155(12):1781–3.

Hollander, E., DeCaria, C. M., Finkell, J. N., Begaz, T., Wong, C. M. & Cartwright, C. (2000). A randomized double-blind fluvoxamine/placebo crossover trial in pathologic gambling. *Biol Psychiatry*, 47(9):813–7.

Hollander, E., Pallanti, S., Allen, A., Sood, E. & Baldini Rossi, N. (2005). Does sustained-release lithium reduce impulsive gambling and affective instability versus placebo in pathological gamblers with bipolar spectrum disorders? *Am J Psychiatry*, 162(1):137–45.

Hollander, E., Buchsbaum, M. S., Haznedar, M. M., Berenguer, J., Berlin, H. A., Chaplin, W. et al. (2008). FDG-PET study in pathological gamblers. 1. Lithium increases orbitofrontal, dorsolateral and cingulate metabolism. *Neuropsychobiology*, 58(1):37–47.

Kim, S. W. (1998). Opioid antagonists in the treatment of impulse-control disorders. *J Clin Psychiatry*, 59(4):159–64.

Kim, S. W. & Grant, J. E. (2001). An open naltrexone treatment study in pathological gambling disorder. *Int Clin Psychopharmacol*, 16(5):285–9.

Kim, S. W., Grant, J. E., Adson, D. E. & Shin, Y. C. (2001). Double-blind naltrexone and placebo comparison study in the treatment of pathological gambling. *Biol Psychiatry*, 49(11):914–21.

Kim, S. W., Grant, J. E., Adson, D. E., Shin, Y. C. & Zaninelli, R. (2002). A double-blind placebo-controlled study of the efficacy and safety of paroxetine in the treatment of pathological gambling. *J Clin Psychiatry*, 63(6):501–7.

Kurlan, R. (2004). Disabling repetitive behaviors in Parkinson's disease. *Mov Disord*, 19(4):433–7.

Lahti, T., Halme, J. T., Pankakoski, M., Sinclair, D. & Alho, H. (2010). Treatment of pathological gambling with naltrexone pharmacotherapy and brief intervention: a pilot study. *Psychopharmacol Bull*, 43(3):35–44.

Leeman, R. F. & Potenza, M. N. (2011). Impulse control disorders in Parkinson's disease: clinical characteristics and implications. *Neuropsychiatry (London)*, 1(2):133–47.

Leeman, R. F. & Potenza, M. N. (2012). Similarities and differences between pathological gambling and substance use disorders: a focus on impulsivity and compulsivity. *Psychopharmacology (Berl)*, 219(2):469–90.

Lim, K. D. (2001). A case of pathological gambling – its features and management. *Singapore Med J*, 42(5):217–9.

McElroy, S. L., Nelson, E. B., Welge, J. A., Kaehler, L. & Keck, P. E., Jr (2008). Olanzapine in the treatment of pathological gambling: a negative randomized placebo-controlled trial. *J Clin Psychiatry*, 69(3):433–40.

Meroni, M. C., Lo Giudice, A., Kotzalidis, G. D. & Biondi, M. (2004). Improvement of pathologic gambling symptoms after administration of sertraline: a case report. *J Clin Psychopharmacol*, 24(3):350–1.

Milovanovic, S., Leposavic, L., Barisic, J. & Nikolic-Balkoski, G. (2006). [Record of successful sertraline treatment of a pathological gambler.] *Srp Arh Celok Lek*, 134(1–2):60–3.

Monterosso, J. R., Flannery, B. A., Pettinati, H. M., Oslin, D. W., Rukstalis, M., O'Brien, C. P. et al. (2001). Predicting treatment response to naltrexone: the influence of craving and family history. *Am J Addict*, 10(3):258–68.

Moskowitz, J. A. (1980). Lithium and lady luck: use of lithium carbonate in compulsive gambling. *N Y State J Med*, 80(5):785–8.

Muller, C. A., Banas, R., Heinz, A. & Hein, J. (2011). Treatment of pathological gambling with disulfiram: a report of 2 cases. *Pharmacopsychiatry*, 44(2):81–3.

Mutschler, J., Buhler, M., Diehl, A., Mann, K. & Kiefer, F. (2010). Disulfiram, an old drug with new potential in the treatment of pathological gambling? *Med Hypotheses*, 74(1):209–10.

Mutschler, J., Buhler, M., Grosshans, M., Diehl, A., Mann, K. & Kiefer, F. (2010). Disulfiram, an option for the treatment of pathological gambling? *Alcohol Alcohol*, 45(2):214–6.

Myrseth, H., Molde, H., Støylen, I., Johnsen, B., Holsten, F. & Pallesen, S. (2011). A pilot study of CBT versus escitalopram combined with CBT in the treatment of pathological gamblers. *International Gambling Studies*, 11(01):121–41.

Nicolato, R., Romano-Silva, M. A., Correa, H., Salgado, J. V. & Teixeira, A. L. (2007). Lithium and topiramate association in the treatment of comorbid pathological gambling and bipolar disorder. *Aust N Z J Psychiatry*, 41(7):628.

O'Brien, C. P. (2005). Anticraving medications for relapse prevention: a possible new class of psychoactive medications. *Am J Psychiatry*, 162(8):1423–31.

Padala, P. R., Madaan, V. & Sattar, S. P. (2007). Bupropion therapy for pathological gambling. *Ann Pharmacother*, 41(3):529.

Pallanti, S., Baldini Rossi, N., Sood, E. & Hollander, E. (2002). Nefazodone treatment of pathological gambling: a prospective open-label controlled trial. *J Clin Psychiatry*, 63(11):1034–9.

Pallanti, S., Quercioli, L., Sood, E. & Hollander, E. (2002). Lithium and valproate treatment of pathological gambling: a randomized single-blind study. *J Clin Psychiatry*, 63(7):559–64.

Pallanti, S., Haznedar, M. M., Hollander, E., Licalzi, E. M., Bernardi, S., Newmark, R. et al. (2010). Basal Ganglia activity in pathological gambling: a fluorodeoxyglucose-positron emission tomography study. *Neuropsychobiology*, 62(2):132–8.

Petry, N. M. (2007). Gambling and substance use disorders: current status and future directions. *Am J Addict*, 16(1):1–9.

Petry, N. M., Stinson, F. S. & Grant, B. F. (2005). Comorbidity of DSM-IV pathological gambling and other psychiatric disorders: results from the National Epidemiologic Survey on Alcohol and Related Conditions. *J Clin Psychiatry*, 66(5):564–74.

Raj, Y. P. (2010). Gambling on acamprosate: a case report. *J Clin Psychiatry*, 71(9):1245–6.

Rotondo, A., Bosco, D., Plastino, M., Consoli, A. & Bosco, F. (2010). Clozapine for medication-related pathological gambling in Parkinson disease. *Mov Disord*, 25(12):1994–5.

Saiz-Ruiz, J., Blanco, C., Ibáñez, A., Masramon, X., Gomez, M. M., Madrigal, M. et al. (2005). Sertraline treatment of pathological gambling: a pilot study. *J Clin Psychiatry*, 66(1):28–33.

Seedat, S., Kesler, S., Niehaus, D. J. & Stein, D. J. (2000). Pathological gambling behaviour: emergence secondary to treatment of Parkinson's disease with dopaminergic agents. *Depress Anxiety*, 11(4):185–6.

Sevincok, L., Akoglu, A. & Akyol, A. (2007). Quetiapine in a case with Parkinson disease and pathological gambling. *J Clin Psychopharmacol*, 27(1):107–8.

Stein, D. J. & Grant, J. E. (2005). Betting on dopamine. *CNS Spectr*, 10(4):268–70.

Tarrant, N., Cavanna, A. E. & Rickards, H. (2010). Pathological gambling associated with modafinil. *J Neuropsychiatry Clin Neurosci*, 22(1):123 E27–8.

Toneatto, T., Brands, B. & Selby, P. (2009). A randomized, double-blind, placebo-controlled trial of naltrexone in the treatment of concurrent alcohol use disorder and pathological gambling. *Am J Addict*, 18(3):219–25.

Thomas, A., Bonanni, L., Gambi, F., Di Iorio, A. & Onofrj, M. (2010). Pathological gambling in Parkinson disease is reduced by amantadine. *Ann Neurol*, 68(3):400–4.

Wardle, H., Sproston, K., Orford, J., Erens, B., Griffiths, M., Constantine, R. et al. (2007). British Gambling Prevalence Survey 2007. London: National Centre for Social Research (978-0-11-703792-2).

Wareham, J. D. & Potenza, M. N. (2010). Pathological gambling and substance use disorders. *Am J Drug Alcohol Abuse*, 36(5):242–7.

Weintraub, D., Koester, J., Potenza, M. N., Siderowf, A. D., Stacy, M., Voon, V. et al. (2010). Impulse control disorders in Parkinson disease: a cross-sectional study of 3090 patients. *Arch Neurol*, 67(5):589–95.

Weintraub, D., Sohr, M., Potenza, M. N., Siderowf, A. D., Stacy, M., Voon, V. et al. (2010). Amantadine use associated with impulse control disorders in Parkinson disease in cross-sectional study. *Ann Neurol*, 68(6):963–8.

Zack, M. & Poulos, C. X. (2007). A D2 antagonist enhances the rewarding and priming effects of a gambling episode in pathological gamblers. *Neuropsychopharmacology*, 32(8):1678–86.

Zack, M. & Poulos, C. X. (2009). Effects of the atypical stimulant modafinil on a brief gambling episode in pathological gamblers with high versus low impulsivity. *J Psychopharmacol*, 23(6):660–71.

Zimmerman, M., Breen, R. B. & Posternak, M. A. (2002). An open-label study of citalopram in the treatment of pathological gambling. *J Clin Psychiatry*, 63(1):44–8.

Chapter 12

Family interventions in gambling

Sanju George and Henrietta Bowden-Jones

Aim

> 1   To introduce the 5-step intervention for families affected by their loved one's gambling problem.

Introduction

Across cultures, most people gamble recreationally, with no resultant adverse impact on themselves or others. However, between 1% and 3% of the population worldwide gamble problematically and it is further estimated that many times this number are at future risk of developing gambling problems. Apart from the various physical, psychological and social consequences on the gambler him- or herself, it can also result in wide-ranging and devastating harms (often 'hidden') to the gambler's family and/or social network. It is estimated that for every gambling addict, between eight and ten others could also be adversely affected (Lobsinger & Beckett, 1996): spouses, children and family members being the most commonly affected. Still, existing gambling treatment services are very often not skilled and resourced to meet the needs of families of gambling addicts.

In a previous chapter, Velleman et al. discussed in detail the various negative effects a person's gambling can have on his/her family. The main purpose of this chapter is to describe one specific psychosocial family intervention: the 5-step intervention, for families of gambling addicts, adapted from work with families of alcohol and drug misusers. Before we discuss the 5-step intervention, we will briefly mention some other family interventions that hold promise.

Other family interventions in gambling

Although not yet adequately developed or studied, various psychosocial interventions for families offer promise. However, an important caveat to bear in mind when interpreting results of the various family-intervention studies are their methodological limitations: small sample sizes, female bias, specialised treatment-seeking groups, predominance of Gamblers Anonymous (GA) attendees, non-random samples, 'uncontrolled' study designs and lack of follow-up assessments.

The most commonly provided but perhaps the least well-studied interventions are those provided by gambling helplines that are available in most countries. These interventions range from advice, information, support, 1:1 (face to face or online) counselling and group therapies. Gam-Anon, the family counterpart of Gamblers Anonymous, is also available widely and it too offers help to families of gambling addicts. Although not systematically evaluated, studies have looked at GA and Gam-Anon attendees and generally concluded that family involvement produced beneficial effects both in terms of reductions in gambling and better relationships with the spouse. More recently, some other more structured family interventions have also been evaluated.

Makarchuck et al. (2002) evaluated the efficacy of CRAFT (Community Reinforcement and Family Training), a cognitive-behavioural intervention first developed for use in spouses of alcoholics. Thirty-one significant others of gambling addicts were randomly allocated to two groups to receive either a control intervention or a CRAFT self-help-manual-based intervention, and they were re-assessed after three months. The treatment group reported reductions in gambling, found the self-help manual to be helpful, felt less guilty and felt better in themselves.

Yet another intervention studied is Congruence Couple Therapy (CCT) (Lee, 2009). CCT employs humanistic and systems principles and views the person as an interactive dynamic of four human dimensions: intrapsychic, interpersonal, intergenerational and universal-spiritual. It is offered as a 12-session couple therapy for the gambler and the spouse and works towards 're-connection and congruence within and among the four dimensions'. Twenty-four pathological gamblers and their spouses received CCT and it resulted in a statistically significant reduction in gambling urges and behaviours, and an improvement in spousal relationship.

We now discuss the 5-step intervention that is derived from the Stress Strain Coping Support (SSCS) model which Krishnan and Orford (2002) initially suggested would be 'an appropriate framework for understanding problem gambling and the family'.

The 5-step intervention

In essence, this is 'a brief psychosocial intervention to support family members in their own right who have a close relative with a gambling addiction' (Copello et al., 2010).

Each of the above-noted tenets (stress, strain, coping and social support) is incorporated into the 5-step intervention in a step-wise fashion. This intervention could either be delivered in five separate sessions, or if need be, condensed into fewer ones or even one single session. Copello et al. (2012) have recently developed a 5-step self-help handbook for family members of those with gambling problems.

Origins of the 5-step method

The basic premise of the SSCS model is that having a close relative with an addiction problem is a stressful life event, and often a longstanding one. This in turn places considerable strain on the family member/s, putting them at risk of physical and/or psychological ill health. Two other crucial tenets of this model are coping and social support. Social support is crucial to helping family members cope with the stress of their loved one's addiction. In essence, the 5-step intervention is a means of enhancing the positive social support (emotional support, good information and material help) available to the family member from professional sources.

Using a mixed qualitative–quantitative study design, Krishnan and Orford (2002) explored how family members coped with their relatives' gambling addiction and also the nature and sources of support they received. Using the Stress Strain Coping Support (SSCS) model developed from their work with families of alcoholics and drug users, they also compared coping strategies employed by families of gambling addicts to that of alcoholics and drug users. They found that gambling addiction placed considerable stress on family members and its impact was broadly similar to that of drugs and alcohol. Family members were also seen to employ specific coping strategies such as engagement and tolerance that are associated with ill health. They also noted that relatives often felt unsupported: they appreciated positive emotional and practical support for themselves.

Five steps to support family members affected by addiction problems

Step 1

- Listen, reassure and explore concerns
- Allow family member to describe situation
- Identify relevant stresses
- Identify need for further information
- Communicate realistic optimism
- Identify need for future contacts

Step 2

- Provide relevant, specific and targeted information
- Increase knowledge and understanding
- Reduce stress arising from lack of knowledge or misconceptions

Step 3

- Explore coping responses
- Identify current coping responses
- Explore advantages and disadvantages of current coping responses
- Explore alternative coping responses
- Explore advantages and disadvantages of alternative ways of coping

Step 4

- Discuss social support
- Draw a social network diagram
- Aim to improve communication within the family
- Aim for a unified and coherent approach
- Explore potential new sources of support

Step 5

- Discuss and explore further needs
- Is there a need for further help?
- Discuss possible options with family member
- Facilitate contact between family member and other sources of specialist help

For an in-depth description of each of the five steps and how to deliver them, please read the self-help book by Copello et al. (2012). For brevity purposes we will limit ourselves to some of the key principles and a brief discussion of the 5-step intervention.

Four key principles of the 5-step method

1   The method is focused on affected and concerned family member/s.
2   The method takes a view of family members as ordinary people attempting to respond to highly stressful experiences.
3   The method is very effective and adaptable to a range of settings and circumstances.
4   The orientation of the person delivering the 5-step method is highly important.

Step 1: getting to know the family member and the problem: exploring stresses and strains

Aim: to understand and think about how the gambler's behaviour is affecting the family member and others in the family.

Developers of this intervention see Step 1 as one of the most important, and essentially encompasses the following: eliciting from the family member their perception of how their relative's gambling problem is affecting them and the rest of the family; identifying stresses faced by the family member, and their impact; and promoting realistic optimism. Some of the most commonly noted stressors for such family members are given below:

Universal stressors for family members facing addiction problems

- Concern over the gambler's health or performance
- Gambler not being pleasant to live with
- Financial irregularities and effects
- Impact on the whole family and the home
- Other members of the community get involved
- Concern over frequency, quantity or form of the relative's gambling
- Gambler disappears or comes and goes
- Social life for the family member or while family affected
- Incidents, crises.

Step 2: providing relevant information

Aim: to increase the family member's knowledge and confidence by finding out more information about gambling.

As lack of sufficient knowledge about gambling and its associated problems is often a major contributor to stress experienced by family members, Step 2 tries to equip family members with useful information. Types of information provided include possible signs that someone is gambling problematically, how people can develop a problem with gambling (see Figure 12.1 for an illustration of how individual vulnerabilities for developing a gambling problem is discussed in a treatment session), types and patterns of gambling behaviours, motivation to change and seek help. In this step it is also useful to share with the family member details of agencies/organisations that offer advice, support and treatment for family members – and this could include places/organisations to get more information on gambling (the National Problem Gambling Clinic, Gam Care, Gamblers Anonymous, etc.) and also organisations that provide information on issues that may not be directly related to gambling (social services, housing association, Citizens Advice Bureau, family rights group, etc.).

Step 3: exploring and discussing coping behaviours

Aim: to look at how the family member responds to and copes with the gambler's behaviour. This step also looks at the advantages and disadvantages of how they respond, and looks to identify ways of responding and coping that are best for the individual and for that situation.

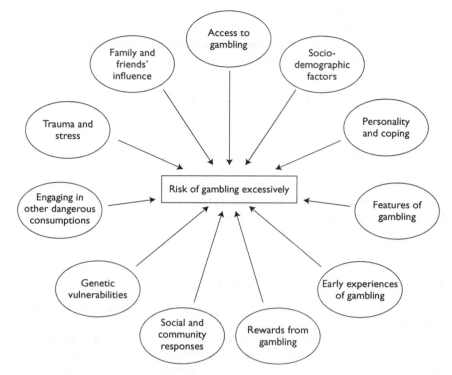

Figure 12.1 Risk factors for problematic gambling.

Coping in this context refers to 'any actions, feelings or positions that family members adopt in response to the gambling problem'. Researchers have identified three broad ways of coping among family members of those with an addiction problem:

1   'standing up to it'
2   'putting up with it'
3   'becoming independent'

In brief, Step 3 consists of four key tasks: to explore the family member's current ways of coping; to look at the advantages and disadvantages of these coping methods, as perceived by the family member; to explore alternative ways of coping; and to explore the advantages and disadvantages of these alternative coping methods.

Step 4: exploring and enhancing social support

Aim: to look at who could support the family member and the family so they can better deal with the gambler's behaviour.

As the amount of social support available to the family member can impact on their stress levels and ability to cope, this step focuses on social support. This includes both exploring the existing level of social support available to the family member, and trying to build a stronger support (family or wider social) system. Types of support in this context include emotional support, informational support and material support. There are both helpful and unhelpful forms of support and the key features of each are illustrated below:

Step 5: ending and exploring additional needs and further sources of help

Aim: to identify whether the family member needs further help for themselves and their family.

Often in the course of delivering this intervention, other needs might emerge, and this might mean referring the family member for further specialist help. Such further needs might be identified for the family member who received the intervention, another family member including children, the gambler, or the whole family. Examples of some specific areas of help requested by family members include further training and education needs, jobs, financial advice, etc. There may also be some specific issues family members may want more help with. Some of the commonly reported are: supporting children; supporting their relative if he/she wishes to access treatment; dealing with domestic violence and abuse; getting help for other issues (health problems, family planning, couples counselling, legal advice, etc.).

Conclusion

Despite the clearly evidenced huge negative impact of gambling addiction on families, surprisingly this area has not been adequately studied or appropriately resourced. Or perhaps it is unsurprising that as a non-substance addiction, gambling in general and as a relatively 'hidden' and intangible harm, and its effects on families specifically, are not key priorities for clinicians, researchers or policy makers. We call for future evaluations of the 5-step intervention and other family interventions in clinical settings to test their feasibility and effectiveness. Entirely aware of the resource restrictions and competing priorities in the health sector currently, we acknowledge that the road ahead to address this 'hidden harm' may be long and arduous, but that is no excuse not to start the journey.

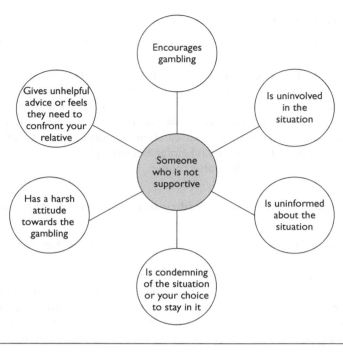

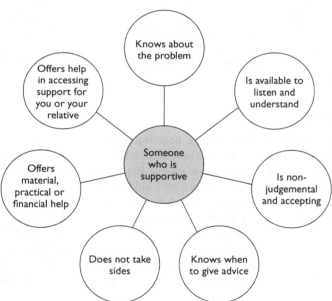

Figure 12.2 Types of support and their key features.

Key points

1 The 5-step family intervention offers considerable promise for those affected by their loved one's gambling.
2 Further systematic research needs to be done to establish the effectiveness of the 5-step method in families of problem gamblers.

References

Copello, A., Ibanga, A., Orford, J., Templeton, L. & Velleman, R. (2010). An introduction to the supplement. *Drugs: Education, Prevention and Policy*, 17(S1):6–7.

Copello, A., Bowden-Jones, H., Cousins, J., Orford & J., George, S. (2012). *Gambling, the Family and You: A Self-help Handbook for Family Members*. The National Problem Gambling Clinic and the UK ADF Research Group.

Krishnan, M. & Orford, J. (2002). Gambling and the family from the stress-coping support perspective. *International Gambling Studies*, 2, 61–83.

Lee, B. K. (2009). Congruence Couple Therapy for pathological gambling. *International Journal of Mental Health and Addiction*, 7(1).

Lobsinger, C. & Beckett, L. (1996). *Odds on the Break-even: A Practical Approach to Gambling Awareness*. Canberra: Relationships Australia, Inc.

Makarchuck, K., Hodgins, D. C. & Peden, N. (2002). Development of a brief intervention for concerned significant others of problem gamblers. *Addictive Disorders and Their Treatment*, 1:126–34.

Chapter 13

Women and gambling

Jasbir Dhillon

Aims

1   To explore the research available on the prevalence, profile and experience of women gamblers.
2   To discuss the treatment needs and treatments currently available for women gamblers.

Introduction

Traditionally gambling has been viewed as a male activity, with problem gamblers being identified as dominantly male. Over the last 30 years, however, research has seen changes in the gambling environment, finding an increase in women gamblers, and women problem gamblers. There is little gender specific research in the UK and internationally, however this chapter endeavours to briefly explore the research currently available on the prevalence, profile and experience of women gamblers. This chapter will also discuss the treatment needs of women gamblers, and the treatments available for women at the National Problem Gambling Clinic in London.

Prevalence

The British Gambling Prevalence Survey reports that around 451,000 adults are classified as problem gamblers (Wardle et al., 2010). The typical problem gambler identified by the National Problem Gambling Clinic is a high-functioning white-collar male in his thirties (National Problem Gambling Clinic, 2009). Although men were found to be more likely to gamble than women (75% for men and 71% for women), the British Gambling Prevalence Survey found that gambling amongst women was on the increase (65% in 2007 and 71% in 2010).

An increased prevalence of past-year gambling among women gamblers was found specifically for the use of slot machines, betting on horse races, buying scratch cards and taking part in other lotteries. The same survey also reported an increase in online casino, bingo and online slot-machine gambling between 2007 and 2010, with this increase being greater in women than men. Women have also been found to participate in a lesser number of gambling activities than men (Sproston et al., 2000; Wardle et al., 2010).

Demographic information

A higher prevalence of gambling was found between the age ranges of 16 and 24 in women by the British Gambling Prevalence Survey 2010. Men however, have been found to have an earlier age of onset for gambling behaviour (Grant & Kim, 2002). DSM-IV notes that 'Pathological gambling typically begins in early adolescence in males and later in life in females' (APA, 1994). Women problem gamblers have been found to progress to pathological gambling sooner after beginning to gamble, which has been described as a 'telescoping effect' (Tavares et al., 2001).

Gambling preferences

Women gamblers have been found to engage more frequently in gambling activities such as scratch cards and bingo (Hing & Breen, 2001; Wardle et al., 2010), and a review showed that women were at least twice as likely to be involved in bingo playing than men (Griffiths & Bingham, 2002). In a national survey carried out amongst 7166 bingo players in clubs throughout the UK, it was found that the clientele of commercial bingo was overwhelmingly female (85%) (Dixey, 1987), with a recent study also finding that 86% of respondents in a convenience sample were women (Griffiths & Bingham, 2002). Bingo gamblers have also described the activity as more of a woman's game (24%) than a man's game (4%). Qualitative research suggests that gambling activities such as bingo and national lottery play are not seen as being at odds with perceptions of 'responsible' womanly behaviour (Casey, 2003). Bingo and lottery players are also able to restrict how much they spend prior to taking part in the activity, making it possible for women gamblers to build a 'suitable' gambling space for themselves, also allowing their gambling to fit into the 'economic constraints of their lives'. The Australian Productivity Commission (1999) discussed the influence of the availability and social acceptance of different types of gambling for men and women, and have suggested that gambling preferences are culturally based.

Feminisation of gambling

Gambling has traditionally been perceived as a male activity, however, researchers have reported on the increasing 'feminisation of gambling' (Volberg, 2001), stating that gambling sources have slowly changed and become more gender-neutral (Griffiths, 2011). Due to technological developments and newer forms of gambling such as online gambling, more appealing sources and opportunities to gamble are now available. Women gamblers have described online gambling as less intimidating and stigmatising, and more anonymous and safe, in comparison to gambling in a venue such as a bookmakers (Griffiths, 2001), suggesting that Internet gambling is perceived as a more accessible source of gambling for women gamblers. Studies from outside the UK also report that machine gambling has increasingly become a problem for women however (Trevorrow & Moore, 1998), and studies predict that the prevalence of gambling, and problem gambling in women will increase (Potenza et al., 2001).

Why women gamble

Both men and women were most likely to report gambling for excitement or to make money, according to the British Gambling Prevalence Study 2010. The study also found that for both male and female gamblers the least-endorsed reasons for gambling were to impress others, relieve tension or to compete with others. Studies from outside the UK report that for some women problem gamblers, loneliness is a major trigger to gamble (Grant & Kim, 2002), as well as boredom and depression (Hraba & Lee, 1996; Ohtsuka et al., 1995) and to escape negative affective states (Beaudoin & Cox, 1999; Ladd & Petry, 2002) or take an emotional 'time out' (Brown & Coventry, 1997).

Research further suggests that women who live 'unconventional lifestyles' may experience boredom, depression and frustration, leading to their 'integration into a social world of gambling'.

Research has also found that women gamblers may use gambling as a way of escaping personal and social pressures (Lesieur, 1993; Lesieur & Rosenthal, 1991; Schull, 2002). Some studies suggest that women may gamble specifically to escape from their care-giving role, using gambling as a way of coping with anxiety and tension from excess relational demands in the workplace and socially. One early study stated that the 'demand to be superwomen, juggling family and career, has created a whole new set of problems for women who feel that they should, but do not, measure up' (Greenspan, 1983), with gambling possibly becoming a mechanism for some women gamblers to escape from these 'excess demands and responsibilities' (Schull, 2002).

Impact of gambling

A recent study examining gender differences in online gamblers found that women gamblers experienced online gambling differently to men, and reported increased feelings of guilt and shame for gambling (McCormack et al., 2012), and over spending money (Lesieur & Blume, 1991). Women gamblers are also more likely than men to report anxiety and suicide attempts, or suicidal ideation, attributed to gambling (Boughton & Brewster, 2002; Potenza et al., 2001; Shaffer et al., 2002) and depression (Boughton & Brewster, 2002). Gambling has also been reported to have a negative impact on relationships, with women reporting loss of trust and respect, breaking promises, arguments and having to lie or manipulate others (Boughton & Brewster, 2002).

Psychiatric co-morbidities

Depression, anxiety and alcohol and prescription drug misuse have been found to be common psychiatric co-morbid disorders in women gamblers (Ibáñez et al., 2003; Specker et al., 1996; Westphal and Johnson, 2003). One study also found a stronger association between symptoms of problem gambling and dysthymia, panic disorder and nicotine dependence in women (Desai & Potenza, 2007). Alcohol and drug use and disordered eating have also been found to occur at higher rates in women problem gamblers in comparison to the general female population (Boughton & Falenchuk, 2007).

Given below are some gender-specific issues to hold in mind during the assessment and treatment of women gamblers (George et al., 2011).

- Prevalence of gambling is slightly lower among women but the gender gap is narrowing.
- Women gamblers prefer fruit/slot machines and bingo, whereas men prefer card games and sport-related gambling activities.
- Women start gambling later than men.
- Although women initiate gambling later than men, they develop gambling-related problems sooner, referred to as the 'telescoping effect'.
- When asked the reasons for gambling, women report gambling to 'escape' from problems, whereas men say it is for the thrill and excitement.
- Women gamblers tend to have higher rates of co-existing psychiatric disorders such as depression and anxiety.
- As a result of their gambling, women tend to have more financial problems, whereas men report more legal problems.
- Women are more likely to present with emotional issues, whereas men present with employment and legal issues.
- Women are under-represented in gambling treatment programmes.
- Women often find it harder to access gambling treatment services (because of limited choice of female workers, opening hours not suiting child care, lack of specialised services for women, etc.).
- Women are more reluctant to seek help because of feelings of shame, guilt, fear of children being 'taken away', etc.
- Increased likelihood of domestic violence.
- Impact on children.

Figure 13.1 The woman gambler: summary of gender-specific issues.

Treatment

What we know so far

Addiction research has demonstrated that women have unique cultural and gender characteristics that can be best addressed in gender-specific treatment (Currie, 2001). One meta-analysis of 20 studies of group treatment and found that women show lower levels of discussion and participation during group treatment when they are treated alongside men (Currie, 2001). There is a lack of research exploring gender-specific treatments in the field of gambling addiction (Grant & Potenza, 2004), and no studies from the UK exist to provide effectiveness of specific interventions in the treatment of women problem gamblers.

One Canadian qualitative study of 14 women with problem gambling identified that the following contributed to effective practice in the treatment of women problem gamblers: group accessibility, providing gender-specific groups and having a specific treatment format followed during group meetings (Piquette-Tomei et al., 2008). This study found that evening groups, within a closed environment where confidentiality was consistently reinforced and an all-female environment is maintained, were favoured. Participants also suggested that groups with a specific format that included psychoeducational presentations, and guest speakers on topics alongside methods to journal their recovery process would be helpful. Barriers to treatment identified included: personal issues (e.g. guilt/shame), inter-personal issues (justifying absence to attend treatment to partner/family) and finding treatment that allows them to feel valued.

Some evidence has also been demonstrated regarding the usefulness of women-only treatment groups more generally, with women being found to experience increased self-esteem and personal power (Wilke, 1994). Traditional mixed-sex group-based support methods, such as Gamblers Anonymous (GA) groups, may not always feel helpful or accessible to women gamblers. An early study made the assumption that the lack of women attendees at Gamblers Anonymous sessions suggested that women were significantly less likely to be compulsive gamblers (Livingston, 1974). A recent case study, however, suggests that too few female attendees at GA meetings may lead to new women group members ceasing to attend, due to a feeling of psychological isolation and being unable to relate to group members (Griffiths, 2003). It is noted, however, that as a case study these results are not generalisable to all women gamblers, and further research engaging a larger sample of women gamblers is necessary.

Gender-specific treatments currently available in the UK

The National Problem Gambling Clinic piloted a treatment pathway specifically for women at the beginning of 2012 for six months. The clinic began providing its traditional cognitive-behavioural-therapy-based treatment to women gamblers in an individual format, as well as providing it in a new group-based session to explore and understand their gambling, with a view to using this exploration to help them reduce or cease their gambling behaviour.

The individual treatment provided clients with four sessions to cover practical strategies to help restrict their access to gambling opportunities and access to money, with the remaining three sessions providing clients with a space to cover the areas of their gambling they struggled with the most (e.g. cravings, thoughts about gambling). The group session was run on a weekly basis, at a fixed time and location, with the group being a female-only space. All parts of the treatment pathway were facilitated by female therapists, including individual and group-based intervention. Each session began with an opportunity for clients to inform the group about their week, and ended with clients being given a chance to 'check-out' and discuss their experience of the session. Each weekly session had no particular topic or format, with material or topics for discussions brought to the group by clients. Topics and issues discussed during the group included conflict within relationships, difficulties communicating emotions and difficult feelings such as loneliness or a lack of belonging.

Gambling behaviour was tracked using a self-report measure developed by the service, which was given to clients for completion every four weeks. Clients also completed a Treatment Outcome Profile (TOP), an outcome measure commonly used to assess outcomes in the drug-using population, at the beginning and end of individual treatment, and at three- and six-month follow up. Due to inconsistent attendance at the group sessions, and low numbers of attendees, reliable quantitative data were not available to analyse treatment efficacy. Changes were made to the treatment pathway for women following a review of the pilot stage.

The National Problem Gambling Clinic now has a treatment pathway for women, consisting of a weekly group-based treatment for women, based on the clinic's traditional cognitive-behavioural treatment, but with the addition of emotional regulation techniques. Cognitive-behavioural-therapy-based treatment is provided in a psychoeducational group format over eight weeks, in order to teach clients self-management techniques, as well as provide them a space to be supported, and to discuss and learn from their peers. This treatment programme supports its female clients to use practical strategies to manage their thoughts and behaviours, as well as learn emotional regulation techniques, which have been found to be helpful in the treatment of other addictive problem behaviours (Axelrod et al., 2011; Azizi et al., 2010; Berking et al., 2011). The group continues to be run by experienced female psychologists, creating a safe female-friendly environment for clients. It is not yet possible to assess the efficacy of this women's treatment group for gambling treatment and client satisfaction, due to the limited data collected as yet.

Suggestions for future research

Mark and Lesieur (1992) reviewed diverse topics concerning problem gamblers for its gender-related content and found a male bias in research, with the gender of respondents and gender-related findings not being examined or discussed. As a result of this bias, assumptions have been made about women gamblers (Casey, 2003), from existing research using predominantly male samples. Researchers need to remain vigilant to ensure that women are included in numbers which are sufficient for data analysis, as women continue to be under-represented by research samples (NRC, 1999), making it difficult to gain meaningful and representative information about women gamblers.

It is predicted that due to increased accessibility to gambling, and gambling sources creating more appealing and female-friendly gambling environments, the number of women who gamble and experience problems with their gambling will increase. More gender-specific gambling research is now necessary to develop a better understanding of women gamblers and the treatment needs of women problem gamblers, in order for clinicians to begin building helpful and effective interventions for female clients.

Key points

1   There has been an increase in the prevalence of past-year gambling among women gamblers, specifically for the use of slot machines, betting on horse races, buying scratch cards and taking part in other lotteries.
2   Triggers for gambling in women include boredom, loneliness, negative affective states and 'escapism'.
3   Women find it more difficult to access gambling treatment programs and are under-represented in such programs.
4   Despite some evidence to support gender-specific treatment programs, there are very few such facilities available.

References

American Psychiatric Association (APA) (1994). *Diagnostic and Statistical Manual of Mental Disorders (4th edn)*. Washington, DC: American Psychiatric Association.
Australian Productivity Commission (1999). Australia's Gambling Industries: Draft Report. Cited in N. Hing & H. Breen (2001), Profiling lady luck: an empirical study of gambling and problem gambling amongst female club members. *Journal of Gambling Studies*, 17(1):47–69.
Axelrod, S. R., Perepletchikova, F., Holtzman, K. & Sinha, R. (2011). Emotion regulation and substance use frequency in women with substance dependence and borderline personality disorder receiving dialectical behaviour therapy. *American Journal of Drug and Alcohol Abuse*, 37(1):37–42.
Azizi, A., Borjali, A. & Golzari, M. (2010). The effectiveness of emotion regulation training and cognitive therapy on the emotional and addictional problems of substance abusers. *Iranian Journal of Psychiatry*, 5(2):60–65.

Beaudoin, C. & Cox, B. J. (1999). Characteristics of problem gambling in a Canadian context: a preliminary study. Cited in N. Piquette-Tomei, E. Norman, S. S. Dwyer & E. McCaslin (2008). Group therapy for women problem gamblers: a space of their own. *Journal of Gambling*, 22.

Berking, M., Margraf, M., Ebert, D., Wupperman, P., Hofmann, S. G. & Junghanns, K. (2011). Deficits in emotion-regulation skills predict alcohol use during and after cognitive-behavioral therapy for alcohol dependence. *Journal of Consulting and Clinical Psychology*, 79(3):307–18.

Boughton, R. & Brewster, J. (2002). *Voices of Women Who Gamble in Ontario: A Survey of Women's Gambling, Barriers to Treatment and Treatment Service Needs.* Toronto: Ontario Ministry of Health and Long-Term Care. Retrieved 2 October 2012 from http://www.gamblingresearch.org/contentdetails.sz?cid=2375.

Boughton, R. & Falenchuk, O. (2007). Vulnerability and co-morbidity factors of female problem gambling. *Journal of Gambling Studies*, 23(3):323–34.

Brown, S. & Coventry, L. (1997). Queen of Hearts: the needs of women with gambling problems. Cited in N. Hing & H. Breen (2001), Profiling lady luck: an empirical study of gambling and problem gambling amongst female club members. *Journal of Gambling Studies*, 17(1):47–69.

Casey, E. (2003). Gambling and consumption: working-class women and UK National Lottery play. *Journal of Consumer Culture*, 3:245.

Currie, J. (2001). Best practices: treatment and rehabilitation for women with substance use problems. Ottawa, Ontario: Health Canada. Retrieved 15 April 2005 from http://www.hc-sc.gc.ca/hl-vs/alt_formats/hecs-sesc/pdf/pubs/adp-apd/bp_womenmp_femmes/women-e.pdf.

Desai, R.A. & Potenza, M. N. (2007). Gender differences in the associations between past-year gambling problems and psychiatric disorders. *Social Psychiatry and Psychiatric Epidemiology*, 43:173–83.

Dixey, R. (1987). It's a great feeling when you win: women and bingo. *Leisure studies*, 6:199–214.

George, S., Ekhthari, H. & Bowden-Jones, H. (2011). Gambling addiction in women. *MIMS Women's Health*, 6(3):43–5.

Grant, J. E. & Kim, S. W. (2002). Gender differences in pathological gamblers seeking medication treatment. *Comprehensive Psychiatry*, 43, 56–62.

Grant, J. E. & Potenza, M. N. (2004). Pathological gambling: a clinical guide to treatment. Cited in N. Piquette-Tomei, E. Norman, S. S. Dwyer & E. McCaslin (2008). Group therapy for women problem gamblers: a space of their own. *Journal of Gambling*, 22 December.

Greenspan, M. (1983). A new approach to women and therapy. Cited in R. Boughton (2003). A feminist slant on counselling the female gambler: key issues and tasks. *eGambling: The Electronic Journal of Gambling Issues*, 8.

Griffiths, M. D. (2001). Internet gambling: preliminary results of the first UK prevalence study. *Journal of Gambling Issues*, 5.

Griffiths, M. D. (2003). Fruit machine addiction in females: a case study. *Journal of Gambling Issues*, 8. Retrieved on 31 October 2010 from http://www.camh.net/egambling/issue8/clinic/griffiths/index.html.

Griffiths, M. D. (2011). Technological trends and the psychosocial impact on gambling. *Casino and Gaming International*, 7(1):77–80.

Griffiths, M.D. & Bingham, C. (2002). Bingo playing in the UK: the influence of demographic factors on play. *International Gambling Studies*, 2:51–60.

Hing, N. & Breen, H. (2001). Profiling lady luck: an empirical study of gambling and problem gambling amongst female club members. *Journal of Gambling Studies*, 17(1):47–69.

Hraba, J. & Lee, G. (1996). Gender, gambling and problem gambling. *Journal of Gambling Studies*, 12(1):83–101.

Ibáñez, A., Blanco, C., Moreryra, P. & Saiz-Ruiz, J. (2003). Gender differences in pathological gambling. *Journal of Clinical Psychiatry*, 64(3):295–301.

Ladd, G. T. & Petry, N. M. (2002). Gender differences among pathological gamblers seeking treatment. *Experimental and Clinical Psychopharmacology*, 10(3):302–9.

Lesieur, H. R. (1993). 'Female pathological gamblers and crime', gambling behaviour and problem gambling. Cited in N. Hing & H. Breen (2001). Profiling lady luck: an empirical study of gambling and problem gambling amongst female club members. *Journal of Gambling Studies*, 17(1):47–69.

Lesieur, H. R. & Blume, S. B. (1991). When lady luck loses: women and compulsive gambling. In N. Van Den Bergh (ed.), *Feminist Perspectives on Addiction*, pp. 181–197. New York: Springer Publishing.

Lesieur, H. R. & Rosenthal, R. J. (1991). Pathological gambling: a review of the literature (prepared for the American Psychiatric Association Task Force on DSM-IV committee on disorders of impulse control). *Journal of Gambling Studies*, 7:5–39.

Livingston, J. (1974). Compulsive gamblers: observations on action and abstinence. Cited in M. E. Mark & H. R. Lesieur (1992). A feminist critique of problem gambling research. *British Journal of Addiction*, 87:549–65.

Mark, M. E. & Lesieur, H. R. (1992). A feminist critique of problem gambling research. *British Journal of Addiction*, 87:549–65.

McCormack, A., Shorter, G. W. & Griffiths, M. D. (2012). An empirical study of gender differences in online gambling. *Journal of Gambling Studies*, 25 October.

National Problem Gambling Clinic (2009). Problem gamblers in the UK are white-collar males in mid-30s. *Problem Gambling Addiction*. Retrieved from http://problem gamblingaddiction.com/gambling-addiction/problem-gamblers-in-the-uk-arewhite -collar-males-in-mid-30s/.

National Research Council (NRC), National Academy of Sciences, Committee on the Social and Economic Impact of Pathological Gambling (1999). *Pathological Gambling: A Critical Review*. Washington, DC: National Academy Press.

Ohtsuka, K., Bruton, E., Borg, V., DeLuca, L. & Imms, T. (1995). Gender differences in pathological gamblers using gaming machines. Cited in N. Hing & H. Breen (2001). Profiling lady luck: an empirical study of gambling and problem gambling amongst female club members. *Journal of Gambling Studies*, 17(1):47–69.

Piquette-Tomei, N., Norman, E., Dwyer, S. S. & McCaslin, E. (2008). Group therapy for women problem gamblers: a space of their own. *Journal of Gambling Issues*, 22 December.

Potenza, M. N., Steinberg, M. A., McLaughlin, S. D., Wu, R., Rounsaville, B. J. & O'Malley, S. S. (2001). Gender-related differences in the characteristics of problem gamblers using a gambling helpline. *International Journal of Psychiatry*, 158(9):1500–05.

Schull, S. D. (2002). Escape mechanism: women, caretaking, and compulsive machine gambling. Center for Working Families. Cited in N. Piquette-Tomei, E. Norman, S. S.

Dwyer & E. McCaslin (2008). Group therapy for women problem gamblers: a space of their own. *Journal of Gambling Issues*, 22 December.

Shaffer, H. J., LaBrie, R. A., LaPlante, D. A. & Kidman, R. C. (2002). The Iowa Department of Public Health Gambling Treatment Services: Four Years of Evidence (Technical Report #101102-200). Boston: Harvard Medical School. Retreived on 31 October 2010 from www.1800betsoff.org/common/pdf/Iowa_harvard_report.pdf.

Specker, S. M., Carlson, G. A., Edmonson, K. M., Johnson, P. E. & Marcotte, M. (1996). Psychopathology in pathological gamblers seeking treatment. *Journal of Gambling Studies*, 12(1):67–81.

Sproston, K., Erens, B. & Orford, J. (2000). *Gambling Behaviour in Britain, Results from the British Gambling Prevalence Survey.* London: National Centre For Social Research.

Tavares, H., Zilberman, M., Beites, F. & Gentil, V. (2001). Gender differences in gambling progression. *Journal of Gambling Studies*, 17(2):151–9.

Trevorrow, K. & Moore, S. (1998). The association between loneliness, social isolation and women's electronic gaming machine gambling, *Journal of Gambling Studies*, 14:263–84.

Volberg, R. A. (2001). When the chips are down: problem gambling in America. Cited in M. D. Griffiths (2007). Gambling addiction in the UK. In K. Gyngell (ed.), *Breakthrough Britain: Ending the Costs of Social Breakdown*, pp. 393–426. London: Social Justice Policy Group.

Wardle, H., Moody, A., Spence, S., Orford, J., Volberg, R., Jotangia, D., Griffiths, M., Hussey, D. & Dobbie, F. (2010). The British Gambling Prevalence Survey 2010. Retrieved on 31 October 2010 from http://www.gamblingcommission.gov.uk/PDF/British%20Gambling%20Prevalence%20Survey%202010.pdf.

Westphal, J. & Johnson, J. (2003). Gender differences in psychiatric comorbidity and treatment seeking among gamblers in treatment. *eGambling: The Electronic Journal of Gambling Issues*, 8.

Wilke, D. (1994). Women and alcoholism: how a male-as-norm bias affects research, assessment and treatment. *Health & Social Work*, 19(1):29–35.

Chapter 14

Young people and problem gambling

Xenia Anastassiou-Hadjicharalambous and Cecilia A. Essau

Aims

1 To look at some of the risk factors for problem gambling in young people.
2 To discuss some of the gambling assessment tools used in young people.
3 To discuss some key prevention and treatment strategies.

Introduction

Problem gambling has, over the last few years, started to be recognised as a major public-health problem with debilitating effects on the affected individuals, their families and society. Gambling Disorder, as determined by the most recent revision of DSM (Diagnostic and Statistical Manual of Mental Disorders, DSM-5), is characterised by persistent and recurrent problematic gambling behaviour leading to clinically significant impairment or distress (APA, 2013). It has been documented to be associated with other psychiatric conditions, and to significantly impact on the quality of life, psychosocial impairment and suicidality. Of greater societal concern is the problem/pathological gambling in children and youth. Research on gambling in young people has revealed that they start engaging in gambling as young as nine years of age (Derevensky & Gupta, 2004). The types of gambling that were reported by young respondents included card playing, lottery-ticket purchasing, bingo playing and wagering on their own video games. Of major concern are the more recent forms of electronic gambling including electronic gambling machines, and gambling on the Internet and mobile phone.

Prevalence rates of gambling in young people are very difficult to establish and vary depending upon availability of gambling venues and age prerequisites. Studies conducted in America, Canada, Australia and Europe (e.g. Becona, 1997; Clarke & Rossen, 2000; Dickson et al., 2002; Fisher, 1999; Griffiths, 1995; Gupta & Derevensky, 1998; Jacobs, 2004; Johanson, & Götestam, 2003; Lupu et al., 2002; Olason et al., 2006a, 2006b; Wood & Griffiths, 2004) have documented that 60-80% of youth aged 13–17 are involved in some form of gambling at least once a year. More worrying is the 3% to 6% of youth aged 13–17, that the majority of investigations documented to be systematically involved in gambling and to display pathological characteristics similar to adult pathological gamblers (e.g. Clarke & Rossen, 2000; Dickson et al., 2002; Griffiths, 1995; Fisher, 1999; Gupta & Derevensky, 1998; Jacobs, 2004; Skokauskas & Satkeviciute, 2007). These characteristics include extreme preoccupation with gambling, chasing after losses, lying to parents and peers, neglecting school, etc.

Risk factors and etiological perspective

A variety of risk factors have been documented to be associated with – but not restricted to – pathological gambling in youth. These risk factors refer to personality attributes, as well as environmental characteristics, and situational variables. Common factors identified in empirical literature are: low impulse control, depression, low self-esteem, history of physical and sexual abuse, parenting style characterised by low levels of parental bonding, monitoring and supervision, learning difficulties and lack of connection to school community (Derevensky & Gupta, 2004; Dickson et al., 2004). These risk factors have been documented to be quite common not only in gambling, but also in other high-risk behaviours. Additionally, factors more specific to adolescent gambling have been reported to be parental addiction, parental and community norms that enable access to gambling venues, specific personality traits such as low conformity and low self-discipline, boredom susceptibility, cheerfulness and excitability (Gupta et al., 2006). Gambling in adolescence has further been reported to be correlated with other high-risk behaviours such as smoking, alcohol abuse and drug abuse (Potenza et al., 2000).

Alternatively, it has been argued that gambling in youth is the result of extreme levels of stress deriving from the inability to cope with adverse life events (Jacobs, 1987). As per this account, gambling is considered a maladaptive way of coping with these adverse life events (Bergevin et al., 2006).

Assessment

A comprehensive assessment will enable the clinician with sufficient information to prepare an effective treatment plan, and for this the following elements are vital: perinatal and developmental history, medical history, comprehensive mental state examination, family psychiatric history, detailed psychiatric history including elaborate history of the presenting problem and other co-morbid conditions (i.e. detailed assessment of Axis I and Axis II co-morbid conditions, including substance abuse disorders that are often co-morbid with gambling), and assessment of suicide risk. Critical to the treatment plan, is the detailed history of the presenting problem – i.e. gambling. This should include information on the kind of gambling that the young person is involved in, when it started and under what conditions, what were the possible factors related to the initiation, how it developed, what factors maintain it, how often it takes place, how severe it is (as reflected in how much money is spent and how dependent the young gambler is) and so on.

Several assessment tools have been specifically adapted or developed for adolescent gambling research, clinical use and treatment planning. The Teen-Addiction Severity Index (T-ASI) is a 133-item interview (Kaminer et al., 1993) which takes approximately 30 minutes to complete and is administered by a trained mental health professional. The T-ASI is an age-appropriate modification of the Addiction Severity Index for Pathological Gamblers (ASI-PG) (Lesieur & Blume, 1992), which taps gambling severity as reflected in gambling frequency on a number of different gambling activities, and problems associated with gambling. The T-ASI rates six domains: psychoactive substance abuse, school or employment status, family functioning, peer and social relationships, legal status and psychiatric status. It has demonstrated a consistency reliability of .78.

The South Oaks Gambling Screen – Revised for Adolescents (SOGS-RA) (Winters et al., 1993, 1995) is the most widely utilised adolescent-gambling screen. It is a revised version of SOGS (Lesieur & Blume, 1987) and was designed in order to more accurately assess adolescent gambling problems. It is a 16-item scale assessing gambling behaviours and gambling-related problems. SOGS-RA scaled items assess negative behaviours and feelings as a result of gambling involvement. The items include lying about gambling, gambling more than planned, conflict with family and friends, and borrowing/stealing to gamble in the last 12 months. The internal consistency reliability of the SOGS-RA was reported to be .80 (Poulin, 2002). Reviews of the assessment instruments of gambling literature (Ladouceur et al., 2000; Rossen, 2001; Wiebe et al., 2000) have identified a number of issues with it. Firstly, because the rate and severity of gambling in females is relatively low, the psychometric properties could not be determined for females in the original testing. Secondly, items do not contribute equally to the total score, and in effect the items that are better indicators of problem gambling, should be more heavily weighed. Thirdly, the instrument should not be used for children under the age of 11 since prior to this age children do not cognitively apprehend the meaning of items (Ladouceur et al., 2000). Finally, preoccupation with gambling is not adequately addressed when clinical practice has documented that the preoccupation needs to be incorporated in every gambling screen.

The Diagnostic and Statistical Manual-IV Multiple Response Adapted for Juveniles (DSM-IV-J) (Fisher, 2000b) is a 12-item screen for measuring 'pathological' gambling during adolescence. It is modelled after the DSM-IV criteria for diagnosis of adult 'pathological' gambling. The DSM-IV-MR-J assesses a number of important variables related to pathological gambling: progression and preoccupation, tolerance, withdrawal and loss of control, escape, chasing, lies and deception, illegal activities, and family and school disruption. Internal consistency reliability for this scale has been reported to be .78. It has further discriminated between social and pathological gamblers, thus presenting good construct validity. The weakness of this assessment tool is that it does not have adequate data on validity and has not been widely used in gambling literature, nor in large-scale studies.

The Gamblers Anonymous 20 Questions (GA-20) (Gamblers Anonymous, 2005) is a brief screening instrument that is primarily used to help gamblers and their families to assess the existence and severity of a gambling problem. In a study designed to compare the GA-20, the DSM-IV-MR-J, the SOGS-RA and a questionnaire assessing gambling behaviour in the youth, it was found that the DSM-IV-MR-J was the most stringent gambling screen, while the GA-20 was the least conservative, in classifying more adolescents as having higher levels of problematic behaviour than the other two screens (Derevensky & Gupta, 2000). One further finding worth noticing from this comparative study was that while DSM-IV-J, SOGS-RA and GA-20 identified between 3.4% and 5.8% of participants as probable pathological gamblers, only 1.1% of individuals classified themselves as such. The authors concluded that it seems that either youth underestimate the severity of their gambling problems, or the gambling screens overestimate prevalence rates.

The Gambling Expectancy Questionnaire (GEQ) (Gillespie et al., 2007) is a 23-item instrument designated to assess the influence of outcome expectancies on gambling behaviour. The GEQ consists of three positive expectancy scales (enjoyment/arousal, self-enhancement, money) and two negative expectancy scales (over-involvement, emotional impact). Internal consistency of each of the five factors of this gambling expectancy instrument was reported to be adequate to good (enjoyment/arousal $\alpha = .86$, over involvement $\alpha = .91$; self-enhancement $\alpha = .81$; emotional impact $\alpha = .85$; and money $\alpha = .78$).

Prevention

Evidence pertaining to prevention of gambling in youth mostly relies on the empirical literature and theoretical formulations extrapolated from other addictive and high-risk behaviours. Many prevention experts have argued for the development of intervention strategies that address multiple high-risk behaviours (see Derevensky et al., 2004). At the level of primary prevention, efforts have focused on avoiding, or delaying the onset of gambling-related behaviours. These efforts have been particularly important, given the empirical evidence suggesting that the younger the age of onset in pathological gamblers, the greater the impairment (Dickson et al., 2004; Jacobs, 2004). Whether indeed the traditional aim of primary prevention aiming to no gambling in youth is plausible, has been a theme of debate for many years in the field of gambling. It has been argued that provided a substantial number of youth (70%–80%) report having engaged in some form of gambling from a very early age, the most logical approach would be the adoption of a harm-reduction strategy in those adolescents who have already engaged in gambling, rather than attempts to eliminate gambling (Dickson et el., 2004). It has been considered unrealistic to expect these adolescents to stop gambling completely, given that despite in the underage youth access is prohibited to government-controlled gambling forms and venues, adolescents still have easy access to gambling activities organised among peers and family members (Jacobs, 2000, 2004). Harm-reduction strategies in those adolescents who already have engaged in some form of gambling include psychoeducation on the risks of excessive gambling, promotion of responsible behaviour, altering misperceptions and beliefs and enhancing self-control techniques (Gupta & Derevensky, 2008). Considering that in many societies various forms of gambling are socially acceptable, the employment of harm-reduction strategies for those youths who are already engaged in some forms of gambling has been considered more promising by several, but not all, gambling experts (for a discussion see Gupta & Derevensky, 2008).

Treatment

Here, treatment paradigms for adults have been extrapolated to young people. These treatment paradigms are based on the following models: psychoanalytic or psychodynamic (e.g. Rosenthal, 1987), behavioral (e.g. Blaszczynski & Silove, 1995), cognitive and cognitive-behavioral (e.g. Ladouceur & Walker, 1998), pharmacological (e.g. Grant et al., 2003), physiological (Carlton & Goldstein, 1987), biological/genetic (e.g. Hollander et al. 1992), addiction-based (e.g. Lesieur & Blume, 1991), and self-help (e.g. Brown, 1987) (for comprehensive review of these models see Griffiths, 1995; Rugle et al., 2001).

Case reports of young pathological gamblers provide a clinical picture of young gamblers, and are not just based on mistaken beliefs and desire to get money (Gupta & Derevensky, 2008). The clinical picture of the affected youth is much more complicated, and it is typically underpinned by physiological substrates (i.e. abnormal resting physiological state that predisposes them to addictive behaviours). Further, it is often co-morbid with other addictive disorders, depression, anxiety, and higher levels of dissociation when gambling (Gupta & Derevensky, 2008).

Most young gamblers are neither referred to, nor do they seek treatment. This failure to seek treatment is related to a diverse set of factors. Certain affected adolescents are characterised by fear of stigmatisation; others perceive themselves as invulnerable, and in effect do not perceive their gambling behaviour as problematic; and some others believe in spontaneous remission (see Derevensky & Gupta, 2004). Given the small number of young gamblers who are referred to or seek treatment, the empirical data on treatment efficacy are scarce. In effect, it is very hard to develop *empirically validated treatment designs* (Toneatto & Ladouceur, 2003). The rigorous criteria for *empirically validated treatment designs* incorporate randomisation of participants into treatment conditions, replicability of findings, inclusion of matched control group, and utilisation of adequate number of participants for sufficient statistical power.

In one of the few empirically-based treatment studies, Ladouceur and colleagues (Ladouceur et al., 1994) studied four adolescent pathological gamblers, using a cognitive-behavioural paradigm. This paradigm postulates that the persistence patterns of gambling in the pathological gamblers can be explained by the erroneous belief that they will recover their losses. This erroneous belief is underpinned by lack of understanding of independence of events, perceived level of skilfulness in predicting the outcome of chance events, and illusions of control (Ladouceur & Walker, 1998). The treatment components of the Ladouceur et al. (1994) program were: psychoeducation, cognitive interventions, problem-solving, social-skills training and relapse prevention. It consisted of 17 individual sessions that resulted in significant gains across the three adolescents who remained abstinent six months post intervention.

More recently, Gupta and Derevensky, over a period of eight years, developed the McGill Treatment Paradigm (see Gupta & Derevensky, 2000, 2004). Treatment goals of this paradigm included: understanding the motives for gambling, analysing the gambling episodes, establishing a baseline of gambling behaviour and encouraging decrease, challenging cognitive distortions, determining the underlying causes of stress and anxiety, evaluating and improving coping abilities, restoring interpersonal relations, restructuring free time, developing effective money-management skills, and relapse prevention. The McGill Treatment Paradigm was tested empirically on over 60 young pathological gamblers aged 14 to 21, with significant gains as reflected in self-reports of abstinence and psychological wellbeing in general.

However, despite these significant gains in treatment studies, the treatment of young gamblers with multiple addictions coupled with multiple co-morbid conditions is yet a major treatment challenge for clinicians. Young pathological gamblers with co-morbid substance abuse disorders (Ladd & Petry, 2003), anxiety, impulsivity, and depression are treated both for gambling, as well as for their co-morbid conditions, which often complicate treatment, and place greater demands for good treatment outcomes. In the most complex cases where gambling is underpinned by high levels of impulsivity, pharmacotherapy is incorporated in the treatment protocol, intending to reduce the levels of impulsivity in the young pathological gambler. Empirical data have provided corroborative evidence that pharmacotherapy is indeed useful in reducing levels of impulsivity that underpin gambling behaviour (Grant, et al., 2003, 2004).

Brief case studies illustrating diverse profiles of young gamblers

It is crucial for clinicians to understand that young gamblers may present diverse profiles and with diverse developmental trajectories. While empirical data on these diverse trajectories are minimal, the two brief case studies given below aim to illustrate this diversity.

Case study 1

Andreas, an 18-year-old male, primarily gambled on sports and in casinos (spending around €900 per week depending on how much he would win, or obtain from thefts and manipulation). From the clinical interview, further supported by complementary assessment instruments and information derived from significant others, it became clear that Andreas had an extreme preoccupation with gambling, needed to gamble with increasing amounts of money in order to achieve desired excitement, would chase after losses, would steal money from his father, mother and peers, and would manipulate his mother in order to obtain money to gamble. Andreas was a student and he had a lot of absences, and was running the risk of failing. He would work for a few hours a week in his father's company. Motivators of Andreas' gambling were the thrill and adventure that he would find from gambling, accompanied by an erroneous belief that the casino 'owes' him an amount of €30,000 – which he lost while playing and which he would retrieve. In terms of psychiatric co-morbidity, he also suffered from substance abuse disorders, antisocial personality disorder and attention deficit/hyperactivity disorder. Establishing a therapeutic plan for Andreas was a major challenge for the clinician, given the multiple co-morbidities. Therapeutic goals were targeted towards controlling the symptoms of impulsivity. Further, Andreas would show no remorse for stealing and manipulation, and in effect, a major goal of therapy was directed towards these features and the associated psychopathology. The treatment plan also focused on the erroneous belief system underpinning Andreas' problem gambling.

Case study 2

Maria, a 15-year-old female, primarily gambled on sports and in casinos. She gambled until she spent all the money she had available (around €500 per week), and would be preoccupied to chase after losses. Maria had a part-time job, the income of which was solitarily spent on gambling, since she was staying with her family and her expenses were covered. She would regularly take cash advances on her credit card, which would be covered by her father, who was also a problem gambler. As it emerged from the clinical interview, further structured assessments and information gathered from significant others, Maria had long had academic difficulties, and would leave behind schoolwork in order to gamble. As motivators for her gambling, Maria reported it was a way for her to feel special, but, also, to come closer to her father. For Maria, gambling was a means for dealing with anxiety, low self-esteem and depression. She had a history of repeated suicidal ideations. Her mother had a long history of depression. Based upon comprehensive evaluation and identification of Maria's underpinning stressors and unresolved issues, treatment goals were determined. These goals focused on Maria's excessive gambling, alongside addressing depression and anxiety, and improving her coping skills and adaptive behaviour. In addition, it was obvious that family processes through the years were implicated in Maria's gambling behaviour, and so the whole family was referred for family treatment. Maria's treatment process was slow, but after 38 sessions of cognitive-behaviour therapy, significant gains were achieved. This was reflected in her remaining abstinent one and a half years post-intervention.

The diversity in the clinical profile of young gamblers, as illustrated by these case studies, places additional burden on the clinician, since the diversity coupled with co-morbid conditions often complicates treatment.

Conclusion

The fact that the rate of young problem gamblers is greater than that of adult problem gamblers remains a major concern. While aetiology remains unclear, a variety of factors discussed above (i.e. poor impulse control, history of abuse, low levels of parental bonding, monitoring and supervision often associated with parental gambling behaviour, etc.) seem to interact and place vulnerable adolescents at greater risk. For clinicians and researchers it is vital to conceptualise problem gambling in the youth as a heterogeneous entity that is developed and sustained by a complex interplay of a diverse set of multiple biological and psychosocial determinants.

While severe gambling in the youth is assumed to remain relatively small, the short-term and longer-term effects on the affected youth and their families are devastating. Also, new forms of gambling appear, such as Internet gambling, that are much more difficult to control, and more youths are becoming affected, with devastating consequences (Derevensky et al., 2006).

From a public-health/policy perspective, whilst several governments are seeking to restrict Internet gambling, others provide licence, regulate or even operate gambling sites. The fact that gambling is not socially disapproved and that underage youths are exposed through popular media such as TV, mobile phones and the Internet, places the youth at greater risk. Of paramount importance is the adoption of a healthy attitude towards gambling, which will be clear to children from when they are very young. At the level of primary prevention, in the family, issues of parental bonding, as well as monitoring and supervision, need to be addressed. At a more specific level, parental attitude towards gambling needs to be one that does not facilitate underage children to engage in excessive gambling. There are other forms of interesting games that they can entertain their children with, which would not involve gambling, and would not give the message to the developing child that gambling is a positive kind of entertainment.

From a clinical perspective, problem gambling in youth is often referred to as the 'hidden' addiction and it often goes unnoticed by clinicians. It is therefore important that clinicians are encouraged to routinely screen for this condition as part of all psychiatric/psychological assessments. While preliminary research findings provide promising trends in pharmacological and cognitive-behavioural treatments, treatment outcome studies are still in their infancy.

Key points

1   Problem gambling among young people can have devastating consequences on themselves and their families.
2   Particular risk factors for gambling by young people include low impulse control, depression, low self-esteem, history of physical and sexual abuse, parenting style characterised by low levels of parental bonding, monitoring and supervision, learning difficulties, lack of connection to school community, parental addiction, and parental and community norms that enable access to gambling venues.
3   There are several screening and assessment instruments with good reliability and validity.
4   Public-health policy measures should target gambling in young people.
5   Psychological interventions are the mainstay of treating problem gambling in young people.

References

American Psychiatric Association (APA) (2013). *Diagnostic and Statistical Manual of Mental Disorders (5th edition)*. Washington, DC: American Psychiatric Association.

Becona, E. (1997). Pathological gambling in Spanish children and adolescents: an emerging problem. *Psychological Reports*, 81:275–87.

Bergevin, T., Gupta, R., Derevensky, J. & Kaufman, F. (2006). Adolescent gambling: understanding the role of stress and coping. *Journal of Gambling Studies*, 22:195–208.

Blaszczynski, A. P. & Silove, D. (1995). Cognitive and behavioral therapies for pathological gambling. *Journal of Gambling Studies*, 11:195–220.

Brown, R. I. (1987). Dropouts and continuers in gamblers anonymous: IV. Evaluation and summary. *Journal of Gambling Behavior*, 3:202–10.

Carlton, P. L. & Goldstein, L. (1987). Physiological determinants of pathological gambling. In T. Galski (Ed.): *Handbook on Pathological Gambling*. Springfield, IL: Charles C. Thomas.

Clarke, D. & Rossen, F. (2000). Adolescent gambling and problem gambling: a New Zealand study. *New Zealand Journal of Psychology*, 29:10–16.

Derevensky, J. L. & Gupta, R. (2000). Prevalence estimates of adolescent gambling: a comparison of the SOGS-RA, DSM-IV-J and the GA20 questions. *Journal of Gambling Studies*, 16(2–3):227–51.

Derevensky, J. & Gupta, R. (2004). Adolescents with gambling problems: a synopsis of our current knowledge. *e-Gambling: The Electronic Journal of Gambling Issues*, 10:119–40.

Derevensky, J., Gupta, R. & Dickson, L. (2004). Adolescent gambling problems: prevention and treatment implications. In J. E. Grant & M. N. Potenza (eds), *Understanding and Treating Pathological Gambling*, pp. 159–68. Washington, DC: APPI Press.

Derevensky, J., Gupta, R. & McBride, J. (2006). Internet gambling among youth: a cause for concern. Paper presented at the Global Remote and E-Gambling Research Institute Conference, Amsterdam, The Netherlands, August.

Dickson, L., Derevensky, J. L. & Gupta, R. (2002). The prevention of youth gambling problems: a conceptual model. *Journal of Gambling Studies*, 18:161–84.

Dickson, L., Derevensky, J. L. & Gupta, R. (2004). Harm reduction for the prevention of youth gambling problems: lessons learned from adolescent high-risk prevention programs. *Journal of Adolescent Research*, 19:233–63.

Fisher, S. (1999). A prevalence study of gambling and problem gambling in British adolescents. *Addiction Research*, 7:509–38.

Fisher, S. E. (2000a). Measuring the prevalence of sector-specific problem gambling: a study of casino patrons. *Journal of Gambling Studies*, 16:25–51.

Fisher, S. E. (2000b). Developing the DSM-IV-MR-J criteria to identify adolescent problem gambling in non–clinical populations. *Journal of Gambling Studies*, 16:253–73.

Gamblers Anonymous (2005). *Twenty Questions*. Los Angeles, CA: Gamblers Anonymous. Retrieved 1 July 2012 from http://www.gamblersanonymous.org/20questions.html .

Gillespie, M., Derevensky, J. & Gupta, R. (2007). Adolescent problem gambling: developing a gambling expectancy instrument. *Journal of Gambling Issues*, 19:51–68.

Grant, J. E., Kim, S. W. & Potenza, M. N. (2003). Advances in pharmacotherapy of pathological gambling disorder. *Journal of Gambling Studies*, 19:85–109.

Grant, J. E., Chambers, A. D. & Potenza, M. N. (2004). Adolescent problem gambling: neurodevelopment and pharmacological treatment. In J. Derevensky and R. Gupta (Eds), *Gambling Problems in Youth: Theoretical and Applied Perspectives*, pp. 81–98. New York: Kluwer Academic/Plenum.

Grant, J. E., Steinberg, M. A., Kim, S. W., Rounsaville, B. J. & Potenza, M. N. (2004). Preliminary validity and reliability testing of a structured clinical interview for pathological gambling (SCI–PG). *Psychiatry Research*, 128:79–88.

Griffiths, M. D. (1995). *Adolescent Gambling*. London: Routledge.

Gupta, R. & Derevensky, J. (1998). Adolescent gambling behaviour: a prevalence study and examination of the correlates associated with excessive gambling. *Journal of Gambling Studies*, 14, 319–345.

Gupta, R. & Derevensky, J. (2000). Adolescents with gambling problems: from research to treatment. *Journal of Gambling Studies*, 16:315–42.

Gupta, R. & Derevensky, J. (2004). A treatment approach for adolescents with gambling problems. In J. Derevensky and R. Gupta (eds), *Gambling Problems in Youth: Theoretical and Applied Perspectives*, pp. 165–188. New York: Kluwer Academic/Plenum Publishers.

Gupta, R. & Derevensky, J. (2008). Gambling practices among youth: etiology, prevention and treatment. In C. A. Essau (ed.), *Adolescent Addiction: Epidemiology, Assessment and Treatment*, pp. 207–30. London: Elsevier.

Gupta, R., Derevensky, J. & Ellenbogen, S. (2006). Personality characteristics and risk-taking tendencies among adolescent gamblers. *Canadian Journal of Behavioural Science*, 38(3):201–13.

Hollander, E., DeCaria, C. M. & Mari, E. (1998). Short-term single-blind fluvoxamine treatment of pathological gambling. *American Journal of Psychiatry*, 155:1781–3.

Hollander, E., Frenkel, M., DeCaria, C., Trungold, S. & Stein, D. (1992). Treatment of pathological gambling with clomipramine. *American Journal of Psychiatry*, 149:710–11.

Jacobs, D. F. (1987). A general theory of addictions: application to treatment and rehabilitation planning for pathological gamblers. In T. Galski (ed.), *The Handbook of Pathological Gambling*, pp. 169–194. Springfield, IL: Charles C. Thomas.

Jacobs, D. F. (2000). Juvenile gambling in North America: an analysis of long-term trends and future prospects. *Journal of Gambling Studies*, 16:119–52.

Jacobs, D. F. (2004). Youth gambling in North America: long-term trends and future prospects. In J. Derevensky & R. Gupta (eds), *Gambling Problems in Youth: Theoretical and Applied Perspectives*, pp. 1–26. New York: Kluwer Academic/Plenum Publishers.

Johanson, A. & Götestam, K. G. (2003). Gambling and problematic gambling with money among Norwegian youth (12–18 years). *Nordic Journal of Psychiatry*, 57:317–21.

Kaminer, Y., Wagner, E., Plummer, B. & Seifer, R. (1993). Validation of the Teen Addiction Severity Index (T-ASI): Preliminary findings. *American Journal on Addictions*, 2:250–4.

Ladd, G. T. & Petry, N. M. (2003). A comparison of pathological gamblers with and without substance abuse treatment histories. *Experimental and Clinical Psychopharmacology*, 11, 202–9.

Ladouceur, R. & Walker, M. (1998). Cognitive approach to understanding and treating pathological gambling. In A. S. Bellack & M. Hersen (eds), *Comprehensive Clinical Psychology*, pp. 588–601. New York: Pergamon.

Ladouceur, R., Boisvert, J-M. & Dumont, J. (1994). Cognitive-behavioral treatment for adolescent pathological gamblers. *Behavior Modification*, 18:230–42.

Ladouceur, R., Bouchard, C., Rheaume, N., Jaques, C., Ferland, F. & Leblond, J. (2000). Is the SOGS an accurate measure of pathological gambling among children, adolescents and adults? *Journal of Gambling Studies*, 16, 1:1–21.

Lesieur, H. R. & Blume, S. B. (1987). The South Oaks Gambling Screen (SOGS): a new instrument for the identification of pathological gamblers. *American Journal of Psychiatry*, 144:1184–8.

Lesieur, H. R. & Blume, S. B. (1991). Evaluation of patients treated for pathological gambling in a combined alcohol, substance abuse, and pathological gambling treatment unit using the Addiction Severity Index. *British Journal of Addictions*, 86:1017–28.

Lesieur H. R. & Blume S. B. (1992). Modifying the Addiction Severity Index for use with pathological gamblers. *American Journal of Addictions*, 1:240–7.

Lupu, V., Onaca, E. & Lupu, D. (2002). The prevalence of pathological gambling in Romanian teenagers. *Minerva Medica*, 93:413–18.

Olason, D. T., Sigurdardottir, K. J. & Smari, J. (2006a). Prevalence estimates of gambling participation and problem gambling among 16–18 year old students in Iceland: a comparison of the SOGS-RA and DSM-IV-MR-J. *Journal of Gambling Studies*, 22:23–39.

Olason, D. T., Skarphedinsson, G. A., Jonsdottir, J. E., Mikaelsson, M. & Gretarsson, S. J. (2006b). Prevalence estimates of gambling and problem gambling among 13–15-year-old adolescents in Reykjavík: an examination of correlates of problem gambling and different accessibility to electronic gambling machines in Iceland. *Journal of Gambling Issues*, 18:39–56.

Potenza, M. N., Steinberg, M. A., McLaughlin, S. D. et al. (2000). Illegal behaviours in problem gambling: analysis of data from a gambling helpline. *Journal of the American Academy of Psychiatry and the Law*, 28(4):389–403.

Poulin, C. (2002). An assessment of the validity and reliability of the SOGSRA. *Journal of Gambling Studies*, 18:67–93.

Rosenthal, R. J. (1987). The psychodynamics of pathological gambling: a review of the literature. In T. Galski (ed.), *The Handbook of Pathological Gambling*, pp. 41–70. Springfield, IL: Charles C. Thomas.

Rossen, F. (2001). *Youth Gambling: A Critical Review of the Public Health Literature*. New Zealand: Centre for Gambling Studies, University of Auckland.

Rugle, L., Derevensky, J., Gupta, R., Winters, K. & Stinchfield, R. (2001). The Treatment of Problem and Pathological Gamblers. Report prepared for the National Council for Problem Gambling, Center for Mental Health Services (CMHS) and the Substance Abuse and Mental Health Services Administration (SAMHSA), Washington, DC.

Skokauskas, N. & Satkeviciute, R. (2007) Adolescent pathological gambling in Kaunas, Lithuania. *Nordic Journal of Psychiatry*, 61(2):86–91.

Toneatto, T. & Ladouceur, R. (2003). Treatment of pathological gambling: a critical review of the literature. *Psychology of Addictive Behaviours*, 17:284–92.

Wiebe, J. M. D., Cox, B. J. & Mehmel, B. G. (2000). The South Oaks Gambling Screen Revised for Adolescents (SOGS-RA): further psychometric findings from a community sample. *Journal of Gambling Studies*, 16(2/3):275–88.

Winters, K. C., Stinchfield, R. & Fulkerson, J. (1993). Toward the development of an adolescent gambling problem severity scale. *Journal of Gambling Studies*, 9:63–84.

Winters, K. C., Stinchfield, R. & Kim, L. (1995). Monitoring adolescent gambling in Minnesota. *Journal of Gambling Studies*, 11:165–83.

Wood, R. T. & Griffiths, M. D. (2004). Adolescent lottery and scratch card players: do their attitudes influence their gambling behaviour? *Journal of Adolescence*, 27:467–75.

Chapter 15

Remote gambling

An overview of Internet gambling, mobile phone gambling and interactive television gambling

Mark Griffiths

Aims

> 1 To examine three types of remote gambling (Internet gambling, mobile phone gambling and interactive television gambling).
> 2 To discuss factors that may influence problem gambling in remote-gambling environments.
> 3 To describe online help and treatment for remote gamblers.

Introduction

It has been claimed that remote types of gambling have provided the biggest cultural shift in gambling in the past decade (Griffiths, 2011; Griffiths, et al., 2006) and that the introduction of remote gambling has the potential to lead to increased levels of problematic gambling behaviour (Griffiths, 2003; Griffiths & Parke, 2002). To date, knowledge and understanding of how the remote media affects gambling behaviour is sparse (particularly in relation to gambling via mobile phone and interactive television). Globally speaking, proliferation of remote-gambling access is still an emerging trend and it will take some time before the effects on gambling behaviour surface. The impact of gambling technology has been widespread and there are many observed trends around the world that appear to have resulted from technological innovation, e.g. gambling coming out of gambling environments, gambling becoming a more asocial activity, widespread deregulation and increased opportunities to gamble (Griffiths, 2011).

This chapter therefore examines three types of remote gambling (Internet gambling, mobile phone gambling, and interactive television gambling). This is then followed by an examination of 1) factors that may influence problem gambling in remote-gambling environments, and 2) online help and treatment for remote gamblers.

Internet gambling

To date, there have been a relatively small number of studies on Internet gambling and even fewer that have examined problem gambling and online gambling addictions. Furthermore, there have been a variety of different studies and methodologies examining different aspects of Internet gambling. These have included representative national survey studies on adult Internet gambling (e.g. Gambling Commission, 2008; Griffiths, 2001; Griffiths et al., 2009; 2011; Wardle, Moody, Griffiths, et al., 2011), national survey studies on adolescent Internet gambling (e.g. Griffiths & Wood, 2007; Ipsos MORI, 2009), regional survey studies of Internet gamblers (e.g. Ialomiteanu & Adlaf, 2001; Olason et al., 2011; Wood & Williams, 2007; Wong, 2010), studies on self-selected samples of Internet gamblers (e.g. Gainsbury, et al., 2012; Griffiths & Barnes, 2008; International Gaming Research Unit, 2007; Lloyd et al., 2010; Matthews et al., 2009; McBride & Derevensky, 2009; Wood & Williams, 2011; Wood et al., 2007), studies examining behavioural tracking data of Internet gamblers from online gaming sites (e.g. Broda et al., 2008; Dragicevic et al., 2011; LaBrie et al., 2007; LaBrie et al., 2008; Xuan & Shaffer, 2009), qualitative interview studies (Corney & Davis, 2010; McCormack & Griffiths, 2012a; Parke & Griffiths, 2011a, 2011b, 2012; Valentine & Hughes, 2008), Internet gambling case studies (Griffiths & Parke, 2007), studies examining very specific forms of gambling such as online poker (Griffiths et al., 2010; Hopley & Nicki, 2010; McCormack & Griffiths, 2012b; Wood & Griffiths, 2008; Wood, et al., 2007), experimental studies of online gambling (e.g. Cole et al., 2011), and studies examining Internet gambling and social responsibility features (Griffiths, Wood & Parke, 2009; Sevigny et al., 2005; Smeaton & Griffiths, 2004).

The largest survey of Internet gamblers was carried out by the International Gaming Research Unit (2007). A total of 10,865 Internet gamblers completed an online survey (58% male and 42% female), with the majority of respondents being between the ages of 18–65 years. Respondents from 96 countries participated, and a broad range of occupations was represented. It was reported that the typical Internet casino player was likely to: be female (54.8%), be aged 46–55 years (29.5%), play two to three times per week (37%), have played for two to three years (22.4%), play for between one to two hours per session (26.5%), and wager between $30–$60 (18.1%) per session. It was also reported that the typical Internet poker player was likely to: be male (73.8%), be aged 26–35 years (26.9%), play two to three times per week (26.8%), have played for two to three years (23.6%), and play for between one to two hours per session (33.3%). However, online gambling addiction was not assessed. (Despite the size of the survey, it should be noted that the sample was not representative as it comprised a self-selected sample).

Griffiths & Wardle et al. (2009) provided the first ever analysis of a representative national sample of Internet gamblers. Using participant data from the 2007 British Gambling Prevalence Survey (n = 9003 adults aged 16 years and over), all participants who had gambled online, bet online, and/or who had used a betting exchange in the last 12 months (n = 476) were compared with all other gamblers who had not gambled via the Internet. Overall, results showed a number of significant socio-demographic differences between Internet gamblers and non-Internet gamblers. When compared to non-Internet gamblers, Internet gamblers were more likely to be male, relatively young adults, single, well educated, and in professional/managerial employment. Further analysis of DSM-IV scores showed that the problem gambling prevalence rate was significantly higher among Internet gamblers (5%) than non-Internet gamblers (0.5%). It was also found that some items on the DSM-IV were more heavily endorsed by Internet gamblers, including gambling preoccupation and gambling to escape. However, it may be that the medium of the Internet is a less protective environment for vulnerable players (e.g. problem gamblers).

Wardle and Griffiths (2011) have asked what exactly is an 'online gambler'? Very few people only gamble online, and most online gamblers also gamble offline (Griffiths et al., 2009). In the 2007 British Gambling Prevalence Survey (Wardle et al., 2007) there were 476 people (out of 9003 people who participated in the survey) who reported gambling online in the past year. Of these, only nine people did not report also participating in some kind of offline gambling activity. In other words, over 98% of online gamblers also gambled offline. These data suggest that 'pure' online gamblers (i.e. gamblers who gamble online and online only) are relatively rare.

According to secondary analysis from the latest BGPS study (Wardle, Moody, Griffiths et al., 2011), the number of 'online only gamblers' had slightly increased to 2%, but the data suggest there were a number of distinct ways to categorise gamblers, based on the medium in which they gamble and what activities they gamble on in those mediums. The 2011 BGPS report surveyed 7756 adult gamblers. Approximately one in seven respondents (14%) had gambled online in the past year (i.e. had gambled on at least one gambling activity, such as gambling at online casinos and/or playing the lottery online). However, for the first time ever, the authors created four new groups of gamblers for comparison. These were those who:

- Gambled offline only (i.e. had gambled on at least one activity such as buying a lottery ticket in a shop or playing roulette at an offline casino, but hadn't gambled online in the past year).
- Gambled online only (i.e. had gambled on at least one activity such as gambling on a betting exchange or gambling at an online casino, but hadn't gambled offline in the past year).
- Gambled both online and offline but on different activities (i.e. had gambled on at least one activity online and one activity offline, but these were different activities such as gambling on a slot machine in an amusement arcade and playing blackjack in an online casino).

- Gambled both online and offline but on the same activities (i.e. had gambled on at least one activity both online and offline such as gambling at both an online and offline casino).

Perhaps unsurprisingly, most gamblers were those who gambled offline only (80.5%), and the smallest group comprised those who gambled online only (2.1%). Of far more interest were the rates of problem gambling among these four groups. The highest prevalence rates of problem gambling were amongst mixed-mode gamblers who gambled on different activities (4.3%), followed by mixed-mode gamblers who gambled on the same activities (2.4%), those who only gambled offline (0.9%), and those who only gambled online (0%).

The most interesting statistic is arguably the fact that *there wasn't a single case of problem or pathological gambling among those gamblers who only gambled online*. Extreme caution must be given, as the player base for 'online only' gamblers was very small when compared to the other groups. However, this certainly opens up an area for future research as to whether those who only gamble online are more resilient to developing gambling problems than those who engage in mixed modes of gambling. Socio-demographic information from the BGPS studies suggest that those who gamble online are more educated and in better occupations than those who have never gambled online. Maybe these demographic factors are also protective factors when it comes to the development of gambling problems? The limited data (to date) suggest that it is not the medium of gambling that is more problematic *per se*, but that to vulnerable people (e.g. problem gamblers), the Internet may be providing easily accessible 'convenience' gambling that perhaps explains why problem gambling prevalence rates among online gamblers appear to be much higher than non-online gamblers.

Another British national prevalence survey examined Internet gambling among adolescents. In a survey of 8017 children aged between 12 and 15 years old, Griffiths and Wood (2007) reported that 8% of their sample (n = 621) had played a National Lottery game on the Internet. Boys were more likely than girls to say they had played National Lottery games on the Internet (10% and 6%, respectively), as were young people who were Asian and black. Not surprisingly, young people classified as 'problem gamblers' (as defined by the DSM-IV-J) were more likely than 'social gamblers' to have played a National Lottery game on the Internet (37% compared with 9%). When asked which of a series of statements best describes how they played National Lottery games on the Internet, nearly three in ten adolescents who played online reported playing free games (29%), one in six reported that the system let them register (18%), slightly fewer played along with their parents (16%), and one in ten used their parent's online National Lottery account either with their permission (10%) or without it (7%). However, it should be noted that a third of online players said they 'couldn't remember' (35%). Overall these findings indicate that, of all young people (and not just players), 2% have played National Lottery games online with their parents or with their permission and 2% have played independently or without their parents. Those who have played independently are most likely to have played free games, with just 0.3% of young people having played National Lottery games on their own for money.

More recently, Ipsos MORI (2009), in a survey of 8598 students, aged 11–15 years from 201 schools, reported that overall, 1% of youth gambled on the Internet for money in the past seven days. They also reported that 28% of their sample had participated in money-free gambling of some sort in the week preceding the survey. Just over a quarter of adolescents had played in 'money-free mode' in the week preceding the survey, with opportunities on the social networking sites four or five times more popular than those presented on actual gambling sites. Using statistical modelling to further examine the same data, Forrest, McHale and Parke (2009) reported that gambling in money-free mode was the single most important predictor of whether the child had gambled for money and one of the most important predictors of problem gambling. However, it should be noted that this relationship is correlational and not necessarily causal. The possibility and extent to which money-free gambling is responsible for real gambling participation and gambling-related risk and harm could only be confirmed using longitudinal data.

In a number of studies (e.g. Griffiths & Barnes, 2008; Griffiths & Wood, 2007; Griffiths, et al., 2009, 2010, 2011; Hopley & Nicki, 2010; Ladd & Petry, 2002; Matthews, et al., 2009; McBride & Derevensky, 2009; Olason, et al., 2010; Petry, 2006; Petry & Weinstock, 2007; Wong, 2010; Wood & Williams, 2007, 2011; Wood, et al., 2007), the prevalence of Internet gambling addiction (pathological) and/or problematic Internet gambling were assessed. From those who gamble online, a minority appears to develop an addiction to Internet gambling. Kuss and Griffiths (2012) recently reviewed all the known studies on Internet gambling and concluded that with regards to the reported prevalence of Internet gambling addiction, the results of the studies vary substantially. Of Internet users, Kuss and Griffiths reported that based on the studies they evaluated, 12–23% appear to have online gambling problems, whereas 5–20% were found to be pathological gamblers. Student Internet gamblers, on the other hand, had higher prevalence rates, suggesting that 18–77% suffer from pathological gambling online. Kuss and Griffiths also noted that the prevalence rates of problem gambling for adolescents were between 8 and 25% of those who gambled on the Internet. Naturally, from these estimates no definite conclusions can be deducted. However, Kuss and Griffiths also noted several methodological limitations in interpreting these studies.

Firstly, a large majority of studies included in this review did not comprise samples that were representative of the general population (i.e. self-selected samples were used). As a consequence, this limits the external validity of results. Secondly, the methodologies applied to assess Internet gambling addiction were diverse, and researchers used a number of different classifications. The distinction between problematic and pathological gambling was somewhat unfeasible, therefore somewhat restricting construct validity. Thirdly, the reliance on self-reports brings into question the reliability of the reported findings. A solution to this problem may be to include significant others of problem/pathological gamblers in determining whether and to what extent the latter's gambling behaviours can be classified as being clinically relevant.

Despite these shortcomings/the methodological shortcomings, it appears that in general the results support the prevalence estimates for land-based pathological gamblers, indicating that the prevalence of pathological gambling is higher in adolescents and college students. The dissimilarity of findings for prevalence rates may therefore be related to 1) measures and conceptualisations, 2) cut-off points, and 3) samples used. Concerning the former, valid comparisons are only possible when similar diagnostic tools are used. Moreover, with regards to the latter, future researchers are additionally advised to conduct cross-cultural studies in order to control for the effect of culture on pathology status.

With regards to specific risk factors for the development of pathological gambling online, it appears that those identified in Kuss and Griffiths' (2012) review were very similar to the results of other studies concerned with land-based pathological gambling. The results with regards to specific personality and socio-demographic characteristics as well as mood status associated with pathological Internet gambling were in line with the findings regarding pathological gambling in general (e.g. higher impulsivity, younger age, male gender, increased emotional distress, being single, and having higher rates of depression and maladaptive coping).

Mobile phone gambling

Gambling has taken another step towards convergence and convenience with the advent of gambling and gaming via mobile phone. This is gaming on the move, whenever and wherever. Obviously, mobile gambling and gaming via handheld consoles have been around since the early 1990s, but it is only more recently that wireless networked gaming has emerged. Since it is unnatural to be always near a computer or console, handheld devices (including mobile phones) make the medium convenient for mobile gambling and gaming. A player/gamer can be occupied by gambling/gaming whenever they have time to spare, for example whilst in transit and during work breaks. These activities have helped satellite and cable television, video and the Internet. The wireless world of the mobile phone may not be too different. The most successful communities look to 'mobilise' and then 'monetise' (Griffiths, 2004).

Gamers are 'techno-savvy' to begin with, and are likely to be less cautious with new forms of technology. Mobile phone gambling and gaming is anonymous, and can provide immediate gratification, any time, anywhere. The penetration of wireless mobile gambling and gaming will mostly be contingent upon the market penetration of wireless web users in general. The mobile phone market is already large in many parts of the world. The number of international mobile phone users has already passed the two billion mark (Griffiths, 2007a). The new generation of mobile phones already have the capability to play typical 'casino style' games like blackjack, poker and slots. The limiting aspects of the technological and protocol demands of mobile gambling (graphics, sound and displays on mobile devices) are largely being resolved through technological advance.

These advances allow gamblers to watch sporting events live on their phones while wagering in real time. Consider the following scenario as outlined by Griffiths (2008).

A betting service that knows where you are and/or what you are doing has the capacity to suggest something context-related to the mobile user to bet on. For instance, if the mobile phone user bought a ticket for a soccer match using an electronic service, this service may share this information with a betting company. If in that match the referee gives a penalty for one team, a person's mobile could ring and give the user an opportunity (on screen) to bet whether or not the penalty will be scored. On this type of service, the mobile phone user will only have to decide if they want to bet, and if they do, the amount of money. Two clicks and the bet will be placed. Context, timeliness, simplicity, and above all user involvement look like enough to convince also people that never entered a bet-shop (p. 39).

Mobility also facilitates an increase in 'personalised' gambling, e.g. the types of service offered by Eurobet's match service, where bettors gamble against each other, rather than the house. Gambling (for some people) appears to be becoming part of the match-day soccer experience. Griffiths (2008) says that a typical scenario might involve a £10 bet with a friend on a weekend soccer match. The gambler can text their friend via SMS and log on to the betting service to make their gamble. If the friend accepts, the gambler has got the chance to win (or lose). Soccer clubs get a share of the profits from the service. Clubs are keen to get fans using branded mobile devices where they can simply hit a 'bet' button and place a wager with the club's mobile phone partner.

It is clear that mobile phone gambling and gaming is still a relatively untapped area, and the functional capabilities of mobile phones are getting better all the time. Market research by the companies Mintel and Juniper (cited by Griffiths, 2007a) raised the possibility that almost unlimited access to mobile phone gaming will lead to more problem gaming (although this includes gambling as well as video gaming). However, there has been little empirical research specifically in the area of mobile phone gambling, with most writings raising the issue and speculating about potential social impact rather than providing empirical data (e.g. Griffiths, 2004, 2006a, 2007a; Kangas, 2004; Moore & Rutter, 2004; Phillips & Blaszczynski, 2008; Phillips et al., 2011; Shchiglik & Scornavacca, 2004). The most recent British Gambling Prevalence Survey (BGPS) included data on gambling via mobile phone (Wardle, Moody, Spence et al., 2011). However, the number of people who gambled via their mobile phone was much less than 1% and there were too few in the sample for any reliable statistical analysis. This figure is similar to an online international survey carried out by Bryce et al. (2004) of 600 mobile phone users.

Phillips and Blaszczynski (2010) carried out a survey for Gambling Research Australia on gambling and the impact of new and emerging technologies and associated products, comprising 900 Australian residents. Using the Canadian Problem Gambling Index (CPGI), the respondents were classed into one of four groups – non-problem gamblers (72.6%), low-risk gamblers (14.8%), moderate-risk gamblers (9.6%) and problem gamblers (3.1%). Problem gamblers did not use their mobile phones any more than other individuals. The authors speculated that this may be because the survey asked about work or personal uses, whereas other applications may be of more interest to gamblers. Participants were asked the number of minutes in a typical week they spent using their mobile phone to play games. On average participants spent nine minutes per week playing games on their mobile phones. Problem gambling status significantly influenced the amounts of time people reported spending playing games on their mobile phones (i.e. problem gamblers spent more time playing games than other groups), although low-risk gamblers also spent similar amounts of time per week playing games – non-problem gamblers (six minutes a week playing mobile phone games), low-risk gamblers (21 minutes a week), moderate-risk gamblers (seven minutes a week) and problem gamblers (22 minutes a week).

The authors further argued that a clearer indicator of willingness to engage in financial transactions on mobile phones is the purchase of items using the mobile phone. Therefore, participants were also asked how often they used their mobile phone to purchase items in a typical week (e.g. ringtones). Although respondents rarely used their mobile phone to make purchases (0.18 times a week on average), problem gamblers were significantly more likely than other groups to make commercial purchases – non-problem gamblers 0.04 purchases a week, low-risk gamblers 0.67 purchases a week, moderate-risk gamblers 0.12 purchases a week and problem gamblers 1.54 purchases a week.

Participants were asked how often they used SMS on their mobile phone to enter cash prize competitions in a typical week. Again, the average was relatively low (1.14 times a week) but problem gamblers entered prize competitions significantly more than other groups – non-problem gamblers 0.92 times a week, low-risk gamblers 1.05 times a week, moderate-risk gamblers 2.2 times a week and problem gamblers 3.2 times a week.

Because mobile phones provide access to services anywhere and at any time, the study also examined how problems controlling mobile phone use (on the Mobile Phone Problem Use Scale) may possibly interact with problem gambling status. A significant effect was reported for mobile phone problems upon the amount of game playing reported (i.e. as participants became more dependent upon their mobile phone, they were more likely to report playing games). Problem gamblers were significantly more likely than other groups to be contacted by companies asking them to participate in prize competitions. However, no relationship was found between problem gambling status, problem mobile phone use status and amount of prize competitions entered via SMS.

Further statistical analysis was conducted to determine which variables predicted the playing of games on mobile phones. People who reported playing more games on their mobile phones were more likely to report problems limiting their use of their mobile phones, and were more likely to report problems limiting their Internet use. Age was not a significant predictor of game play on mobile phones (in fact, interest in the technology, rather than age, appears to be the issue when playing games on mobile phones). A similar analysis was also conducted to determine which variables predicted the use of mobile phones to enter competitions. Problem gamblers were more likely to report problems, when using their mobile phones to enter competitions in magazines. People using SMS to enter competitions were more likely to report problems limiting their Internet use and to be less well educated. Prize competitions are of interest to problem gamblers, but this is not an activity that appears to attract a specific age range. Overall, Phillips and Blaszczynski (2010) argue that their data suggest that gamblers and people with problems controlling their technology use are more interested in access to electronic services.

Interactive television gambling

In recent years, the television industry has invested heavily in digital infrastructure in anticipation of the predicted financial boom that was to come from interactive television (i-TV). However, revenue from i-TV has been relatively slow to materialise (Griffiths, 2008). Despite the relatively slow start, industry analysts (e.g. Wise & Hall, 2005) believed i-TV would bring financial rewards for the television industry. Early i-TV revenue projections forecast robust growth in interactive advertising and television-based commerce, but ultimately these were not as lucrative as consumer-driven applications, such as video-on-demand.

For television companies to flourish in an evolving digital landscape, Griffiths (2008) notes that they have formulated strategies for targeting particular segments of the industry. Platform operators have deployed consumer-driven applications, such as gambling and gaming. They have created an environment where content originators and channel operators can innovate and create (potentially) profitable interactive broadband content. Interactive television is seen as a way of rapidly expanding gaming and gambling, because of its naturalness and ease of use.

Interactive television gaming covers a wide range of activities. This includes such activities as playing video games like Tetris, and playing along with television game shows like *Who Wants to Be a Millionaire?* There appears to be an increasing wave of interactive television applications aimed at viewers drawn to the allure of gambling. This interest in all things interactive directly results from growing competition between Internet service providers, satellite TV and cable-TV outfits. All these different providers are looking for features to differentiate themselves. One of the most potentially lucrative vehicles for this has therefore been interactive television gaming and gambling.

Interactive television (i-TV) services are increasingly being linked to actual television programmes (Griffiths, 2006b). Over the last few years in the UK, there has been a significant increase in the number of television shows raising revenue through the use of interactive programming. One of the most popular methods has viewers call into the television show using a premium-rate telephone service to either answer simple quiz questions or vote somebody out of a reality TV show (Griffiths, 2007b). The television programmers clearly see this as a way of raising extra revenue. There are also those who argue that this form of television programming is gambling in another guise. Whether this television phenomenon is a *bona fide* type of gambling is debatable, but some elements certainly resemble gambling.

This innovative form of interactive viewing experience raises many questions about whether viewers are being exploited or whether such programming is just another enjoyment-enhancing dimension of the viewing experience. However, there is a fine line between customer enhancement and customer exploitation (Griffiths, 2003). Programmers will argue that when viewers 'put their money where their mouth is', the viewing experience is enhanced. This is very similar to the gambling industry's maxim that 'it matters more when there's money on it'. However, callers are usually charged at a premium rate even if they fail to get through to register their answer. Typically, on failing to connect, callers get a recorded message saying, 'Even though you haven't got through this time, we still want you to be a winner.'

It could also be argued that in many i-TV quizzes, viewers are participating in a lottery (Griffiths, 2007b). For instance, viewers are typically asked to call a premium-rate telephone line to answer a very simple question (e.g. 'Rearrange the following letters to make the name of a top rock group – STOLLING RONES'). A winner is then chosen from all those viewers with the correct answer. This, to all intents and purposes, is a lottery. However, unlike lotteries, those participating do not know what their probability of winning is. Furthermore, viewers are staking money (through the cost of the premium-rate telephone call) on the outcome of a future event (i.e. whether they will get the correct answer). Such a scenario could be defined as a form of gambling (Griffiths, 2007b).

Griffiths (2007b) has also argued that viewers who participate in late-night and 'through-the-night' interactive quiz programming in the UK (such as *The Mint, Make Your Play, Quiz Call, The Great British Quiz*) may be some of the most vulnerable and susceptible. These viewers are more likely to be those who do not work and therefore are on low incomes and can least afford to participate (e.g. the unemployed, the retired and elderly). Viewers may also be making decisions to play in an intoxicated state (as these programmes typically start just as people get in from an evening's drinking) and/or in a state where they are not fully alert (i.e. at 3 am). They may also be participating because they think their chances of winning are better, in the belief that there are very few other people awake at 3 am. In fact, this latter point highlights the fact that no one participating has any idea what the odds are of winning (Griffiths, 2007b).

Lots of companies have done well financially in Europe and Asia where more than 30% of television shows have an interactive element to them (Griffiths,

2008). Television gambling appears to be particularly popular in Europe. Interactive Systems Worldwide (ISWI) was one of the first companies to develop an interactive television play-by-play betting system. Their software system enabled interface between SportXction and the satellite television broadcast of its first interactive television partner. SportXction is a patented, real-time software system that allows TV viewers to make play-by-play gambles on a sporting event while the event is in progress. Gambling can be conducted while viewing a live or televised sporting event, or listening to it on the radio. The wagers offered are mostly oriented to short-term action like the penalty kick, or whether the next play will be a run or a pass. The wagers have odds associated with them, which relate to the probable outcome of the proposition being wagered upon, and the odds are adjusted in real time to balance the pool using proprietary artificial intelligence software to reflect player sentiment, as derived from the betting patterns. The system can be used with virtually any sport.

Many media service providers' networks still need work to enable cutting-edge interactivity like multiplayer gaming, but this is beginning to happen. Digital pay-TV software makers are beginning to roll out technology that can enable feature-rich games even on a 'primitive' set-top box. Using software that sits on a provider's server, games can be made graphically complex (e.g. game sequences that give the viewer an impression of flying through a house). Exactly how successful interactive television gambling and gaming will become cannot be answered at present.

Factors that may influence problem gambling in remote-gambling environments

According to Griffiths (2003), there are a number of factors that make remote-gambling activities potentially addictive. These include: anonymity, convenience, escape, dissociation/immersion, accessibility, event frequency, interactivity, disinhibition, simulation and asociability. Outlined below are some of the main variables that may account for acquisition and maintenance of some online behaviours (adapted from Griffiths, 2003; Griffiths et al., 2006). It would also appear that remote-gambling environments have the potential to provide short-term comfort, excitement and/or distraction.

Accessibility

Access to the Internet, mobile phones and interactive television is now commonplace and widespread, and can be done easily from the home and/or the workplace (and in the case of mobile phones, almost anywhere). Increased accessibility may also lead to increased problems. Increased accessibility of gambling activities enables the individual to rationalise involvement in gambling by removing previously restrictive barriers such as time constraints emanating from occupational and social commitments. With reductions in time required to select, place wagers and collect winnings, gambling as a habitual activity appears more viable, as social and occupational commitments are not necessarily compromised (Griffiths et al., 2006).

Affordability

Given the wide accessibility of the Internet, mobile phones and interactive television, it is now becoming cheaper and cheaper to use the online and mobile services on offer. Griffiths et al. (2006) noted that the overall cost of gambling has been reduced significantly through technological developments. For example, the saturation of the online and mobile gambling industry has led to increased competition, and the consumer is benefiting from the ensuing promotional offers and discounts available on gambling outlay. Regarding interactive wagering, the emergence of peer-to-peer gambling through the introduction of betting exchanges has provided the customer with commission-free sporting gambling odds, which in effect means the customer needs to risk less money to obtain potential revenue. Finally, ancillary costs of face-to-face gambling, such as parking, tipping and purchasing refreshments, is removed when gambling within the home, and therefore the overall cost of gambling is reduced, making it more affordable.

Anonymity

The anonymity of remote environments allows users to privately engage in gambling without the fear of stigma. This anonymity may also provide the user with a greater sense of perceived control over the content, tone and nature of the online experience. Anonymity may also increase feelings of comfort since there is a decreased ability to look for, and thus detect, signs of insincerity, disapproval or judgment in facial expression, as would be typical in face-to-face interactions. For activities such as gambling, this may be a positive benefit, particularly when losing, as no one will actually see the face of the loser. Griffiths et al. (2006) believe that anonymity, like increased accessibility, may reduce social barriers to engaging in gambling, particularly skill-based gambling activities such as poker that are relatively complex and often possess tacit social etiquette. The potential discomfort of committing a structural or social *faux pas* in the gambling environment because of inexperience is minimised, since the individual's identity remains concealed.

Convenience

Interactive online and mobile applications provide convenient mediums to engage in gambling behaviours. Remote gambling will usually occur in the familiar and comfortable environment of home or workplace, thus reducing the feeling of risk and allowing even more adventurous behaviours that may or may not be potentially addictive. For the gambler, not having to move from their home or their workplace may be of great positive benefit.

Escape

For some, the primary reinforcement to engage in remote gambling will be the gratification they experience online. However, the experience of remote gambling itself may be reinforced through a subjectively and/or objectively experienced 'high'. The pursuit of mood-modifying experiences is characteristic of addictions. The mood-modifying experience has the potential to provide an emotional or mental escape and further serves to reinforce the behaviour. Excessive involvement in this escapist activity may lead to addiction. In a qualitative interview-based study of 50 problem gamblers, Wood and Griffiths (2007a) identified that gambling to escape was the primary motivator for problem gamblers' continued excessive gambling. Remote-gambling behaviour can provide a potent escape from the stresses and strains of real life.

Immersion/dissociation

The medium of the Internet (and possibly other remote environments) can provide feelings of dissociation and immersion and may facilitate feelings of escape. Dissociation and immersion can involve lots of different types of feelings. This can include losing track of time, feelings of being someone else, blacking out, and being in a trance-like state. In extreme forms it may include multi-personality disorders. All of these feelings when gambling remotely may lead to longer play, either because 'time flies when you are having fun' or because the psychological feelings of being in an immersive or dissociative state are reinforcing.

Disinhibition

Disinhibition is clearly one of the Internet's key appeals, as there is little doubt that the Internet makes people less inhibited (Joinson, 1998). Online users appear to open up more quickly online and reveal themselves emotionally much faster than in the offline world. Walther (1996) referred to this phenomenon as 'hyperpersonal communication'. Walther argued that this occurs because of four features of online communication:

- The communicators usually share social categories, so will perceive each other as similar (e.g. all online poker players).
- The message-sender can present him- or herself in a positive light, and so may be more confident.
- The format of online interaction (e.g. there are no other distractions, users can spend time composing messages, mix social and task messages, users don't waste cognitive resources by answering immediately).
- The communication medium provides a feedback loop whereby initial impressions are built upon and strengthened.

For the gambler, being in a disinhibited state may lead to more money being gambled, particularly if they are motivated to maintain their initial persona (e.g. as a skilful online poker player).

Event frequency

The event frequency of any gambling activity (i.e. the number of opportunities to gamble in a given time period) is a structural characteristic designed and implemented by the gaming operator. The length of time between each gambling event may indeed be critical as to whether some people might develop problems with a particular type of gambling. Obviously gambling activities that offer outcomes every few seconds (e.g. slot machines) will probably cause greater problems than activities with outcomes less often (e.g. bi-weekly lotteries). The frequency of playing, when linked with the two other factors – the result of the gamble (win or loss) and the actual time until winnings are received – exploits certain psychological principles of learning. This process (operant conditioning) conditions habits by rewarding behaviour, i.e. through presentation of a reward (e.g. money), reinforcement occurs. Rapid event frequency also means that the loss period is brief, with little time given over to financial considerations, and, more importantly, winnings can be re-gambled almost immediately. Internet gambling has the potential to offer visually exciting effects similar to slot machines and video lottery terminals (two of the most problematic forms of gambling).

Furthermore, the event frequency can be very rapid, particularly if the gambler is subscribed or visits several sites. Griffiths et al. (2006) concluded that the high event frequency in skill-based games like online poker provides increased motivation to participate in such gambling activities. Online poker, in relative terms, provides significant opportunity for an individual to manipulate the outcome of the gambling event. However, the individual's profitability is still determined to an extent by random probability. The online poker gambler may rationalise that with the increased frequency of participation, deviations from expected probability will be minimised (i.e. bad luck), increasing the effect of skill in determining gambling outcomes over the long term. Because of technological developments, poker gamblers can participate in several games simultaneously, and with reduced time limits for decision making in comparison to traditional poker games, games are also completed at a substantially faster rate.

Interactivity

The interactivity component of remote gambling may also be psychologically rewarding and different from other more passive forms of entertainment (e.g. television). It has been shown that the increased personal involvement in a gambling activity can increase the illusion of control (Langer, 1975) that in turn may facilitate increased gambling. The interactive nature of the Internet may therefore provide a convenient way of increasing such personal involvement.

Simulation

Simulations provide an ideal way in which to learn about something and tend not to have any of the possible negative consequences. However, Internet gambling simulations may have effects that were not originally thought of. For instance, many online gambling sites have a practice-mode format, where a potential customer can place a pretend bet in order to see and practise the procedure of gambling on that site. Although this activity cannot be regarded as actual gambling as there is no real money involved, it can be accessed by minors and possibly attract an underage player into gambling. Also, gambling in practice modes available within the gambling website may build self-efficacy and potentially increase perceptions of control in determining gambling outcomes, motivating participation in the 'real cash' counterparts within the site (Griffiths et al., 2006).

Asociability

One of the consequences of remote gambling has been to reduce the fundamentally social nature of gambling to an activity that is essentially asocial. Those who experience problems are more likely to be those playing on their own (e.g. those playing to escape). Retrospectively, most problem gamblers report that at the height of their problem gambling, it is a solitary activity. Gambling in a social setting could potentially provide some kind of 'safety net' for over-spenders, i.e. a form of gambling where the primary orientation of gambling is for social reasons, with the possibility of some fun and a chance to win some money (e.g. bingo). However, it could be speculated that those individuals whose prime motivation was to constantly play just to win money, would possibly experience more problems. One of the major influences of remote technology appears to be the shift from social to asocial forms of gambling. From this it could be speculated that as gambling becomes more technological, gambling problems will increase due to its asocial nature. However, it could also be argued that for some people, the Internet (including online gambling) provides a social outlet that they would not otherwise have. This is particularly true for women who may feel uncomfortable going out on their own, unemployed people and retired people.

Because of the apparent vacuous social component within remote gambling, Griffiths et al. (2006), Parke & Griffiths (2011a, 2011b, 2012) emphasise that alternative methods of peer interaction are available within interactive gambling activities that retain the socially reinforcing aspects of the behaviour. Individuals can communicate via computer-mediated communication within the game itself and even post-gambling through involvement in online gambling web-communities. An increasing trend is for online gambling websites to provide a customer forum to facilitate peer interaction and therefore increase the social element of the game. Some firms have even introduced an Internet radio facility that entertains their customers as they gamble, while simultaneously drawing attention to significant winners within the site. Effectively, the structural design of remote gambling removes the social safety net that is integral to maintaining responsible gambling practice without reducing the socially rewarding aspects inherent in traditional gambling environments (Griffiths et al., 2006).

Furthermore, there are many other specific developments that look likely to facilitate uptake of remote-gambling services, including sophisticated gaming software, integrated e-cash systems (including multi-currency), multi-lingual sites, increased realism (e.g. 'real' gambling via webcams, player and dealer avatars), live remote wagering (for both gambling alone and gambling with others) and improving customer care systems.

Online help and treatment for remote gamblers

Although an overview of treatment for problem gamblers is beyond the scope of this chapter, it is worth noting that online treatment interventions may be an effective medium in helping remote-gambling addicts. Griffiths and Cooper (2003) reviewed the main issues in the area and examined the advantages and disadvantages of online therapy, and the implications for the treatment of problem gamblers. There appear to be three main types of website where psychological help for problem gamblers is provided – information and advice sites, websites of traditional helping agencies (e.g. Gamblers Anonymous) and individual therapists. Despite a number of possible downsides to online therapy (e.g. establishing client rapport, possible client referral problems, confidentiality issues), there are many positive advantages including convenience, cost-effectiveness for clients, overcoming barriers that may prevent people seeking help in the first place, and overcoming social stigma.

Wood and Griffiths (2007b) reported one of the first ever studies that evaluated the effectiveness of an online help and guidance service for problem gamblers. GamAid is an online advisory, guidance and signposting service whereby the client can either browse the available links and information provided and/or talk to an online advisor. If the problem gambler connects to an online advisor, then a real-time image of the advisor appears on the client's screen in a small webcam box. Next to the image box is a dialogue box where the client can type messages to the advisor and in which the advisor can type a reply. Although the client can see the advisor, the advisor cannot see the client. The advisor also has the option to provide links to other relevant online services, and these appear on the lefthand side of the client's screen, remaining there after the client logs off from the advisor. The links that are given are in response to statements or requests made by the client for specific (and where possible) local services (e.g. a local debt advice service, or a local Gamblers Anonymous meeting).

In Wood and Griffiths' study, a total of 80 clients completed an in-depth online evaluation questionnaire, and secondary data were gathered from 413 distinct clients who contacted a GamAid advisor. They reported that the majority of clients who completed the feedback survey were satisfied with the guidance and 'counselling' service. Most participants agreed that GamAid provided information for local services where they could get help, agreed that they had or would follow the links given, felt the advisor was supportive and understood their needs, would consider using the service again and would recommend the service to others. Being able to see the advisor enabled the client to feel reassured, whilst at the same time, this one-way feature maintained anonymity, as the advisor cannot see the client.

An interesting aside is the extent to which GamAid was meeting a need not met by other gambling help services. This was examined by looking at the profiles of those clients using GamAid in comparison with the most similar service currently on offer, that being the UK GamCare telephone helpline. The data recorded by GamAid advisors during the evaluation period found that 413 distinct clients contacted an advisor. The types of gambling engaged in and the preferred location for gambling showed little similarity to the data collected in the two British national prevalence surveys to date (e.g. Wardle et al., 2011). Unsurprisingly (given the medium of the study), online gambling was the single most popular location for clients to gamble, with 31% of males and 19% of females reporting that they gambled this way. By comparison, the GamCare helpline found that only 12% of their male and 7% of their female callers gambled online. Therefore, it could be argued that the GamAid service is the preferred modality for seeking support for online gamblers. This is perhaps not surprising given that online gamblers are likely to have a greater degree of overall competence in using, familiarity with, and access to Internet facilities. Problem gamblers may therefore be more likely to seek help using the media that they are most comfortable in.

GamAid advisors identified gender for 304 clients of which 71% were male and 29% were female. By comparison, the GamCare helpline identified that 89% of their callers were male and 11% were female. Therefore, it would appear that the GamAid service might be appealing more to women than other comparable services do. There are several speculative reasons why this may be the case. For instance, online gambling is gender-neutral and may therefore be more appealing to women than more traditional forms of gambling, which (on the whole) are traditionally male-oriented (with the exception of bingo) (Wardle et al., 2007).

It is likely that online gamblers are more likely to seek online support than offline gamblers. Women may feel more stigmatised as problem gamblers than males and/or less likely to approach other help services where males dominate (e.g. GA). If this is the case, then the high degree of anonymity offered by GamAid may be one of the reasons it is preferred. Most of those who had used another service reported that they preferred GamAid because they specifically wanted online help. Those who had used another service reported that the particular benefits of GamAid were that they were more comfortable talking online than on the phone or face-to-face. They also reported that (in their view) GamAid was easier to access, and the advisors were more caring.

Online therapy is clearly not for all problem gamblers, and those participating should at the very least be comfortable expressing themselves through the written word. In an ideal world, it would not be necessary for those in serious crisis – some of whom could be problem gamblers (where non-verbal cues are vital) – to need to use computer-mediated communication-based forms of help. However, because of the Internet's immediacy, if this kind of therapeutic help is the only avenue available to individuals and/or the only thing they are comfortable using, then it is almost bound to be used by those with serious crises.

Gambling in a multi-media world

The rise and challenges of remote gambling and remote-gambling addictions cannot be seen in isolation, particularly as there is ever-increasing multi-media integration between the Internet, mobile phones and interactive television (i-TV). It may be that people are more likely to spend money in particular media. For instance, the Internet can be described as a 'lean forward' medium. This means that the user (who is usually alone) takes an active role in determining what they do. Computers are better at displaying text than television and have a wider range of fine-tuning controls through the mouse and keyboards. This makes them more suitable for complex tasks such as obtaining insurance quotations or travel itineraries. In contrast, the television is a 'lean back' medium where the viewer (often as part of a group) is more passive and seeks less control over what is going on. The television is better at displaying moving images than computers. This may have implications for the types of gambling done in particular media.

Furthermore, i-TV may also help in one other important area – trust. People appear to trust their television even though it is accessing the Internet in the same way as a computer. However, as argued above, i-TV is a 'lean back' service. If a person is relaxed sitting back on their sofa, it will make television the key to creating a true mass market for online commercial activity (including gambling). In addition, some i-TV services can be linked to actual television programs (such as betting on horse races). Browsing and buying by i-TV is still in its infancy, but looks set to expand significantly in the future.

Conclusions

Technology has always played a role in the development of gambling practices and will continue to do so. Analysis of the technological components in gambling activities indicates that situational characteristics impact most on acquisition, and that structural characteristics impact most on development and maintenance. Furthermore, the most important of these factors appear to be accessibility of the activity and event frequency. It is when these two characteristics combine that the greatest problems could occur in remote gambling. It can be argued that games that offer a fast, arousing span of play, frequent wins and the opportunity for rapid replay are associated with problem gambling.

There is no doubt that frequency of opportunities to gamble (i.e. event frequency) is a major contributory factor in the development of gambling problems (Griffiths, 1999). Addictions are essentially about rewards and the speed of rewards. Therefore, the more potential rewards there are, the more addictive an activity is likely to be. However, there is no precise frequency level of a gambling game at which people become addicted, since addiction will be an integrated mix of factors, in which frequency is just one factor in the overall equation. Furthermore, Parke and Griffiths (2004) point out that the most effective way to control the effects of the idiosyncratic features of Internet gambling on development of problematic gambling behaviour is to provide individuals with a scrutinised, regulated Internet gambling industry. All over the world, the recognition of the inability to prohibit Internet gambling successfully has led various jurisdictions to turn attention to developing harm-minimisation regulations.

To date, empirical research into remote gambling has mostly been carried out on Internet gambling (rather than mobile phone and interactive television gambling). Based on this limited empirical research, gambling on the Internet appears to be more associated with problematic gambling than is land-based gambling. A reason for this may be the structural characteristics of the Internet inherent to this technology, namely availability, ease of access, anonymity and convenience (Griffiths, 2003; Griffiths & Parke, 2002). In line with this, Wood and Williams (2007) point out that although 'Internet gambling is an exacerbating rather than a causal factor for most problem gamblers who gamble on the Internet, the nature of online gambling still makes it inherently more problematic than most other forms of gambling' (p. 95). It follows logically that the prevalence of problematic gambling in Internet gamblers is higher than in land-based gamblers. Therefore, the Internet cannot be claimed to be addictive *per se*, but rather to facilitate the engagement in addictive behaviours, such as gambling. Future research is needed to highlight the addictive potential of other Internet applications. This will inform both prevention efforts and potential treatment modalities.

Key points

1   Remote types of gambling (Internet, mobile and television) have provided the biggest cultural shift in gambling in the past decade, and their introduction has the potential to lead to increased levels of problematic gambling behavior.

2   There are a number of factors that make remote-gambling activities potentially addictive: anonymity, convenience, escape, dissociation/immersion, accessibility, event frequency, interactivity, disinhibition, simulation and asociability.

3   Online treatment interventions may be an effective medium in helping remote-gambling addicts.

4   So far, most of the research into remote gambling has focused on Internet gambling, but future research is needed to highlight the addictive potential of other Internet applications, such as mobile phone gambling and interactive television gambling.

References

Broda, A., LaPlante, D. A., Nelson, S. E., LaBrie, R. A., Bosworth, L. B. & Shaffer, H. J. (2008). Virtual harm reduction efforts for Internet gambling: effects of deposit limits on actual Internet sports gambling behaviour. *Harm Reduction Journal*, 5:27.

Bryce, J., Moore, K. & Rutter, J. (2004). Mobile entertainment users: headline results from an online survey. In K. Moore & J. Rutter (eds), *Proceedings of the 'Mobile Entertainment: User-Centred Perspectives' Conference*, pp. 86–99. Manchester: ESRC Centre for Research on Innovation and Competition.

Cole, T., Barrett, D. K. R. & Griffiths, M. D. (2011). Social facilitation in online and offline gambling: a pilot study. *International Journal of Mental Health and Addiction*, 9:240–7.

Corney, R. & Davis, J. (2010). The attractions and risks of Internet gambling for women: qualitative study. *Journal of Gambling Issues*, 24:121–39.

Dragicevic, S., Tsogas, G. & Kudic, A. (2011). Analysis of casino online gambling data in relation to behavioural risk markers for high-risk gambling and player protection. *International Gambling Studies*, 11:377–91.

Forrest, D. K., McHale, I. & Parke, J. (2009). Appendix 5: Full report of statistical regression analysis. In Ipsos MORI (2009) *British Survey of Children, the National Lottery and Gambling 2008–09: Report of a quantitative survey*. London: National Lottery Commission.

Gainsbury, S., Wood, R., Russell, A., Hing, N. & Blaszczynski, A. (2012). A digital revolution: comparison of demographic profiles, attitudes and gambling behavior of Internet and non-Internet gamblers. *Computers in Human Behavior*, 28:1388–98.

Gambling Commission (2008). *Survey Data on Remote Gambling Participation*. Birmingham: Gambling Commission.

Griffiths, M. D. (1999). Gambling technologies: prospects for problem gambling. *Journal of Gambling Studies*, 15:265–83.

Griffiths, M. D. (2001). Internet gambling: preliminary results of the first UK prevalence study, *Journal of Gambling Issues*, 5. Retrieved 17 June 2009 from http://www.camh.net/egambling/issue5/research/griffiths_article.html.

Griffiths, M. D. (2003). Internet gambling: issues, concerns and recommendations. *CyberPsychology and Behavior*, 6:557–68.

Griffiths, M. D. (2004). Mobile phone gambling: preparing for takeoff. *World Online Gambling Law Report*, 8(3):6–7.

Griffiths, M. D. (2006a). Internet trends, projections and effects: what can looking at the past tell us about the future? *Casino and Gaming International*, 2(4):37–43.

Griffiths, M. D. (2006b). Interactive television and gaming. *World Online Gambling Law Report*, 5(2):12–13.

Griffiths, M. D. (2007a). Mobile phone gambling. In D. Taniar (ed.), *Encyclopedia of Mobile Computing & Commerce*, pp. 553–6. Pennsylvania: Information Science Reference.

Griffiths, M. D. (2007b). Interactive television quizzes as gambling: a cause for concern? *Journal of Gambling Issues*, 20:269–76.

Griffiths, M. D. (2008). Digital impact, crossover technologies and gambling practices. *Casino and Gaming International*, 4(3):37–42.

Griffiths, M. D. (2011). Technological trends and the psychosocial impact on gambling. *Casino and Gaming International*, 7(1):77–80.

Griffiths M. D. & Barnes, A. (2008). Internet gambling: an online empirical study among gamblers. *International Journal of Mental Health Addiction*, 6:194–204.

Griffiths, M. D. & Cooper, G. (2003). Online therapy: implications for problem gamblers and clinicians. *British Journal of Guidance and Counselling*, 13:113–35.

Griffiths, M. D. & Parke, J. (2002). The social impact of Internet gambling. *Social Science Computer Review*, 20:312–20.

Griffiths, M. D. & Parke, J. (2007). Betting on the couch: a thematic analysis of Internet gambling using case studies. *Social Psychological Review*, 9(2):29–36.

Griffiths, M. D. & Wood, R. T. A. (2007). Adolescent Internet gambling: preliminary results of a national survey. *Education and Health*, 25:23–7.

Griffiths, M. D., Parke, A., Wood, R. T. A. & Parke, J. (2006). Internet gambling: an overview of psychosocial impacts. *Gaming Research and Review Journal*, 27(1):27–39.

Griffiths, M. D., Wood, R. T. A. & Parke, J. (2009). Social responsibility tools in online gambling: a survey of attitudes and behaviour among Internet gamblers. *CyberPsychology and Behavior*, 12:413–21.

Griffiths, M. D., Wardle, J., Orford, J., Sproston, K. & Erens, B. (2009). Socio-demographic correlates of Internet gambling: findings from the 2007 British Gambling Prevalence Survey. *CyberPsychology and Behavior*, 12:199–202.

Griffiths, M. D., Parke, J., Wood, R. T. A. & Rigbye, J. (2010). Online poker gambling in university students: further findings from an online survey. *International Journal of Mental Health and Addiction*, 8:82–9.

Griffiths, M. D., Wardle, J., Orford, J., Sproston, K. & Erens, B. (2011). Internet gambling, health. Smoking and alcohol use: Findings from the 2007 British Gambling Prevalence Survey. *International Journal of Mental Health and Addiction*, 9:1–11.

Hopley, A. A. B. & Nicki, R. M. (2010). Predictive factors of excessive online poker playing. *Cyberpsychology, Behavior & Social Networking*, 13:379–85.

Ialomiteanu, A. & Adlaf, E. (2001). Internet gambling among Ontario adults. *Electronic Journal of Gambling Issues*, 5. Retrieved 17 June 2009 from http://www.camh.net/egambling/issue5/research/ialomiteanu_adlaf_articale.html.

International Gaming Research Unit (2007). The global online gambling report: an exploratory investigation into the attitudes and behaviours of Internet casino and poker players. Report for eCOGRA (e-Commerce and Online Gaming Regulation and Assurance). Nottingham.

Ipsos MORI (2009). *British Survey of Children, the National Lottery and Gambling 2008–09: Report of a Quantitative Survey*. London: National Lottery Commission.

Joinson, A. (1998). Causes and implications of disinhibited behavior on the Internet. In J. Gackenback (ed.), *Psychology and the Internet: Intrapersonal, Interpersonal, and Transpersonal Implications*, pp. 43–60. New York: Academic Press.

Kangas, S. (2004). International comparison of mobile entertainment. In K. Moore & J. Rutter (eds), *Proceedings of the 'Mobile Entertainment: User-Centred Perspectives' Conference*, pp. 32–46. Manchester: ESRC Centre for Research on Innovation and Competition.

Kuss, D. & Griffiths, M. D. (2012). Internet gambling behavior. In Z. Yan (ed.), *Encyclopedia of Cyber Behavior*, pp. 735–53. Pennsylvania: IGI Global.

LaBrie, R. A., LaPlante, D. A., Nelson, S. E., Schumann, A. & Shaffer, H. J. (2007). Assessing the playing field: a prospective longitudinal study of Internet sports gambling behavior. *Journal of Gambling Studies*, 23:347–63.

LaBrie, R. A., Kaplan, S., LaPlante, D. A., Nelson, S. E. & Shaffer, H. J. (2008). Inside the virtual casino: a prospective longitudinal study of Internet casino gambling. *European Journal of Public Health*, doi: 10.1093/eurpub/ckn021.

Ladd, G. T. & Petry, N. M. (2002). Disordered gambling among university-based medical and dental patients: a focus on Internet gambling. *Psychology of Addictive Behaviours*, 16:76–9.

Langer, E. J. (1975). The illusion of control. *Journal of Personality and Social Psychology*, 32:311–28.

Lloyd, J., Doll, H., Hawton, K., Dutton, W. H., Geddes, J. R., Goodwin, G. M. & Rogers, R. D. (2010). How psychological symptoms relate to different motivations for gambling: an online study of Internet gamblers. *Biological Psychiatry*, 68:733–40.

Matthews, N., Farnsworth, W. F. & Griffiths, M. D. (2009). A pilot study of problem gambling among student online gamblers: mood states as predictors of problematic behaviour. *CyberPsychology & Behavior*, 12:741–6.

McBride, J. & Derevensky, J. L. (2009). Internet gambling behavior in a sample of online gamblers. *International Journal of Mental Health and Addiction*, 7:149–67.

McCormack, A. & Griffiths, M. D. (2012a). Motivating and inhibiting factors in online gambling behaviour: a grounded theory study. *International Journal of Mental Health and Addiction*, 10:39–53.

McCormack, A. & Griffiths, M. D. (2012b). What differentiates professional poker players from recreational poker players? A qualitative interview study. *International Journal of Mental Health and Addiction*, 10:243–57.

Moore, K. & Rutter, J. (2004). Understanding consumers' understanding of mobile entertainment. In K. Moore & J. Rutter (eds), *Proceedings of the 'Mobile Entertainment: User-Centred Perspectives' Conference*, pp. 49–65. Manchester: ESRC Centre for Research on Innovation and Competition.

Olason, D. T., Kiristjansdottir, E., Einarsdottir, H., Haraldsson, H., Bjarnason, G. & Derevensky, J. L. (2011). Internet gambling and problem gambling among 13 to 18 year old adolescents in Iceland. *International Journal of Mental Health and Addiction*, 9:257–63.

Parke, A. & Griffiths, M. D. (2004). Why Internet gambling prohibition will ultimately fail. *Gaming Law Review*, 8:297–301.

Parke, A. & Griffiths, M. D. (2011a). Poker gambling virtual communities: the use of Computer-Mediated Communication to develop cognitive poker gambling skills. *International Journal of Cyber Behavior, Psychology and Learning*, 1(2):31–44.

Parke, A. & Griffiths, M. D. (2011b). Effects on gambling behaviour of developments in information technology: a grounded theoretical framework. *International Journal of Cyber Behaviour, Psychology and Learning*, 1(4):36–48.

Parke, A. & Griffiths, M. D. (2012). Beyond illusion of control: an interpretative phenomenological analysis of gambling in the context of information technology. *Addiction Research and Theory*, 20:250–60.

Parke, J. & Griffiths, M. D. (2007). The role of structural characteristics in gambling. In G. Smith, D. Hodgins & R. Williams (eds), *Research and Measurement Issues in Gambling Studies*, pp. 211–43. New York: Elsevier.

Petry, N. M. (2006). Internet gambling: an emerging concern in family practice medicine? *Family Practice*, 23(4):421–6.

Petry, N. M. & Weinstock, J. (2007). Internet gambling is common in college students and associated with poor mental health. *American Journal on Addictions*, 16(5):325–30.

Phillips, J. G. & Blaszczynski, A. (2008). Mobile phone gambling. Paper presented at the Sixth International Conference on Pervasive Computing, Sydney, Australia, May.

Phillips, J. G. & Blaszczynski, A. (2010). Gambling and the Impact of New and Emerging Technologies and Associated Products. Final Report prepared for Gambling Research Australia.

Phillips, J. G., Ostojic, P. & Blaszczynski, A. (2011). Mobile phones and inappropriate content. In M. C. Barnes & N. P. Meyers (eds), *Mobile Phones: Technology, Networks and User Issues*. Hauppauge, NY: Nova Science Publishers.

Sevigny, S., Cloutier, M., Pelletier, M. & Ladouceur, R. (2005). Internet gambling: misleading payout rates during the 'demo' period. *Computers In Human Behavior*, 21:153–8.

Shchiglik, C. & Scornavacca, E. (2004). Consumer perceptions towards WAP Games. In K. Moore & J. Rutter (eds), *Proceedings of the 'Mobile entertainment: Use-centredperspectives' conference*, pp. 66–81. Manchester: ESRC Centre for Research on Innovation and Competition.

Smeaton, M. & Griffiths, M. D. (2004). Internet gambling and social responsibility: an exploratory study. *CyberPsychology and Behavior*, 7:49–57.

Valentine, G. & Hughes, K. (2008). *New Forms of Gambling Participation: Problem Internet Gambling and the Role of the Family*. London: Responsibility in Gambling Trust.

Walther, J. B. (1996). Computer-mediated communication: impersonal, inter-personal, and hyperpersonal interaction. *Communication Research*, 23:3–43.

Wardle, H. & Griffiths, M. D. (2011). Defining the 'online gambler': the British perspective. *World Online Gambling Law Report*, 10(2):12–13.

Wardle, H., Sproston, K., Orford, J., Erens, B., Griffiths, M., Constantine, R., Pigott, S. (2007). British Gambling Prevalence Survey 2007. London: National Centre for Social Research.

Wardle, H., Moody. A., Spence, S., Orford, J., Volberg, R., Jotangia, D., Griffiths, M.D., Hussey, D. & Dobbie, F. (2011). British Gambling Prevalence Survey 2010. London: The Stationery Office.

Wardle, H., Moody, A., Griffiths, M. D., Orford, J. & and Volberg, R. (2011). Defining the online gambler and patterns of behaviour integration: evidence from the British Gambling Prevalence Survey 2010. *International Gambling Studies*, 11:339–56.

Wardle, H., Moody. A., Spence, S., Orford, J., Volberg, R., Jotangia, D., Griffiths, M. D., Hussey, D. & Dobbie, F. (2011). British Gambling Prevalence Survey 2010. London: The Stationery Office.

Wise, T. & Hall, D. A. (2005). Interactive TV Services: take advantage of time to define roles, identify capabilities. Retreived on 5 October 2014 from http://www.accenture.com/SiteCollectionDocuments/PDF/a4_interactive_tv.pdf.

Wong, I. L. K. (2010). Internet gambling: a school-based survey among Macau students. *Social Behavior and Personality*, 38(3):365–71.

Wood, R. T. A. & Griffiths, M. D. (2007a). A qualitative investigation of problem gambling as an escape-based coping strategy. *Psychology and Psychotherapy: Theory, Research and Practice*, 80:107–25.

Wood, R. T. A. & Griffiths, M. D. (2007b). Online guidance, advice, and support for problem gamblers and concerned relatives and friends: An evaluation of the *Gam-Aid* pilot service. *British Journal of Guidance and Counseling*, 35:373–89.

Wood, R. T. A. & Griffiths. M. D. (2008). Why Swedish people play online poker and factors that can increase or decrease trust in poker websites: a qualitative investigation. *Journal of Gambling Issues*, 2:80–97.

Wood, R. T. A. & Williams, R. J. (2007). Problem gambling on the Internet: implications for Internet gambling policy in North America. *New Media & Society*, 9:520–42.

Wood, R. T. & Williams, R. J. (2011). A comparative profile of the Internet gambler: demographic characteristics, game play patterns, and problem gambling status. *New Media & Society*, 13:1123–41.

Wood, R. T. A., Griffiths, M. D. & Parke, J. (2007). The acquisition, development, and maintenance of online poker playing in a student sample. *CyberPsychology and Behavior*, 10:354–61.

Xuan, Z. M. & Shaffer, H. (2009). How do gamblers end gambling: longitudinal analysis of Internet gambling behaviors prior to account closure due to gambling related problems. *Journal of Gambling Studies*, 25(2):239–52.

National Problem Gambling Clinic CBT group programme

The eight-session group programme offered at the National Problem Gambling Clinic is a treatment programme that has showed to be successful in helping people to reduce and stop their problem gambling.

The programme is based on Cognitive Behavioural Theory, which means that the sessions focus on the problem behaviour, in this case gambling, and address the 'here and now'. You will learn to identify and manage the triggers to gambling, challenge irrational thinking associated with gambling and find better ways to cope with feelings, thoughts and urges that you may experience before a gambling episode.

The sessions cover a different topic each week and last for 90 minutes. You will have the chance to practise and reinforce what you have learned at the sessions by putting different strategies into practice, whilst keeping a record of your successes and introducing new hobbies in your life.

Below is a brief summary of the different topics covered in the programme.

Session 1: Stimulus control

In this session you will learn how to manage your gambling impulses and reduce the opportunity for gambling. Limiting access to cash, excluding yourself from bookmakers and blocking websites are some of the strategies that you will discuss. You will also explore the different sides of your gambling in order to gain a more balanced picture, and create a cue card to act as a reminder.

Session 2: Tracking and rewards

In this session you will learn how your brain's 'reward system' works in relation to gambling. You will also explore possible solutions to tackle the 'gambling loop' and new ways to reward yourself.

Session 3: Increasing pleasant activities

When gambling takes over your life it tends to fill all your free time and replace most of the recreational activities that you used to do. In this session you will be able to assess the balance of the 'shoulds' and 'wants' in your life and plan for new pleasant activities.

Session 4: Coping with cravings and urges to gambling

After stopping gambling, people often have thoughts related to gambling that can make them feel edgy or anxious. In this session you will learn to be more aware of these thoughts and feelings and what different strategies you could use to cope with your urges to gamble.

Session 5: Triggers to gambling

In this session you will have a chance to identify what triggers lead you to gambling and how to deal with them. It could be specific places, certain people, certain thoughts and different feelings. It's about being prepared and using foresight in order to prevent lapses.

Session 6: A functional analysis of your gambling

The more you know about gambling, the more you will be able to exert some control over it. A functional analysis is a detailed account of what happens before and after a gambling episode. This session will help you to understand the triggers that lead to gambling, and the short-term consequences that reinforce the gambling behaviour.

Session 7: Challenging gambling thinking beliefs

In this session you will learn how thoughts and emotions are interlinked and what the main thoughts and erroneous beliefs are behind your gambling. Once you are aware of these thoughts, you can begin to challenge them with your rational mind and use different strategies to cope with them.

Session 8: Future planning

In this last session you will look at what situations could increase your risk of gambling, and how to keep yourself safe and committed to your goal. You will also develop an emergency plan in case a gambling crisis arises in the future.

Assessment form for problem gambling

CNWL National Problem Gambling Clinic assessment form

PERSONAL DETAILS	
NAME:	**DOB:**
DATE:	**REFERRER:**
ASSESSED BY:	

CURRENT PROBLEM GAMBLING	
	<u>DSM-IV CRITERIA (5+)</u> Preoccupation Tolerance Recurrent relapses Withdrawal Emotional coping Chasing losses Concealment Illegal acts Loss or damage to relationships/ career Financial reliance on others after gambling * *NOT related to mania*

PAST HISTORY OF PROBLEM GAMBLING – include estimated total losses

CURRENT DEBTS – how much to whom	**PAST TREATMENT** – where, when, abstinence

PSYCHIATRIC HISTORY AND SUBSTANCE MISUSE – suicidal ideation past and present, impulsivity

		Score	Severity	
	PHQ			
	GAD			

FORENSIC HISTORY – include any illegal acts to finance gambling

MEDICAL HISTORY – include allergies and current medication

FAMILY PSYCHIATRIC HISTORY – include PG in family

FAMILY STRUCTURE AND IMPACT OF GAMBLING ON FAMILY – complete genogram, include information on children's age, where living and caregivers

SAFEGUARDING – if children of school age and safeguarding is a concern, enquire of social service contact, and what schools children go to

CURRENT EMPLOYMENT and employment history

PERSONAL HISTORY – include childhood physical, emotional or sexual abuse

MENTAL STATE EXAMINATION

Appearance and behaviour	
Speech	
Mood and affect	
Thought	
Perception and cognition	
Insight	

CAPACITY

Might this person have impairment or disturbance of mental functioning (such as an intellectual disability, dementia or other cognitive impairment, acquired brain injury or mental illness) that is sufficient to affect their capacity to make a particular decision?

(Circle)	**YES**	**NO**

If **YES**, you must undertake a formal assessment of capacity

CLINICAL IMPRESSION

DIAGNOSIS – specify Lifetime or Current where applicable, record all ICD-10 codes				
ICD-10 Classifications	**Classification**	**Code**	**Lifetime**	**Current**
Pathological gambling		F63.0		
Mood disorder				
Anxiety disorder				
Substance misuse issues				
Psychosis				
Other disorders: Specify:_____				
Screening severity rating		**Low**	**Moderate**	**High**

Probable management plan: TBC following MDT discussions		
Psychology	**Tick**	**Comments/reasons**
Evening CBT group		
Day group		
Homeless group		
Women's group		
Additional individual CBT		Formulation/Co-morbid/Gambling+
Individual CBT manual		
Individual remote CBT		
Low-intensity brief x 4		
Motivational Enhancement x 4		
Family support		
Carers' group		
Workbook		
Therapy		

Psychiatric review		
Money management	Yes/No	
Research	Yes/No	
No treatment offered		
Community Care Co-ordinator: (name and designation)		

Client-administered questionnaire

Self-administered NPGC client assessment form

Date of Assessment ☐☐ / ☐☐ / ☐☐☐☐

Client Name: _____

1. GAMBLING SEVERITY

1.1 Problem Gambling Severity Index

	Thinking about the past 12 months:	Never	Sometimes	Most of the time	Almost always
a.	How often have you bet more than you could afford to lose?	0	1	2	3
b.	How often have you needed to gamble with larger amounts of money to get the same feeling of excitement?	0	1	2	3
c.	How often have you gone back another day to try to win back the money you lost?	0	1	2	3
d.	How often have you borrowed money or sold anything to get money to gamble?	0	1	2	3
e.	How often have you felt that you might have a problem with gambling?	0	1	2	3

f.	How often have people criticised your betting, or told you that you had a gambling problem, regardless of whether or not you thought it was true?	0	I	2	3
g.	How often have you felt guilty about the way you gamble or what happens when you gamble?	0	I	2	3
h.	How often has your gambling caused you any health problems, including stress or anxiety?	0	I	2	3
i.	How often has your gambling caused any financial problems for you or your household?	0	I	2	3

1.2 How troubled or bothered have you been in the past 28 days by these gambling problems? (Please circle one.)

Not at all	Slightly	Moderately	Considerably	Extremely
0	I	2	3	4

1.3 In the last 12 months what proportion of the time that you consider to be *free to yourself* have you spent gambling? This includes actual gambling, thinking about gambling and activities relating to gambling, such as managing debts.

None	Not very much	Some of my free time	Most of my free time	All of my free time
0	I	2	3	4

2. HEALTH

Patient Health Questionnaire (PHQ-9).

Over the last two weeks, how often have you been bothered by any of the following problems? (Circle the number that most closely matches your answer.)

		Not at all	Several days	More than half the days	Nearly every day
a.	Little interest or pleasure in doing things.	0	1	2	3
b.	Feeling down, depressed or hopeless.	0	1	2	3
c.	Trouble falling or staying asleep, or sleeping too much.	0	1	2	3
d.	Feeling tired or having little energy.	0	1	2	3
e.	Poor appetite or overeating.	0	1	2	3
f.	Feeling bad about yourself – or that you are a failure or have let yourself or your family down.	0	1	2	3
g.	Trouble concentrating on things, such as reading the newspaper or watching television.	0	1	2	3
h.	Moving or speaking so slowly that other people could have noticed. Or the opposite – being so fidgety or restless that you have been moving around a lot more than usual.	0	1	2	3
i.	Thoughts that you would be better off dead or of hurting yourself in some way.	0	1	2	3

2.2 If you mentioned *any* problems, how *difficult* have these problems made it for you to do your work, take care of things at home or get along with other people?

Not difficult at all		Somewhat difficult		Very difficult		Extremely difficult	

2.3 Generalised Anxiety Disorder (GAD-7)

Over the last two weeks, how often have you been bothered by any of the following problems? (Circle the number that most closely matches your answer.)

		Not at all	Several days	More than half the days	Nearly every day
a.	Feeling nervous, anxious or on edge.	0	1	2	3
b.	Not being able to stop or control worrying.	0	1	2	3
c.	Worrying too much about different things.	0	1	2	3
d.	Trouble relaxing.	0	1	2	3
e.	Being so restless that it is hard to sit still.	0	1	2	3
f.	Becoming easily annoyed or irritable.	0	1	2	3
g.	Feeling afraid as if something awful might happen.	0	1	2	3

3. SUBJECTIVE HEALTH AND SOCIAL FUNCTIONING

Please reflect back across the past four weeks. We would like you to think about various aspects of your life during that period: your psychological health, your physical health and your overall quality of life.

How would you rate yourself on these aspects on a scale from 0 to 20, where zero is very poor indeed – the worst it could be – and 20 is very good, pretty much the best it could be? (Please circle number)

3.1 Rating of mental health status (anxiety, depression, problem emotions and feelings) in last 30 days:

Poor   0_1_2_3_4_5_6_7_8_9_10_11_12_13_14_15_16_17_18_19_20   **Good**

3.2 Rating of physical health status (extent of physical symptoms and bothered by illness) in last 30 days:

Poor	0_1_2_3_4_5_6_7_8_9_10_11_12_13_14_15_16_17_18_19_20	Good

3.3 Rating of quality of life (e.g. able to enjoy life, gets on well with family and partner) in last 30 days:

Poor	0_1_2_3_4_5_6_7_8_9_10_11_12_13_14_15_16_17_18_19_20	Good

4. TOBACCO

4.1	Have you ever smoked?	Yes	No
		(If No go to 4.5)	
4.2	Do you currently smoke?	Yes	No
4.3	If 'yes':		
	a) For how long have you smoked?	__ years	__ months
	If 'no':		
	b) How long did you smoke before giving up?	__ years	__ months
	c) How long has it been since you smoked?	yrs/ mths/days*	
		*delete as applicable	

4.4	During the past month, on average how many of the following products do you smoke each day?	Yes	No
a.	Manufactured cigarettes		
b.	Hand-rolled cigarettes		
c.	Other (specify)		

4.5	Do you currently use chewing/smokeless tobacco? If so, how often? (Circle *one* answer.)		
Daily	Less than daily	Not at all	Don't know

5. ALCOHOL

5.1	Have you drunk alcohol in the past year?		Yes	No

5.2 AUDIT-C (Alcohol Use Disorders Identification Test – Consumption Questions)

a.	How often do you have a drink containing alcohol?			
Never	**Monthly or less**	**2–4 times a month**	**2–3 times a week**	**4 or more times a week**
0	1	2	3	4

b.	How many drinks containing alcohol do you have on a typical day when you are drinking?			
1 or 2	**3 or 4**	**5 or 6**	**7 to 9**	**10 or more**
0	1	2	3	4

c.	WOMEN: How often have you had 6 or more units on a single occasion in the last year? MEN: How often have you had 8 or more units on a single occasion in the last year?			
Never	**Less than monthly**	**Monthly**	**Weekly**	**Daily or almost daily**
0	1	2	3	4

6. INVOLVEMENT WITH OTHER SERVICES

6.1 Have you used any of the following in the last three months?

	Yes	No
Gamblers Anonymous		
GamCare		
Gordon Moody Association/Gordon Moody House		
Other therapy (please state)		

Thank you for taking the time to complete this assessment questionnaire.

These questions are part of the routine evaluation of the treatment programme offered at the National Problem Gambling Clinic. They are repeated at set time-points during the treatment journey. They are important as they provide further information for the decisions that are made about individual care. They also help the clinic in understanding how well the treatment is working.

Please hand to the facilitator at the beginning of your session.

Index

Note: Pages numbers in **bold** are for figures.

11C-raclopride ligand 54, 60–1
[11C]PHNO tracer 61
[123-I]FP-CIT tracer 61
[18F]fallypride tracer 61
Abbott, M. W. 29, 31, 118
abuse, physical/verbal 94, 96, 110, 117
acamprosate 149
acceptability 18
access/accessibility: remote gambling
   205–6; treatment services 22, 176
Adams, P. J. 22, 24, 25
Addiction Research Center Inventory
   (ARCI) 145
Addiction Severity Index (ASI) 29, 184
addiction-spectrum disorders 65
adequacy schemas 45
Adlaf, E. 107, 196
adolescents *see* children and young people
advertising: bans on 21, 23, 24, 25;
   controls 25
aetiology *see* risk factors
affective arousal 47–9
affordability, remote gambling 206
Afifi, T. O. 110, 117
age 8, 9, 10, 29
Agrawal, A. 98
Akitsuki, Y. 63
Albein-Urios, N. 65
alcohol, and social marketing campaigns 21
alcohol industry 23, 24
alcohol misuse 8, 20, 41, 56, 98, 99, 143,
   156; co-morbidity with 33, 76, 77, 78,
   109, 134, 154; in women gamblers 175;
   in young people 183
alcohol use disorders identification test
   (AUDIT) 154
Alessi, S. M. 57
ALSPAC report 20
amantadine 148–9
American Psychiatric Association (APA)
   110; Diagnostic and Statistical Manual
   see DSM
amphetamine 60
Anderson, C. 118
Anderson, G. 40
anger, co-morbid 126–7
anonymity of remote environments 206
anterior cingulate cortex 63
Antisocial Impulsivists 30, 32, 33, 56
antisocial personality disorder 33, 78, 79,
   116
anxiety/anxiety disorders 98, 138;
   co-morbidity with 32–3, 78, 79, 81, 82,
   109, 115, 138–9, 186; in family
   members 117; women gamblers 174,
   175; young people 186, 187
Aragay, N. 76, 134
Argo, T. 81
arousal 40–1, 42, 44; affective 47–9;
   control over 42
Ashley, L. L. 30, 34
Ashrafioun, L. 58
Asian/Asian–British groups 9, 18–19, 20,
   31, 198

asociality of remote gambling 209–10
assessment: of client motivation to engage in treatment 114–16; of consequences of problem gambling 116–18; core content 114–18; of gambling behaviour 114; interviewing style 113–14; of personal history 118; of psychiatric co-morbidity 82–4, 115–16; purpose of 113; sample form for 221–5; young people 183–5
'at-risk' gamblers 8–9
Atherton, M. 3
attachment to gambling 41
Attention Deficit Hyperactivity Disorder (ADHD) 33, 80, 85, 142; checklist 141, 142
Australian Productivity Commission 22, 29, 90, 95, 97, 173
avoidant coping 50–1
avoidant personality disorder 79, 116
Axelrod, S. R. 177
Ayton, P. 63
Azizi, A. 177

Bagby, R. M. 78
Balodis, I. M. 59, 60
Barker, J. 91
Barnes, A. 196, 199
Barratt Impulsiveness Scale (BIS-11) 148
Battersby, M. W. 108
Beaudoin, C. M. 115, 174
Bechara, A. 53, 55
Beck, A. T. 44–5, 46, 48
Beck depression inventory (BDI) 154
Beckett, L. 163
Becona, E. 190
behavioural accounts 34, 39–40
Behavioural Conditioned groups 30, 31
behavioural economics 56–7
Behrens, T. E. 63
Ben-Tovim, D. 108
Bergevin, T. 183
Bergh, C. 60
Berking, M. 177
Berlin, H. A. 147–8
Berridge, K. C. 60
bettors/betting 7, 9, **10**, 11, 201; horse-race 3, 6, 11, 40, 173; spread 11

Bickel, W. K. 53, 56
Bingham, C. 173
bingo 3, 10, 173, 182
bio-psycho-social model **43**
bipolar affective disorder (BAD) 78
bipolar disorder, co-morbidity with 76, 149–50
Black, D. W. 75, 79, 80, 81, 98, 115, 116, 140, 141–2, 151
Black/Black-British groups 31
Blanco, C. 124, 136
Bland, R. C. 77, 78, 79, 115
Blaszczynski, A. 23, 28, 30, 31, 32, 40, 51, 56, 78, 109, 115, 117, 186, 201, 202–3
Blum, K. 59, 77
Blume, S. B. 54, 76, 110, 174, 184, 186
Boehlke, K. K. 30, 34
Boileau, I. 61
Bondolfi, G. 29, 109
borderline personality disorder (BPD) 33, 78
boredom 40, 44, 45, 174
Bosco, D. 155
Boughton, R. 174, 175
Bowden-Jones, H. 64
Bowirrat, A. 59
Boyer, M. 58
brain imaging *see* functional Magnetic Resonance Imaging (fMRI); Positron Emission Tomography (PET)
Brecksville Gambling Craving Scale (BGCS) 145
Breen, H. 173
Brennan, J. 109, 110
Brewer, J. A. 134
Brewster, J. 174, 175
Brief Bio-Social Gambling Screen (BBGS) 105
brief interventions 22, 128–30, 154
British Gambling Prevalence Survey series (BGPS) 4–12, 19, 29, 30, 31, 90, 97, 99, 172, 173, 174; Internet gambling 196, 197–8; key findings 6–8; limitations 5–6; methodology 5; mobile phone gambling 201
Broda, A. 196
Brown, R. I. 124, 186
Brown, R. J. F. 40

Brown, S. 174
Bryce, J. 201
Buchel, C. 57
Buckholtz, J. W. 61
bupropion 137, 140–2
Burge, A. N. 29

Calvete, E. 50
Cambridge Gambling Task 56, 57
Campbell-Meiklejohn, D. 63–4
Canadian Problem Gambling Index (CPGI) 22, 55, 107, 202
carbamazepine 151
Carlbring, P. 126, 130
Carlton, P. L. 186
Casarella, T. 57
case studies, young gamblers 187–9
Casey, E. 173, 178
casino games 10, 40, 173, 196
Castellani, B. 80, 90
causal factors see risk factors
Cavedini, P. 56
CBT see cognitive-behavioural therapy
Chalmers, H. 29
Chase, H. W. 62
'chasing' behaviour 45–6, 47–9, 51, 63–4, 65, 112, 123, 184
children and young people 19, 98–9, 182–94; abuse of 96, 110, 117; and advertising 23; assessment 183–5; case studies 187–9; Internet gambling 182, 189, 198–9; and parental gambling 20, 95–7, 117; pocket money amounts 20; prevalence rates of gambling 182–3; prevention of gambling 20–1, 185–6, 190; psychiatric co-morbidity 182, 183, 186, 187; risk factors 20, 34, 183; treatment 186–7
Chinese community 31
Chung, S. K. 137
Cilia, R. 61
citalopram 138, 157
Clapson, M. 3
Clark, L. 53, 54, 55, 56, 61, 62, 64, 65
Clarke, D. 29, 30, 31, 182, 183
Clarke, H. 21
Clarkson, J. 31
Cleaver, H. 95

Clinical Global Impressions (CGI) scale 136, 139, 140, 141, 142, 145, 147, 148, 150, 151, 152, 153, 157
clomipramine 135, 143
Cloninger, C. R. 79
clozapine 146
co-morbidity 44, 92, 126–7; see also psychiatric co-morbidity
Cocco, N. 40
cognitive biases 42
cognitive distortions 50–1, 62–4
cognitive therapy 127
cognitive-behaviour models/accounts 34, 39, 41–52, 186, 187; developmental model of substance abuse (Liese and Franz) 44–5; Orford, Morison and Somers 41; Sharpe 42–4; Sharpe and Tarrier 41–2
cognitive-behavioural therapy (CBT) 125–7, 128, 129, 130, 139, 154, 157, 164; Internet-based 126, 131; National Problem Gambling Clinic group programme 219–20; women gamblers 176–7; workbooks 128, 131
Cole, T. 196
Coman, G. J. 32
Comings, D. E. 59
conditional beliefs 45
Congruence Couple Therapy (CCT) 164
control: attempts at 114; failure of 111, 123; illusory 63, 65, 208
Cooper, G. 210
Copello, A. 164–5, 166
coping skills/strategies 42, 44, 50–1, 125, 166, 167–8
core beliefs 44–51
Coricelli, G. 63
Corney, R. 196
Cottler, L. B. 78
Coulombe, A. 41
Coventry, L. 174
Cox, B. J. 115, 174
CRAFT (Community Reinforcement and Family Training) 164
criminality 9, 16, 30, 54, 117
Criteria for Control of Pathological Gambling Questionnaire (CCPGQ) 138
Crockford, D. N. 58, 152

Cronce, J. M. 31
cue reactivity 58, 60
Cummings, K. M. 21
Cunningham, J. A. 130
Cunningham-Williams, R. M. 77, 78, 79,
    109
Currie, J. 176
Custer, R. 91
cyclothymia 136, 149, 151

Damasio, A. R. 53
Damasio, H. 53
Dannon, P. N. 137, 141, 148
Darbyshire, P. 95
Davis, J. 196
DeCaria, C. M. 80
De la Gandara, J. 140
De Ruiter, M. B. 58, 64
debt problems 16, 117
decision making 53, 54, 55–7, 62, 65
delay discounting 56–7, 59
Delfabbro, P. 33
Delgado, M. R. 59
Dell'Osso, B. 151
demographic features 9, 10, 19, 28–31,
    173, 197, 198, 200
dependent personality disorder 79
depression 32, 78, 92, 98, 109, 115, 138; in
    family members 117; in women
    gamblers 174, 175; in young people
    183, 187
depressive symptoms 33, 78; in children 97
deprivation 19, 20, 30
Derenevsky, J. 21, 182, 183, 185, 186,
    187, 189, 196, 199
Desai, R. A. 29, 76, 175
Desire to Gamble Scale (DGS) 145
diagnosis 110–13, 123–4; psychiatric
    co-morbidity 81, 82, 83
Diagnostic and Statistical Manual of
    Mental Disorders see DSM
dialectical behaviour therapy 127
Dickerson, M. G. 40, 50, 58
Dickson, L. 182, 183, 185
Dickson-Swift, V. A. 92, 94
disinhibition, and Internet gambling 207–8
Diskin, K. M. 130
dissociation 207

disulfiram 143–4
divorce rates 94
Dixey, R. 173
Dixon, M. R. 57
domestic abuse/violence 94, 110
dopamine 42, 64
dopamine receptors 53, 54, 60, 64
dopaminergic system 60–1, 134;
    medication targeted at 53–4, 140–6
dorsal striatum 59
dorsolateral prefrontal cortex (PFC) 58
dorsomedial prefrontal cortex (PFC) 58
Dowling, N. 97–8, 99, 126, 128
Draganski, B. 65
Dragicevic, S. 196
drug use/addiction 8, 58, 60–1, 64, 65, 98,
    143; co-morbidity with 20, 33, 57,
    76–7, 109–10; and social marketing
    campaigns 21; in women gamblers 175;
    in young people 183
DSM-III 107
DSM-IV 6, 8, 11, 12, 19, 29, 76, 82, 84,
    107, 110–13, 123, 197; screening tools
    based on 8, 105, 106
DSM-IV Multiple Response Adapted for
    Juveniles (DSM-IV-MR-J) 184–5, 198
DSM-IV-TR 182
DSM-5 55, 64, 110, 123–4, 134
Dussault, F. 32, 33
dysthymia 78, 175

early life experiences 44–51
Early Maladaptive Schemas (EMS) 46–51
early wins 42
Echeburúa, E. 78, 116
educational background 8
educational opportunities, loss of 9, 113, 123
EEG studies 59
Eisen, S. A. 98
el-Guebaly, N. 114, 152
electronic gaming machines (EGMs) 22,
    25, 44, 182
Ellenbogen, S. 183
Elliott, R. 63
Emond, A. 20
Emotionally Vulnerable groups 30, 31,
    32–3
employment status 9, 19, 20, 30

endogenous opioid system 62
escape, gambling as 40, 44, 174, 184, 197, 206, 207–8
escitalopram 138–9
Estevez, A. Y. 50
ethnicity 8, 9, 20, 31
EuroQuol Five Dimension quality of life survey (EQ-5D) 154
event frequency 208, 212–13; *see also* opportunity for gambling
executive function 55, 56
expectancy scales 185
Eysenck Impulsivity Questionnaire (EIQ) 142

F-DOPAligand 61
Fabian, T. 117
Falenchuk, O. 175
families, effects on 90–103, 116–17, 166–7; adult members 91–5, 116–17; children 20, 95–7, 117; emotional and physical health impact 94–5, 117–18; financial impact 92–3; relational impact 93–4
family history/attitudes 20, 31, 42, 83–4, 97–9, 190
family interventions 163–71; 5-step intervention 164–9
Farnsworth, W. F. 196
Feigelman, W. 30, 33
feminisation of gambling 173–4
Fernández-Montalvo, J. 78
Ferris, J. 8, 55, 107
financial impact/problems 113, 117–18, 123; and families 92–3
Fischer, I. 63
Fisher, S. E. 182, 183, 184
Fixed Odd Betting Terminals (FOBTs) 11
fluoxetine 140, 157
fluvoxamine 135–7
follow-up evaluations 22, 128, 131, 137, 164
Fong, T. 144–5
football pools 3, 11
Forbush, K. T. 56, 79
Forrest, D. 9, 18, 20, 199
Fortune, E. E. 62
Franklin, J. 95
Franz, R. A. 44–5

freewill 18
French, M. T. 109
Friend, K. B. 21, 23
Frost, R. 32
Fuentes, D. 56
functional Magnetic Resonance Imaging (fMRI) 54, 55, 58–60, 63, 64, 134, 137

GABA 62
gabapentin 157
Gainsbury, S. 196
Gam-Anon 164
GamAid 210–11
Gambino, B. 97
Gamblers Anonymous 20 Questions (GA-20) 185
Gamblers Anonymous (GA) 124, 125, 128, 164, 176
gambler's fallacy 42, 45, 63
Gambling Act (2005) 3–4, 15
Gambling Beliefs Questionnaire 62
Gambling Commission 4, 5, 196
gambling environment, risk-reduction in 22–3
Gambling Expectancy Questionnaire (GEQ) 185
gambling industry: and government, inter-dependence of 24–5; government revenue from 21; regulation of 3–4, 15, 23–4, 25, 213; support for good causes 24
gambling opportunities 2–3, 18, 30, 42, 208, 212–13
Gambling Related Cognitions Scale 62
Gambling Research Australia 202
Gambling Symptom Assessment Scale (G-SAS) 139, 140, 142, 147, 148–9, 152, 153, 155, 156, 157
GamCare 4; telephone helpline 211
games/machine players 6, 10; *see also* electronic gaming machines (EGMs); slot machines
Gebauer, L. 105
gender 29
genetic vulnerability 42, 98
George, S. 175
Gerdner, A. 33
Gerstein, D. R. 77

Gettings, B. 58
Getty, H. 32
Gillespie, M. 185
Ginsburg, D. 3
Global Assessment of Functioning (GAF)
    157
glutamate 62
glutamatergic system 134; medication
    targeted at 146–9
Go–No–Go tasks 56
Goldstein, L. 186
Goodie, A. S. 57, 62
Gordon, L. M. 62
Gostin, L. O. 18
Goudriaan, A. 28, 55, 56, 58
government: conflict of interest within 24;
    and gambling industry, inter-
    dependence of 24; revenues 21, 25
GPs, role of 21
Grall-Bronnec, M. 33
Grant, J. E. 56, 77, 80, 128, 138–9,
    139–40, 146–7, 152, 153, 155–6, 157,
    173, 176, 186, 187
Greenspan, M. 174
Griffiths, M. D. 2–9, 97, 173, 174, 176,
    182, 183, 186, 195, 196–7, 199, 200,
    201, 203, 204, 205, 206, 207, 208, 209,
    210–11, 212, 213
guilt 9, 48, 91, 94, 111, 112, 174, 176
Gupta, R. 182, 183, 185, 186, 187
Gütestam, K. G. 182

Hall, D. A. 203
Hall, G. 30
Hall, M. N. 28
Haller, R. 151
haloperidol 60, 145
Hamilton Anxiety Scale (HAM-A) 139
Hamilton Depression Rating Scale
    (HDRS) 141, 142
Hamilton Rating Scale for Depression
    (HAM-D) 151
harm, gambling-related 16–17
harm-reduction approach 129, 185–6
Harman, H. 4
Harris, C. R. 29
Hay, G. 15
health economics 17

Health Survey for England (HSE) 12
Health and Well-Being Boards 25
Heinz, A. 60, 61
helplines 23, 164, 211
Hewig, J. 59
hindsight bias 63
Hing, N. 173
Hinterhuber, H. 151
hippocampus 58
histrionic personality disorder 79
Hodgins, S. 33, 81, 108, 114–15, 117, 124,
    128, 130
Hoinville, G. 3
Holden, C. 134
Hollander, E. 135, 136, 149, 150, 151, 186
Hommer, D. W. 60
Hopley, A. A. B. 196, 199
horse-race betting 3, 6, 11, 40, 173
hot cognitions 47–8
'hot hand' belief 63
Hraba, J. 174
Hughes, K. 93, 196
hypomania 78

Ialomiteanu, A. 196
Ibáñez, A. 32, 33, 75, 77, 175
ICD-10 29, 82, 83, 84, 113
identifying gambling problems 21–2
illegal activities 112–13, 123–4, 184; see
    also criminality
illusory control 63, 65, 208
immersion 207
impulse control disorders (ICDs) 149;
    co-morbidity with 76, 80, 115
impulsivity 29, 33, 42, 44, 56–7, 61, 80,
    116, 142–3, 187; reflection 56
incentive salience hypothesis 60
income 8, 19
Index of Multiple Deprivation (IMD) 19
information provision for families 167
Ingle, P. J. 117
Interactive Systems Worldwide (ISWI) 205
interactive television (i-TV) gambling 195,
    203–5, 206
interactivity, remote gambling 208
intermittent explosive disorder 80
intermittent reinforcement model 22, 25, 40
International Gaming Research Unit 196

Internet gambling 10, 11, 174, 195, 196–200, 212, 213; accessibility 205–6; affordability 206; asociality of 209–10; convenience 206; and disinhibition 207–8; as escape 207–8; event frequency 208; immersion/dissociation feelings and 207; interactive nature of 208; regulation of 213; simulations 209; women and 174, 211; young people and 182, 189, 198–9
Internet-based treatments: CBT 126, 131; for remote gamblers 210–12
interventions 20–1; family 163–71; with young people 20–1, 25, 185–6; see also treatment
Intimate Partner Violence (IPV) see domestic abuse/violence
Iowa Gambling Task 54, 55–6, 58, 59, 61, 62
Ipsos MORI 196, 199
irrational beliefs, challenging 44

Jackson, A. C. 34
Jacobs, D. 95, 96, 182, 183, 185, 186
Jiménez-Murcia, S. 123
jobs/job opportunities, loss of 9, 113, 118
Johansson, A. 28, 29, 32, 182
Johnson, E. E. 106
Johnson, J. 175
Joinson, A. 207
Joutsa, J. 61, 64, 65
Judgment and Decision Making (JDM) 57

Kalischuk, R. G. 91
Kalyoncu, Ö. 28
Kaminer, Y. 184
Kanetkar, V. 50, 51
Kangas, S. 201
Kassinove, J. I. 62
Kausch, O. 32, 109, 115
Kemsley, W. 3
Kennedy, J. L. 60
Kertzman, S. 56
Kessler, R. C. 77, 79, 80
Kim, S. W. 77, 80, 139, 152, 153, 156, 157, 173, 187
Koepp, M. J. 61
Korman, L. M. 117, 126–7
Krishnan, M. 92, 93, 164, 165

Kroll, B. 95
Kurlan, R. 146
Kushner, M. G. 77, 81, 82, 84
Kuss, D. 199, 200

LaBrie, R. A. 196
Ladd, G. T. 21, 23, 77, 174, 187, 199
Ladouceur, R. 33, 62, 118, 127, 184, 186, 187
Lahti, T. 154–5
lamotrigine 157
Langenbucher, J. 77
Langer, E. J. 63, 208
lateral prefrontal cortex (PFC) 58, 59, 63
Lawrence, A. J. 56, 57, 65
Leary, K. 40
Leblond, J. 116
Ledgerwood, D. M. 32
Lee, B. 61
Lee, B. K. 164
Lee, G. 174
Leeman, R. F. 55, 62, 143
legislation 23–4; see also Gambling Act (2005)
Leiserson, V. 56
Lesieur, H. R. 8, 54, 76, 92, 94, 96, 97, 107, 110, 118, 174, 177–8, 184, 186
licensing regime 4
Lie-Bet questionnaire 106
Liese, B. S. 44–5
life events 32, 44, 91, 183
Light, R. 4
Ligneul, R. 57
Likuk, N. M. 75
Lim, K. D. 136–7
Linden, R. D. 81
Linnet, J. 61, 64
lithium 149–51, 157
Livingston, J. 176
Livingstone, C. 22
Lloyd, J. 196
Lobo, D. S. 60
Lobsinger, C. 163
loneliness 91, 174, 177
longitudinal studies 82
Lorenz, V. C. 91, 94, 95, 95–6
loss chasing 46, 47–9, 51, 63–4, 65, 112, 123

lotteries 3, 6, 10, 24, 173, 182; *see also* National Lottery
lovability schemas 45
Ludo-Cage test 140
Lupu, V. 182
lying about gambling 9, 106, 112, 123, 184

Mabia Rating Scale (MRS) 151
Maccallum, F. 109
Madden, G. J. 57
maintenance responses 50
major depressive disorder (MDD) 78, 138
Makarchuck, K. 117, 164
Manes, F. 53
Marissen, M. A. 58
marital status 19
Mark, M. E. 177–8
Marsch, L. A. 53, 56
Martinez, D. 60, 61, 63, 64
Martinez-Pina, A. 30
Matching Familiar Figures Test 56
Matthews, N. 198, 199
May, A. 65
McBride, J. 196, 199
McBride, O. 124
McClure, S. M. 57
McComb, J. L. 92
McConaghy, N. 30, 33, 109, 115
McCormack, A. 174, 196
McCormick, R. A. 50, 77
McCready, J. 107
McCusker, C. G. 58
McElroy, S. L. 80, 144
McGill Treatment Paradigm 187
McHale, G. 20
McHale, I. 199
McLellan, T. 29
McManus, S. 8
McMillan, J. 107
measurement of gambling behaviour 4–6
medication *see* pharmacotherapy
Melamed, L. 56, 80
memantine 147
men 8, 9, 10, 29, 98, 172, 173, 211
mental-ill health 16; and problem gambler's family members 94–5; *see also* psychiatric co-morbidity

Meroni, M. C. 138
Messerlin, C. 21
methylphenidate 61
Meyer, G. 117, 118
Michalczuk, R. 56, 57
Miedl, S. F. 54, 59, 60
Miller, M. 91
Milovanovic, S. 138
Milt, H. 91
mindfulness 44
Mini International Neuropsychiatric Interview (MINI) 141
Minnesota Impulsive Disorders Interview 115
Mischel, W. 56
Mitzner, G. B. 55, 64
Miyake, A. 56
mobile phone gambling 182, 195, 200–3, 205, 206
Mobile Phone Problem Use Scale 202
modafinil 142–3
Monaghan, S. 23
money problems 19; *see also* debt; financial impact on families
money-free gambling 199
Monterosso, J. R. 156
mood disorders: co-morbidity with 76, 78, 81, 82; *see also* bipolar disorder; cyclothymia; depression; dysthymia; major depressive disorder (MDD)
mood stabilisers 157, 159–51
Moody, A. 196, 197, 201
Moore, K. 201
Moore, S. 174
Morasco, B. J. 126
Moreyra, P. 28
Morison, V. 41
Moskowitz, J. A. 149–50
motivation for treatment, assessment of client 114–15
motivational interventions 128–30, 154
Moyer, T. 75, 79, 80, 115, 116
Muelleman, R. 94, 110
Muller, C. A. 143–4
multi-interest gamblers 7, 8, 9, **10**, 11
Mutschler, J. 143
Myrick, H. 58
Myrseth, H. 139

N-Acetyl Cysteine (NAC) 146–7
Najavits, L. M. 33, 75, 79
nalmefene 155–6, 157
naltrexone 62, 77, 84, 137, 141, 152–5,
    156, 157
narcissistic personality disorder 78, 116
NatCen Social Research 5
National Co-morbidity Survey 79
National Epidemiological Survey on
    Alcohol and Related Conditions
    (NESARC) 105
National Lottery 3, 6, 7, 9, 10, 173, 198–9
National Problem Gambling Clinic 172,
    176–7; CBT group programme 219–20
near-miss outcomes 62–3, 65
nefazodone 140
neurobiology 53–74, 77, 134–5
neurochemistry 60–2, 135
neuropsychology 55–7
Nicki, R. M. 196, 199
Nicolato, R. 148
NODS-CLiP 106
noradrenaline 42, 62
noradrenergic system 134
Nordin, C. 79
norepinephrine 143
Nower, L. 28, 30, 31, 51, 56, 78
Nylander, P. O. 79

Oberg, S. A. 59
O'Brien, C. P. 156
Obsessive Compulsive Disorder (OCD) 135,
    138; co-morbidity with 32, 79, 80–1
obsessive-compulsive personality disorder
    (OCPD) 79, 116
occupational situation see employment;
    unemployment
Odlaug, B. L. 56
Oei, T. P. 38, 62, 128
Ohtsuka, K. 174
olanzapine 144–5, 157
Olason, D. T. 182, 196, 199
online gambling see Internet gambling
operant conditioning 41, 208
opioid antagonists/agonists 152–6, 157;
    see also naltrexone
opportunity for gambling 2–3, 18, 30, 42,
    208, 212–13

orbitofrontal cortex 57
Orford, J. 4, 41, 92, 93, 124, 164, 165
Oscar-Berman, M. 59
Oskarsson, A. T. 63
O'Sullivan, S. S. 61
overcompensation responses 50
overconfidence 57

Padala, P. R. 141
Pallanti, S. 140, 150–1
panic disorder, co-morbidity with 76, 79,
    175
paranoid personality disorder 78, 79
parental gambling 20, 31, 95–9
parental norms/attitudes 20, 183, 190
parenting style 183, 190
parents, working with 20
Parke, A. 196, 199, 209, 213
Parkinson's Disease (PD) 53–4, 60, 61, 64,
    143, 145–6, 148–9, 155
paroxetine 139–40, 157
Pathways Model of Problem Gambling 28,
    30, 31–3, 51
personal history 118
personality disorders, co-morbidity with
    33, 78–9, 81, 85, 115, 116
Peters, J. 57
Petry, N. M. 33, 57, 64, 75, 76–7, 78, 79,
    123, 125, 126, 128, 129, 130, 134, 174,
    187, 199
PG-CGI see Clinical Global Impressions
    (PG-CGI) scale
PG-YBOCS see Yale Brown Obsessive
    Compulsive Scale
pharmacotherapy 62, 77, 84, 134–62, 186,
    187; dopaminergic 53–4, 140–6;
    glutamatergic 146–9; mood stabilisers
    149–51, 157; multi-pharmacoptherapy
    chart review 157; opioid antagonists/
    agonists 152–6, 157; placebo-controlled
    randomised clinical trials (RCTs)
    135–57; serotonergic 135–40, 157; see
    also names of individual drugs
Phillips, J. G. 201, 202–3
physical exercise 44
physical health impact, on family of
    problem gamblers 95
physiological substrates 186

Pihl, R. O. 56
Piquette-Tomei, N. 176
poker 40, 196, 208
Positron Emission Tomography (PET) 54,
    60–1, 64, 134, 150
post-traumatic stress disorder (PTSD)
    32–3, 79
Potenza, M. N. 29, 55, 58, 62, 76, 117,
    134, 138–9, 143, 174, 175, 176, 183,
    187
Poulin, C. 184
Poulos, C. X. 60, 142, 145
pramipexole 64
prefrontal cortex (PFC) 55, 58; dorsolateral
    58; dorsomedial 58; lateral 58, 59, 63;
    ventral 59; ventromedial (vmPFC) 53,
    55, 56, 58, 59, 64, 134
preoccupation with gambling 111, 123,
    184
prevalence of gambling behaviour 2–3;
    increase in (1999–2010) 10–11;
    Internet gambling 197, 198; problem
    gambling 8–9, 18–19, 172–3, 183, 197,
    198 (changes in 11–12); women 172–3;
    young people 182–3; see also British
    Gambling Prevalence Survey series
    (BGPS)
prevention 20–1, 25, 185–6, 190
prison population 6, 19
probability decisions 56, 57
probability discounting 59
Problem Gambling Research and
    Treatment Centre (PGRTC) 105
Problem Gambling Severity Index (PGSI)
    8, 106, 107
Problem and Pathological Gambling
    Measure (PPGM) 108–9
problem-solving skills 42, 44, 187
Profile of Mood States (POMS) 145
profiles: problem gamblers 9; regular
    gamblers 8
Prospect Theory 57
psychiatric co-morbidity 32–3, 34, 75–89;
    anxiety disorders 32–3, 78, 79, 81, 82,
    115, 138–9, 175, 186, 187; assessment
    of 82–4, 115–16; Attention Deficit
    Hyperactivity Disorder (ADHD) 33,
    80, 85; Axis 1 76, 115, 116, 183; Axis

2 116, 183; depression 32, 78, 92, 98,
    109, 115, 175, 186; impulse control
    disorders 76, 80, 115; methodological
    limitations of studies investigating
    81–2; mood
disorders 76, 78, 81, 82; Obsessive
    Compulsive Disorder (OCD) 32, 79,
    80–1; personality disorders 33, 78–9,
    81, 85, 115, 116; substance misuse 75,
    81, 82, 109–10, 115, 116, 126–7, 134,
    187 (alcohol 33, 76, 77, 78, 134, 154,
    175; drugs 20, 33, 57, 76–7, 175);
    suicidality 78, 79, 115; treatment issues
    84, 85, 116; women gamblers 175;
    young gamblers 182, 183, 186, 187
psychoeducation 84, 176, 177, 186, 187
psychosocial treatments/intervention
    123–33; brief and motivational
    interventions 22, 128–30, 154;
    cognitive therapy 127; with families
    163–71; follow-up evaluations 128,
    131; Gamblers Anonymous (GA) 124,
    125, 128, 164, 176; and gambling
    outcomes 131; and therapeutic alliance
    131; see also cognitive-behavioural
    therapy (CBT)
psychotic disorders 76, 82
public health 15–27, 134
Pulford, J. 109

Qi, S. 62
quetiapine 146

Raj, Y. P. 149
Raylu, N. 28, 62
reactive coping styles 32
reflection impulsivity 56
reflective coping styles 32
Regard, M. 56
regular gamblers 7–8, 10–11; sub-groups
    by number and type of activities 7;
    typical profile 8
regulation: of gambling industry 3–4, 15,
    23–4, 25, 213; public-health 17, 18, 24
Reid, R. L. 62
reinforcement 22, 25, 40, 208; delayed 42;
    partial 40
reinforcement processing 58–60

Reith, G. 3
relationship problems 9, 44, 54, 113;
    within families 93–4
relative glucose metabolic rate (rGMR)
    150
remote gambling 195–218; accessibility
    factors 205–6; affordability 206;
    anonymity 206; asociality of 209–10;
    convenience 206; as escape 207–8;
    event frequency 208; interactivity
    component of 208–10; online help and
    treatment 210–12; *see also* interactive
    television (i-TV) gambling; Internet
    gambling; mobile phone gambling
resilience, development of 20–1
'responsible gambling' 16
Responsible Gambling Strategy Board 16
Reuter, J. 59
reward deficiency hypothesis 59–60
Reynolds, B. 57
risk assessment 83
risk factors 18–20, 28–34, 183, 189, 200;
    age 29; criminality 30; ethnicity 9, 20,
    31; gender 29; parental gambling 20,
    31; and pathways model of problem
    gambling 31–3; socio-economic status
    and occupation 19, 30, 197, 200
risk reduction 17, 22–3
risperidone 145–6
Robinson, T. E. 60
Rogers, R. D. 56
Rönnberg, S. 30, 97
Rosenberg, H. 58
Rosenthal, M. D. 8
Rosenthal, R. J. 174, 186
Rossen, F. 182, 183, 184
Rothschild, H. 96, 97
Rotondo, A. 146
Rugle, L. 56, 80, 186
Rupcich, N. 109
Rushworth, M. F. 63
Rutter, J. 201

Saiz-Ruiz, J. 138
Satkeviciute, R. 183
Schare, M. L. 62
schema processes 50–1
schema theory 45–51

schema therapy 46
Scherrer, J. F. 30, 32, 33
schizoid personality disorder 79, 116
schizophrenia/schizoaffective disorder 76
Schlosser, S. 75, 80
Schneider, G. 96
schools-based interventions 20, 25
Schreiber, L. 98
Schull, S. D. 174
Schultz, W. 60
Scornavacca, E. 201
Scottish Health Survey (2012) 12
scratch cards 3, 6, 10, 173
screening 21, 22, 104–10; purpose of
    104–5; tools 105–9
Seedat, S. 146
Seguin, M. 115
Select Committee Inquiry into the
    Gambling Act (2011) 12
selective serotonin reuptake inhibitors
    (SSRIs) 135–40, 157
self-directed interventions 131
self-exclusion 23
self-help 117, 164, 165, 166, 186
self-reports 78, 139, 142, 199–200
Sellitto, M. 57
sensation seeking 40
serotonergic system 134; medication
    targeted at 135–40, 157
serotonin 42, 62, 64
serotonin reuptake inhibitors (SRIs) 135;
    see also selective serotonin reuptake
    inhibitors (SSRIs)
sertraline 138, 157
Sevigny, S. 196
Sevincok, L. 146
sexual behaviour, compulsive 80, 115
Shaffer, H. 28, 174, 196
shame 48, 50, 51, 109, 112, 117, 174, 176
Sharpe, L. 40–1, 41–4
Shaw, M. C. 94, 98, 117
Shchiglik, C. 201
Shead, N. W. 29, 30, 32, 33, 117
Sheehan Disability Scale (SDS) 141, 155,
    156
Shenassa, E. D. 33
Shepherd, L. 50
Shokauskas, N. 183

Shuttleworth, D. E. 94
Silove, D. 186
Sims, M. 18
simulations, Internet gambling 209
Skinner, B. F. 39–40
slot machines 6, 10, 54, 145, 173
Slutske, W. 33, 55, 56, 79, 124
'smart' pre-commitment systems 25
Smeaton, M. 196
Smith, G. 77, 81, 82
Smith, N. 32
smokers/smoking 8, 9, 17, 18, 20, 21, 23, 24, 58
social gambling 31, 209
social marketing campaigns 21
social support for families 169
socio-economic features 8, 19, 30, 197, 198, 200
Somers, M. 41
South Oaks Gambling Screen (SOGS) 54, 107–8
South Oaks Gambling Screen — Revised for Adolescents (SOGS-RA) 184, 185
Specker, S. M. 75, 79, 80, 81, 175
SportXction 205
spread betting 11
Sproston, K. 5, 173
Spunt, B. 109
Steel, Z. 115
Steenbergh, T. A. 62
Steeves, T. D. 61
Stein, D. J. 146
Stevens, M. 108
Stewart, R. M. 124
Stinchfield, R. 77, 78, 107, 108, 123
Stop-Signal Task (SST) 142
streak effects 63, 65
stress 40, 41, 42, 44, 166–7
Stress Strain Coping Support (SSCS) model 164, 165
striatum 58; dorsal 59; ventral 59, 61, 62, 63, 64, 134
Stroop test 58
structural magnetic resonance imaging 65
structured interviews 82, **83**
student population 6, 199, 200
Studer, B. 54

substance misuse 117, 143; co-morbidity with 33, 75, 76–7, 81, 82, 109–10, 115, 116, 126–7, 134, 187; cognitive developmental model of 44–5; see also alcohol; drug use/addiction
suicidality 78, 79, 115, 117, 174
Sullivan, S. 109
superstitious conditioning 63
Svensson, K. 33
Svetieva, E. 81, 107
Sylvain, C. 127

Taber, J. I. 32
Tanabe, J. 58, 64
Tarrant, N. 143
Tarrier, N. 40–1, 41–2
Tavares, H. 173
Taylor, A. 95
Teen-Addiction Severity Index (T-ASI) 184
telescoping effect 173, 175
television see interactive television (i-TV) gambling
Temperament and Character Inventory (TCI) 79
Templeton, L. 95, 97
terminology, problems of 81
thalamus 59
therapeutic alliance 131
'think aloud' procedure 62
Thompson, W. N. 118
Thoms, D. 95
tobacco industry 23–4; government revenue from 21
Toce-Gerstein, M. 55, 106, 124
Tolchard, B. 108
tolerance 111, 123, 184
Toneatto, T. 63, 109, 110, 117, 154, 186
TOP (Treatment Outcome Profile) 177
topiramate 137, 147–8, 157
treatment 17, 44; access to 22, 176; motivation to engage in 114–15; psychiatric co-morbidity 84, 85, 116; women gamblers 176–7; young people 186–7; see also Internet-based treatments; pharmacotherapy; psychosocial treatments/intervention
Trevorrow, K. 174

Tricomi, E. M. 63
triggers for gambling 44, 174
twin studies 98

unemployment 9, 10, 30
urgency 61
US National Gambling Impact Study
    Commission 96

Vachon, J. 98
Valentine, G. 93, 196
valproate 150–1
van Holst, R. J. 59, 60, 65
Velleman, R. 95, 97, 99
ventral prefrontal cortex 59
ventral striatum (VS) 59, 61, 62, 63, 64,
    134
ventromedial prefrontal cortex (vmPFC)
    53, 55, 56, 58, 59, 64, 134
Verdejo-Garcia, A. 65
Victorian Gambling Screen (VGS) 107,
    108
Visual Analogue Craving Scale (PG-VAC)
    139
Vitaro, F. 33, 55, 56, 97
Volberg, R. A. 29, 30, 31, 105, 108, 118,
    173
Volkow, N. D. 60, 61, 64
Voon, V. 54, 60
voxel-based morphometry 54

Walker, M. 61, 62, 107, 186, 187
Walters, G. 98
Walther, J. B. 207
Wardle, H. 5, 7, 9, 10, 11, 15, 18, 19, 90,
    97, 134, 172, 173, 196, 197, 201, 211
Wareham, J. D. 134
Weinstock, J. 92, 199
Weintraub, D. 54, 60, 149
Welte, J. W. 28, 30, 31, 33, 77, 109
Wensel, M. 107
Westphal, J. 175
Wheeler, B. W. 30
White, C. 99
white-matter tractography 54
White/White-British groups 8, 9, 31
Wiebe, J. M. D. 184

Wilber, M. K. 29
Wilke, D. 176
Williams, R. 81, 105, 108
Williams, R. J. 196, 199, 213
Willoughby, T. 29
win chasing 46, 47, 112
Winters, K. C. 29, 30, 31, 33, 77, 78, 81,
    82, 84, 107, 184
Wisconsin Card Sort Test 54, 56
Wise, T. 203
withdrawal symptoms 111–12
wives of gamblers, impact on 91
Wolfling, K. 58
women gamblers 8, 9, 10, 29, 98, 172–81;
    gender-specific issues **175**; impact of
    gambling on 174–5; online gambling
    174, 211; prevalence of 172–3;
    psychiatric co-morbidity 175; treatment
    176–7; triggers for gambling 174; types
    of gambling engaged in 173
Won Kim, S. 78
Wong, I. L. K. 196, 199
Wood, R. T. A. 97, 182, 196, 199, 207,
    210–11, 213
workbook-delivered treatments 128, 131
working memory 55, 65
Wulfert, E. 107
Wynne, H. 8, 55, 107

Xuan, Z. M. 196
Xue, G. 63

Yaffe, R. A. 91, 94, 95
Yale Brown Obsessive Compulsive Scale
    (PG-YBOCS) 136, 138, 139, 140, 141,
    142, 144, 146, 147, 148, 149, 150, 151,
    153, 154, 155, 156, 157
Yi, S. 50, 51
Yip, S. W. 30, 32, 33
Young, Jeffrey 45, 46, 48, 50
Young, M. 108
young people *see* children and young
    people; student population

Zack, M. 60, 142, 145
Zimmerman, M. 75, 76, 124, 138